BizTalk Server 2016
Performance Tuning and Optimization

Agustín Mántaras

Apress®

BizTalk Server 2016: Performance Tuning and Optimization

Agustín Mántaras
Dubai, United Arab Emirates

ISBN-13 (pbk): 978-1-4842-3993-3   ISBN-13 (electronic): 978-1-4842-3994-0
https://doi.org/10.1007/978-1-4842-3994-0

Library of Congress Control Number: 2018965175

Managing Director, Apress Media LLC: Welmoed Spahr
Acquisitions Editor: Smriti Srivastava
Development Editor: Siddhi Chavan
Coordinating Editor: Shrikant Vishwakarma

Cover designed by eStudioCalamar

Cover image designed by Freepik (www.freepik.com)

Distributed to the book trade worldwide by Springer Science+Business Media New York, 233 Spring Street, 6th Floor, New York, NY 10013. Phone 1-800-SPRINGER, fax (201) 348-4505, e-mail orders-ny@springer-sbm.com, or visit www.springeronline.com. Apress Media, LLC is a California LLC and the sole member (owner) is Springer Science + Business Media Finance Inc (SSBM Finance Inc). SSBM Finance Inc is a Delaware corporation.

For information on translations, please e-mail rights@apress.com, or visit http://www.apress.com/rights-permissions.

Apress titles may be purchased in bulk for academic, corporate, or promotional use. eBook versions and licenses are also available for most titles. For more information, reference our Print and eBook Bulk Sales web page at http://www.apress.com/bulk-sales.

Any source code or other supplementary material referenced by the author in this book is available to readers on GitHub via the book's product page, located at www.apress.com/978-1-4842-3993-3. For more detailed information, please visit http://www.apress.com/source-code.

Printed on acid-free paper

For my father, mother, wife, and friends, even though I know none of them will read it. Oh, yes, and for the rest of my family; otherwise, I would have a problem (Houston).

Table of Contents

About the Author

Agustín Mántaras discovered BizTalk Server back in 2004, working on its implementation in one of Spain's largest banks. His passion for developing and architecting BizTalk solutions continued to grow and, in 2008, he joined Microsoft as a Premier Field Engineer, a job that has taken him around the globe to work on some the biggest BizTalk Server implementations. He is currently based in United Arab Emirates, delivering BizTalk and Azure services to clients in the Middle East, Africa, and Europe.

About the Technical Reviewers

Jean-Pierre Accounie is passionate about code development. He started his career at Microsoft in 1992 as a Support Engineer for Visual Basic 1.0 for DOS and Windows and then moved quickly to supporting Windows SDK via Quick C and C++ 6.0 and then Visual C++ and its famous MFCs.

After several years being an SME on the MTS/COM+ Microsoft middleware products line, he joined the integration world and started to support BizTalk 2002 and BizTalk 2004.

There he created a support tool that, in one click, gathered all the information about a BizTalk configuration. He also made this tool public because of its popularity inside MS. Its current version, named BizTalk Health Monitor, is used today by all MS engineers and almost all BizTalk admins to monitor their platform.

After 26 years at Microsoft, Jean-Pierre Accounie still works in its Support division, supporting its Integration offers (BizTalk, Logic Apps, MSMQ, WFM, etc.).

Originally from Dayton, OH, **Clint Huffman** is a senior software engineer at Microsoft and a published author on Windows performance analysis. He is probably best known as the creator of the Performance Analysis of Logs (PAL) tool and regularly teaches the Windows architecture.

Felipe Senso has worked in the integration space for more than 18 years now. His main areas of expertise are BizTalk Server and Azure Hybrid Integration, with a strong .NET Development background. In 2012, he joined Microsoft as Support Engineer, assisting many mission-critical hot issues worldwide, making him a great resource within complex reactive troubleshooting. In 2015, he moved to the Premier Field Engineer Integration role in the EMEA region, delivering proactive services such as stabilization and optimization of the BizTalk Server platform, and BizTalk/Azure training for developers and administrators.

As the founder of BizTalk360, **Saravana Kumar** fulfills the role of CTO, where he is responsible for the strategic direction of the company and most importantly, the clients. A Microsoft Integration MVP since 2007, Saravana was awarded the "Integration MVP of the Year 2013" by Microsoft. With more than a decade of experience handling BizTalk customers across the world, Saravana was frustrated seeing customers struggling with the same challenges again and again when it came to BizTalk Server administration and operations. The idea of BizTalk360 came to him over a cup of coffee with his fellow MVPs, and therefore he started a pet project to address some of the challenges faced by BizTalk administrators. This slowly turned out into full-blown commercial product that helps customers across the world.

Saravana is a very active member of the BizTalk Server community. A popular speaker, he often presents at various BizTalk conferences, user groups, local colleges, etc. across Europe, the United States, and India. If you are a BizTalk programmer or administrator, it's likely that you've read something from him or heard him speak on BizTalk-related topics.

Acknowledgments

I am sure I wrote half of the book in airplanes and trains, and during long hotel nights. Time that I could not use if I were not working for a company that refreshed my life completely. Thank you.

None of this would have been possible without the valuable help of my technical reviewers, as I truly believe they made this book what it is today—Clint, Jean-Pierre, Saravana, and especially Felipe, as he reviewed most of the code during his vacation—I will not forget!

I also want to thank Smriti Srivastava, as she was the one who made me believe I could actually complete this amazing journey with Apress; to Shrikant Vishwakarma, for his patience when I got lost and delayed; and to my development editors, James Markham and Siddhi Chavan.

Finally, I want to thank my wife, for being supportive and probably the most patient person I ever met in my life.

Introduction

A long time ago, in a datacenter far, far away, Microsoft BizTalk Server became to life. It was back in 2000 when we saw it for the first time. Although it was not until version 2004 when it really transformed the integration landscape using Microsoft technologies, it indeed changed my life completely.

The book that you have in your hands it is a journey that starts by revealing what is under the hood of the product at a low level. Even though you have strong BizTalk Server knowledge, I recommend you not skip it, because it provides base knowledge for the rest of the chapters.

I wrote Chapters 2 and 3 to explain almost everything I know about performance counters, analysis techniques, and public tools that are related to the scope of the book.

Chapter 4 is all about optimizing the BizTalk Server platform using essential configurations that you can apply to a BizTalk environment, proactively and reactively. If you expect a compilation of how to solve all the issues you can ever face, you will get probably disappointed. The idea of the chapter is to create a solid foundation so that you will be able design a BizTalk Server application thinking of a concept that I call: application priority levels.

Especially for mission-critical solutions, and BizTalk Server usually handles them, troubleshooting and fixing bugs on time is essential, as these applications frequently require zero downtime. Therefore, efficient application instrumentation becomes crucial to reduce the time of finding issues and to start working in the bug as soon as possible. This topic is explained in Chapter 5, where you will learn how to implement Event Trace for Windows and to leverage in the Business Activity Monitoring feature to log important events and data related to the flow.

Chapter 6 will drive you to the most common actions you can take as a developer to make sure your applications will help the production server run them smoothly. You will learn how to improve your schemas definitions, maps, orchestrations, and pipelines. As we consider that custom pipelines components are essential for low latency scenarios (among others), you will also learn how to develop custom pipeline components.

Chapter 7 explains how take advantage of a Microsoft .NET Framework feature called side-by-side versioning. You will learn how to use it in your BizTalk Server projects to reduce downtime at maximum. Additionally, it provides an introduction to business rules and performance recommendations related to it. You might wonder why I have decided to include business rules. Well, although it's not a topic explicitly related to performance, it provides huge benefits in terms of reducing application downtime and orchestration complexity.

A mature BizTalk Server infrastructure should be able to proactively monitor every aspect of BizTalk Server and for that propose I have decided to write about a fantastic tool called BizTalk 360. This is all detailed in Chapter 8.

Successfully designing and evolving a BizTalk Server platform are tasks that require including unit and performance testing procedures as part of the application development lifecycle. Chapter 9 dives into these topics using Microsoft Visual Studio Testing features.

Finally, Chapter 10 closes the journey with real-life scenarios explained through a fictitious company called ACME corporation.

I hope you learn as much reading the book as I did while writing it.

Who Is This Book For?

If this is the first contact you've had with BizTalk Server, I am not going to lie to you—you are most likely going to get lost. This book assumes that you have already the following knowledge:

- BizTalk Server administration and troubleshooting experience

- Strong development .NET Framework experience

- Familiarity with Microsoft Windows Communication Foundation

You will not learn about the BizTalk Server basic stuff. No. You will learn about the techniques that make the difference.

If you are passionate about BizTalk Server and performance, it does not matter if you are an architect, administrator, developer, or a TV presenter. This book is for you!

Requirements and Source Code

Along the book you will find several walkthroughs that contain step-by-step instructions to develop BizTalk Server solutions that are relevant to the discussed topic. The source code is available on GitHub via the book's product page, located at `www.apress.com/978-1-4842-3993-3`.

To compile the code, you need the following system setup:

- **Microsoft BizTalk Server 2016 Developer edition**—The full installation is recommended, as you will create solutions with BAM as well (no need to install EDI as this book does not cover it). The Enterprise edition of the product will work also.

- **Microsoft Visual Studio Enterprise edition**—Chapter 9 requires you to have this edition because is all about testing features and those are not available in the Microsoft Visual Studio version. The Community edition is not supported.

- **Microsoft Windows 10 or Microsoft Windows Server 2016 (preferred)**—Windows 10 is fine for running the code, but if you want to practice some of the optimizations detailed in Chapter 4, you must have Windows Server 2016.

- **Microsoft Internet Information Server**—There is a lab in Chapter 9 that deploys a WCF service, so you will need to install IIS in your machine.

BizTalk Server 2016 has several requirements that must be in place as well. I recommend that you read the following Microsoft documentation:
`https://docs.microsoft.com/en-us/biztalk/install-and-config-guides/hardware-and-software-requirements-for-biztalk-server-2016`

Good luck!

CHAPTER 1

Revealing the Black Box

Most of the people who start their journey with BizTalk Server are usually not aware of how BizTalk Server receives, process, and sends messages. They instinctively believe that it is something that just happens, driven by a mysterious hidden force. While at the beginning this can be something even pleasant, when you deploy a solution to production and problems arise, troubleshooting BizTalk Server without knowing how the engine works can create confusion, delays, and in the worst of the scenarios, frustration. During my career as a premier field engineer, I have assisted customers with several critical situations, and you would be surprised how many times I heard the sentence:

"What is happening with this black box! I do not understand it!"

In this chapter, you learn how BizTalk Server works from an internal point of view. This topic is crucial if you want to become an expert BizTalk Server developer or a solution architect, but also if you want to master the tuning techniques required to adjust your platform to every situation. The chapter reviews the following topics:

- Essential XML principles and how BizTalk Server uses them

- How BizTalk Server works internally

- Hosts and host instances

- Subscriptions

- Messages

- Publishers

- Subscribers

- The Message Box database

- Publication and dequeue processes

1

© Agustín Mántaras 2019
A. Mántaras, *BizTalk Server 2016*, https://doi.org/10.1007/978-1-4842-3994-0_1

If you are a seasoned BizTalk Server user, you might notice some content missing here, such as tracking and BAM. Although these topics are important from a functionality point of view, they have been moved to further chapters of the book for clarification and simplification proposes. This chapter focuses on the pieces of the engine that BizTalk Server uses to process messages. Do not worry, the book covers tracking and BAM functionalities in detail in Chapters 4 and 5.

Having a solid foundation of the topics discussed in this chapter allows you to create robust BizTalk Server solutions. Hopefully, you will never say again: "What is happening with this black box!"

XML Language Premier

Although the book assumes you have a strong knowledge of XML, this section covers all the XML topics that the engine uses to operate.

BizTalk Server works with messages encoded in XML format. The W3C (World Wide Web Consortium) provides rules and guidelines for creating standard XML definitions. Schemas created by BizTalk Server follow this specification, so you can import BizTalk Server schemas to any other XML tools that follow this specification without too much effort (and vice versa).

If you want to master your XML skills, you could visit the World Wide Web Consortium web page at http://www.w3.org/.

XML Schema Concepts Used by BizTalk Server

In this section, you learn about the XML elements that BizTalk Server uses to implement a message definition.

Attribute

An XML attribute is a data container used to save additional information related to an XML element; they are like properties of an element. Attributes can be associated with any of the simple data types but cannot be nested (elements can be nested when using complex types though). Because of this restriction, you cannot create attributes as complex types, only as simple data types.

In the following example, Book is an element with a value of "La Perla Negra". As you can see, the ISBN is the attribute of the Book element and has a value of 00078743649332.

```
<Book ISBN="00078743649332">La Perla Negra</Book>
```

Namespace

BizTalk Server uses the concept of NameSpace to avoid confusion between elements and attributes names (see Figure 1-1). In this way, unique elements and attributes can be granted for the same schema definition and provided in an XML instance. In addition to this, the BizTalk engine uses this concept implemented as the targetNameSpace property (tNS) in several ways:

- To identify the message within the message box database

- To create subscriptions based on particular properties called promoted properties

- To publish the message along with the binary information

```
<?xml version="1.0" encoding="UTF-16"?>
- <xs:schema xmlns:xs="http://www.w3.org/2001/XMLSchema" targetNamespace="http://Module2.Books" xmlns:b="http://schemas.microsoft.com/BizTalk/2003"
  xmlns="http://Module2.Books">
  - <xs:element name="Book">
    - <xs:complexType>
      - <xs:sequence>
          <xs:element name="ISBN" type="xs:string"/>
          <xs:element name="Title" type="xs:string"/>
        - <xs:element name="Pages">
          - <xs:simpleType>
              <xs:restriction base="xs:integer"/>
            </xs:simpleType>
          </xs:element>
        - <xs:element name="WritenDate">
          - <xs:simpleType>
              <xs:restriction base="xs:dateTime"/>
            </xs:simpleType>
          </xs:element>
        </xs:sequence>
      </xs:complexType>
    </xs:element>
  </xs:schema>
```

Figure 1-1. *Example of the namespace definition*

Element

Elements are the building blocks of an XML. They can behave as containers to hold text, elements, and attributes. Elements classified as simple or complex (see Figure 1-2).

- Simple: Simple data types (such as integer, DateTime, and string)

- Complex: Elements that contain other elements and attributes (such as include and import options)

Figure 1-2. *Simple and complex elements*

Note   It is crucial to note that element names are case sensitive. That implies that, for the BizTalk Server engine, the element name `price` is different than `Price` (because the first character is uppercase). You should pay attention to this fact because if you provide the wrong element names, the BizTalk engine might not identify the message, or the initial validation can fail.

As shown in Figure 1-2, the next elements are simple:

- `ISBN` (string)

- `Title` (string)

- `Pages` (integer)

- `WrittenDate` (DateTime)

However, the record `Writer` is complex.

BizTalk and XML Namespaces in Detail

An XML document may contain elements or attributes from more than one XML definition (more than one namespace declared in the document).

For instance, imagine that you are dealing with an XML document designed to define book information (see Figure 1-3). Every book has a field called ID that is used to identify the book. Similarly, there is an ID field to identify the writer of the book, as shown in Figure 1-3.

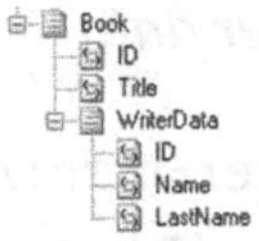

```
⊟─▣  Book
     ▣  ID
     ▣  Title
⊟─▣  WriterData
     ▣  ID
     ▣  Name
     ▣  LastName
```

Figure 1-3. *XML definition example*

As you can see, the schema definition has two IDs. To avoid confusion, you can create two different schema definitions: The first one defines the whole schema, and the second one defines only the writer structure (see Figure 1-4).

```
<BookInformation xmlns="http://http://Books.com/BookInformation"
                 xmlns:writer="http://Books.com/Writer">
    <Book>
            <ID>56554798922</ID>
            <Title>La Perla Negra</Title>
            <WriterData>
                  <writer:id>00000023</writer:id>
                  <writer:Name>Agustin</writer:Name>
                  <writer:LastName>Mantaras</writer:LastName>
            </WriterData>
    </Book>
</BookInformation>|
```

Figure 1-4. *Default and custom namespaces definition*

The Declaration

BookInformation xmlns="http://http://Books.com/BookInformation" is what is called the default namespace, and it applies to all elements in the schema that do not have a custom namespace definition.

On the other hand, xmlns:writer="http://Books.com/Writer" represents a custom namespace.

Notice that the writer data has the prefix ":writer" and the default namespace does not have such a definition. Using this prefix later in the XML document allows you to identify all the elements in the custom namespace and not in the default one. As outlined in the previous example, the writer element has its definition, shown in Figure 1-5.

```
<WriterData>
        <writer:id>00000023</writer:id>
        <writer:Name>Agustin</writer:Name>
        <writer:LastName>Mantaras</writer:LastName>
</WriterData>
```

Figure 1-5. Custom namespace writer data

The custom namespace xmlns:writer=http://Books.com/Writer defines the elements of the child record WriterData (Id, Name, and LastName).

As BizTalk Server implements custom functionality that is not used by any other software, it can leverage the XML namespace technology to access this information. BizTalk Server adds the following two namespaces in every BizTalk Server schema:

- Target Namespace. When you create a new schema using the BizTalk Editor, a target namespace is added by default (see Figure 1-6). The engine uses this information along with the root node name of the document to identify the message. The identification is implemented by the targetNameSpace property of the schema and by default is constructed as shown here:

```
http://VisualStudioProjectName.NameOfTheSchema
```

```
<?xml version="1.0" encoding="UTF-16"?>
<xs:schema xmlns:xs="http://www.w3.org/2001/XMLSchema"
targetNamespace="http://Module2.NameSpaceBook"
xmlns:b="http://schemas.microsoft.com/BizTalk/2003"
xmlns="http://Module2.NameSpaceBook">
  - <xs:element name="Book">
    - <xs:complexType>
      - <xs:sequence>
          <xs:element name="ID" type="xs:string"/>
          <xs:element name="Title" type="xs:string"/>
        - <xs:element name="WriterData">
          - <xs:complexType>
            - <xs:sequence>
                <xs:element name="ID" type="xs:string"
                    minOccurs="1" maxOccurs="1"/>
                <xs:element name="Name" type="xs:string"/>
                <xs:element name="LastName" type="xs:string"/>
              </xs:sequence>
            </xs:complexType>
          </xs:element>
        </xs:sequence>
      </xs:complexType>
    </xs:element>
</xs:schema>
```

Figure 1-6. Default name space definition

- Extensions Namespace. If the schema is representing a flat file or an EDI schema, BizTalk adds a reference to this namespace:

  `xmlns:b="http://schemas.microsoft.com/BizTalk/2003"` (see Figure 1-7)

```
<?xml version="1.0" encoding="UTF-16"?>
- <xs:schema xmlns:xs="http://www.w3.org/2001/XML Schema"
  targetNamespace="http://FlatFileWozard.BookOrders" xmlns:b="http://schemas.microsoft.com/BizTalk/2003"
  xmlns="http://FlatFileWozard.BookOrders">
  - <xs:annotation>
    - <xs:appinfo>
        <schemaEditorExtension:schemaInfo
            xmlns:schemaEditorExtension="http://schemas.microsoft.com/BizTalk/2003/SchemaEditorExtensions"
            standardName="Flat File" extensionClass="Microsoft.BizTalk.FlatFileExtension.FlatFileExtension"
            namespaceAlias="b"/>
        <b:schemaInfo root_reference="BookOrder" compile_parse_tables="false"
            allow_message_breakup_of_infix_root="false" early_terminate_optional_fields="false"
            allow_early_termination="false" generate_empty_nodes="true" suppress_empty_nodes="false"
            lookahead_depth="3" parser_optimization="speed" count_positions_by_byte="false" pad_char_type="char"
            default_pad_char=" " codepage="65001" standard="Flat File"/>
    </xs:appinfo>
  </xs:annotation>
```

Figure 1-7. *Annotation definition under a custom namespace*

BizTalk uses this prefix within the message to add the flat file extensions that contain delimiter and positional information in the form of annotations.

The elements within the annotation are used during the disassembling stage at the pipeline level to create the XML representation of a specific flat file.

Identification of an Incoming Message

When BizTalk receives a message, the message engine extracts the default namespace (target namespace) and the main root node name. These values are internally concatenated (`targetNamespace#rootNodeName`) and written in the context of the message as a property called Message Type. You will learn about message properties later in the chapter.

The Message Type must be unique so that the BizTalk Server engine can determine the correct schema and apply it to the received instance. If you deploy schemas with the same message type, BizTalk Server always gets the same type (usually the one created in the first place), and it ignores the rest. The consequences of this action could be very unpredictable because the engine could publish messages into the wrong host queue table, or raise a routing failure exception as subscribers might not exist for that message.

We will dig into this topic later in the message engine section.

BizTalk Server Schemas

A schema for BizTalk Server is like the definition of the message itself. It contains the specification by adding elements, attributes, types, complex types, and more.

BizTalk schemas can be created by using third-party schema creation tools and the BizTalk Schema Editor, shipped with the product and fully integrated into Microsoft Visual Studio 2015. Developers should consider the use of the BizTalk Editor tool as the preferred method for creating BizTalk Server schemas, since Microsoft guarantees that the schemas created using this tool are fully supported.

BizTalk Server Schema Types

As discussed previously, BizTalk Server 2016 can natively process structured messages using the following formats:

- Flat file schemas

- XML schemas

- JSON (with a little help of JSON pipelines)

- Flat file schemas

There are two types of flat file schemas:

- Delimited—This is the case when a specific character separates records or fields.

- Positional—The length of the elements itself identifies the field. In other words, elements are constructed using the position in the file.

Because public XSD by the W3C does not natively support the flat file structure, BizTalk uses the annotation capabilities (flat file extensions) of the XML technology to provide all the required functionality. The example in Figure 1-8a shows flat file annotations used in BizTalk schemas.

```
<xs:annotation>
  - <xs:appinfo>
      <b:schemaInfo pad_char_type="char" early_terminate_optional_fields="false" root_reference="SalesOrder" standard="Flat File" compile_parse_tables="false"
        allow_message_breakup_of_infix_root="false" allow_early_termination="false" generate_empty_nodes="true" suppress_empty_nodes="false"
        lookahead_depth="3" parser_optimization="speed" count_positions_by_byte="false" default_pad_char=" "/>
      <schemaEditorExtension:schemaInfo xmlns:schemaEditorExtension="http://schemas.microsoft.com/BizTalk/2003/SchemaEditorExtensions"
        standardName="Flat File" extensionClass="Microsoft.BizTalk.FlatFileExtension.FlatFileExtension" namespaceAlias="b"/>
  </xs:appinfo>
</xs:annotation>
```

Figure 1-8a. *Flat file annotation*

Delimited Flat Files

A delimited file contains one or more fields separated by a delimiter character. The most common characters are:

- Comma (,)

- Semicolon (CSV files;)

- Pipe (|)

However, you can work with any desired character. It is important to note that if you set up a separator, that character should not appear as part of the text, as BizTalk Server considers that character a field separator. To overcome this problem, you can enclose the text that contains the separator using double quotes.

For instance, consider the following flat file:

Agustin, Mantaras, Rodriguez, "BizTalk 2016, Developing" ¶«

In this scenario, you can see four columns because the double quotes enclose the book title (see Figure 1-8b).

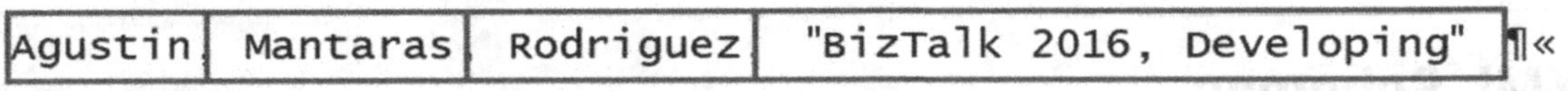

| Agustin | Mantaras | Rodriguez | "BizTalk 2016, Developing" | ¶« |

Figure 1-8b. *Flat file annotation*

On the other hand, look at this one:

Agustin, Mantaras, Rodriguez, BizTalk 2016, Developing ¶«

You can see five columns, as BizTalk considers all the comma characters as column separators (see Figure 1-8c).

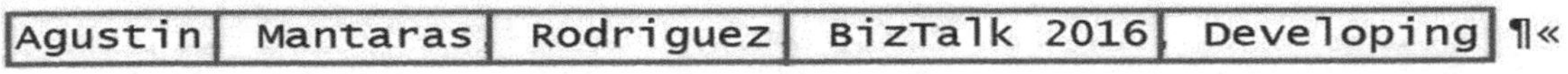

| Agustin | Mantaras | Rodriguez | BizTalk 2016 | Developing | ¶« |

Figure 1-8c. *Flat file annotation*

Positional Flat Files

Usually, in this type of flat file, every line identifies a different record because at the end of the line there is an end-of-record character. This character is considered the delimiter character, and in most of the cases, it is represented by a carriage return (¶«). Fields are identified within that record using a fixed length.

Look at the following message instance:

```
Agustin    Mantaras  Rodriguez BizTalk 2016, Developing        ¶«
```

The length of the elements itself identify the individual columns within the record, as shown in Figure 1-8d.

```
      10              10            10                  30
Agustin     Mantaras   Rodriguez BizTalk 2016, Developing        ¶«
```

Figure 1-8d. *Flat file annotation*

Four columns with a fixed length of 10 characters and one with 30. You can see the record separator at the end (in this case ¶«).

XML Schemas

An XML schema represents the definition of an XML message. XML documents are formed in a typed hierarchical structure that is defined by the schema. BizTalk uses schemas to validate the message and define the data associated with it. It is represented physically by an XSD file.

Figure 1-9 shows the user-friendly view generated by the BizTalk Editor.

Figure 1-9. *Visual XML representation*

Figure 1-10 shows the pure XML representation.

```xml
<?xml version="1.0" encoding="UTF-16"?>
<xs:schema xmlns:xs="http://www.w3.org/2001/XMLSchema" targetNamespace="http://Module2.NameSpaceBook"
  xmlns:b="http://schemas.microsoft.com/BizTalk/2003" xmlns="http://Module2.NameSpaceBook">
  <xs:element name="Book">
    <xs:complexType>
      <xs:sequence>
        <xs:element name="ID" type="xs:string"/>
        <xs:element name="Title" type="xs:string"/>
        <xs:element name="WriterData">
          <xs:complexType>
            <xs:sequence>
              <xs:element name="ID" type="xs:string"/>
              <xs:element name="Name" type="xs:string"/>
              <xs:element name="LastName" type="xs:string"/>
            </xs:sequence>
          </xs:complexType>
        </xs:element>
      </xs:sequence>
    </xs:complexType>
  </xs:element>
</xs:schema>
```

Figure 1-10. *XML representation*

JSON Messages

Although JSON messages are not implemented using XML technology, I decided to include them in this section as BizTalk Server, since version BizTalk 2013 R2 can receive and send messages using JSON pipelines.

JSON is a lightweight data format, natural for humans to read and write. It's widely used in devices communication through modern API interfaces and client-side Java scripts.

The main benefit of the JSON format and the reason why it became popular very fast is the reduced data size. In XML messages, there are lots of repeating element and attributes names.

Figure 1-11 shows an example of a JSON message.

```
{
  "PO": {
    "poNum": "poNum_0",
    "poDate": "1999-05-31",
    "shipDate": "1999-05-31",
    "subTotal": "10.4",
    "shipCost": "10.4",
    "shipMethod": "shipMethod_0",
    "paymentMethod": "paymentMethod_0",
    "totalQty": "10",
    "poTotal": "10.4",
    "discount": "10.4",
    "status": "status_0",
    "fulfillment": "fulfillment_0",
    "customer": {
      "customerID": "customerID_0",
      "companyName": "companyName_0",
      "address": "address_0",
      "city": "city_0",
      "state": "state_0",
      "zip": "zip_0",
      "country": "country_0",
      "phone": "phone_0",
      "email": "email_0"
    },
    "shipTo": {
      "customerID": "customerID_0",
      "companyName": "companyName_0",
      "address": "address_0",
      "city": "city_0",
      "state": "state_0",
      "zip": "zip_0",
      "country": "country_0",
      "phone": "phone_0",
      "email": "email_0"
    },
    "items": {
      "item": {
        "lineNo": "10",
        "partNum": "partNum_0",
        "productName": "productName_0",
        "qty": "10",
        "itemPrice": "10.4",
        "itemTotal": "10.4",
        "manufacturer": "manufacturer_0"
      }
    }
  }
}
```

Figure 1-11. *Example of a JSON message*

Envelope Schemas

You can use envelopes to wrap one or more XML instance documents into a single XML instance message. You could usually find them in a typical batch file that contains one or more child schemas.

Property Schemas

BizTalk Server uses property schemas for property promotion. Property promotion is the process of extracting field element values from a message and inserting them into the message context. We will see this topic later in the book.

Now that you have learned how BizTalk Server uses the XML technology, it is time to reveal what is happening under the hood of the black box.

The Message Engine

What is it that makes BizTalk Server work? Before getting into the details of the BizTalk Server engine, it is essential to understand the different parts that help the engine provide the functionality of receiving, processing, and sending information. BizTalk Server bases the engine in the publish and subscribe model (see Figure 1-12), where incoming information is published to a central store and, in later stages, consumed by subscribers. There are many publish and subscribe models, but BizTalk Server works only by accessing the content of the publication itself. See Table 1-1.

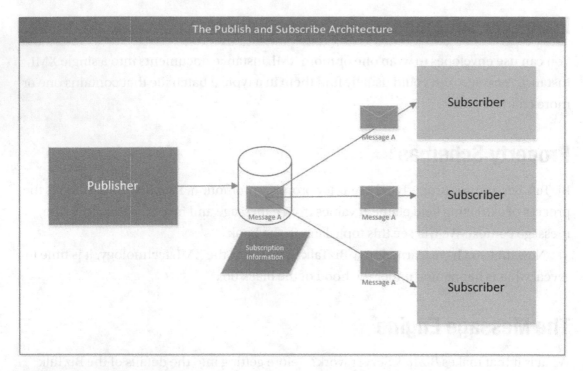

Figure 1-12. *The publish and subscribe architecture*

Table 1-1. *Relationship Between the Standard Publish and Subscribe Model and BizTalk Server Elements*

Publish and Subscribe Model	BizTalk Server Concept
Publications	Messages
Publishers	Receive ports and orchestrations
Subscribers	Send ports and orchestrations
Store	Message Box database

In this model, subscribers sign up for the types of publications that are of interest to them by setting up several requirements that publications (messages) must meet. The message is evaluated at the moment of publication, and all subscribers receive a copy of it. It is crucial to note that BizTalk Server does not use the content of the message only, but also uses additional information provided by the context of the message. See Figure 1-13.

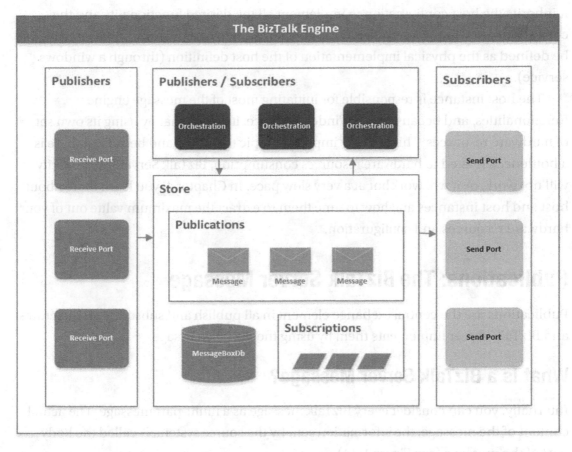

Figure 1-13. *BizTalk Server implementation of the publish and subscribe architecture*

In the next sections, you learn about these elements and how they relate to each other.

Host and Host Instances

If you have a developer background, it might help to extrapolate the host and host instance definitions with classes and object instances. In the object programming model, developers create classes (with methods and properties) that define how the objects of that class will behave when they are instantiated as object instances. You can think of the same way for host and host instances. The host defines how an instance of that host will behave regarding the execution model (32-bit or 64-bit), tracking functionality, and much more. Once a host instance is created using the BizTalk administration console or any other supported method such as WMI, PowerShell, or the OEMExplorer DLL, it inherits the host configuration to implement all the desired functionality and the correspondent windows service is created. Therefore, in other words, a host instance can be defined as the physical implementation of the host definition (through a windows service).

The host instance is responsible for initiating most of the message engine functionalities, and because it is a Windows service, it will do that by using its own set of hardware resources. This is a very important topic to understand because if there is a bottleneck related to hardware resources consumption, BizTalk Server functionality will not work, or it will work but at a very slow pace. In Chapter 4, you learn more about host and host instances and how to tune them to extract the maximum value out of your hardware resources and configuration.

Publications: The BizTalk Server Message

Publications are the central exchange element in all publish and subscribe architectures, and BizTalk Server implements them by using the BizTalk message.

What Is a BizTalk Server Message?

Internally, you can consider every BizTalk message as a multi-part message. The actual content of the message, the information sent by the source system, is called the body part of the message (see Figure 1-14).

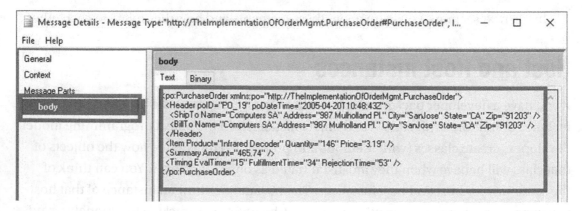

Figure 1-14. *Message body part*

> **Note**   Most BizTalk Server adapters create messages with only one part. However, the POP3 adapter can create several parts to construct the message definition.

Messages are created at the receiving stage using streaming mechanisms provided by the receiving adapter and pipelines and implementing the following interfaces:

```
Microsoft.BizTalk.Message.Interop.IBaseMessage
Microsoft.BizTalk.Message.Interop.IBasePart interfaces
```

Since at the moment of publishing messages to the database you could potentially have more than one subscriber, the engine might not know the number of active subscribers that are expecting that message.

> **Note**   As all subscribers must receive a copy of the original untouched message, messages are immutable. This means that as soon as a message gets published, it cannot be modified using any method.

At this point, if you are an experienced BizTalk Server developer, you might think that it is possible to modify messages in an orchestration by calling an external .NET component. True. However, to accomplish this task, BizTalk Server forces you to insert a construct shape in the orchestration and this action indeed publishes a new message into the Message Box database. This is when orchestrations can also take the publisher role.

BizTalk Server uses the Message Box database to store all messages using the table structure shown in Figure 1-15.

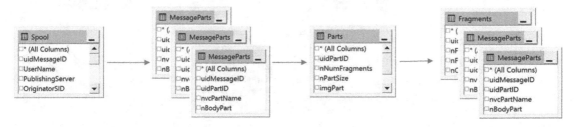

Figure 1-15. *BizTalk Messages structure*

Notice that the `uidMessageID` is present in all tables. When a message gets published, the engine assigns a unique `MessageID` property by generating a new GUID.

The `Spool` table is probably the most important table in the Message Box database. It contains references to all the published messages. We will see this table in more detail later in the book, as it is related to several important areas.

All BizTalk messages are multi-part messages; this means that they are composed of zero to n parts. The `MessageParts` table is used by the engine to store them.

Every part is composed of fragments. As soon as a message gets published, BizTalk Server evaluates the size of the binary data and inserts several chunk fragments into the fragment tables. The large message size setting regulates this process. You will learn about this setting in Chapter 4.

The Message Context

When a document is received, an important BizTalk Server artifact called *adapter* attaches context data to the document. This data is called the *message context,* as shown in Figure 1-16.

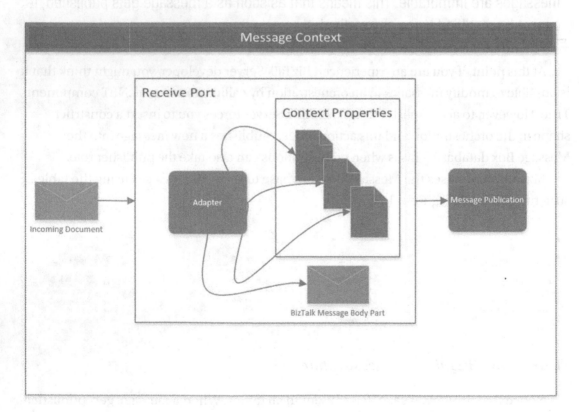

Figure 1-16. *Message context creation*

The message context is a container for several extended properties that BizTalk Server uses internally to operate and for routing reasons. Each property in the message context has four elements:

- Name: The actual name of the property.

- Value: Fulfilled by the adapter or the pipeline.

- Type: It could be Promoted or Not Promoted (detailed later in this chapter).

- Namespace: When adapters fulfill properties, they assign them to a specific namespace. For an in-depth dive into BizTalk namespaces, see the previous section of this book.

We can classify properties into the following categories:

- System-related

- Distinguished properties

- User-related

- Adapter-related

Let's review all of them.

System-Related Properties

BizTalk uses these properties to populate valuable information about system properties like:

- ReceivePortName: Name of the port that received the message.

- InboundTransportType: Name of the adapter used to receive the message.

- ReceiveLocationName: Name of the location used to receive the message through the port.

- MessageType: Probably the most important property of the BizTalk engine. We discuss it in the following section.

Out-of-the-box adapters and the BizTalk engine promote properties into the context to implement BizTalk Server functionality. All system promoted properties are created using any of the following namespaces:

19

- `http://schemas.microsoft.com/BizTalk/2003/messageagent-roperties`

- `http://schemas.microsoft.com/BizTalk/2003/messagetracking-properties`

- `http://schemas.microsoft.com/BizTalk/2003/system-properties`

There are tons of system-related properties and documenting all of them is out of the scope of this book.

Distinguished Properties

All distinguished properties are written into the message context using the following namespace:

`http://schemas.microsoft.com/BizTalk/2003/btsDistinguishedFields`

Developers can create custom distinguished properties (see Figure 1-17) to access specific business data through orchestrations. BizTalk Server can create them at the adapter or pipeline level using Microsoft Adapters (Swift is an excellent example of this).

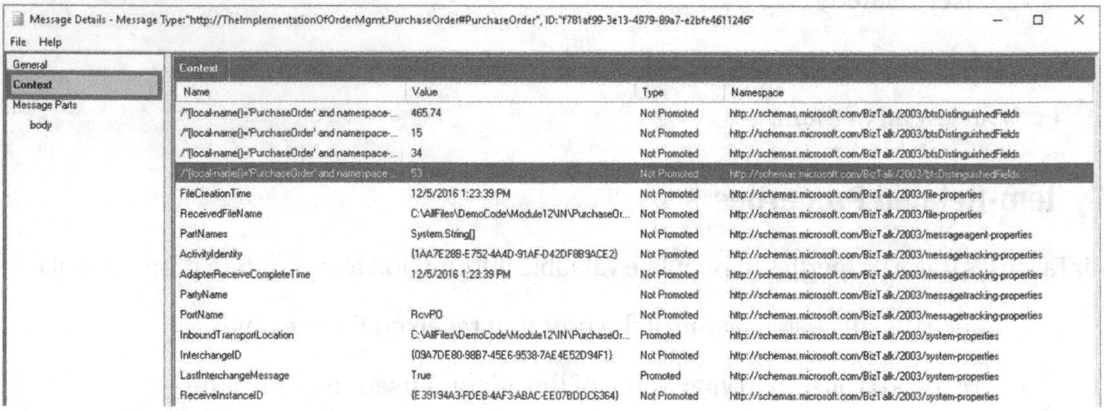

Figure 1-17. Distinguished properties

User-Related Properties

Developers can create custom context properties in two ways:

- Creating a custom adapter that creates custom properties.

- Creating a custom pipeline that adds or changes properties to the context.

All user-related properties use custom namespaces, and they usually appear associated with the target namespace property of the incoming XML.

Adapter-Related Properties

The adapter uses these properties to fulfill information related only to the adapter. Examples of these properties are:

- `FileCreationTime`: Creation time of the actual file.

- `ReceivedFileName`: Full path and name of the file.

All adapter-related properties are created under the namespace:

`http://schemas.microsoft.com/BizTalk/2003/adapterName-properties`

Where `adapterName` changes based on the adapter used.

For a detailed list of all context properties generated by BizTalk engine and its adapters, visit `https://msdn.microsoft.com/en-us/library/aa562116.aspx`.

The Message Type Property

As mentioned previously, when BizTalk Server receives a document, it generates all the context properties for the message. Among all of them, the pipeline constructs the `MessageType` property. It is composed of the target namespace plus the main root node name, as shown in Figure 1-18.

Figure 1-18. *MessageType property view*

In Figure 1-18, the received message has the following target namespace property:

`http://FlatFileWizard.BookOrdersCompleted`

And the following XML Main Root node name:

`BookOrdersCompleted`

Pipelines, within the disassembling stage, concatenate both values using the hash character, #. As a result, the following `MessageType` property is generated:

`http://FlatFileWizard.BookOrdersCompleted#BookOrdersCompleted`

Notice two important things:

- The property type is promoted. This process will not only create and insert this property into the context, but it will also promote it so that it becomes accessible for routing and internal engine operations. The XML and flat file disassemblers promote the message type on the flight, as they are processing the message. If you are developing a custom pipeline component, you should implement a disassembler stage that promotes this property (ensuring proper routing).

- The namespace used is `http://schemas.microsoft.com/BizTalk/2003/sytem-properties`. This namespace indicates that the system has generated the property.

Note   Message type property is a crucial concept in BizTalk Server, as the engine and developers use this property to identify a received message, for routing proposes, advanced developer tasks, and even for troubleshooting issues.

Since the pipeline generates the message type property, what is happening when you set up the receive location to use a pass-through pipeline? Well, in this case, the message type property is not generated as no disassembling stage could be executed. This is the typical scenario where BizTalk Server is receiving a binary chunk of data, and the logic of accessing the content of the message is implemented using custom code (by calling a .NET component or an expression shape in orchestrations).

Message Properties

Message properties are the properties generated by the adapter and pipelines that belong to the message context. As outlined in previous sections, properties can be written to the context or promoted into the context. The message property type reflects this concept. The type could be Promoted or Not Promoted, as shown in Figure 1-19.

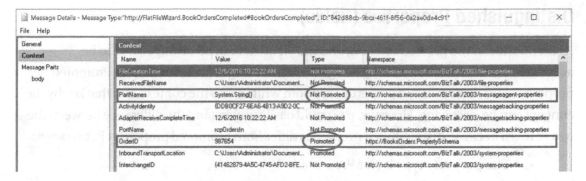

Figure 1-19. *Types of message properties*

Note   The difference between these two types is that promoted properties can be used as conditions in message routing, while written properties cannot.

Non-promoted properties can be distinguished, allowing orchestrations to access them using expression shapes. As you have learned previously, these properties belong to the following namespace:

`http://schemas.microsoft.com/BizTalk/2003/btsDistinguisedFields`

The adapter can promote properties directly from written properties. However, if you want to add custom promoted properties, you can do so in two ways:

- Based on a schema definition. This is the situation when you want to route based on an element in a specific message. In this case, the promoted property is assigned to the `Microsoft.XLANGs.BaseTypes.MessageDataPropertyBase` type.

- Any other property not based on a schema definition. This is the situation when you want to create a custom promoted property inside a custom pipeline component and access it later. In this case, the promoted property is based on the `Microsoft.XLANGs.BaseTypes.MessageContextPropertyBase` type.

Both procedures require that you a create a property schema that contains a definition for the property. Also, you must deploy the property schema to BizTalk Server management database.

23

Distinguished Properties (fields)

As mentioned in the previous section, schema elements can be distinguished to be accessible by orchestrations during design time and using expression shapes. Promoted properties and distinguished properties are both written into the context, and that is why the concept can be deceiving. However, you could easily understand the difference between the two of them because distinguished properties differ from promoted properties in two ways:

- The property type is Not Promoted.

- They do not require the property schema file.

For these reasons, you cannot use distinguished properties for routing proposes as the engine cannot access them at the moment of evaluating the subscription.

Message Properties Design Considerations

You should take the following points into consideration while thinking of promoting and writing properties into the message context:

- The maximum length of a promoted property is 256 characters. This limitation exists to guarantee smooth performance. In the POP3 adapter the part name could be created with a very long name description. This will cause engine errors because message properties can reference the part name.

  Something similar can happen for the file adapter as the total length of the file path, file mask, and filename cannot exceed 256 characters. Keep this limitation in mind.

- Record nodes cannot be distinguished.

- Record nodes can be promoted if they are non-repeated records (single nodes).

Non-promoted properties have no length limitation, as you cannot use them in context routing. Examples of written properties are:

- Distinguished fields

- Non-promoted system properties written to the context

- Custom properties added by developers through a custom pipeline component or custom .NET adapters

Message Properties Performance Recommendations

The following is a list of performance recommendations that you should consider at early stages of project development. Take all of them very seriously, especially if you are developing a low latency solution.

- Reduce the number of written and promoted properties and eliminate those that are not strictly necessary.

- XPath expressions can be very long, primarily when the element is located very deep in the message. Therefore, the more distinguished fields you have, the larger the context size. This situation affects the overall performance of the platform. Whenever possible, consider moving the deep elements at the beginning of the schema.

- It is recommended to reduce the property name length as much as possible. Shorter names ensure that the engine consumes less memory and still provides business functionality. This fact is especially true for distinguished fields as they do not have 256-character limitation.

- If you are not planning to use the property for routing, do not promote it! Just distinguish it. Promoted properties consume more resources as the engine inserts them into the subscriptions table, while distinguished properties are not inserted. Also, if you enable property tracking, SQL Server process consumes more memory, processor, and IO resources as it must insert the tracking information into the tracking data tables within the message box and then to the tracking database. These two facts might not be relevant while you are coding, but when the solution goes live and must process millions of instances per day, believe me: it matters!

- Especially for flat file scenarios, performance is affected by the position of the promoted property within the schema definition. Promoted properties are found faster if you position them at the beginning of the schema.

- If the messages are small (fewer than 100 kilobytes), you can de-serialize the message into a .NET class object and access the public static fields and properties (instead of using XPath). If the message needs complex business rules, accessing data using the properties exposed by an instance of a .NET object is faster than using XPath expressions because XPath loads the full message into the memory every time it executes.

The following code shows an example of a serialized message that exposes distinguished properties:

```
using System;
using Microsoft.XLANGs.BaseTypes;

namespace NetClass
{
    [Serializable]
    public class MyBookNameSpace
    {
        public MyBook()
        {
            iSBN = "101928818910111";
            bookTitle = "BizTalk Server 2016 book";
        }

        [DistinguishedFieldAttribute()]
        public String iSBN;

        [DistinguishedFieldAttribute()]
        public int bookTitle;
    }
}
```

The code to create an instance of this object should be implemented within the context of a construct shape because the properties are implementing the DistinguishedFieldAttribute (defined in Microsoft.XLANGs.BaseTypes). The following code is checking if the ISBN property equals "101928818910111" and if yes, it changes the bookTitle property to "BizTalk 2016, performance tuning and optimization".

```
msgMessageIn = new MyBookNameSpace.MyBook();
if (msgMessageIn.iSBN== "101928818910111"}
{
        msgMessageIn.bookTitle ="BizTalk 2016, performance tuning and
        optimization"
}
```

Subscriptions

In the publish and subscribe architecture, subscriptions are the link between the publication and subscribers. For BizTalk Server, a subscription is a set of conditions statements called predicates. The BizTalk Server engine creates these statements based on:

- Values extracted from the message context

- Values related to the subscription itself

Predicates are saved in the Predicates tables within the Message Box database, while subscription-related information like priority, order delivery sequence, and convoy configuration is stored in a SQL Server table called Subscriptions. The action of saving data to these tables is executed when the subscriber (normally a send port or an orchestration) is enlisted. At this stage, the following two stored procedures are called by the engine:

- Bts_CreateSubscription_HostName—Inserts data into the Subscriptions table.

- Bts_InsertPredicate_HostName—Inserts data into the Predicates table.

When you deploy BizTalk artifacts, like ports or orchestrations, and you do not enlist them, the message engine does not insert the subscription information into the previous tables. This means that the subscription is not active and because of that, the engine will not forward messages to any subscriber (creating a routing failure report—RFR—attached to the message context).

The following predicates tables can be found in Message Box database:

- LessThanPredicates

- GreaterThanPredicates

- `NotEqualsPredicates`

- `LessThanOrEqualsPredicates`

- `GreaterThanOrEqualsPredicates`

- `FirstPassPredicates`

- `ExistsPredicates`

- `EqualsPredicates2ndPass`

- `BitwiseANDPredicates`

- `EqualsPredicates`

Using the information stored in this set of tables, the Message Agent and the End Point Manager decide how to route messages to subscribers.

For instance, if you have a send port called `sndPortSubscriptions` and you create a send port filter with the following expression:

```
BTS.ReceivePortName  = rcvPortSubscriptions
```

After enlisting the send port, BizTalk Server inserts the information shown in Figure 1-20 into the `Subscription` and `EqualsPredicates` tables (see Figure 1-21).

	nID	dtTimeStamp	nvcName	uidSubID
1	70051	2016-12-10 22:31:59.723	sndPortSubscriptions: {6855F367-ABE5-4AE1-8656-4F8071B...	6855F367-ABE5-4AE1-8656-4F8071BC4C22
2	70050	2016-12-10 21:03:08.890	SendPortBookTrackId: {7A4C2E67-24F2-4E58-9A69-C4D26...	7A4C2E67-24F2-4E58-9A69-C4D265DE7E9C
3	70049	2016-12-10 21:00:31.487	SendPort1: {39A668D3-0BD1-4019-A784-BD0B7D69E6E5}	39A668D3-0BD1-4019-A784-BD0B7D69E6E5
4	70048	2016-12-10 20:51:53.313	Cache: BIZTALK2016	38962BB7-2D78-4647-8E49-C7D4348575A8
5	40038	2016-12-06 13:55:48.153	PCSendPort: {5228BEC3-336A-4900-B9B0-926F776FA1D2}	5228BEC3-336A-4900-B9B0-926F776FA1D2
6	40035	2016-12-06 10:19:05.873	Activate: BooksOrders.RecevingOrders{9144e607-42df-f1db-...	644C0697-C596-465E-996E-1E4E123B2C04

Figure 1-20. *Subscription table information*

Figure 1-21 shows the EqualsPredicates table.

	nID	uidPropID	vtValue
9	70069	A2DB8C35-EF73-4C89-9866-5661E330CCE4	{39A668D3-0BD1-4019-A784-BD0B7D69E6E5}
10	20032	A2DB8C35-EF73-4C89-9866-5661E330CCE4	{3C37B3AF-EF3B-4CC4-8C00-76C2CAD5826D}
11	20034	A2DB8C35-EF73-4C89-9866-5661E330CCE4	{4169503C-F32B-4A52-A5A6-F176FD5706BC}
12	40056	A2DB8C35-EF73-4C89-9866-5661E330CCE4	{5228BEC3-336A-4900-B9B0-926F776FA1D2}
13	70073	A2DB8C35-EF73-4C89-9866-5661E330CCE4	{6855F367-ABE5-4AE1-8656-4F8071BC4C22}
14	70071	A2DB8C35-EF73-4C89-9866-5661E330CCE4	{7A4C2E67-24F2-4E58-9A69-C4D265DE7E9C}
15	40055	798D8A34-3A4E-4DD9-8AB5-99AD2AEB16...	PCReceivePort
16	70072	798D8A34-3A4E-4DD9-8AB5-99AD2AEB16...	rcvPortSubscriptions

Figure 1-21. *EqualsPredicates table*

The engine inserts the condition statement into the EqualsPredicates table because you used the equals operator to build the filter expression (=).

BizTalk Server works with two types of subscriptions:

- Activation Subscriptions

- Instance Subscriptions

Activation Subscriptions

These types of subscriptions activate a new instance of the subscriber when a specific message is received. For instance, in the following cases you can find activation subscriptions:

- Send ports with filters

- Send ports bound to an orchestration

- Orchestration receive shapes with the Activate property set to true

Send Ports with Filters

The message engine evaluates subscriptions, and when a send port filtering expression is met, the send port is activated and the message is sent out. See Figure 1-22.

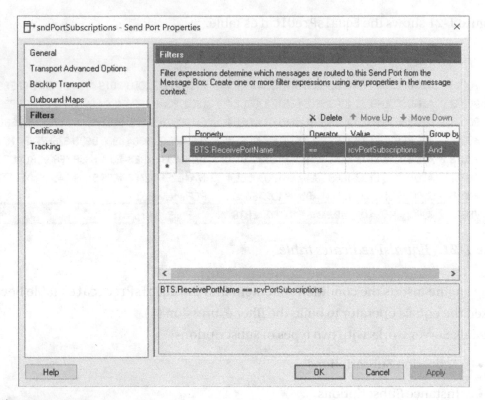

Figure 1-22. *Send port filter exampleSend ports bound to an orchestration*

This situation is very similar to the previous scenario, as the message engine works in the same way, but in addition, the orchestration ID is part of the condition that activates the send port, and it is automatically inserted into the `EqualsPredicate` table. See Figure 1-23.

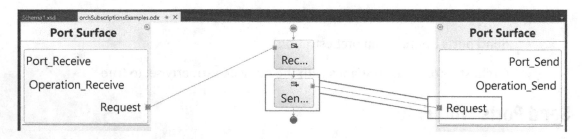

Figure 1-23. *Send port bound to an orchestration*

Orchestration Receive Shapes with Activate Property Set to True

In this case, the BizTalk engine will start an orchestration instance when the receiving ports receive a new message. Additionally, you can add filter expressions to the subscription, as shown in Figure 1-24.

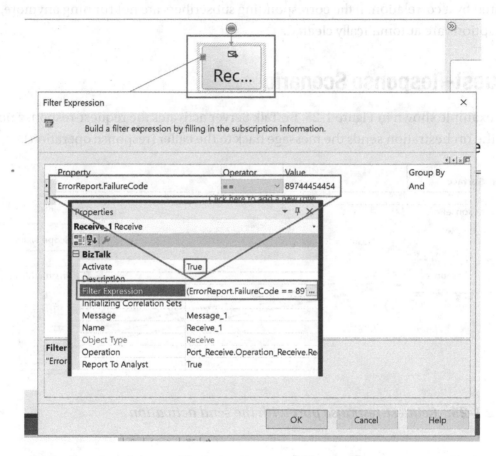

Figure 1-24. *Receive shape with activation and filter subscriptions*

The previous orchestration is extending the subscription by picking up messages that contain an error report structure within the context.

Instance Subscriptions

This type of subscription does not activate a new subscriber. Messages received are routed to existing orchestrations instances that are already running or waiting for a response using a Request/Response (receive port) scenario or an interchange regulated by a correlation. If the corresponding subscribers are not running anymore, subscriptions are automatically cleared.

Request-Response Scenario

In the example shown in Figure 1-25, BizTalk Server activates the request-response port when the orchestration sends the message back to the caller (response operation).

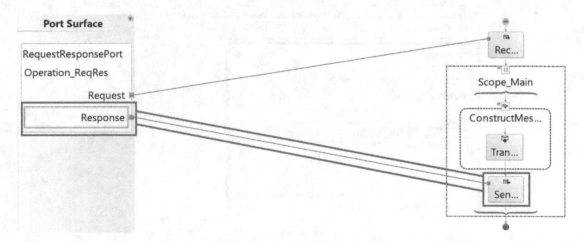

Figure 1-25. *Request-response port with the send activation*

Solicit-Response Scenario

In this case, BizTalk Server activates the orchestration when the solicit-response port receives a new correlated message. See Figure 1-26.

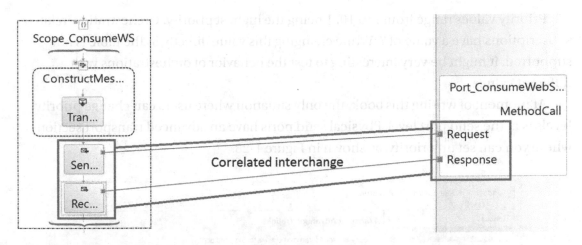

Figure 1-26. *Solicit-response port with correlation*

Subscription Priority

When the engine generates a subscription, the creation process sets a priority level for that subscription into the Subscriptions table, as shown in Figure 1-27.

	nID	dtTimeStamp	nvcName	snPriority
1	19	2016-11-22 20:05:31.740	ResendPort: WCF-WSHttp	5
2	18	2016-11-22 20:05:31.740	ResendPort: WCF-NetTcp	5
3	3	2016-11-22 20:05:05.083	Activate: Microsoft.BizTalk.Edi.RoutingOrchestration.BatchR...	7
4	40038	2016-12-06 13:55:48.153	PCSendPort: {5228BEC3-336A-4900-B9B0-926F776FA1D2}	5
5	15	2016-11-22 20:05:31.740	ResendPort: WCF-Custom	5
6	13	2016-11-22 20:05:31.740	ResendPort: MQSeries	5
7	40034	2016-12-06 10:19:04.850	sndSendORders: {0DCC7ED3-0A15-419B-ACEA-EFDC6890...	5
8	5	2016-11-22 20:05:31.740	ResendPort: HTTP	5
9	14	2016-11-22 20:05:31.740	ResendPort: WCF-BasicHttp	5
10	20021	2016-12-02 12:17:21.473	SendShipNotice: {3C37B3AF-EF3B-4CC4-8C00-76C2CAD58...	5
11	6	2016-11-22 20:05:31.740	ResendPort: SOAP	5
12	4	2016-11-22 20:05:15.613	Activate: Microsoft.BizTalk.Edi.UpgradeBatchingOrchestratio...	7
13	40035	2016-12-06 10:19:05.873	Activate: BooksOrders.RecevingOrders{9144e607-42df-f1db-...	7
14	20022	2016-12-02 12:17:21.533	SendPOAck: {4169503C-F32B-4A52-A5A6-F176FD5706BC}	5
15	2	2016-11-22 20:04:53.517	Activate: Microsoft.BizTalk.Edi.BatchingOrchestration.Batchi...	7
16	23	2016-11-22 20:05:31.740	ResendPort: WCF-NetTcpRelay	5

Figure 1-27. *Priority of subscriptions*

Priority values range from 1 to 10, 1 being the highest priority. Orchestration-related subscriptions have a value of 7. While changing this value directly in the table is not supported, it might be very interesting to test the behavior of orchestrations with a different value.

At moment of writing this book, the only situation where users can change priority levels is at the send port level. Physical send ports have an advanced transport section where you can set up priority, as shown in Figure 1-28.

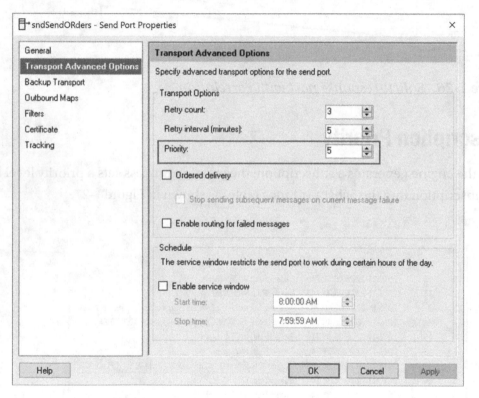

Figure 1-28. *Priority of send ports*

This setting is very useful when you want BizTalk Server to send messages to a specific destination system with a higher priority. For instance, if you change the Send Port priority to 1, this action is reflected in the Subscriptions table, as shown in Figure 1-29.

	nID	dtTimeStamp	nvcName	snPriority
1	19	2016-11-22 20:05:31.740	ResendPort: WCF-WSHttp	5
2	18	2016-11-22 20:05:31.740	ResendPort: WCF-NetTcp	5
3	3	2016-11-22 20:05:05.083	Activate: Microsoft.BizTalk.Edi.RoutingOrchestration.BatchR...	7
4	40038	2016-12-06 13:55:48.153	PCSendPort: {5228BEC3-336A-4900-B9B0-926F776FA1D2}	5
5	15	2016-11-22 20:05:31.740	ResendPort: WCF-Custom	5
6	13	2016-11-22 20:05:31.740	ResendPort: MQSeries	5
7	5	2016-11-22 20:05:31.740	ResendPort: HTTP	5
8	14	2016-11-22 20:05:31.740	ResendPort: WCF-BasicHttp	5
9	20021	2016-12-02 12:17:21.473	SendShipNotice: {3C37B3AF-EF3B-4CC4-8C00-76C2CAD58...	5
10	70052	2016-12-14 13:35:18.160	sndSendORders: {0DCC7ED3-0A15-419B-ACEA-EFDC6890...	1
11	6	2016-11-22 20:05:31.740	ResendPort: SOAP	5
12	4	2016-11-22 20:05:15.613	Activate: Microsoft.BizTalk.Edi.UpgradeBatchingOrchestratio...	7
13	40035	2016-12-06 10:19:05.873	Activate: BooksOrders.ReceivingOrders{9144e607-42df-f1db-...	7

Figure 1-29. *Priority at Send port level changed to 1*

From now on, every time BizTalk Server has to send messages using this port, it will assign the highest priority as the stored procedures that query the host queue tables will retrieve these operations first.

Searching for Subscription Information

When troubleshooting, you might need to search for a specific subscription. You can use the BizTalk Administration Console to query subscription information. To do that, follow these steps:

1. Open the BizTalk Administration Console.

2. Click on BizTalk Group and Select the New Query tab, as shown in Figure 1-30.

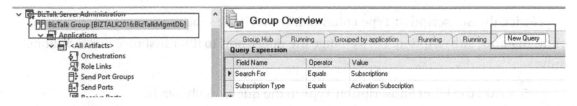

Figure 1-30. *Accessing the New Query tab*

3. In the Search for option, choose Subscriptions, as shown in
    Figure 1-31.

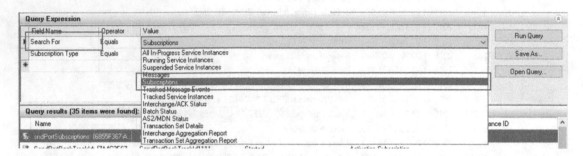

Figure 1-31. *Search for option*

4. The query will list all subscriptions in the system, as shown in
    Figure 1-32.

Name	Service Name	State	Subscription Type	Service Instance ID
sndPortSubscriptions: (6855F367-A...	sndPortSubscriptions	Stopped	Activation Subscription	
SendPortBookTrackId: (7A4C2E67-...	SendPortBookTrackId1111	Started	Activation Subscription	
SendPort1: (39A668D3-0BD1-4019-...	SendPort1	Started	Activation Subscription	
Cache: BIZTALK2016	BizTalkCachingService	Started	Instance Subscription	f2e75276-be3e-4286-b65b-262c27b...
PCSendPort: (5228BEC3-336A-490...	PCSendPort	Started	Activation Subscription	
Activate: BooksOrders.RecevingOr...	BooksOrders.RecevingOrders. Book...	Started	Activation Subscription	
sndSendORders: (0DCC7ED3-0A15...	sndSendORders	Started	Activation Subscription	
Activate: TheImplementationOfOrde...	TheImplementationOfOrderMgmt.Or...	Started	Activation Subscription	
SendPOAck: (4169503C-F32B-4A5...	SendPOAck	Started	Activation Subscription	
SendShipNotice: (3C37B3AF-EF3B-...	SendShipNotice	Started	Activation Subscription	
Cache: BIZTALK2016	BizTalkCachingService	Started	Instance Subscription	89160b89-df86-468d-8dac-112f24a...
ResendPort: MSMQ	ResendPort	Started	Activation Subscription	
ResendPort: FILE	ResendPort	Started	Activation Subscription	
ResendPort: SMTP	ResendPort	Started	Activation Subscription	
ResendPort: SB-Messaging	ResendPort	Started	Activation Subscription	

Figure 1-32. *Visualization of the Subscription type*

Notice the Subscription Type column. It shows if the subscription is an Activation
or an Instance subscription. Let's change the query now to filter Instance Subscriptions
only.

5. Add the Filter Subscription Type to the query, as shown in
    Figure 1-33.

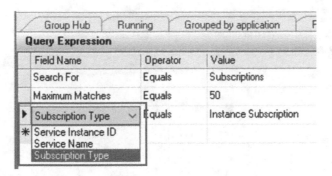

Figure 1-33. *Subscription Type filter*

6. Select Instance Subscription as the subscription type, as shown in
    Figure 1-34.

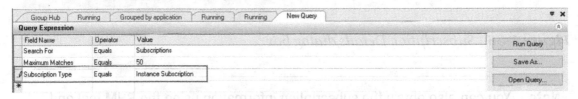

Figure 1-34. *Subscription Type filter (Instance Subscription)*

7. Click Run Query. All instance subscriptions will be shown, as you
    can see in Figure 1-35.

Query results (2 items were found):				
Name	Service Name	State	Subscription Type	Service Instance ID
Cache: BIZTALK2016	BizTalkCachingService	Started	Instance Subscription	f2e75276-be3e-4286-b65b-262c27b...
Cache: BIZTALK2016	BizTalkCachingService	Started	Instance Subscription	89160b89-df86-468d-8dac-112f24a...

Figure 1-35. *Instance Subscription results*

8. You can now right-click any of the query results to access the
    Subscription Details dialog box, as shown in Figure 1-36.

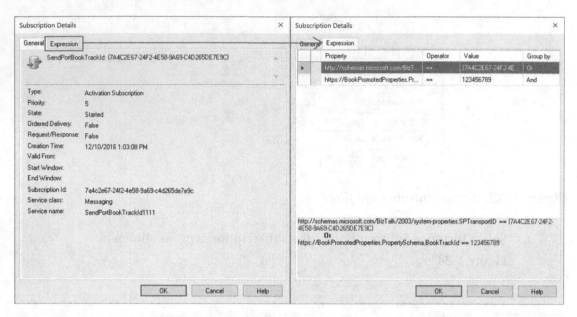

Figure 1-36. *Subscription Details dialog box*

Note   You can also obtain the subscription information using the BHM tool and accessing the Subscriptions query.

Publishers

Publishers are BizTalk Server artifacts that publish messages to the Message Box database. BizTalk Server works with the following publisher types:

- Receive ports: Usually, the main entry point for BizTalk messages.

- Orchestrations: Every time an orchestration creates a new message using a construct shape, it publishes a new message to the Message Box.

Note   Keep in mind that construct shapes are used in combination with message assignment or transform shapes only.

The publication process (Figure 1-37) is initiated mainly by the host instance process that is running receive locations and/or orchestrations. It executes a set of SQL Server stored procedures that evaluate the subscriptions and insert the message in the right host queue table. This process is outlined in Figure 1-37.

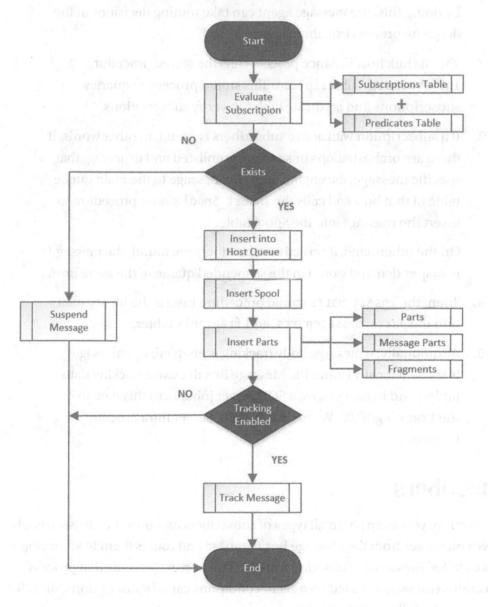

Figure 1-37. *Message publication process*

Here are the detailed steps:

1. The message agent component that is running in the host instance
    inserts the values of the promoted properties and predicates
    values from the message context into the Message Box database.
    By doing this, the message agent can take routing decisions in the
    dequeue process explained later.

2. The BizTalk host instance process calls the stored procedure
    `int_evaluate_subscription`. This stored procedure queries
    subscriptions and predicate tables to verify subscriptions.

3. If a subscription with active subscribers is found, in other words, if
    there are orchestrations or send ports enlisted and expecting that
    specific message, the engine adds the message to the main queue
    table of that host and calls the `Insert_Spool` stored procedure to
    insert the message into the Spool table.

    On the other hand, if no active subscribers are found, the message
    is suspended and stored in the suspended queue of the same host.

4. Then, the `insert_parts` stored procedure inserts the binary data
    into the `parts`, `messageparts`, and `fragments` tables.

5. Additionally, if message body tracking is enabled, the message
    is tracked locally within the Message Box database tracking data
    tables, and in later stages, a SQL Server job moves this data to
    the `trackingDTADB`. We review the SQL Server infrastructure in
    Chapter 3.

Subscribers

In this section, you learn about all types of subscribers and how the message engine
retrieves messages from the Message Box database and routes them to subscribers.

As detailed previously, subscribers are BizTalk Server elements that process
publications (messages) based on a set of conditions called subscriptions. BizTalk Server
implements the following subscribers:

- Orchestrations. Orchestrations can be subscribed to messages using
  the following approaches:

- • Receiving messages from a Receive shape.

- • Receiving messages directly from the Message Box database.

- • Receiving messages from nested orchestrations.

- Send ports. Send ports can be subscribed to messages in the
  following ways:

  - • When they are bound to an orchestration.

  - • When they are not bound to orchestration, but they have filtering
    conditions (message routing).

- System. The message engine creates a special internal subscription in
  these situations:

  - • Correlation scenarios.

  - • Calling an inline pipeline inside an orchestration.

Subscribers receive their a copy of the message through a process called *dequeue*.

The Dequeue Process

BizTalk host instances execute a stored procedure called `bts_DeQueueMessages` within
the Message Box database. The frequency at which these calls occur is regulated
by a host setting called the Messaging Polling Interval and by default is set to 500
milliseconds (twice per second).

As messages are published, host instances poll their respective queues within the
Message Box database to retrieve new messages.

Note   While there are rows in the host queue table, the Pooling Interval setting is
not used, but once the queue has zero rows, the host instance will poll the queue
at intervals based on this setting until more messages are published.

You can find this setting using the BizTalk Administration Console by clicking on
settings action, as shown in Figure 1-38.

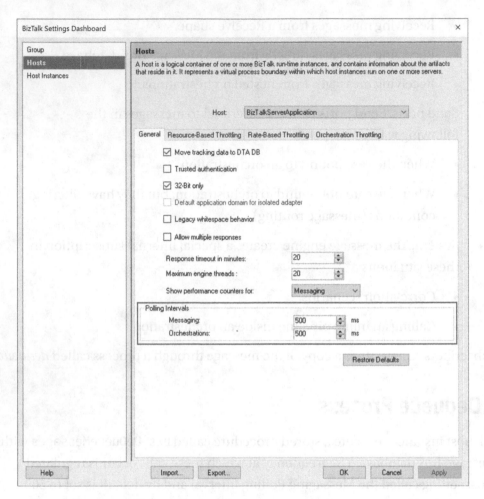

Figure 1-38. *Pooling intervals for BizTalk Server hosts*

Note   There are two settings:

Messaging Frequency at which host instances poll the Message Box database to retrieve new messages to subscribers.

Orchestrations Frequency at which host instances poll the Message Box database to run new Orchestration instances.

By default, BizTalk Server is configured to perform under balanced latency conditions (closer to high throughput scenarios rather than low latency).

The best practice is to leave the default balanced setting of 500 milliseconds unless the host has specific low latency requirements. In these circumstances, lowering this value can reduce overall latency but, on the other hand, SQL Server and BizTalk Servers can consume more resources as the host instances perform more round trips to the Message Box database.

You will see how to adjust this setting for several scenarios in the book.

Warning!   Decreasing the value of pooling intervals may cause excessive CPU utilization on the SQL Server computer that houses the Message Box database instance.

When the bts_DeQueueMessages stored procedure is called, it analyzes the Subscriptions, Instances, and HostMainQueue tables and loads batches of 20 messages into the in-memory queue of the host instance. The EndPoint Manager Subservice sends the messages to the original subscribers, designated by the Subscription table, and subscribers deliver the appropriate message to the destination systems.

Once all the active subscribers use that message, the engine marks that message as consumed, and it removes it from all the Message Box tables (calling a set of stored procedures and SQL Server agent jobs).

Figure 1-39 outlines the full process.

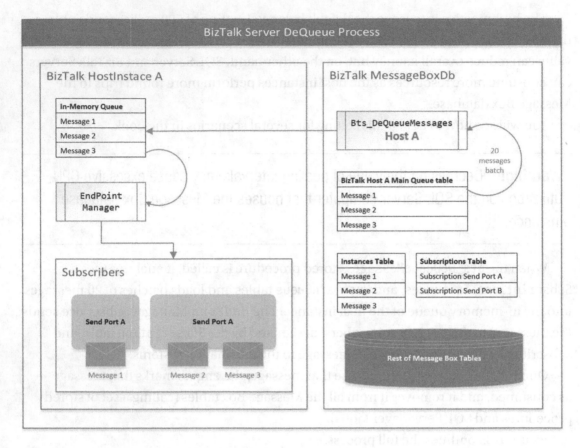

Figure 1-39. *BizTalk Server Dequeue process*

Adapters

The adapter is used to exchange messages with source and destination systems. Most of the adapters are .NET components that have the protocol knowledge to access and transfer messages through an NTFS folder, a WCF service, a SQL Server database, and many others. By design, BizTalk implements receiving and sending adapters. On top of the apparent action of receiving messages, the receive adapter also adds properties to the message context. Some of them are generic and exist in all adapters such as ReceiveLocationName, receivingPortname, messageID, and processingServer. Others are related to a specific adapter.

As outlined in previous sections, the receiving adapter also sends the message to the engine to check for active subscriptions.

When all host instances start, all the receive adapters that have receiving locations enabled are instantiated. However, send adapters work in an entirely different way: All out-of-the-box BizTalk send adapters are not instantiated when host instances start; they do this in a way that is called lazy creation. This means that the adapter starts when the Message engine gets the first message from the internal message queue and delivers it to the send port. By acting this way, BizTalk Server saves system resources when send adapters are not configured in send ports.

In some scenarios, BizTalk applications require interaction with systems that cannot be accessed using the out-of-the-box adapters. For this reason, third-party companies have written adapters to support additional protocols. After you review all the available adapters, you might reach a point in which you need to develop an adapter. Writing a custom adapter is one of the most challenging things in BizTalk Server. The Adapter Framework, in combination with the examples in the SDK, is meant to simplify the creation process. This is out of the scope of this book; therefore, if you have a specific need, you can search in MSDN, and you will find plenty of public resources related to this task.

As BizTalk uses the publish and subscribe architecture, the engine needs to store messages and subscription information. BizTalk Servers uses a SQL Server database called the Message Box database.

The MessageBox Database

While all BizTalk Server databases are essential, the Message Box database is the heart of the engine and gives BizTalk Server the ability to store the following information:

- Subscriptions, which were detailed previously in the Subscriptions section
- Binary message data
- Host queues
- Spool table
- Orchestration persistent points
- Debugging information
- Tracking temporary data

Host Tables

Host tables are a set of tables within the Message Box database that are created as part of the process of adding a new host to a BizTalk Server group. These tables are used in message publication, the dequeue process, orchestration states, and host throttling mechanisms. They are classified into two categories: Queue tables and System tables.

Queue Tables

These tables are used by the engine to access messages that are related to a specific host.

- *Main queue*—Contains references to messages that are pending to deliver to a host and are not suspended. Ideally, this table should not grow too large (the threshold for raising an alarm is directly linked to performance service level agreements). The number of rows in this table indicates the number of messages waiting to be processed for a host.

- *Suspended queue*—Where references to suspended messages are stored. This is important. When a message gets suspended it remains in the Message Box until resume or terminate actions occur. So, if the suspended queue is growing, performance is affected. A suspended message can occur due to validating errors, failed transmissions, or the impossibility to find an active subscription (among others).

- *Scheduled queue*—Contains documents that have been processed and are waiting to be sent based on the service window that was specified for the port.

- *InstanceStateMessageReferences*—The State queue table saves the list of messages that have been processed by an instance but might be needed later. This is used mainly in orchestrations when the developer creates a BizTalk message using a construction shape. Because the message might be used everywhere in the code, the Message engine saves a reference to it in the State Queue table.

System Tables

These tables are used by the engine to create temporary information related to several engine functionalities, like subscription generation, dequeue processing, and routing.

- MessageRefCountLog—When a message has more than one subscriber, the BizTalk Server engine use this table to correlate this information with the rest of reference tables. Every time a message is used, the engine increments a reference counter within this table. When this counter decreases to zero, the message is marked as "to be purged" and SQL Server jobs will remove references to that message so that subscribers will not pick them up again.

- DynamicStateInfo—Stores all orchestration persistent points. It is saving real-time data, so if you query this table without having any running orchestration, it will be empty. Dehydration and rehydration processes will use this table to restore orchestrations to previous states.

- DeQueueBatches—When a message is delivered to all the available subscribers and it is not in the InstanceStateMessageReferences table, it is inserted into this table, so the bts_DeQueue stored procedure can delete all references to the message.

Spool Table

The Spool table is an important BizTalk Server table because the engine uses it to hold all the current references (binary data that's saved in the fragment tables) to messages that are still alive in the system (see Figure 1-40). Alive messages are:

- Messages that are being consumed in active service instances (subscribers to that message are orchestrations and send ports mostly).

- Messages that are queued because they need to be sent to a scheduled send port.

- Messages that are being used by retrying send ports.

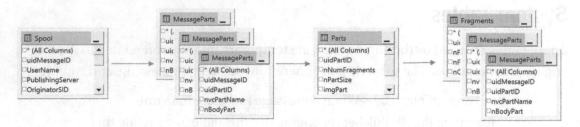

Figure 1-40. *Messages table structure and spool table relationship*

Knowing the Number of Messages in the Spool Table

There are two ways to gather the number of rows in the Spool table: by counting the number of rows of the Spool table or by querying the Spool performance counter.

To count the number of rows of the Spool table, use the following:

```
SELECT COUNT(*) FROM Spool WITH (noLock)
```

The use of the WITH (NoLock) statement here prevents the query from affecting locked data. It is essential to keep this in mind when performing SQL Server queries against a BizTalk Server database. This is especially true for the Message Box database.

To query the Spool performance counter, choose BizTalk ➤ Message Box ➤ General Counters. This counter tracks the size of the spool over a Message Box database on a specific server. If the environment is using multiple Message Boxes, you should query the Message Box that is acting as a publisher.

Spool Table as a Performance Indicator

BizTalk Server can queue messages for several reasons. For instance, imagine that destination systems are not available for an extended period. In this scenario, BizTalk Server cannot send messages through those send ports. What would happen with the Spool table in this scenario?

As you might have guessed, the Spool table will become larger since BizTalk Server is keeping those messages as suspended, and it will not remove them until the user decides what to do with them. In this case, you would typically also see that the average total documents received per second performance counter is greater than the documents processed per second performance counter (because BizTalk cannot dequeue messages to the subscribers).

In this situation, the system might have a critical performance issue because BizTalk Server cannot deal with the current load. In other words, the load is not considered sustainable. This context can eventually induce a throttling condition (based on database size) that causes BizTalk Server to perform slowly as message publication is begin throttled. This is especially true if tracking is enabled, as the calculation for message count in the database considers the number of messages in the Tracking Spool tables within the Message Box database.

As you can see in the example in Figure 1-41, the Spool table could be used to detect reactive problems and to monitor the platform for increasing trends over an extended period. We cover these analysis techniques in Chapter 2.

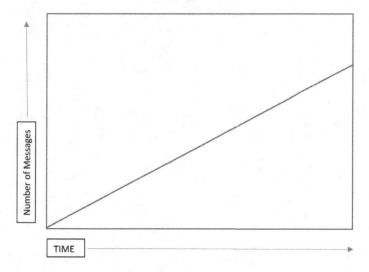

Figure 1-41. *Messages queued in the Spool table*

Summary

In this chapter, you learned how BizTalk Server uses different XML technology elements such as namespaces, attributes, and elements to create a solid foundation for message definitions. You also learned about certain engine behaviors that ensure the functionality of the product.

Also, the chapter went through most of the relevant topics to clarify how BizTalk Server processes information using key elements of the engine, such as messages, publishers, subscribers, and the Message Box database, and how it integrates all of them by implementing the publish and subscribe architecture. Although most of this functionality is implemented by the publishing and dequeuing processes, there are several aspects like subscription priority, large message size settings, and host and host instances configurations that have a direct impact on how BizTalk Server integrates all the pieces together.

Now that you have a deeper picture of what is happening under the hood of BizTalk Server, is time to gain solid knowledge about performance analysis. In the next chapter, you see how you can interpret performance information, a subject that is crucial to learn how to assess your production environment and to interpret the output of your testing procedures.

And remember, do not ever say again: "What is happening with this black box?"

CHAPTER 2

Performance Analysis

Analyzing performance data is not an easy task. There are dozens of performance counters, and if you do not know how to analyze the information correctly, that can mislead you in so many ways and eventually it will cause you get the wrong conclusion. Additionally, hardware and features are rapidly evolving, and your performance testing and analysis methodologies may need to evolve as well. However, as performance counters are always based on samples over time, you can apply the concepts detailed in this chapter to make your life easier when trying to find an issue or a bottleneck. In this chapter, you will learn general analysis techniques that you can use to troubleshoot performance issues. Although the examples used focus on BizTalk Server, you could extrapolate them to any other software that exposes their performance counters.

In this chapter, you learn about the following topics:

- Performance analysis techniques

- Performance analysis guidelines in terms of the most used threshold for specific counters

- How to interpret the latency counters

- BizTalk Server throttling

- Suspended messages

- Tracking

Performance Analysis Techniques

In this section, you learn to use the most common performance analysis techniques that will help you understand performance data.

© Agustín Mántaras 2019
A. Mántaras, *BizTalk Server 2016*, https://doi.org/10.1007/978-1-4842-3994-0_2

Increasing Trends Over Long Periods

Growing trends can often indicate resource leaks or data contention. This is especially true for BizTalk Server counters that are related to queue information such as Spool, number of instances, host queue counters, suspended messages, and all BizTalk Server latency counters. On the contrary, some cumulative counters such as \TCP\Connection Failures will increment indefinitely whenever failures occur, and the underlying problem could not be related to data contention or resource leak.

To analyze these kinds of situations, you can trace an imaginary line that links all the lower values. By doing so, you are detecting not only if a specific resource is leaking, but also if that the leaking condition is getting worse over time.

If the imaginary lines increase the angle of the previous line, the leaking condition gets worse over time. However, if the opposite occurs, it indicates that the situation is getting better over time.

To illustrate this scenario, imagine that the Spool performance capture over a 24-hour period, as shown in Figure 2-1.

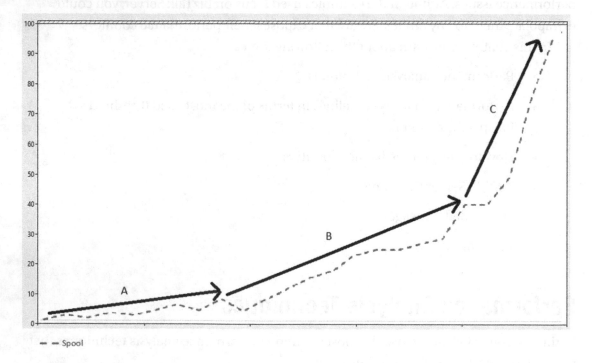

Figure 2-1. *Increasing trend over the Spool table*

As you can see, messages are getting queued in BizTalk as the Spool table is growing over an extended period. On top of that, the situation is getting worse, because the arrows A, B, and C have a more significant upward trend.

Note   Some performance counters are cumulative and show increasing trends as they calculate values in the form of:

`Counter Value = Counter value + n`

The counter `System Up Time` is a perfect example of a cumulative counter.

Figure 2-2 shows server uptime in seconds. It does not indicate a resource leak. Some of the BizTalk Server related counters that exhibit leaks or data contention with increasing trends are:

- Spool

- Suspended messages

- Host queue length

- All the latency counters (inbound, outbound, and request-response)

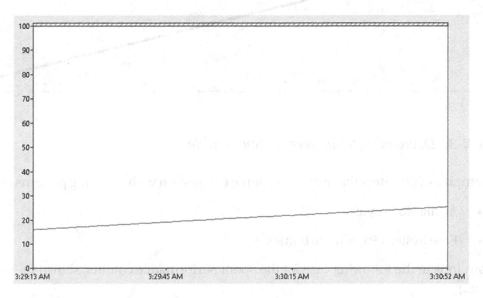

Figure 2-2. *Increasing trend over the Spool table*

System counters:

- Thread count

- Working set

- Private bytes

- Decreasing trends over a long period

- Decreasing trends usually indicate resource exhaustion (see Figure 2-3)

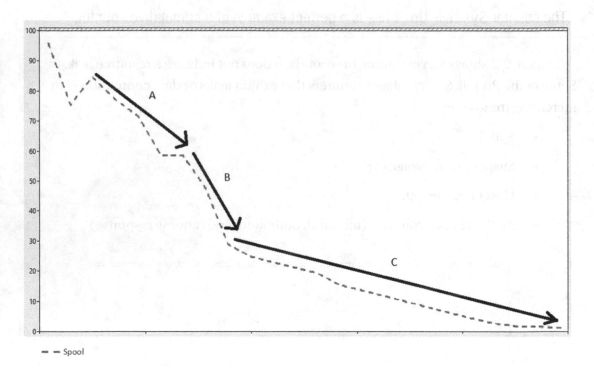

— — Spool

Figure 2-3. *Decreasing trend over the Spool table*

Examples of counters that exhibit resource exhaustion with reducing patterns are:

- Available MBytes

- Free System Page Table entries

Now, look at the following case for the Spool performance counter, shown in Figure 2-4.

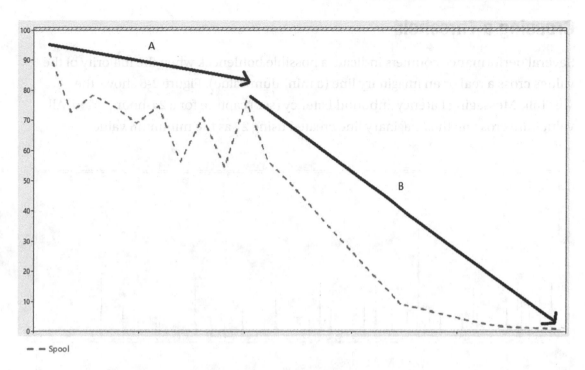

Figure 2-4. *Increasing trend over the Spool table*

What is happening here? The platform is keeping up very well with the current load until the end of arrow A when something odd happens. The Spool counter shows a downward trend until the end of B.

Two things could be happening here:

- The engine is processing messages faster than the rate of incoming messages. As the Spool table holds all the messages that are being processed at a given time, it could indicate that the engine is processing messages very efficiently and, because of that, no backlog is created in the Spool table.

- The platform is not receiving new messages and it is just sending whatever was pending in the Spool. If the platform is usually processing messages without interruptions, you should suspect that all receive locations got disabled, or that IIS is not working (if the platform is receiving most of the requests through IIS).

Crossing a Threshold

Several performance counters indicate a possible bottleneck when the majority of the values cross a real or an imaginary line (a minimum value). Figure 2-5 shows the \BizTalk:Messaging Latency\Inbound Latency (sec) capture for a 24-hour period. All values are crossing the imaginary line created using 27 as the minimum value.

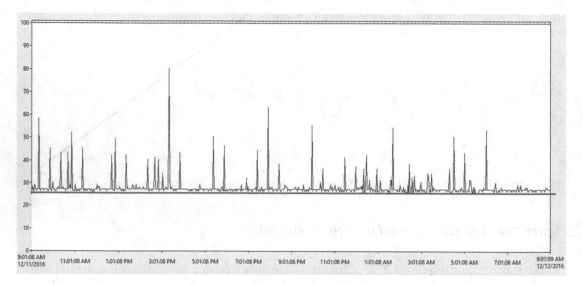

Figure 2-5. *System Queue length crossing threshold*

That means that the engine takes more than 27 seconds to publish a message. On later stages, you should investigate what resource could be causing the this issue.

Inverse Relationships

In most scenarios, analyzing performance data is all about finding the right cause and effect. Two or more performance counters often represent this inverse relationship.

For instance, look at the example in Figure 2-6.

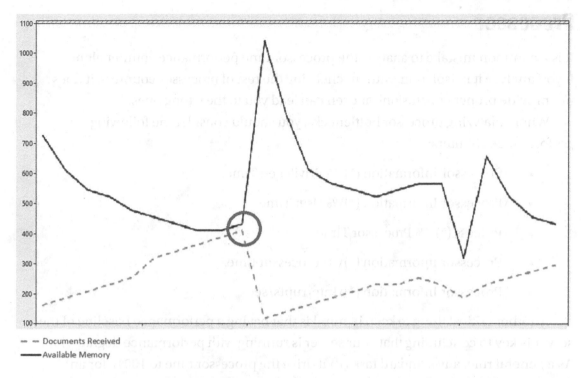

- - Documents Received
——Available Memory

Figure 2-6. *Inverse relationship with documents received and available memory*

The dotted yellow line shows the documents received by a specific host instance and the blue line represents the available memory on the server. As you can see, while the platform is receiving messages, the amount of available memory also decreases until the graph reaches the red circle. That is the moment when the host stops receiving new messages (around 6:20 PM) and the available memory increases to 1050 MB.

Analyzing this kind of relationships is an excellent technique to find issues.

Performance Counters Analysis Guidelines

In this section, you learn how to analyze an essential performance counter set that will help you troubleshoot BizTalk Server performance issues more efficiently.

Keep in mind that this book provides you with a set of initial guidelines and recommendations that for very specific scenarios might not be suitable. The idea is to provide you with a preliminary set of information that you can use as a starting point when it comes to BizTalk Server performance analysis.

Processor

It is a common mistake to analyze the processor time performance counter alone. If you analyze it in isolation, without checking the rest of processor counters, it does not provide proper conclusions or even can lead you to the wrong ones.

When analyzing processor bottlenecks, you should consider the following performance counters:

- \Processor Information (*)\% Privileged Time.

- \Processor Information (*)\% User Time.

- \Process (*)\ % Processor Time.

- \Processor Information (*)\ % Processor time.

- \Processor Information (*)\Interrupts/sec.

Another critical thing to keep in mind is that having a performance baseline of the server is key to concluding that your server is running with performance degradation. As a general rule, any standard tasks that drive the processor time to 100%, for an extended period, should raise alarms.

Once you have identified a processor bottleneck at the BizTalk Server layer, you can use the following actions as an inspiration for compensating the lack of processor capacity:

- Add more servers (also known as scaling-out)—Adding another server provides double the resources (not only CPU), which will provide higher throughput.

- Add more processors (also known as scaling-up)—If you have detected that the cause of the processor bottleneck hides within any of the following factors, you should choose to scale-up instead of scale-out:

    - Large message transforms within the custom code, pipelines, or maps.

    - Large number of messages for an interchange.

- Divide the workload in the BizTalk Server farm—If your BizTalk Servers are running hosts that run all of the BizTalk Server functionalities, you can optimize the resource consumption by dedicating the servers to run only one functionality at a time (receiving, processing, or sending). We will see host separation recommendations later in the book.

- Schedule tasks—When the processor is idle or with low load, some operations such offline batch scenarios, backups, and any other unattended processes that don't have to be completed immediately can be rescheduled for later processing. By doing this, you will be distributing the load during the day and that could alleviate the processor usage under high load. BizTalk Server 2016 offers advanced scheduling options at the port level, so you can enable this setting to distribute the load along the day (of course, if the business requirements allow you to do that).

Percentage of Processor Privileged Time

This counter measures the percentage of time the processor runs in kernel mode. Applications like BizTalk Server, SQL Server, or Notepad run in user mode while operating system components run in kernel mode. Probably the essential difference between kernel and user mode is that, in user mode, threads run under the context of a process and because of that it has its own set of memory resources that are also protected and cannot be accessed from other processes. In kernel mode, all components share the same virtual address space. Therefore if a driver running in kernel mode crashes, the entire operating system can crash as well.

Examples of Windows components that run in kernel mode are:

- File system

- Object manager

- Virtual memory management

As you can see, most of these components are related to hardware resource management.

For instance, if a BizTalk Server adapter access the network to stream data or if a host instance writes messages into the in-memory queue, these functions call components of the Windows operating system that runs in kernel mode. Imagine now that in a particular scenario, the BizTalk platform is receiving one million messages at the same time. Assuming that no BizTalk Server throttling conditions are raised, adapters will run kernel functions thousands of times a second to access memory, disks, and network resources. In this case, high privileged times can occur, and that indicates that the server is busy calling operating system components to access those resources.

The following table can be used as a general guideline to interpret the percentage of the privilege time performance counter.

Percentage	Alert
<20	Acceptable value. The server is not busy.
>=20 and <30	Warning. This situation along with high user mode and high system queue length or high context switching could be part of a processor bottleneck.
>= 30	Critical. Most likely the environment is suffering from a processor bottleneck during the analyzed period if performance degradation is perceived.

Once you suspect you have a kernel mode issue, you can identify which process is the primary cause by analyzing the percentage of \Process (*)\ % privileged time (counter at process level).

Percentage of User Time

This counter measures the percentage of time the processor runs in user mode. As you saw in the Privileged Performance Counter section, applications such as Microsoft BizTalk Server, Microsoft Word, and Microsoft SQL Server run in user mode.

All processes (not related only to a core Windows component) execute a mix of user and kernel code.

The following table can be used as a general guideline to interpret the percentage of user time performance counter.

Percentage	Alert
<50	Acceptable value. The server is not busy.
>=50 and <=80	Warning. This situation along with high privileged percentage could be part of a processor bottleneck (especially if the load increases).
>= 80	Critical. Most likely the environment is suffering from a processor bottleneck during the analyzed period (if performance degradation is perceived).

Now that you also learned about the user time counter, in general, it is easier to diagnose user mode conditions than high privileged time.

Why? Identifying the issue related to user mode is always more manageable as, at the end of the day, the responsible party is always a specific process. Moreover, if the server is suffering from high privileged time, this situation will impact all running processes, especially while they are accessing I/O resources.

Percentage of Processor Time

Processor time shows the percentage of time where the server is processing threads. As you learned previously, threads can run in user or kernel modes. Therefore, this counter sums the counters % User Time and Privileged Time.

There is an unusual situation where hardware devices are failing and affect the overall processor time by adding interrupt time. If a device in your server is working abnormally, it can increase the processor usage. Unfortunately, you cannot determine what device is causing the issue by analyzing performance counters, but you can use the ETW tracing for that propose.

Note   Although this issue can occur, it is recommended that you analyze interrupt time only when the value for this counter is higher than 10%.

The following table can be used as a general guideline to interpret the percentage of processor time counter.

Percentage	Alert
<50	Acceptable value. The processor is not causing an issue if system queue length is under optimum values.
>=50 and <=80	Warning. This situation along high context switching could be part of a processor bottleneck. If high context switching is observed, then reducing the number of active threads could alleviate the condition.
>= 80	Critical. Most likely the environment is suffering from a processor bottleneck during the analyzed period if performance degradation is perceived.

Based on this table, if the counter shows values higher than 50%, check the privileged and user time counters to investigate the cause.

Keep in mind that high values for % Processor Time for the system process can indicate a busy device driver (like a network card). In this case, you could usually see a high percentage of DPC time. DPCs are interrupts that run at a lower priority than normal interrupts (measured by % Interrupt Time).

System Processor Queue Length

This performance counter shows the number of threads that are ready for execution, but they are idle because processors are busy. However, it is not reliable especially on virtualized servers.

When the server is physical, you can use this performance counter to compliment the information, but it should not be used as the only source of information.

Number of Threads	Alert
<2 x processor	Acceptable value. The processor is not causing an issue
>=2 per processor	Further Investigation required. Most likely the environment is suffering from a processor bottleneck during the analyzed period if system percentage of processor time is also high (caused by privileged or user time).

The capture in Figure 2-7 shows 24 hours of performance logging and outlines how the processor queue length counter grows with the processor time when there is a processor bottleneck in the system.

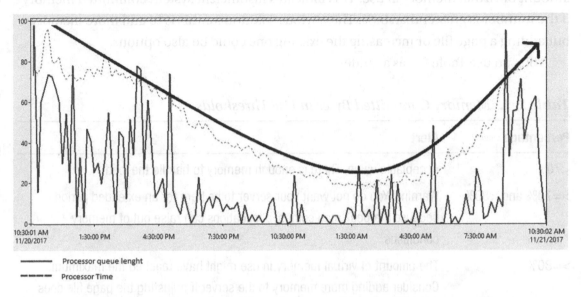

Figure 2-7. Processor queue length analysis combined with processor time

Memory

The following issues usually cause a memory bottleneck:

- Insufficient RAM.

- A memory leak.

- System settings (BCDEdit.exe settings).

- BizTalk Server throttling unnecessary due to a memory condition when the server has still enough available memory. This could be the case of a 64-bit host where the memory threshold is set to the default 25%. In this scenario, the host can enter into a memory condition even though there are still plenty of memory resources in the server.

Memory\% Committed Bytes in Use

This measures the ratio of committed bytes to the commit limit. In other words, the amount of virtual memory in use. This indicates insufficient system committed memory if the number is greater than 80%. The obvious solution for this is to add more memory, but adding a page file or increasing the existing one could be also options.

You can use Table 2-1 as a guide.

Table 2-1. *Memory Committed Bytes in Use Thresholds*

Percentage	Alert
<70%	Acceptable value. There is enough memory to handle the load.
>=70% and <80%	Warning. You do not want your server to be here for an extended period because if a peak load comes, applications can raise out of memory conditions.
>=80%	The amount of virtual memory in use might have reached the maximum. Consider adding more memory to the server if adjusting the page file does not solve the problem.
>90%	If the page file is managed by the system, then it will automatically attempt to increase the page file. Therefore, if this counter reaches 95%, then it means that the page file is not being automatically increased or the page file has been locked to a maximum size. Adjust the page file size, add a new one, or increase server memory.

Memory\Available MBytes

This measures the amount of physical memory, in megabytes, available for running processes. If this value is less than 10% of the total physical RAM, that means there is an insufficient amount of memory, and that can increase paging activity. To resolve this problem, you should first investigate the root cause and later decide if adding more memory will fix the issue.

You can use Table 2-2 as a guide.

Table 2-2. *Memory Available Mbytes Thresholds*

Percentage	Alert
>15%	Acceptable value. There is enough memory to handle operating system load.
>=15% and <10%	Warning. You do not want your server to be here for a long period because if a peak load comes, applications can raise out of memory conditions.
< 10%	Critical. Peaks under high load might be acceptable during small periods of time. If this situation happens frequently and in increasing trends, you should consider adding more memory to the server.

Disks

BizTalk not only stores data in a set of databases, but also elements such as configuration files, Windows Registry, and temporary folders. For obvious reasons, a bottleneck affecting disk performance can have a significant impact on the servers.

If the system is running with insufficient physical memory, the operating system can make excessive use of the page file, and that could eventually affect disk performance (if this condition lasts for an extended period).

You should use the following performance counters to check whether the disks are performing under the expected thresholds:

- Logical Disk (*)\ % Free Space

- Logical Disk (*)\ % Idle Time

- Logical Disk (*)\ % \Avg. Disk Sec/Write

- Logical Disk (*)\ % Avg. Disk Sec/Read

- Logical Disk (*)\ %. Disk Write Queue Length

- Logical Disk (*)\ %. Disk Read Queue Length

What is the difference between physical and logical disks counters? A physical disk is a LUN that is presented to the operating system, while a logical disk is a private unit within a specific physical disk. Logical disks are presented as a volume with a drive letter. You can see this relationship using the disk management tool, as shown in Figure 2-8.

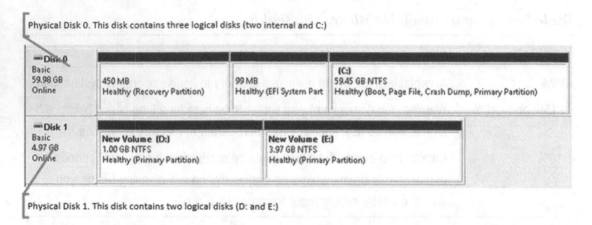

Figure 2-8. *Difference between physical and logical disk counters*

Because the underlying hardware configuration for the disks can be very complicated (virtual disks, new SAN hardware configurations, and more), if you do not know the physical architecture, it's better to start analyzing the LogicalDisk counter sets. This is because it is the closest measurement to what the processes will use.

LogicalDisk\% Free Space

This counter measures the percentage of free space of a logical drive within the physical disk. See Table 2-3.

Table 2-3. *Logical Disk Free Space Thresholds*

Percentage	Alert
>30%	Acceptable value. There is enough disk space to handle the current capacity.
=<30% and >15%	Warning. You do not want your server to be here for a long period because if a peak load comes, the server might run out of space on that drive.
< 15%	Critical if performance degradation is observed. In the context of a single physical drive, the performance can be impacted when low of free space. However, servers often use a SAN, which divides the data among multiple drives and may not suffer any performance degradation.

Keep in mind that this threshold might change for drives holding the BizTalk databases (especially under high load) because these databases are very transactional and the LDF files can grow extremely fast.

Disk Idle Time Percentage

This counter measures the percentage of time the disk had no outstanding IO requests during the capture. It is more important than it seems because you can use it as an indicator whether the disks are busy. See Table 2-4.

Table 2-4. *Disk Idle Time Percentage Thresholds*

Percentage	Alert
>20%	An acceptable value.
<=20% and >10%	Warning. If disks are idle between 20% and 10% for a long period, it might indicate that the disks are getting very busy. Although performance degradation is not perceived yet, you should pay attention.
< 10%	Critical. If the disk is queuing transfers and latency is also high, most likely the disk is overused.

As you can see, if the percentage of disk idle time is less than 10% over long periods, you might need to check the disk queue length and read and writes latency to ensure performance is not affected.

In Figure 2-9, we can see that when the BizTalk platform is processing more messages the idle time for the disk that holds the BizTalk Message Box database is trending to zero. That means that the disk is being used extensively.

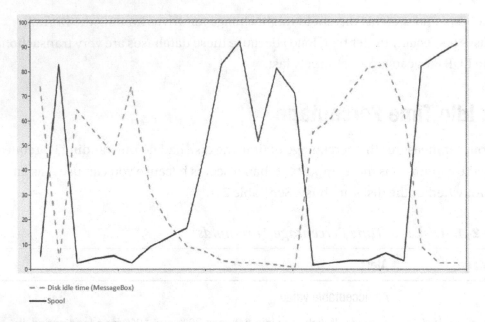

— — Disk Idle time (MessageBox)

——— Spool

Figure 2-9.   *Disk Idle time and the Spool table*

Avg. Disk Sec/Read and Avg. Disk Sec/Write

These counters measure the average access time to perform the requested operation (read or write).

The majority of the storage solutions of today implement very complex scenarios and use a wide range of configurations. Unless you are part of the storage team, keeping in mind elements such as LUN allocations, drive settings, and cabin distribution becomes a very complicated task. On top of that, modern virtualization technologies, and especially cloud environments, relay entirely in virtualized storage solutions where the relationship between physical and logical drives is almost impossible to disguise. For those reasons, these counters, also known as the disk response times, become an essential indicator of the disk performance, as they measure latency as accurate at the disk driver level.

As a general rule, you can follow the thresholds listed in Table 2-5.

Table 2-5. *Normal Load: Avg Disc Sec Read and Writes Thresholds*

Response Time	Alert
<=15 ms	Acceptable value. Latency under optimum values
>15 ms and <=25 ms	Warning. This situation, along with increasing trends over the Spool table, could indicate that the system is getting very close to experiencing a performance issue due to poor disk performance.
>25 ms	Critical. Disk response times are very likely to be affected.

The previous recommendation works well for most of the non-aggressive BizTalk loads. However, if your environment is extremely low latency or very high throughput, especially for the disks holding the BizTalk databases, you might need to reduce these thresholds, as outlined in Table 2-6.

Table 2-6. *High Load: Avg Disc Sec Read and Writes Thresholds*

Response Time	Alert
<=10 ms	Acceptable value. Latency under optimum values.
>10 ms and <=15 ms	Warning. This situation, along with increasing trends over the Spool table, could indicate that the system is getting very close to experiment a bottleneck.
>15 ms	Critical. Business latency can be affected.

Keep in mind that when the disks hosting the BizTalk Server databases perform with reduced response times, BizTalk Server latency might also be affected, and because of that, all BizTalk latency counters might show dilated values as well. In this situation, if your business is being affected, then disks might be causing a bottleneck in your system.

The previous scenario is outlined in Figure 2-10.

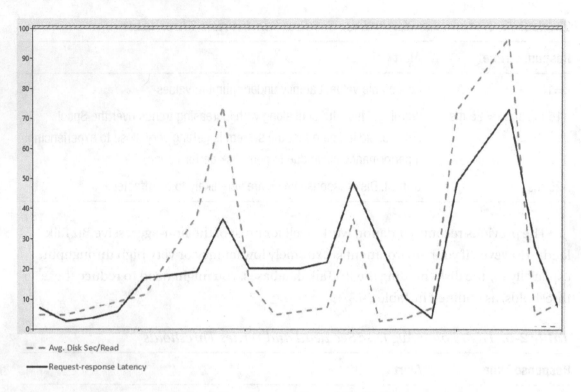

Figure 2-10. *Average disk reads per second and BizTalk request response*

You can see that high read disk response is affecting BizTalk request-response latency.

Avg. Disk Queue Length

Do not confuse this counter with Current Disk Queue Length as they are calculated in completely different ways. Current Disk Queue length shows the number of requests that are outstanding on the disk, whereas the Avg. Queue Length shows an estimated calculation of (Disk Transfers/sec)*(Disk sec/Transfer).

Reads and writes are populated using the following two counters:

- Avg. Disk Read Queue Length

- Avg. Disk Write Queue Length

When no virtualization technology is used this counter is very reliable, and high values on this counter might indicate a disk bottleneck. However, with modern cabin and disk virtualization, the output of this counter can be very deceiving. In this scenario, LUNS can share hardware queues, and the cache has a significant impact on the values of this counter. My recommendation is that you look for increasing trends over a period where disk response times are also high. See Figure 2-11.

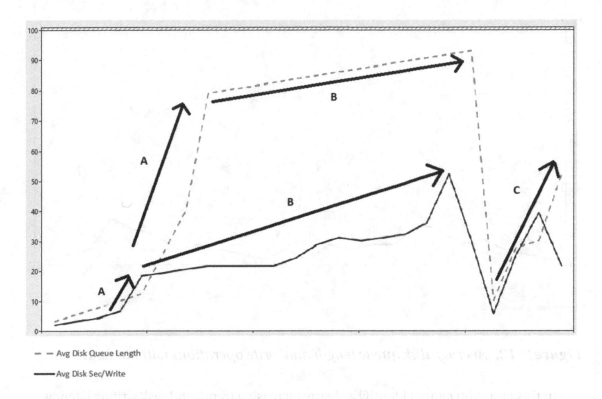

Figure 2-11. *Average disk queue length and write operations*

In Figure 2-11, we can see that the Avg Queue Length shows increasing trends in traces A, B, and C along with high writing latency (more than 15 ms and peaks of around 50). However, look at Figure 2-12.

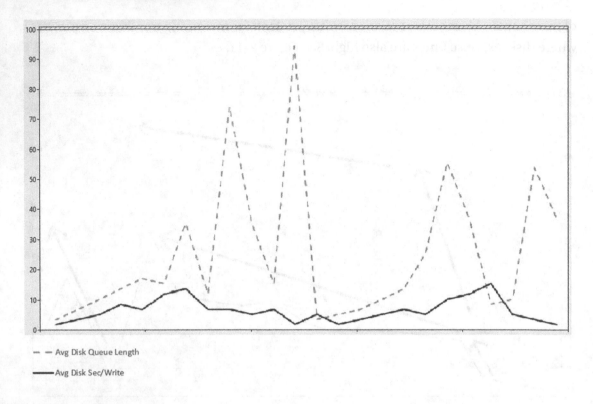

Figure 2-12. *Average disk queue length and write operations without issues*

In this case, you cannot identify a clearly increasing trend, and disk writing latency is under normal values. Most likely there is no writing latency issue here because writes are serviced on time. What you can do though is adjust the disk cache to improve the throughput.

Network

When a network bottleneck occurs, BizTalk will not be able to enlist new DTC transactions against the destination SQL Server and that at the end, will prevent processing messages. This situation can arise because of a malfunction of the networking components, network outage, or because the network is saturated due to outbound port exhaustion. You can analyze the following counters.

Network Interface(*)\Bytes Total/Sec

This counter shows the amount of data in bytes per second that go through the adapter. It computes receiving and sending bytes. As a general rule, more than 60% of the allocated bandwidth for that card should raise an alarm assuming that the network adapter is set for full-duplex mode. Since the counter is showing the information in megabytes, you can use the data in Table 2-7 as thresholds for different network card bandwidth.

Table 2-7. *Network Bytes Total Per Second Thresholds*

Bandwidth	60% Threshold
100 megabits/s	7.5 megabytes/second
1000 megabits/s	75 megabytes/second
10000 megabits/s	750 megabytes/second

If the network is using 60% of the available bandwidth or more during a long period, then you should investigate what is happening with that specific network card.

Network Interface\Output Queue Length

This counter measures the length of the output packet queue, in packets. In an ideal situation, this value should not be greater than zero. You can use Table 2-8 as a guideline when analyzing networking bottlenecks.

Table 2-8. *Network Output Queue Length Threshold*

Number of Packets	Effect
0	The network card is performing well.
<= 2	Warning: Delays can appear, and all BizTalk latency counters start to be affected.
>2	Critical: Most likely BizTalk is being affected by high latency on all the latency counters. Message publication and the dequeue process might also be affected.

The example in Figure 2-13 outlines the effect of poor network performance over the BizTalk latency counters. As packets are getting queued, BizTalk latency increases exponentially over time.

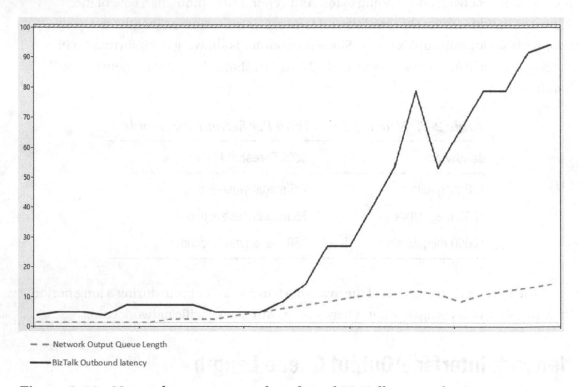

Figure 2-13. *Network output queue length and BizTalk output latency*

Latency

Measuring latency is probably one of the most important concepts when you want to analyze the performance of a BizTalk solution. Latency counters measure the time taken by all the BizTalk events since the adapter receives the message until the message is sent out. All latency counters are at host level. That means that if you want to measure the latency of a specific BizTalk element using these counters, you must isolate that element into a specifically dedicated host.

As seen in Chapter 1, BizTalk comes with settings orientated for high throughput scenarios. The following crucial concepts can change the engine behavior at message publication, dequeue, and orchestration processing:

- Polling intervals (default of 500 ms)—Decreasing this setting reduces latency as BizTalk Server engine will consider this setting when there are new messages or orchestrations to process for a particular host.

- Receiving batch setting of the adapter—Most of the BizTalk adapters receive information in batches. Although all adapters behave differently, this concept is very similar for all of them. The adapter retrieves messages from receive locations until the batch size is surpassed, or there are no more available messages at the source. At this point, all messages of that batch are published to the Message Box database. Increasing the receive batch setting will also increase the latency of individual messages as the engine publishes messages in a batch. On the other hand, setting the batch to 1 will decrease latency, as messages are published individually, and that process will be shorter than processing a larger batch. While there is not a specific recommendation for this setting, you can follow the guidelines in Table 2-9 to tune it.

Table 2-9. *Receiving Batch Adapter Setting Recommendation*

Scenario	Value	Indication
Low latency	>=min* (usually >= 1)	Throughput can be affected.
Mixed	Somewhere in between	None. This is the ideal value for the majority of scenarios.
High throughput	< max*	Latency can be affected.

The max and min values are obtained during the performance test phases of the project—when either the Message Box database or BizTalk Servers become a bottleneck due to the lack of hardware resources (or contention) and throttling based on database size is not occurring unnecessary (or disabled).

- Large message threshold setting—As seen in Chapter 1 this setting controls the number of fragments that are inserted in the Message Box database. Setting a proper value reduces or increases the latency of message publication.

- Host separation policy—Isolating, receiving, processing, and sending functionalities have a very positive effect on performance. Even though the general recommendation is to isolate hosts by functionality, you should only do it when latency is affecting your performance target level agreements. In such a case, if your hosts are running more than one BizTalk functionality and you detect that the latency performance counters are showing delays, you can follow the next isolation advice. See Table 2-10.

Note   Chapter 4 digs into host separation policy recommendations based on several factors that are not related to latency itself, such as business requirements, type of application, and load. You can combine both techniques.

Table 2-10. *Basic Host Separation Policy Recommendation*

Counter	Recommendation
High inbound latency	You might consider creating a new host to dedicate all receive locations to it.
High outbound and adapter latency	You might consider adding a new host to dedicate all send ports to it.
High outbound but not adapter latency	If there is no adapter latency, then the problem might be at the dequeue stage. Decreasing the pooling interval for that host might reduce latency while adding a new sending host might not be useful in this scenario.
High request-response latency	You might consider creating a new host to dedicate all orchestrations to it.

Important: As you learned previously, all latency counters are at the host level. Therefore, you have to perform the changes only to the hosts that are showing the specific behavior.

Note   As every host instance consumes its own set of hardware resources, keep in mind that if you add more hosts to the BizTalk group, the server that runs that new host instance will consume more resources. As always, you have to test what is the maximum number of hosts for your hardware configuration.

Latency Factors

There are several factors that can affect the latency of your solution. The following elements are the most common ones.

Load

For obvious reasons, having a high load and peaks can increase the latency of your solution, especially if hardware resource consumption has reached a level where BizTalk start throttling conditions.

Bad Disk Performance or Overused Disks

The BizTalk engine uses storage in areas such as message publication, dequeue process, and configuration. Therefore, if disks are not performing efficiently, the BizTalk solution will struggle to process messages on time and latency will be directly affected.

Throttling

When throttling occurs, the engine applies a delay to the publishing and the dequeue processes. You will also see that latency counters show higher latency values because the engine is slowing down. The amount of extra time will be reflected by the following throttling performance counters (BizTalk: Message Agent category):

- Message delivery delay (milliseconds)—Delay applied to the dequeue process.

- Message publishing delay (milliseconds)—Delay applied to the publishing process.

Complex Maps

As maps can run at receive port, orchestration, and send port level, the time taken to execute has a direct relationship to the latency of the solution. You will see how you can optimize map execution in Chapter 4.

Complex Orchestrations and Custom Code.

Orchestrations can also increase the latency of the solution as they can process code that it is out of the engine's control. You will see how to optimize orchestrations on Chapter 6.

Size of the Message

BizTalk uses messages in almost any components such as orchestrations, pipelines, maps, business rules, BAM, and the message engine. Therefore, the message size has substantial implications in all those areas. The BizTalk product does not have any limitation by design, but you should consider the message size in initial stages of your solution development because, as message size growths, the messages per second rate decrease and general throughput declines (in some cases exponentially especially when executing maps). Keep in mind also that the larger the message size, the larger the latency you will observe across all the latency counters.

In Chapter 6, we will see how to optimize schemas for performance scenarios.

Latency Performance Counters

Let's review the latency performance counters:

- Request-response

- Inbound

- Outbound

- Outbound adapter

Request-Response Latency

This counter measures the latency in seconds since the message engine receives a message from the adapter until the response message is redirected back to the message engine, just before the message is sent to the original caller (this counter does not measure the time of the final sending operation to the caller). See Figure 2-14.

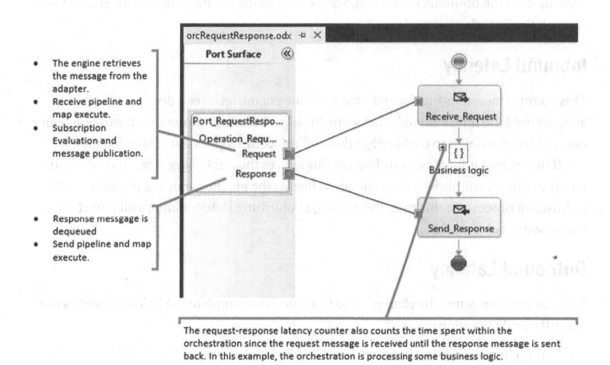

The request-response latency counter also counts the time spent within the orchestration since the request message is received until the response message is sent back. In this example, the orchestration is processing some business logic.

Figure 2-14. *Understanding the request-response latency*

This counter generates the data per host level. If you have more than one orchestration running on that host, the counter calculates average numbers for all the orchestrations. Therefore, if you want to get data related to a specific orchestration, you have to create a new host and configure the orchestration to run under that dedicated host.

Since orchestrations can take the subscriber and publisher roles, the engine can start a throttling condition that would affect both the message publication process and the message dequeue process.

Also, if the orchestration dehydration process is affected by SQL Server performance or restriction settings, latency will also be increased. If you suspect that request-response latency is high because of issues with the dehydration process, you can check the Orchestrations: Dehydrating Orchestrations counter. This counter shows the number of orchestrations that are currently in the process of dehydrating. If you see an increasing trend over the period where request-response latency is detected, then you can investigate if the bottleneck is on SQL Server side, as the database might not able to keep up with the dehydration load.

Inbound Latency

This counter measures the elapsed time since the engine receives a document from the adapter until the time it is published to the Message Box. As you know, orchestrations can also publish messages to the Message Box, but this counter does not reflect that time.

If the system initiates a throttling condition over the publishing stage, the inbound latency counter will show higher latency values as the engine is putting pressure on the publishing process. In this case, the Message Publishing Delay counter will reflect the increased time.

Outbound Latency

This counter measures the elapsed time in seconds to complete the following stages (for an outbound operation):

1. The message is dequeued.

2. Pipeline and maps are executed.

3. The adapter picks up the message and sends it to the destination system.

If the system initiates a throttling condition over the delivery stage, the outbound latency counter will show higher latency values, as the engine is putting pressure on the dequeue process. In this case, the Message Delivery Delay counter will reflect the increased time.

Outbound Adapter Latency

This counter measures the elapsed time in seconds in an outbound operation since the adapter picks up the message and sends it to the destination system.

Note that the difference between the previous counter is that outbound adapter latency counter does not count the time spent during the Dequeue process while the outbound latency counter does.

Latency Thresholds

If you take latency as an essential indicator when the system performance is degraded, what thresholds can you use for latency counters? That is not an easy question to answer, as it depends on lots of external factors such as business requirements, peak loads that can affect overall latency, and hardware configuration.

What is an optimal latency then?

- The one that can be obtained when the business flow is not affected? All load within that specific flow is going in and out under the agreed performance service level agreement (SLA).

- The one that can be obtained when there are no bottlenecks at BizTalk and SQL Server layer?

In my experience, in most of the BizTalk environments where the personnel has an awareness of the latency concept, they choose only the second option to define the latency thresholds, as in most of the cases the business team has not provided the performance requirements or in the best of the scenarios they are entirely obsolete.

Anyway, in both cases, the value should be gathered/verified from performance testing. That is the best approach. Ideally, you will be stressing the testing platform until one of the following conditions are met first:

- The SQL Servers become the bottleneck

- BizTalk become the bottleneck

- Business Performance SLA is not met for the flow

If the business team provides you the required latency, you are lucky! That is it, you got your latency thresholds, and you can size you BizTalk environment to perform within those values. But if not, you need to reach a point where you get a server bottleneck (BizTalk or SQL), gather the latency counter values, and fulfill Table 2-11.

Table 2-11. *General Latency Thresholds*

Seconds	Alert
< x-40%	Acceptable value. Latency under optimum values.
>= x-40% and < x-20%	Warning. This situation, along with increasing trends over the Spool table, could indicate that the system is getting very close to experiment a bottleneck.
>= x-20% and <x-10%	Critical. Latency shows that the performance of the system is close to being in a non-compliant scenario. Where x is the latency value when BizTalk or SQL Servers become the bottleneck.

Let's illustrate this with an example: Imagine that you stress the testing server to a point where BizTalk processor time counter is close to 80% for a long period. That is indicating already a bottleneck at CPU level. You gather the request-response latency counter, and you get a value of 20 seconds.

Now if you fulfill the latency table (x = 20), as shown in Table 2-12.

Table 2-12. *An Example Implementation of Latency Thresholds*

Seconds	Alert
< 12	Acceptable value. Latency under optimum values.
>= 12 and < 16	Warning. This situation, along increasing trends over the Spool table, could indicate that the system is getting very close to experiment a bottleneck.
>= 16 and < 18	Critical. Latency shows that the performance of the system is close to being in a non-compliant scenario.

You can use those latency thresholds to raise an alert when troubleshooting or monitoring.

Important   Remember that this procedure makes sense only when the business team has not provided the performance thresholds. On the contrary, you should use the provided ones and adjust the hardware resources to run under those thresholds.

Keep in mind that when there are increasing trends in all the latency counters related to outbound operations, you will also see that the Spool table is being affected by this fact. The Spool table holds references to messages that are alive in the system. As latency increases, those messages will remain in the Spool table for a longer time, and that can eventually rise a throttling condition based on database size or slow down the message engine as the Message Box database grows.

Throttling

Without a doubt, the BizTalk throttling mechanism is one of the scariest topics for every BizTalk administrator. No one wants to see business users panicking, arriving at your desktop and saying in a solemn voice: "BizTalk is processing messages terribly slow! Can you check what is happening?"

At first glance, this mechanism brings with it a negative conceptions since when throttling enters into action, the system will process messages more slowly or will not process them at all. However, Microsoft designed this mechanism to alleviate pressure and prevent reaching a severe situation.

Note   Think of it this way: When this condition appears, something can still be done to solve the problem. If the throttling mechanism were not implemented, the system would undoubtedly reach a state without a solution.

If you are a seasoned BizTalk expert, one of the first things you should probably check is the status of throttling, because this often is the most likely cause of the slowness.

What Is Throttling?

Throttling is the mechanism that implements the BizTalk messaging engine to reduce the rate at which messages are processed. That includes running any of the basic functionalities of the engine such as receiving, processing, and sending messages.

Why does it need to slow down? When BizTalk is processing messages under high load, to prevent the system from running out of processor, memory and disk resources (on the database side), the message engine initiates a throttling condition. The engine increases latency in two areas:

- Message publication—Messages stored in the Message Box

- Dequeuing process—Messages retrieved from the Message Box

This mechanism monitors the status of the following resources to verify if any of them exceed the established usability threshold:

- Consumed memory—The memory that both the system and the host instances are consuming.

- Number of in-process messages—Messages that are still not processed by any subscriber. This number is directly related to the current system load. The more subscribers with pending messages, the more messages are in the in-process queue. Messages that are in the internal memory queue are excluded from this calculation.

- Number of concurrent database connections established with the SQL Server instance that holds the BizTalk databases—This number is not accumulating over a host instance session.

- Number of threads—Processors assign tasks to threads. The throttling algorithm ensures that the number of threads per processor does not exceed an absolute limit.

- Rate of publishing, delivery, or processing—When the relationship between the publishing and delivering rates is not balanced, BizTalk initiates throttling and applies delay to the function with a higher rate. This one is the most common of throttling conditions, as systems usually receive and send messages in batches (or randomly). Rate in this context indicates messages per second.

- Message count in Message Box database tables—This number is computed by counting the number of rows in these tables within the Message Box database:

  - Main queue tables for the host

  - Spool

  - Tracking tables

If any of these thresholds are reached, the throttling algorithm applies restraint to the publication of messages or to the Dequeuing process, depending on whether the message is received or sent. The severity varies depending on which condition has exceeded its established threshold, as explained in Table 2-13.

Table 2-13. *Severity of the Most Common Throttling Conditions*

Condition	Severity
Memory threshold	5
In-Process threshold	4
Number of threads	3
Message count in database	2
Rest of Throttling conditions	1

A rating of 5 is the most aggressive severity and 1 is the least. The higher the severity, the longer the delay that is applied by the engine.

Note   This severity classification based on numbers is not used internally by the engine; it has been included for clarification reasons.

At the configuration level, you can change the throttling severity using the BizTalk Administration Console, as shown in Figure 2-15.

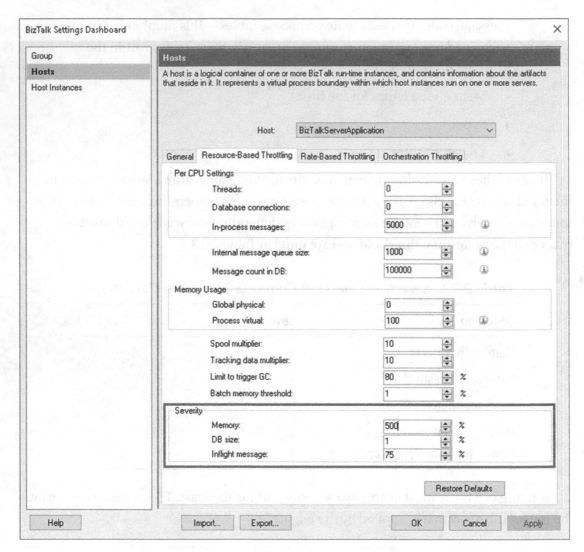

Figure 2-15. *Severity customization for the throttling mechanism*

As you can see in Figure 2-15, if you leave the default settings, the most aggressive throttling condition will be caused by memory situations. In this case, the engine applies a pressure 500% higher than a normal throttling condition.

If you have disk space limitations, it might be interesting to change the severity for the DB size.

Throttling Performance Counters

The throttling mechanism could be overly complicated to analyze. Luckily, the engine uses a set of performance counters that can help you determine the following information:

- If the engine has started a throttling condition

- How long it's been doing throttling

- How aggressive the condition is

- Throttling vital information

When the engine throttles, it will populate several performance counters under the BizTalk Message Agent category:

- Active instance count—Refers to the number of instances that are in the in-memory queue.

- Database session—Number of opened connections to the Message Box database.

- Database size—Sums the number of messages in all host queues and the Spool and tracking data tables within the Message Box (not the tracking database).

- High database session—If the engine enters into a throttling condition based on database size, this counter will show a value of one; otherwise, it shows zero.

- High in-process message count—If the engine enters into a throttling condition based on in-process message count, this counter will show a value of one, otherwise, it will show zero

- High message delivery rate—If the message delivery rate exceeds the message processing rate this counter will show a value of one, otherwise, it will show zero.

- High message publishing rate—If the message publishing rate exceeds the message delivery rate this counter will show a value of one, otherwise, it will show zero.

- High process memory—One if process memory exceeds the process virtual memory threshold, otherwise, it's zero.

- High system memory—One if system memory exceeds the system memory threshold, otherwise, it's zero.

- High thread count—If the number of used threads for the host instances of a specific host in the server exceeds the number of threads per CPU setting, this counter will show a value of one, otherwise, it will show zero.

- In-process message count—Number of in-memory messages for this host.

- Message delivery delay (ms)—If throttling condition is raised, this is the delay in milliseconds that the engine will apply to the dequeue process.

- Physical memory usage (MB)—Physical memory used in the server. This counts even non-BizTalk Server processes.

- Process memory usage (MB)—This is the maximum of the process working set size and the total space allocated for the page file for the process.

As you learned previously, the engine can apply throttling to the publishing or dequeue processes. To reflect that situation, BizTalk populates the following state performance counters:

- Message delivery throttling state

- Message publishing throttling state

Message Delivery Throttling State

This counter indicates whether the engine is throttling the dequeue process. It can show the following values:

Value	Description
0	The engine is not throttling
1	Input rate exceeds the output rate
3	High number of messages in the in-process queue
4	BizTalk host instance reaches the virtual memory threshold
5	System memory reaches the system memory threshold
9	The host instance reaches the number of used threads threshold
10	Throttling due to user override on delivery; occurs when you have changed the message delivery throttling settings for that host

Input Rate Exceeds Output Rate (1)

This throttling condition can occur by high processing complexity, slow sending adapters, or poor system resources such as processor, memory or I/O (disk and network).

This is the situation where the message incoming rate exceeds the message outgoing rate using the following formula: Message publishing outgoing rate* the specified Rate overdrive factor (percent) value.

The rate overdrive factor (percent) parameter is configurable on the Message Publishing Throttling Settings dialog box and by default is set to 125%, as shown in Figure 2-16.

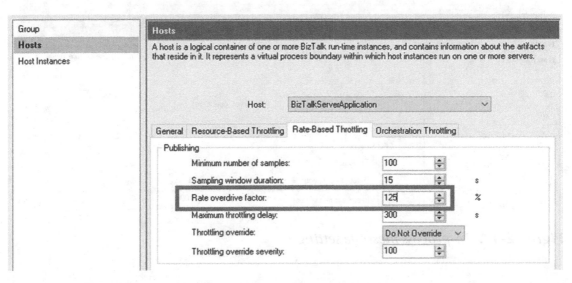

Figure 2-16. *Publishing rate overdrive factor setting*

For simplification, you can think that when the engine is publishing messages 125% faster than delivering, this throttling condition starts.

1. The engine puts pressure on the publishing process.

2. High message publishing rate counter is set to 1.

3. The message publishing throttling state duration counter is reset to reflect the new throttling condition. This counter is measured in seconds.

4. The message publishing delay counter is updated with the delay time induced per message (or message batch).

5. As the publishing process is delayed, you should see also that the inbound latency and request-response latency counters are affected.

High Number of Messages in the In-Process Queue (3)

In Chapter 1, you learned how the dequeue process works. In-process messages are messages that have been retrieved from the in-memory queue and are not yet processed by any subscriber (send ports or orchestrations).

The in-process messages are configurable on the Resource-Based throttling dialog box and by default are set to 1000. See Figure 2-17.

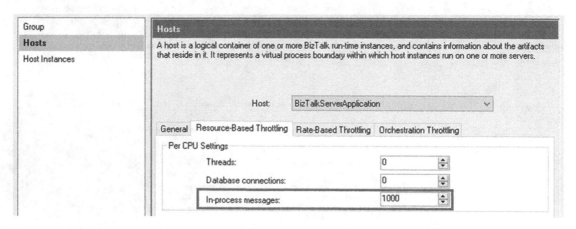

Figure 2-17. *In-process message setting*

1. The engine puts pressure on the delivery process.

2. You can query the in-process message count counter for that host to check the value and to look for increasing trends until the condition has risen.

3. High in-process message count performance counter is set to 1.

4. The message delivery throttling state duration counter is reset to reflect the new throttling condition. This counter is measured in seconds.

5. The message delivery delay counter is updated with the delay time induced per message (or message batch).

6. As the dequeue process is delayed, you should see also that all BizTalk latency counters are affected but the incoming latency that is related to publishing is not.

In my experience, you have to tune this setting in combination with the in-memory queue setting. Let's see an example.

Imagine that you are receiving 5,000 messages simultaneously and that your business SLA is to process each request within one second. The first 1000 request will go extremely fast but then BizTalk will start throttling as the in-process, and the in-memory queue counters values, will cause BizTalk to start throttling. From message 1,001 latency is applied and it might happen that latency will decrease to a point where every individual message takes more than one second to process (remember that the throttling algorithm can apply up to 300 seconds to every message).

In this scenario and optimum value could be 5,000 for both queues. Memory consumption will grow though so you need to increase the available memory of the server because if not, a throttling condition due to available memory will occur, and this condition is the most aggressive one.

Note   If the in-memory size of the incoming files is 500 KB, then 5,000 messages means around 2.5 GB of memory consumption for this process only.

You can have a similar situation when processing large batch files (more than 1000 messages per file).

BizTalk Host Instance Reaches the Virtual Memory Threshold (4)

This situation occurs when the BizTalk process reaches the threshold for virtual memory consumption.

The process virtual memory setting is configurable on the Resource-Based throttling dialog box and by default is set to 25%; see Figure 2-18.

Memory Usage
Global physical:	0
Process virtual:	25

Figure 2-18. *Process virtual setting*

If the host instance enters in this state, the BizTalk engine will apply the highest severity condition, and the system will slow down perceptively.

If the hosts are 64-bit, host instances can address up to 128 TB of virtual address space. In this case, it is recommended to increase this setting up to 100% which gives the process the potential to add the majority of system physical memory into its working set. Be aware though that in most scenarios, there will be more hosts and you do not want to enter into a situation where this host takes all the memory of the servers, blocking the access to memory resources for the rest of the hosts.

System Memory Reaches the System Memory Threshold (5)

This situation occurs when the BizTalk process reaches the threshold for global physical memory consumption. The global physical memory setting is configurable on the Resource-Based throttling dialog box, as shown in Figure 2-19.

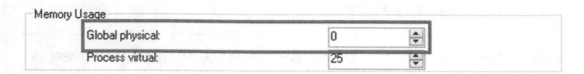

Memory Usage
Global physical:	0
Process virtual:	25

Figure 2-19. *Global Physical memory setting*

By default, it's set to 0. This means that BizTalk will not evaluate the system memory condition. If you change this setting and the host instance enters in this state, the BizTalk engine will apply the highest severity condition, and the system will slow down perceptively.

Do not change this setting unless all your host instances are 32-bit and you have an extremely limited amount of memory. If your host instances are 64-bit, the global physical and process virtual settings behave the same way, as 64-bit host instances can potentially take up to 100% of the available memory of the server.

The Host Instance Reaches the Number of Used Threads Threshold (9)

Each process offers the resources needed to execute a program. A process has a virtual address space, running code, and a base thread priority. Each process is started with a single thread, but can create additional threads as is the case of BizTalk host instances.

BizTalk host instances load a minimum number of threads per CPU dedicated for IO and the rest for operations. These settings can be tuned using the BizTalk Administration Console, as shown in Figure 2-20.

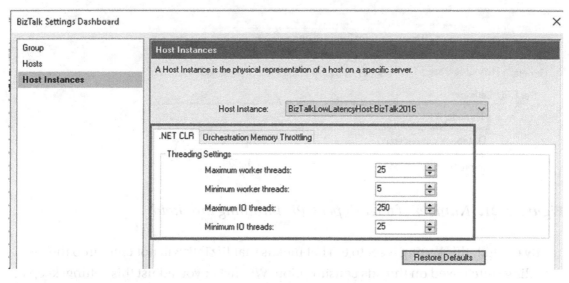

Figure 2-20. .NET CLR threads for host instance usage

Reducing the number of threads that the BizTalk Server engine use can improve performance when processors are showing a high amount of context switching.

Note   The actual CLR is the one owning this thread's resources, but for the propose of this concept, these threads will be also counted by the throttling algorithm.

You can think of these settings like a thread pool. When a host instance starts, it loads 25 threads for I/O (disk and network operations) and another 5 for the rest of the engine tasks. That means that, by default, each host instance will reserve 30 threads "without doing anything".

You can control how BizTalk enters into a throttling condition by adjusting the setting Threads, using the BizTalk Administration Console, as shown in Figure 2-21.

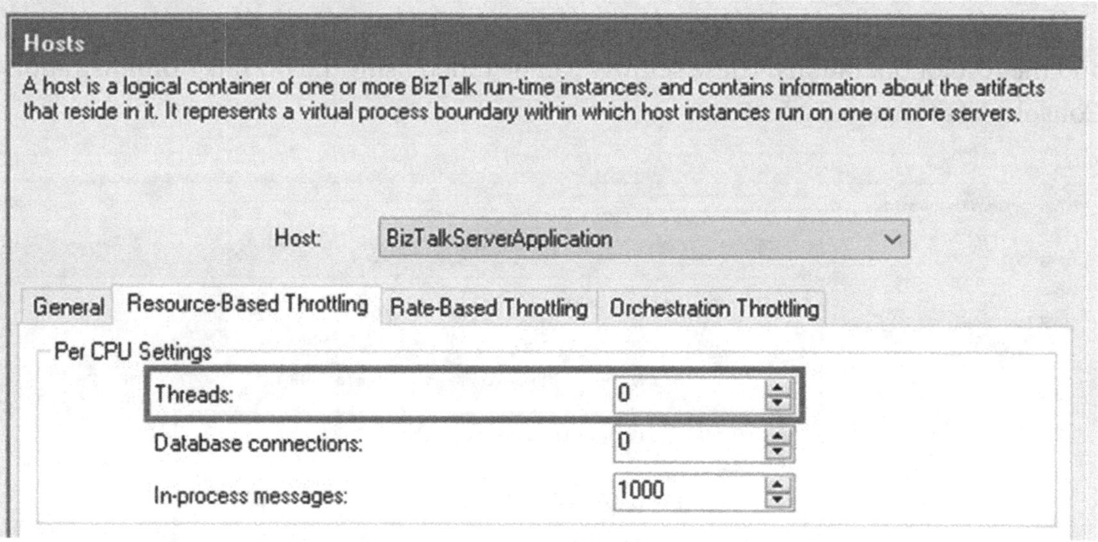

Figure 2-21. *Number of threads per CPU throttling threshold*

By default, this setting is set to 0. That means that BizTalk will not enter into the throttling state based on threads consumption. Whenever you adjust this setting, keep in mind the host instances settings for the .Net CLR, because if you adjust the thread setting for the host to a lower value than the minimum values specified for host instance, all the host instances of that host will not process anything, and the engine will enter into the throttling state as soon as the host instance loads.

Throttling Due to User Override on Delivery (10)

If you change any of the settings related to rate-based throttling, BizTalk will enter into this state.

Message Publishing Throttling State

This counter indicates whether the engine is throttling the publishing process. It can show the following values:

Value	Description
0	The engine is not throttling.
2	Output rate exceeds input rate.
4	BizTalk host instance reaches the virtual memory threshold.
5	System memory reaches the system memory threshold.
6	The number of messages in the Spool and tracking data tables exceeds the defined threshold.
9	The host instance reaches the number of used threads threshold.
11	Throttling due to user override on delivery. This occurs when you changed the message delivery throttling settings for that host.

Output Rate Exceeds Input Rate (2)

This throttling condition can occur by high processing complexity, slow sending adapters, or poor system resources such as processor, memory, or I/O (disk and network). This is the situation when the message output rate exceeds the message input rate using the following formula: Message delivering outgoing rate* the specified Rate overdrive factor (percent) value.

The Rate overdrive factor (percent) parameter is configurable on the Message Publishing Throttling Settings dialog box and by default is set to 125% (see Figure 2-22).

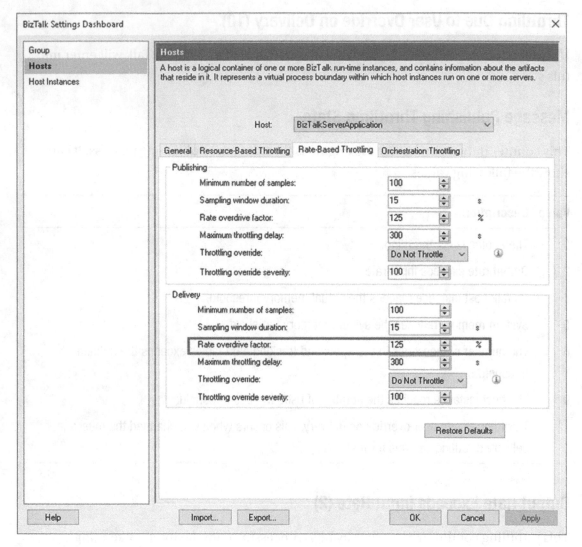

Figure 2-22. *Delivery overdrive factor for the rate-based throttling condition*

For simplification, you can think that when the engine is delivering messages 125% faster than publishing, this throttling condition starts.

1. The engine puts pressure on the publishing process.

2. High message delivering rate counter is set to 1.

3. The message delivering throttling state duration counter is reset to reflect the new throttling condition. This counter is measured in seconds.

4. The message delivering delay counter is updated with the delay time induced per message (or message batch).

5. As the delivering process is delayed, you should see also that the outbound latency and request-response latency counters are affected.

BizTalk Host Instance Reaches the Virtual Memory Threshold (4)

The same behavior as the delivery condition, but BizTalk will apply throttling to the publishing stage.

System Memory Reaches the System Memory Threshold (5)

The same behavior as the delivery condition, but BizTalk will apply throttling to the publishing stage.

Throttling Due to Message Count in Databases (6)

The throttling mechanism is continuously monitoring the size of the following tables within the Message Box database:

- Host message queue size—It contains references to messages that are pending to deliver to a host and are not suspended.

- Host message state queue—The State Queue table saves the list of messages that have been processed by an instance but might be needed later. This is used mainly in orchestrations when the developer creates a BizTalk message using a construction shape. Because the message might be used everywhere in the code, the message engine saves a reference to it in the state queue table.

- Host message suspended queue—The suspended queue is where references to suspended messages are stored.

- Spool table size—As you learned in Chapter 1, this table contains references for all messages in the BizTalk group.

- Tracking tables—The TDDS service (subservice loaded into the host instance that has tracking enabled) moves tracking data and tracking events to the tracking data tables within the Message Box database. Later, the SQL Server job `TrackedMessages_Copy_BizTalkMsgBoxDb` moves this data into the `Tracking` database.

Three settings regulate how the throttling based on database size works:

- Message count in DB—BizTalk will enter into the throttling state when any of the host message queues reaches this threshold. By default, it's set to 50,000.

- Spool multiplier—If the number of messages in the Spool table reaches the message count DB * the Spool multiplier setting, BizTalk will enter into the throttling state.

- Tracking multiplier—If the number of messages in the tracking data tables reaches the message count DB * the tracking multiplier setting, BizTalk will enter into the throttling state.

You can adjust these settings using the BizTalk Administration Console, as shown in Figure 2-23.

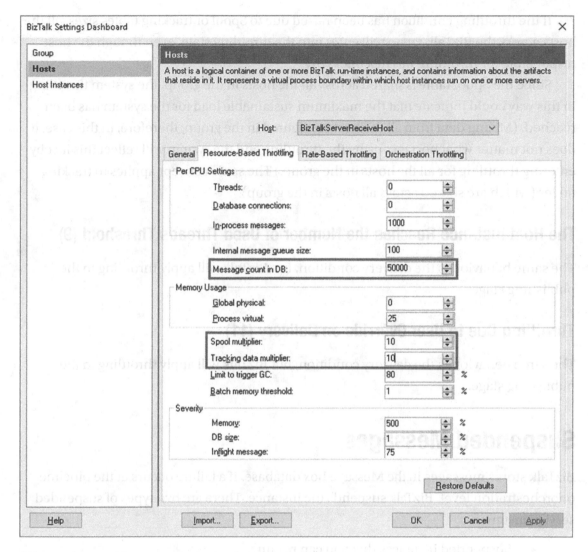

Figure 2-23. *Message count in database settings*

The most common situations when BizTalk enters into a throttling state due to database size are:

- `TrackedMessages_Copy_BizTalkMsgBoxDb` is not running or is running slowly (the SQL Server Agent might be stopped).

- Subscribers are not processing messages from the in-memory queue due to the lack of resources.

- The number of suspended messages is high.

- Maximum sustainable load for the BizTalk group has been reached.

If the throttling condition has been raised due to Spool or tracking tables sizes, all the hosts across the BizTalk group will enter into the throttling state, even though the host responsible for throttling was just one. Why?

Since the Spool table is shared across all the hosts in the group, the system throttling in this way could indicate that the maximum sustainable load for the system has been reached. (Mixing data from all the host configured in the group; therefore, in this case, it does not matter what host is causing the throttling and the system will reflect this fact by entering throttling for all the hosts in the group.) The same concept applies to tracking tables (which are shared across all hosts in the group).

The Host Instance Reaches the Number of Used Threads Threshold (9)

The same behavior as the delivery condition, but BizTalk will apply throttling to the publishing stage.

Throttling Due to User Override on Delivery (11)

The same behavior as the delivery condition, but BizTalk will apply throttling to the publishing stage.

Suspended Messages

BizTalk stores messages in the Message Box database. If a failure occurs at the pipeline or orchestration level, BizTalk suspends the instance. There are two types of suspended service instances:

- Suspended instances that you can resume.

- Suspended instances that you cannot resume. For example, if an instance is corrupt or there is a routing failure (RFR).

BizTalk does not automatically remove suspended instances. Therefore, you have to resume or terminate them manually.

As reviewed in the "Message Engine" section, the engine creates a set of tables for each host within the Message Box database. One of the tables is called the suspended queue and is used to store all suspended messages.

Impact of Suspended Messages

Each suspended message is stored in the suspended queue for that host. This action has several implications that can cause BizTalk to perform slowly:

- Spool table grows since it has references to those suspended messages.

- Latency and throughput. Each internal stored procedure that the BizTalk engine runs must "filter" and execute even more records than usual, and within in a 100,000 execution, it will have a negative impact, even more in a low latency scenario where pooling intervals settings are aggressively reduced.

- Throttling due to message count in database threshold is also affected since suspended messages are included in the message count in database calculation (because of the Spool and Tracking Spool table sizes). Throttling due to message publishing can occur even if BizTalk is experiencing low or no load.

Monitoring Suspended Messages

As suspended messages can impact performance negatively, implementing a solution to monitor them becomes crucial. This can be done using the following methods:

- Performance counter data

- WMI classes

- BizTalk Health Monitor tool (BHM)

- External tools, such as system center operations manager and BizTalk 360 (both tools will be covered in the monitoring section)

The following methods are not detailed in the book, as I assume you have mastered them:

- Reviewing the Windows EventLog

- BizTalk Administration Console

Performance Counters

The following performance counters could be used to monitor suspended messages:

- Host Queue – Suspended Msgs – Length and Documents suspended. Tracks the total number of suspended messages for a specific Host.

- Documents suspended/Sec. Tracks the current number of suspended messages per second for a specific host.

Windows Management Instrumentation Classes

The MSBTS_MessageInstance WMI class can be used to monitor and solve suspended messages instances. It loads message instances from the instances table within the Message Box database. Its most relevant properties are listed in Table 2-14.

Table 2-14. *Properties of the MSBTS_MessageInstance WMI Class*

Property	Description
HostName	Name of the host that published or consumed the message instance
MessageType	Contains the MessageType property

Its most relevant methods are listed in Table 2-15.

Table 2-15. *Methods of the MSBTS_MessageInstance WMI Class*

Property	Description
SaveToFile	Saves the message context and message body part to a location

The MSBTS_ServiceInstance class loads all service instances from the instances table. The difference with the MSBTS_MessageInstance class is that it shows the orchestration instances as well. Its most relevant properties are listed in Table 2-16.

Table 2-16. *Properties of the MSBTS_ServiceInstance WMI Class*

Property	Description
ErrorId	The exception number that raised the error.
ServiceStatus	Status of the service. It can be 16 (Completed with discarded messages)32 (Suspended not resumable)4 (Suspended resumable)
SuspendedTime	Time that the service was suspended.

Its methods are listed in Table 2-17.

Table 2-17. *Methods of the MSBTS_ServiceInstance WMI Class*

Method	Description
Resume	Resumes the suspended instance
Suspend	Suspends an active instance
Terminate	Terminates a suspended instance

BizTalk Health Monitor Tool

Although the BHM tool will be covered in more detail in the monitoring chapter, I include the suspended message section here for your reference.

Once the BHM tool is configured and after you run an analysis, navigate to the Message Box Database section. If the platform has suspended messages, the tool shows an alert like the one in Figure 2-24.

103

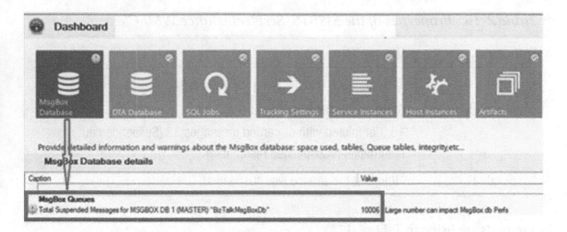

Figure 2-24. *Suspended messages alert in the BHM tool*

In this case, the alert is marked as a warning, but if the number of suspended messages reaches the 50,000 threshold, it would be marked as critical. You can customize the default thresholds by changing the profile settings.

Visual Basic Script to Deal with Suspended Messages

This script is intended to be as a tool to deal with BizTalk suspended messages, especially if the environment is suffering from a massive number of suspended messages.

You can view a full description and how to use it in the TechNet Wiki article I wrote, called "Visual Basic Script to Deal with BizTalk Suspended Messages" and found at `http://social.technet.microsoft.com/wiki/contents/articles/28157.BizTalk-script-to-deal-with-suspended-messages-vbs.aspx`.

Or you can find it in my personal blog here: `http://blogs.msdn.com/b/amantaras/archive/2014/10/26/improved-visual-basic-script-to-deal-with-BizTalk-suspended-messages.aspx`.

The code is published in MSDN Code Gallery, and you can download it from `https://gallery.technet.microsoft.com/Visual-Basic-script-to-8542997`.

Tracking

Tracking is the BizTalk feature that makes it possible to track everything that has happened in the platform during a specified period. The tracking information can be classified into two types:

- Data—BizTalk can track information related to the message content, promoted properties, partner data, schemas, and routing information (since tracking allows you to trace the path of a message as it is routed through the BizTalk, enabling tracking can be useful for troubleshooting errors). The Group Hub can display error codes and routing states for a message so that you can troubleshoot errors in real time.

- Events—This type of tracking is related to the time that the information is tracked than the information itself. BizTalk can track events such as:

  - The start or end of a service

  - When messages are sent or received

  - When a pipeline starts or ends

  - When an orchestration starts or ends

  - The execution of each shape in an orchestration

The tracking feature is completely decoupled from the publishing and subscribe mechanisms, so you can adjust it without affecting the business functionality.

Warning!   It is true that, from a functional viewpoint, this feature detaches from the messaging engine. However, you have to be careful when changing the tracking settings, because if you increase the amount of tracked information, the level of performance requirements will increase, affecting to the SQL Server that hosts the BizTalk databases. If the tracking database is not isolated in a separated SQL Server instance, it could also affect the Message Box database.

The tracking configuration is adjusted using the BizTalk Administration Console. You can track the following types of data or events:

- Inbound and/or outbound event data—For example, message ID, and start and stop times for the artifact.

- Inbound and/or outbound message properties—For example, general and promoted properties for each message that the artifact processes.

- Inbound and/or outbound message bodies and parts—For example, body and parts for each message that the artifact processes.

- Orchestrations—Execution data for orchestration shapes

Tracking Performance Counters

BizTalk exposes the following performance counters related to the Tracking feature:

- Tracking data size—This counter reflects the size of the tracking data in the Message Box. As SQL Server's purging jobs move data from Message Box to tracking database, any increasing trend over a period will indicate that there is probably a bottleneck in the tracking feature and the Message Box database will grow. This will eventually raise a throttling condition based on the database size and the system will process messages very slowly.

- Tracked Msgs Copy (Purge Jobs) and Tracking Spool Clean Up (Purge Jobs)—These two jobs show the time that it took both jobs to complete the task during the last run. Increasing trends over a period will also indicate that the system has a tracking bottleneck. If the tracking data size counter is also growing exponentially while these jobs are taking longer to complete, you should suspect a performance issue on SQL Server (most likely due to IO contention and/or CPU processing).

Summary

In this chapter, you learned several common performance analysis techniques that will help you identify problems related to performance. Using these techniques, in combination with all the knowledge detailed for the most common counters, should give you a great toolset to start analyzing performance issues.

Several books about Windows performance can be written only on processor performance analysis, so keep in mind that this book provides basic guidelines that will orientate you along the right track.

CHAPTER 3

Performance Tools

In this chapter, you learn how to use the most common performance tools that will help you find bottlenecks and resolve performance issues in your BizTalk Server environment.

The tools that you are going to learn about are:

- Performance Monitor
- Performance analysis of logs (PAL)
- LoadGen

Performance Monitor

The Performance Monitor is an essential tool to analyze performance counters. It is included in every Windows server installation and in Windows 10. Windows Performance Monitor uses performance counters, event trace data, and configuration information combined into Data Collector Sets for viewing performance data in real time or offline. It will be your primary out-of-the-box tool to capture and analyze your BizTalk Server platform. The Performance Monitor tool gathers the following data:

- Performance counters are measurements of system state or activity. They can be included in the operating system or can be part of individual applications. Windows Performance Monitor requests the current value of performance counters at specified time intervals.

- Event trace data is collected from trace providers, which are components of the operating system or of individual applications that report actions or events. The output from multiple trace providers can be combined into a trace session.

- Configuration information is collected from essential values in the Windows Registry. Windows Performance Monitor can record the data of a registry key at a specified time or in intervals as part of a log file.

© Agustín Mántaras 2019
A. Mántaras, *BizTalk Server 2016*, https://doi.org/10.1007/978-1-4842-3994-0_3

Setting Up a Performance Counter Capture

The best way to learn how to do this is practicing. In this section, you learn how to create your performance capture using the Performance Monitor tool.

This exercise uses the BizTalk Server performance counters template that you can find in the companion files for Chapter 2, located at `C:\APRESS\Chapter2\Perfmon`:

- Perfmon BizTalk Server `template.xml`

- Perfmon SQL Server template.xml

Follow the same instructions for the SQL Server template.

Note   The instructions provided in this section are meant to capture performance data on an as-needed basis, in the case of a reactive scenario or to asses an environment in a specific situation such as a health check or during application performance testing. If you want to capture the performance data daily, you will need to set up the performance logging for circular capture.

Prerequisites: If the current user is a member of the Performance Log Users security group, then you will have access to the New Data Collector Set Wizard, but will not be able to finish the wizard unless the user has administrator rights or if you specify an account that has administrator rights.

Follow these steps:

1. Open `Perfmon.exe` by typing `perfmon` in the Windows Server search box, as shown in Figure 3-1.

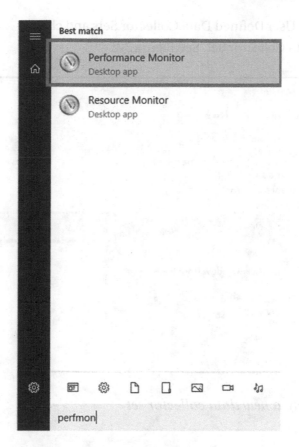

Figure 3-1. *Running the Performance Monitor tool*

2. By default, you can find the tool in the following folder:
    C:\ProgramData\Microsoft\Windows\Start Menu\Programs\
    Administrative Tools

3. Right-click User Defined Data Collector Sets and choose
    New ➤ Data Collector Set. See Figure 3-2.

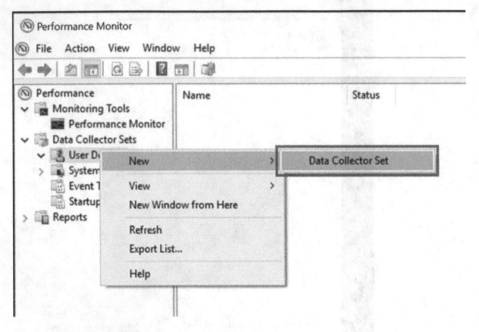

Figure 3-2. *Creating a new data collector set*

4. Type BizTalk performance as the name of the Collector Set. Then
    select the Create From a Template option and click Next, as shown
    in Figure 3-3.

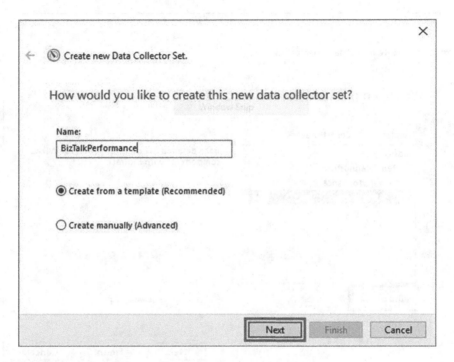

Figure 3-3. *Setting the data collector set name*

5. In the template selection window, click on the browse button and
    locate the template files downloaded from the Apress site. This
    is the BizTalkXMLTemplate.xml or SQLXMLTemplate.xml file. See
    Figure 3-4. Click Next.

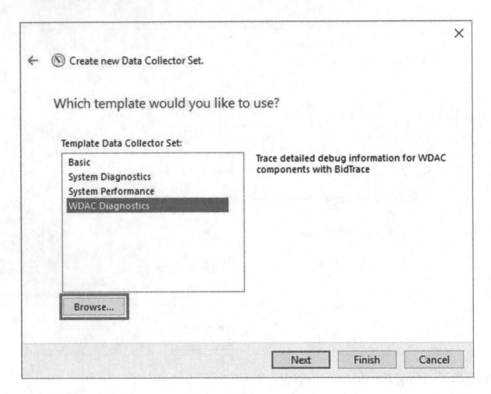

Figure 3-4. Browsing for a template option

6. After you select the template files, the confirmation window in
    Figure 3-5 appears. Click Next.

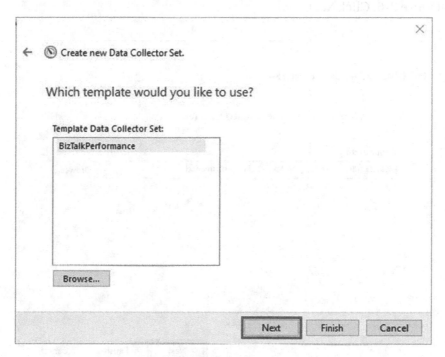

Figure 3-5. *Select the template confirmation*

7. Specify the location of the output BLG file. By default, it is using
    %systemdrive%\PerfLogs\Admin\BizTalkPerformance. See
    Figure 3-6. Click Next.

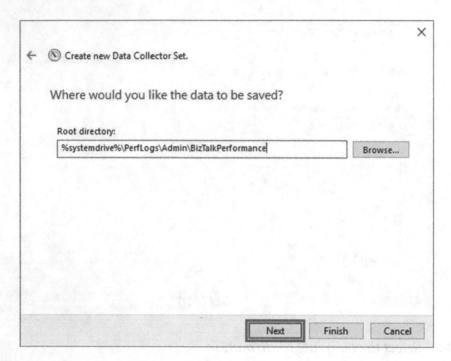

Figure 3-6. *Store location for a data collector set*

8.   Click Finish. See Figure 3-7.

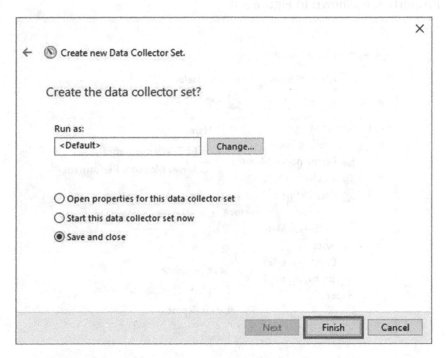

Figure 3-7. *Finishing the wizard for a data collector set*

9. Right-click the already created data collector set and select Properties, as shown in Figure 3-8.

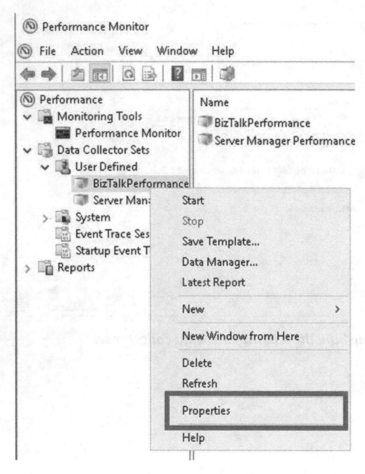

Figure 3-8. *Accessing the properties of the data collector set*

10. In the Properties window, go to the Schedule tab and click the Add
     button, as shown in Figure 3-9.

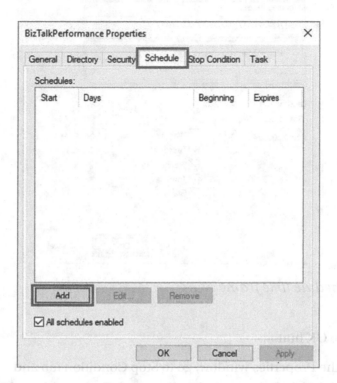

Figure 3-9. *Adding a new schedule*

11. In the Folder Action window, specify the following values
     (see Figure 3-10):

     a. Beginning date: You have to decide the best starting date.

     b. Expiration date: 2 Days after the beginning date.

     c. Start time: Make sure to set up a high load time frame.

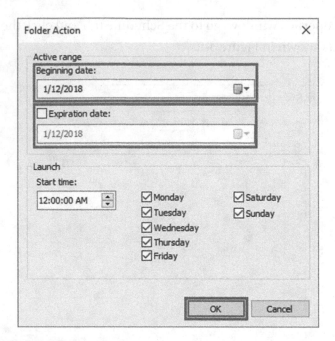

Figure 3-10. *Schedule time frame*

12. Click the OK button.

13. Within the Properties window, go to Stop Condition tab and enable the Overall Duration checkbox. Specify one as the value and choose days as the unit. Click OK to Finish. See Figure 3-11.

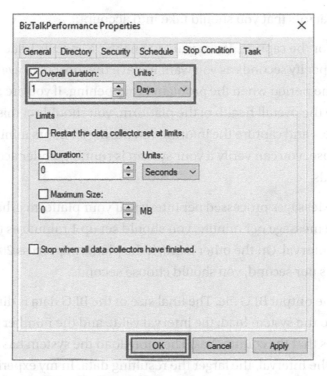

Figure 3-11. *Stop condition by overall duration*

14. Adjust the right sample interval. This value controls how often the
     tool captures the information of the selected counters. You can
     establish the following intervals:

     a. Seconds

     b. Minutes

     c. Hours

     d. Days

     e. Weeks

The interval setting is much more important than it seems since adjusting the
appropriate value depends directly on the scenario you want to capture.

These are the factors that you should take into account:

- Reason for the capture. If you want to analyze a specific issue, you should specify seconds as you want to have the most data available during the period when the problem is happening. If you are going to measure the overall health of the platform, you should set this value to minutes and capture the information during 24 hours minimum. In this case, you can verify if your system is running under acceptable thresholds.

- BizTalk Messages processed per interval. If your platform is handling only one message per minute, you should set up 1 minute as the sample interval. On the other hand, if the platform process 20 messages per second, you should choose seconds.

- Size of the output BLG file. The final size of the BLG data is directly related to the system load, the interval value and the number of instances that the counter has. The more load the system has and the smaller the interval, the larger the resulting data. In my experience, if you set the range to 2 minutes for a 24-hour capture, the output file will have a length between 40 and 80 MB. Therefore, by reducing the value to a few seconds, the output file will grow exponentially and the analysis will become more complicated, as you will have to analyze a larger volume of data.

Follow these steps:

1. Right-click the Performance counter capture, as shown in Figure 3-12.

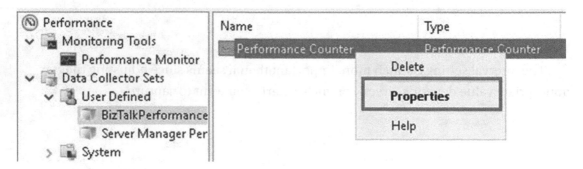

Figure 3-12. *Access to performance counter properties*

2. In the Properties window, set the Sample Interval as required. In this example, set it to capture performance data every two minutes. See Figure 3-13.

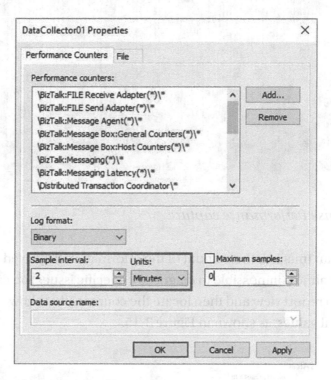

Figure 3-13. *Sample Interval adjustment*

3. Click OK.

4. View as report. In some scenarios, it is beneficial to present performance information in report view. The first time you open a BLG file, the Performance Monitor tool loads all the counters. See Figure 3-14.

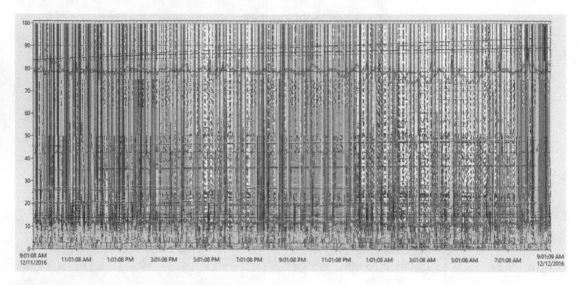

Figure 3-14. *Dense Performance capture*

5. As you can imagine, the amount of the information displayed
    makes it almost impossible to diagnose a specific issue. You can
    switch to report view and then locate the counters that show
    abnormal values, as shown in Figure 3-15.

System

% Registry Quota In Use	2.643
Alignment Fixups/sec	0.000
Context Switches/sec	898.135
Exception Dispatches/sec	7.865
File Control Bytes/sec	417,017.911
File Control Operations/sec	2,331.563
File Data Operations/sec	145.653
File Read Bytes/sec	442,011.167
File Read Operations/sec	62.369
File Write Bytes/sec	87,427.611
File Write Operations/sec	83.284
Floating Emulations/sec	0.000
Processes	70.146
Processor Queue Length	3.757
System Calls/sec	12,493.333
System Up Time	1,417,358.287
Threads	1,265.309

Figure 3-15. *Report view representation of the counters*

6. In this case, this environment is queuing lots of threads on average. You can then select only this counter and analyze what happens during the capture, as shown in Figure 3-16.

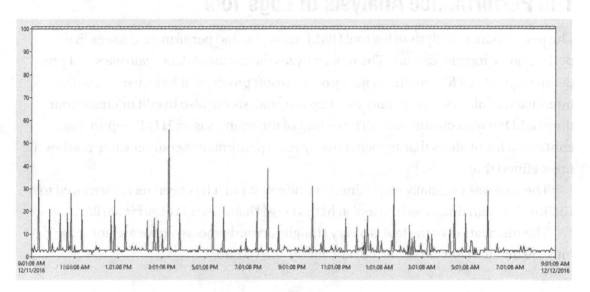

Figure 3-16. *Processor queue length graph detail*

This server is queuing threads with very high peaks. You should investigate the issue by adding processor usage counters.

To view the information as a report, follow these steps:

1. Select the report option view from the toolbox bar, as shown in Figure 3-17.

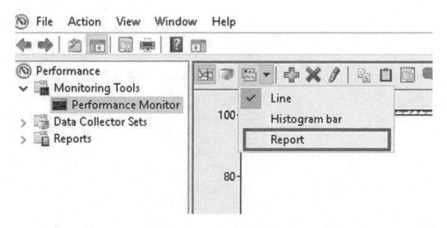

Figure 3-17. *Access to the report view*

2. The tool switches to the report view. Look for abnormal values and filter the log as desired.

The Performance Analysis of Logs Tool

The performance analysis of log tool (PAL) helps you find performance issues in a performance logging capture. The tool analyzes the captured data against a set of pre-defined threshold files for the majority of Microsoft products. It has a user-friendly interface that allows you not only to set up the analysis but also to edit or create your threshold file with custom rules. The output of the analysis is an HTML report that contains a list of alerts that are generated when a performance counter value reaches the pre-defined thresholds.

The tool was originally maintained in Codeplex, but it has been recently moved to GitHub. You can download the tool at `https://github.com/clinthuffman/PAL`.

The installation of the tool is a very straightforward process, so we are not getting into the details. Download the tool and follow the Wizard.

Creating a New Analysis Using PAL Tool

In this section, you learn how to use the PAL tool to analyze a BLG file that has been captured previously using the perfmon tool. Although the instructions provided here will suit the majority of the scenarios, it is recommended that you explore all the options discussed.

Follow these steps:

1. Once the PAL tool loads, click Next on the welcome screen, as shown in Figure 3-18.

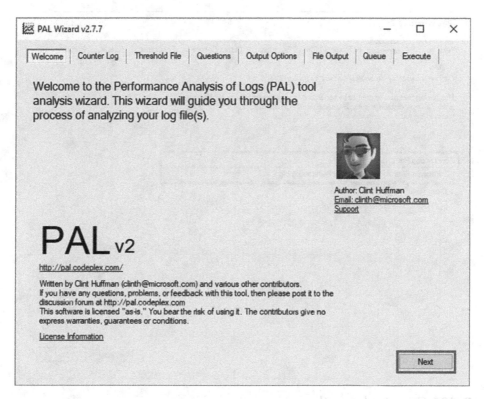

Figure 3-18. The PAL tool welcome screen

2. In the Counter Log section, browse for the location of the BLG
    file that you have captured using the perfmon tool and click Next
    (see Figure 3-19).

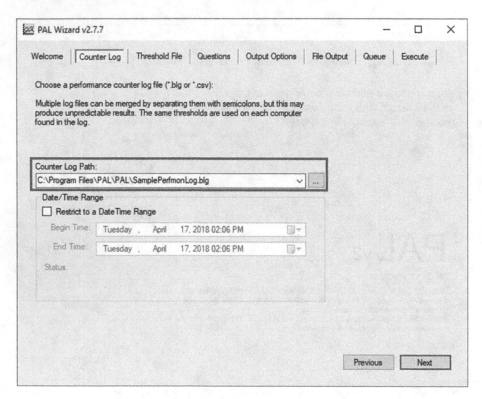

Figure 3-19. *Counter log path*

Notice that you have a Date and Time Selector. Sometimes the BLG files are enormous, or you want to analyze what happened at a specific time range. You can use this option to filter the captured data by a beginning time and an ending time.

3. In the Threshold file section, select the Microsoft BizTalk Server 2006/2009/2010 option from the drop-down box (see Figure 3-20) and click Next.

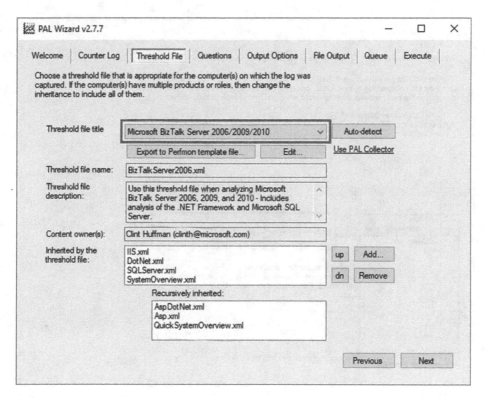

Figure 3-20. *Selecting a threshold file*

Do not worry if BizTalk Server 2016 is not listed. Most of the BizTalk performance counters remain unchanged throughout all the product versions.

4. In the Questions section, navigate through all the available questions and answer them according to the analyzed server (not to the server where you are running the PAL tool). Click Next. See Figure 3-21.

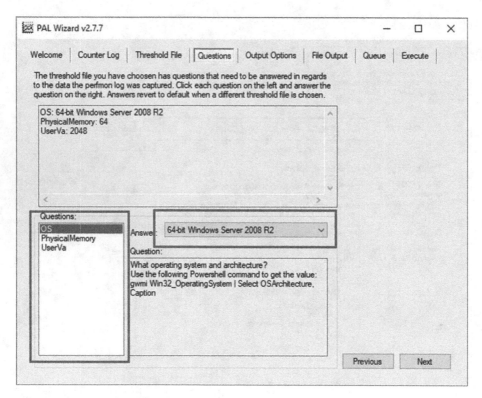

Figure 3-21. *Answering the platform questions*

5. In the Output Options section, select the desired Analysis Interval.
    AUTO is the default value, and it will create 30-time samples. If
    you want a higher level of detail, you can increase this interval by
    selecting a time using the drop-down box. Increasing this value
    will cause the analysis to take longer to complete. See Figure 3-22.
    Click Next.

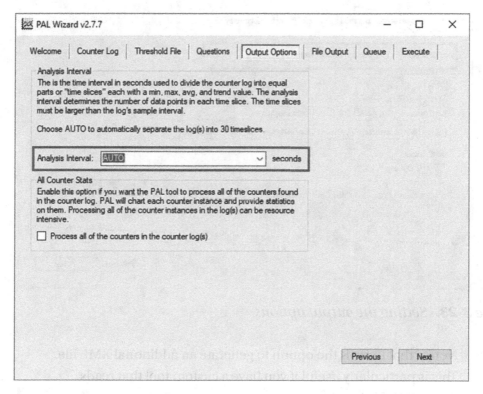

Figure 3-22. *Selecting an analysis interval*

6. Also, notice the Process All of the Counters in the Counter Log(s)
    checkbox. This option is attractive if your BLG files contain
    counters that do not have a threshold defined in the threshold
    file. It could be especially useful if your BizTalk applications are
    creating custom performance counters, and you want to include
    them in the final report.

7. In the File Output section, locate the folder where you want the
    tool to create the output HTML file. See Figure 3-23. Click Next.

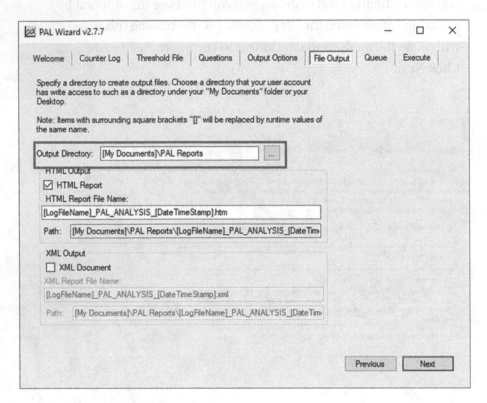

Figure 3-23. *Setting the output options*

8. Notice that there is the option to generate an additional XML file.
    This is particularly useful if you have a custom tool that reads
    those XML files.

9. Click Next in the Queue section. This section will show you the analysis that the tool will run when you complete the wizard. As this is the first analysis, you will get something similar to Figure 3-24.

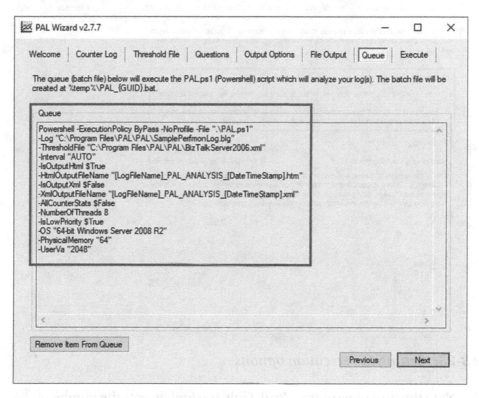

Figure 3-24. *Viewing the queue*

10. In the Execute section, you have three options:

    Execute: It executes the current analysis and all of the queued analysis now.

    Add to Queue: It adds the current analysis to the queue and the wizard will start again from the Counter Log section to add a new analysis.

    Execute and Restart: It executes the current analysis and will restart the wizard again so you can run another analysis in parallel. This option is the preferred one when you have a compelling workstation, as PAL will run all the analysis in parallel.

11. Select the desired option and click Finish, as shown in Figure 3-25.

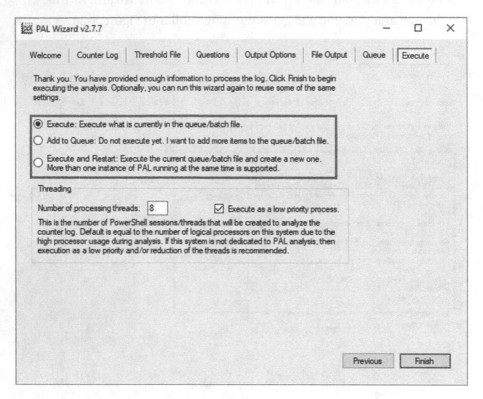

Figure 3-25. *Setting the execution options*

12. Note the threading option. By default, the tool detects the number of cores in your computer and runs using the same number of threads.

13.   Now the tool creates an inline PowerShell script that does all the magic. The PowerShell window shown in Figure 3-26 appears.

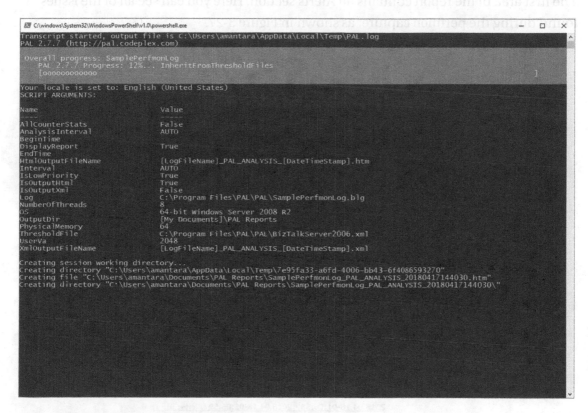

Figure 3-26.   Status of the analysis

14.   Here you can see the status of the analysis. When the tool is about to complete the analysis, you will see the text "Generating HTML Report...". Depending on the size of the BLG, this operation can take from a few seconds to several minutes. Once the report is generated, the tool loads it automatically using your default Internet browser.

Understanding the PAL Output

The first area of the report contains an Alerts section. Here you can see all of the issues found during the perfmon capture, as shown in Figure 3-27.

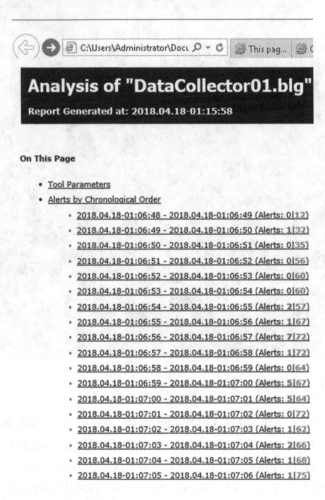

Figure 3-27. *Alerts by chronological order section*

You can click in the links to go to a specific time frame. If you scroll down through the report, you can see see all of the detailed analysis for BizTalk Server and the rest of performance counters, as shown in Figure 3-28.

- BizTalk:Message Agent
  - BizTalk Messaging Publishing Throttling State (Alerts: 0|0)
  - BizTalk Message Delivery Throttling State (Alerts: 0|0)
  - BizTalk High Database Sessions (Alerts: 0|0)
  - BizTalk High Database Size (Alerts: 0|0)
  - BizTalk High In-Process Message Count (Alerts: 0|0)
  - BizTalk High Message Delivery Rate (Alerts: 0|0)
  - BizTalk High Message Publishing Rate (Alerts: 0|0)
  - BizTalk High Process Memory (Alerts: 0|0)
  - BizTalk High System Memory (Alerts: 0|0)
  - BizTalk High Thread Count (Alerts: 0|0)
  - BizTalk Message Delivery Delay (Alerts: 0|0)
  - BizTalk Message Publishing Delay (Alerts: 0|0)
- BizTalk:Message Box:General Counters
  - BizTalk Spool Table Size (Alerts: 0|12)
  - BizTalk Tracking Data Size (Alerts: 0|8)
- BizTalk:Message Box:Host Counters
  - BizTalk Host Queue Length (Alerts: 0|0)
  - BizTalk Host Suspended Messages Queue Length (Alerts: 0|0)

Figure 3-28. The rest of the analysis

Any issues are highlighted, and you can click on them to see the details. For instance, if you click on the spool table analysis, you will get the spool table analysis graph, as shown in Figure 3-29.

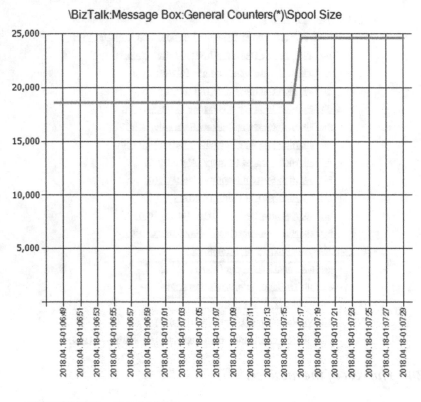

Figure 3-29. *Spool table analysis graph*

The associated alerts are shown in Figure 3-30.

Alerts						
Time Range						
2018.04.18-01:07:17 - 2018.04.18-01:07:18	Condition	Counter	Min	Avg	Max	Hourly Trend
	BizTalk: Increasing trend in spool table	\\BIZTALK2016\BizTalk:Message Box:General Counters(biztalkmsgboxdb:biztalk2016)\Spool Size	24,613	24,613	24,613	744,828
2018.04.18-01:07:18 - 2018.04.18-01:07:19	Condition	Counter	Min	Avg	Max	Hourly Trend
	BizTalk: Increasing trend in spool table	\\BIZTALK2016\BizTalk:Message Box:General Counters(biztalkmsgboxdb:biztalk2016)\Spool Size	24,613	24,613	24,613	720,000
2018.04.18-01:07:19 - 2018.04.18-01:07:20	Condition	Counter	Min	Avg	Max	Hourly Trend
	BizTalk: Increasing trend in spool table	\\BIZTALK2016\BizTalk:Message Box:General Counters(biztalkmsgboxdb:biztalk2016)\Spool Size	24,613	24,613	24,613	696,774
2018.04.18-01:07:20 - 2018.04.18-01:07:21	Condition	Counter	Min	Avg	Max	Hourly Trend
	BizTalk: Increasing trend in spool table	\\BIZTALK2016\BizTalk:Message Box:General Counters(biztalkmsgboxdb:biztalk2016)\Spool Size	24,613	24,613	24,613	675,000
2018.04.18-01:07:21 - 2018.04.18-01:07:22	Condition	Counter	Min	Avg	Max	Hourly Trend
	BizTalk: Increasing trend in spool table	\\BIZTALK2016\BizTalk:Message Box:General Counters(biztalkmsgboxdb:biztalk2016)\Spool Size	24,613	24,613	24,613	654,545
2018.04.18-01:07:22 - 2018.04.18-01:07:23	Condition	Counter	Min	Avg	Max	Hourly Trend
	BizTalk: Increasing trend in spool table	\\BIZTALK2016\BizTalk:Message Box:General Counters(biztalkmsgboxdb:biztalk2016)\Spool Size	24,613	24,613	24,613	635,294
2018.04.18-01:07:23 - 2018.04.18-01:07:24	Condition	Counter	Min	Avg	Max	Hourly Trend
	BizTalk: Increasing trend in spool table	\\BIZTALK2016\BizTalk:Message Box:General Counters(biztalkmsgboxdb:biztalk2016)\Spool Size	24,613	24,613	24,613	617,143
2018.04.18-01:07:24 - 2018.04.18-01:07:25	Condition	Counter	Min	Avg	Max	Hourly Trend
	BizTalk: Increasing trend in spool table	\\BIZTALK2016\BizTalk:Message Box:General Counters(biztalkmsgboxdb:biztalk2016)\Spool Size	24,613	24,613	24,613	600,000
2018.04.18-01:07:25 - 2018.04.18-01:07:26	Condition	Counter	Min	Avg	Max	Hourly Trend

Figure 3-30. *Spool table analysis alerts detail*

Using LoadGen to Test the Environment

In this section, you learn how to run the LoadGen tool in your environment. While in Chapter 4, you will learn how to test your environment using Visual Studio, this tool comes in handy when you are a BizTalk Server administrator, and you are not familiar with Visual Studio testing tools.

You can download the tool at `https://www.microsoft.com/download/details.aspx?id=14925`.

Installation of the tool is very straightforward, and it does not have different dependencies than the BizTalk Server installation. Install the tool following the wizard.

The LoadGen Configuration File

LoadGen uses an XML configuration file to simulate loading your environment.

```xml
<LoadGenFramework>
    <CommonSection>
            <LoadGenVersion>2</LoadGenVersion>
            <OptimizeLimitFileSize>20480000</OptimizeLimitFileSize>
            <NumThreadsPerSection>5</NumThreadsPerSection>
            <SleepInterval>200</SleepInterval>
            <LotSizePerInterval>25</LotSizePerInterval>
            <RetryInterval>10000</RetryInterval>

            <StopMode Mode="Files">
                    <NumFiles>2000</NumFiles>
                    <TotalTime>36000</TotalTime>
            </StopMode>

            <Transport Name="FILE">
<Assembly>FileTransport.dll/FileTransport.FileTransport</Assembly>
            </Transport>

    </CommonSection>

    <Section Name="FileSection">
    <SrcFilePath>C:\Users\Administrator\Documents\BOOK\BooksSolution\
      FIles\FFBooksOrder.txt</SrcFilePath>
        <DstLocation>
                <Parameters>
    <DstFilePath>C:\Users\Administrator\Documents\BOOK\BooksSolution\
      Ports\IN\</DstFilePath>
                </Parameters>
        </DstLocation>
    </Section>
</LoadGenFramework>
```

Table 3-1 shows a list of all the most common configuration settings for a performance load.

Table 3-1. *LoadGen Configuration Settings*

Setting	Description	Value
OptimizeLimitFileSize	If the file is larger than the value here, LoadGen will not use that file. This is to avoid out-of-memory conditions.	20.480.000
NumthreadsPerSection	The number of threads that the tool will use. The best value here is to set it to the number of cores in the running server.	5
SleepInterval	Time in milliseconds between test cycles.	200
LotSizePerInterval	Number of files copied per test.	25
RetryInterval	If the test could not be done, LoadGen will retry after 10.000 milliseconds.	10.000
StopMode	You can choose the stoping condition of the test cycle by assigning this setting. Supported stopping modes are: A) Files. LoadGen stops when the number files is reached. B) TotalTime. LoadGen stops when the test duration reaches the total time value. You can use both and LoadGen will stop where any of those conditions are met.	Files
StopModeNumFiles	Number of files to stop the test cycle.	2.000
StopModeTotalTime	Total duration to stop the test cycle.	36.000

(*continued*)

Table 3-1. (*continued*)

Setting	Description	Value
TransportName	Transport used to test the scenario. Currently LoadGen supports the following out-of-the-box transports: A) File B) HTTP C) MQSeries D) MSMQ E) SOAP F) WSE G) WCF	File
FileTransportDLL	Location of the file transport DLL. LoadGen will use this assembly to emulate the adapter protocol. All the assemblies are located at C:\Program Files (x86)\LoadGen\Bins.	
ScrFilePath	Instance that will be used to test.	Test instance
DstFilePath	Here is where the tool will drop the message instances.	Receive location path

Testing a Solution

In this scenario, you are going to test the book orders solution provided in the Chapter 2 folder.

Follow these steps:

1. Install the application using the MSI file located at C:\APRESS\ Chapter2\BooksSolution\BooksOrders\msi.

2. Start the application.

3. Test that the application works. Using the Windows Explorer, navigate to the C:\APRESS\Chapter2\BooksSolution\Test folder and run the Send1BookOrder.bat file.

4. If the application is installed successfully, you should have an output file located at `C:\APRESS\Chapter2\BooksSolution\Ports\OUT`.

5. Open a command prompt and navigate to the BINS folder where you have installed the LoadGen tool. If you choose the default location, it will be at `C:\Program Files (x86)\LoadGen\Bins`.

The bookOrders solutions comes already with a LoadGen pre-configured file, and it is located at `C:\APRESS\Chapter2\loadgen\Send2000Files.xml`.

Type the following instruction at the command prompt:

```
C:\Program Files (x86)\LoadGen\Bins>LoadGenConsole.exe "C:\APRESS\Chapter2\loadgen\Send2000Files.xml "
```

The process will start and the tool will show the screen in Figure 3-31.

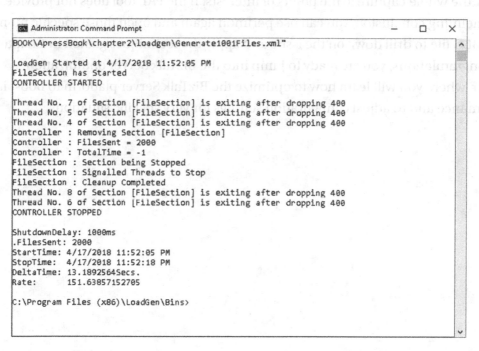

Figure 3-31. *LoadGen output*

6. Wait until the process finishes and review the output folder and the BizTalk Administration console to check that everything runs smoothly.

Now that you know how to use LoadGen tool, you can use Performance Monitor to capture all the BizTalk Server relevant performance data. Then later, you can use the PAL tool to analyze what happened during the test.

Summary

In this chapter, you have learned about the most common tools you will need to asses your BizTalk Server environment. First, you should capture the performance counter information using the Perfmon tool and then you can pass through the output BLG file to the PAL tool to accelerate the discovery of performance issues. PAL will narrow the whole capture to the points of interests. If the PAL tool does not provide an overwhelming conclusion, you can use perfmon again and open those specific moments of the BLG file to drill down on the issue and apply the techniques gained in Chapter 2.

Congratulations, you are ready to jump into the BizTalk Server optimization chapter, where you will learn how to optimize the BizTalk Server platform to boost its performance and to adjust configuration settings for very specific situations.

CHAPTER 4

Optimizing the BizTalk Platform

Probably one of the most missed tasks when designing BizTalk Server solutions is the specification phase. Most of the integration development focuses on providing the business functionality without taking into consideration the impact on performance once the application goes live.

This is especially true for BizTalk Server, as per design, the platform operates ruled by the publishing and subscribe architecture thus, all BizTalk Server messages flow through BizTalk Server message box database. Additionally, if you enable tracking and business activity monitoring, performance factors such as hardware sizing, message size, and the number of transactions (among others) becomes essential. Therefore, there is something you must keep in mind before starting a BizTalk Server project: The solution you are coding might not be the only one running in your production group. Applications compete with available hardware resources. Consequently, this should be your mantra when approaching a new project:

> *Performance! Performance! Performance!*
>
> *Testing! Testing! Testing!*

During the initial phases of the project proper design and formal testing procedures will give you an initial idea of the hardware sizing. If you have vast experience in designing BizTalk Server architectures, intuition could also guide you to an initial hardware estimation. Unfortunately, no systematic process precisely estimates the platform size for any BizTalk Server application. BizTalk Server is usually the core integration system within the organization, and it can potentially integrate a large variety of business implementations that run with their performance specifics.

© Agustín Mántaras 2019
A. Mántaras, *BizTalk Server 2016*, https://doi.org/10.1007/978-1-4842-3994-0_4

So, while an estimate based on existing experience provides a good starting point for planning purposes, the final size of the system will most certainly need to be adjusted along the way through a very structured testing procedure and good design principles.

In this chapter, you learn how to:

- Categorize your applications based on a concept that is called application priority levels.

- Optimize BizTalk and SQL Servers based on those levels.

- Use WMI and PowerShell to automate performance settings.

- Document application performance requirements.

- Use that documentation to size the Message Box and Tracking databases.

Assigning Application Priority Levels (APL)

It is good practice to categorize applications based on priority levels from a business point of view and the rest of the BizTalk Server factors that are relevant to solution architecture. By doing so, you will be taking crucial decisions during all phases of the project. The values used in this book are based on personal experience, but you should overwrite them to fit the project needs.

APL is calculated by combining five essential elements that are directly related to SLA definitions:

- Release stage level (RSL)

- Business priority level (BPL)

- High availability level (HAL)

- Number of transactions level (NTL)

- Performance behavior level (PBL)

You can use the Description field in the application properties section to document the application priority level and any other relevant information, as shown in Figure 4-1.

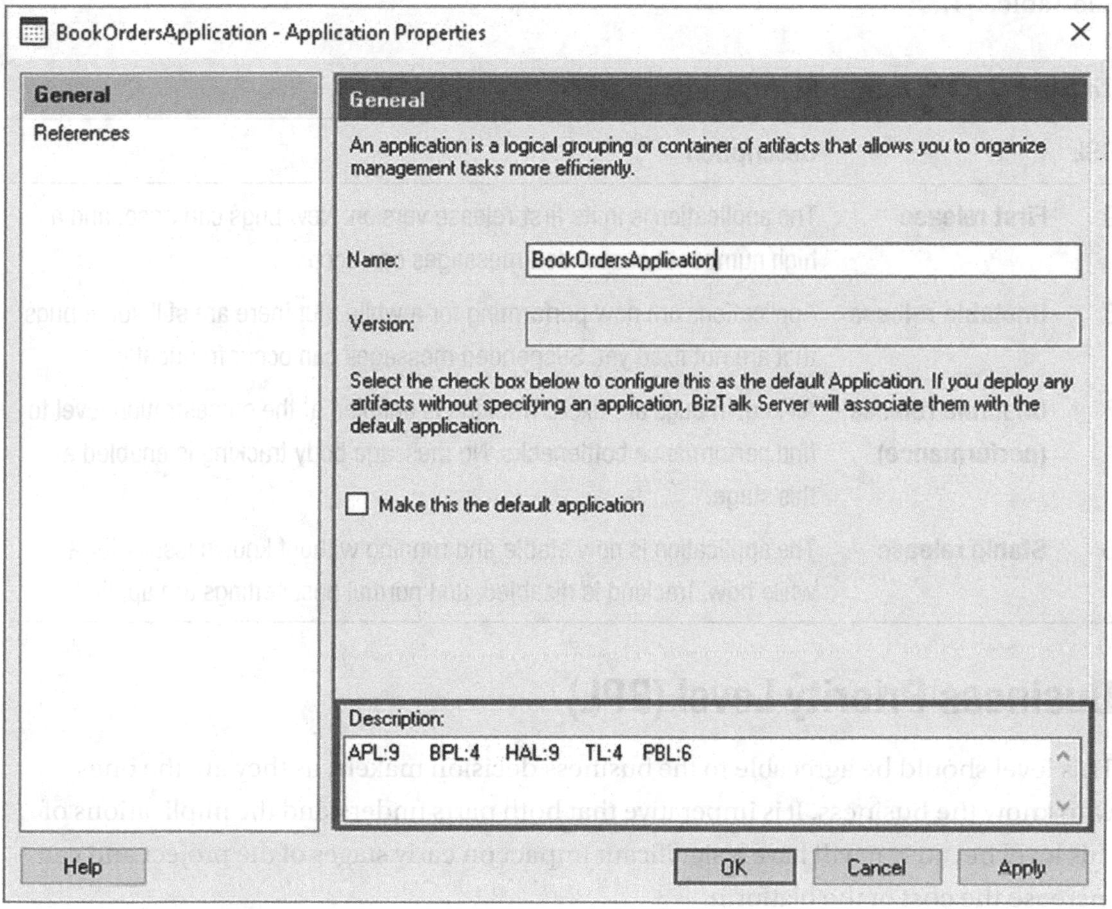

Figure 4-1. Documenting the application priority level using the BizTalk Administration Console

Release Stage Level (RSL)

This level represents how mature the solution is, or in other words, how stable it is. See Table 4-1.

Table 4-1. *Common Release Stage Levels*

RSL		Description
9	**First release**	The application is in its first release version. New bugs can arise, and a high number of suspended messages can occur.
8	**Unstable release**	Applications are now performing for a while, but there are still some bugs that are not fixed yet. Suspended messages can occur frequently.
7	**Unstable release (performance)**	All known bugs are fixed. Tracking is enabled at the orchestration level to find performance bottlenecks. No message body tracking is enabled at this stage.
6	**Stable release**	The application is now stable and running without known issues for a while now. Tracking is disabled, and normal host settings are applied.

Business Priority Level (BPL)

This level should be agreeable to the business decision makers, as they are the ones who know the business. It is imperative that both parts understand the implications of this level because it will have a significant impact on early stages of the project and can increase the cost of the platform.

In BizTalk Server, we can define a mission-critical solution as an integrated system where any of its components (equipment, personnel, process, procedure, software, and so forth) are essential to the business operation. Failure of any of these elements usually results in a severe impact on business operations that can even influence the image of the organization.

Examples of mission-critical systems are

- An online banking system

- Aircraft operating

- Electric power systems

- Electronic bill applications

- Health care systems

- ATM systems

The majority of mission-critical solutions must run 24x7 without downtime. Performance is especially vital, as these implementations operate under very restrictive performance requirements for individual transactions.

Additionally, these systems should remain very secure to prevent malicious attacks and to protect the data that goes through the BizTalk Server databases.

As BizTalk Server is usually deployed to host mission-critical solutions, you will need a solid foundation on the performance factors that make a difference.

The definitions on this section are based on common customer deployments all around the world. Use them as an inspiration when categorizing your own solutions. See Table 4-2.

Table 4-2. *Common Business Priority Levels*

BPL	Example Definition
9	**Mission-critical solution level 1**. Organization operations are affected at a global scale. Failure of this application causes significant failures to other applications. The application has particular performance requirements. Zero downtime. Typically involves long running processes and very low latency scenarios. Performance degradation is not accepted (especially under high load). Usually, these applications are isolated in a dedicated BizTalk Server group, since even the administration team is frequently dedicated to operate these platforms.
8	**Mission-critical solution level 2**. The application is significant from the business point of view, but failures do not affect other applications. The application has particular performance requirements. Zero downtime. Performance degradation is not accepted (especially under high load).
7	**Important application level 1**. Major failure it is an issue. Performance is still a fundamental requirement; an application can have specific performance requirements. Zero downtime
6	**Important application level 2**. Functionality should be granted at any time but if the application run below the performance SLA during certain times is not an issue. The importance here is that all transactions are completed successfully. The business accepts downtime.

(continued)

Table 4-2. (*continued*)

BPL	Example Definition
5	**Medium priority level**. Intermittent failures are accepted as the consumer can resubmit the message. The Destination system or the integration layer can handle duplicated/missed transactions accordingly. The business accepts downtime. Performance degradation for a standard period is accepted as usual (even under high load).
4	**Low priority level**. If the application fails, it will not impact the business operations. This application does not have any specific performance requirement. The application can be manually stopped/resumed without any consequences at any time. Performance degradation is accepted as normal.

High Availability Level (HAL)

This level represents the high availability requirements for the solution. See Table 4-3.

Table 4-3. *Common High Availability Levels*

HAL	Description
9	High availability is required. Zero downtime.
8	High availability is required. Downtime is accepted to fix issues (debugging, stopping instances).
7	High Availability is required. Downtime is also accepted for deployment.
6	Even though high availability is required, it cannot be applied due to platform restriction or adapter behavior. Downtime is accepted.
5	High Availability is not required.

Transaction Levels (TL)

This definition is directly related to the business performance requirement. It is not calculated based on specific hardware configuration. Once the business provides you with the actual volume of transactions, you should design all the performance testing scenarios to size your platform correctly and based on this definition.

Note   Keep in mind that business transactions might not be equivalent to the number of messages that BizTalk Server process per business flow, as usually this relationship is one:many.

TL	Volume Definition	Number of Transactions Per Hour
9	Extremely high	>=3,000,000
8	Very high	>=1,000,000 and < 3,000,000
7	High	>= 300,000 and < 1,000,000
6	Medium	>=100,000 and < 300,000
5	Common	>= 10,000 and < 100,000
4	Low	< 10,000

Performance Behavior Level (PBL)

This application priority level dictates how an application behaves performance wise. In BizTalk Server, applications can be classified into the following categories:

PBL	Name
9	Low latency
8	High throughput
7	Mixed
6	No specific

This is more important than it seems at first glance, as you will have to tune the application based on its most common behavior.

Service-Level Agreements Between the Integrated Parties

A service-level agreement (SLA) is a contract between a service provider and a consumer. Your BizTalk Server environment provides specific business functionalities that must run below the defined SLA agreement. Although services can have very specific custom SLA, for most BizTalk Server solutions your agreement should include one or more of the following SLAs:

- Performance
- Availability

Performance Service Level Agreement

For BizTalk Server, you define performance SLA at the business application level. The concept of an application in integration world is probably quite deceiving as usually, BizTalk Server connects to different services to provide the business functionality. Additionally, mature BizTalk Server deployments have usually shared applications that behave as a framework that provides internal functionality to the business applications or acts as an enterprise service bus.

As most of the performance settings in BizTalk Server are applied at a host level, it is essential that you define a host separation policy that matches the required performance SLA. What does it mean exactly? For example, if you are developing an application that behaves as low latency, the best option is to place all the BizTalk Server artifacts to run in a dedicated set of hosts and apply specific host settings to improve latency. In other words, you can create three hosts for that application: One for receive locations, another one for orchestrations, and one more for sending ports.

In contrast, if the application is running only a few transactions per day, you do not need to create additional hosts; you can have a set of standard hosts to run all the low volume applications.

Adding unnecessary hosts can create overhead in the BizTalk and SQL Server boxes when host instances are started. That is why you have to use common sense when approaching a new BizTalk Server project. Do not just create a new set of receiving, processing, and sending hosts because it is just the Microsoft best practice. Instead, create a generic set of hosts that you will be using for low volume applications, and then you move forward with the specific cases.

We will discuss the host separation policy in more detail in later sections.

To create a performance service level agreement, you have to agree with the integrated parties in the following elements:

- A measure of time—Usually, business decision makers will state that the solution must process a specific number of transactions during a specific time range. An example could be this solution must process one thousand transactions per minute, per second, or two million monthly.

- Latency of individual transactions—Sometimes, especially for low latency scenarios, individual transactions will also have a performance SLA. We define the latency of an individual transactions as the elapsed time since the consumer initiated the request and gets the response from the integration layer (whatever the format of the response is). This, of course, can vary across all of the cases you can imagine but usually low latency scenarios will require an individual transaction time of fewer than 5-2 seconds (down to milliseconds even) If you receive a requirement like this, then you should be automatically thought of a low latency scenario and because of that you should consider applying low latency customizations. In some other cases, the individual transaction time is not essential. What matters in these cases, is the total number of transactions globally. In other words, a high throughput scenario.

- Number of transactions—This is also very important. The number of business transactions creates new BizTalk Server messages. However, that does not necessary means that BizTalk Server will publish the same number of messages as most of BizTalk Server solutions create internal messages to drive the logic through the code. Additionally, orchestrations will be consuming internal services, databases and .Net components that can publish new messages to the Message Box. So, how do we calculate the number of messages in BizTalk Server? There is not an easy answer to that. However, the best thing you could do as a developer is to document all the messages that your solution is using per message flow. This action will become crucial later for testing, sizing, troubleshooting and maintaining the BizTalk Server solution.

- Maximum number of live instances—As messages are stored into
  the message box database, it is a must that you define the maximum
  number of transactions that can be running simultaneously. This
  number is affected by two different aspects:

  - Consumer requests—During the normal operation behavior, the
    consumer of the service will send some transactions. However,
    in the majority of the scenarios, those requests will arrive at
    BizTalk Server at their pace, and it is very complicated to size
    the environment based on that number. To avoid this problem,
    consumer and provider must agree on the maximum number
    of simultaneous transactions that the consumer can request.
    By doing so, you will be sizing the environment based highest
    performance business requirement.

  - BizTalk Server engine behavior—This refers to the transactions
    that are queued in BizTalk Server because of the engine features
    such as throttling, pooling intervals, and in-memory and
    processing queues. Getting a specific value for this is again
    almost impossible. What you could do though is to increment the
    number of maximum requests based on business priority levels:

BPL	The increment of Maximum Transactions
<=5	No increment required
6	+20%
7	+25%
8	+30%
9	+35%

For instance, imagine that you are designing a BizTalk Server solution that you
categorized as priority 6. The business requirement is that the application must handle a
maximum of 200 transactions simultaneously. Therefore, if we applied the formula, you
will have to add 20% on top of the business requirement. That means that BizTalk Server
should be able to process 40 additional transactions caused by the engine behavior.

- Convoy patterns—Achieving some business functionalities will eventually take you to implement convoy patterns. BizTalk Server holds convoys, and the associated message instances, in a separated set of tables within the message box. If the number of messages in convoy is substantial (especially if they are using large messages), you will have to size the Message Box accordingly to include the extra space requirements. Additionally, convoy patterns can cause zombie messages within the Message Box database.

- Recovery behavior—How would affect an error to the business? In case of an error, will the caller system be able to resubmit the transaction again? What about the destination system? Can it handle duplicated transactions by discarding them? For obvious reasons, this is very important for the solution design but also for performance. Why? BizTalk Server has a great feature to recover individual orchestrations from the latest service call in case of a failure. When an orchestration is sending a request to service or, in general, when it is waiting for something to happen (the orchestration is idle), the orchestration engine will dehydrate that orchestration into the Message Box. That means that will store the orchestration state into the database waiting for the timed event to occur. This is very useful too, first it saves hardware resources, and second, it allows the engine to recover the orchestration in case the failure. If the recovery behavior of the calling system is set to resubmit the transaction again, then you do not need the dehydration BizTalk Server feature, and you can disable it. This action alleviates SQL Server resources as orchestrations will not perform extra round trips to the message box. However, keep in mind that the BizTalk Server host instance that runs orchestrations will consume more memory as orchestrations will not be saved to the Message Box.

- Monitoring capabilities—Do the integrated parties need visibility of the data processed by BizTalk Server? If yes, would it be enough by saving the standard BizTalk Server tracking information or do they require business data associated with the process as well? Proactively monitoring performance data should be always considered. Predicting when the system can potentially reach a performance bottleneck will help you to create a healthy platform and to avoid majority of performance problems related to bottlenecks on both, BizTalk and SQL Server side. In Chapter 8, you will learn how to monitor the BizTalk Server platform using BizTalk 360 tool.

- Organization or business data retention policies—Some organizations, or even individual entities within the organization, will have specific regulations to save tracking data during a period that is far beyond the limit that should be used for troubleshooting. In this situation, you might need to keep tracking data for more extended periods of time. In this case, the Tracking database can become a performance bottleneck over time. Therefore, you should be ready to tune the SQL Server platform, so it has enough hardware resources to deal with all the tracking feature. Unfortunately, at the moment of writing this book, the configuration of the tracking purging job applies globally to the whole BizTalk group and does not purge specific application tracking data.

Out of-the-box, BizTalk Server can tune a specific host to improve its behavior within the following areas:

- Message publication

- Message delivery

- Polling the Message Box database

- Dehydration behavior

These topics are discussed later in this chapter and in Chapter 6.

Availability SLA

In information technology, high availability refers to a system or component that is uninterruptedly operational for an appropriate length of time. Availability can be measured relative to "100% operational" or "never failing." A widely-held but difficult-to-achieve standard of availability for a system or product is known as "five 9s" (99,999%) availability. While from infrastructure point of view you can provide the majority of the necessary considerations to provide high availability, it is also at development stage where developers can use techniques to get the availability level closer to 99,999%. In Chapter 7, you learn about these techniques.

This book does not focus on high availability, therefore, the recommendations in this section should be taken as initial steps.

Within application priority levels, you must agree with the integration layers and the high availability level. The following aspects should come up in this discussion:

- Recovery downtime—In case of a significant failure, do the business accepts downtime for recovering?

- Troubleshooting SLA—What is the maximum downtime of the service in case of troubleshooting?

- Deployment downtime—To fix bugs and to provide new functionality, deployments might be quite frequent. This is very dependent on the release stage level of the solution. If it is the case, what is the maximum amount of time that the business accepts for deployment situations?

- Adapter considerations—Depending on the adapters used to integrate the systems involved, you will have to consider different strategies to provide high availability.

The following elements in BizTalk Server are crucial regarding high availability because if any of them fails, the system will not be able to process messages, in other words, these elements are single point of failures in any BizTalk Server environment.

- Hosts Instances—Host instances initiate most of the activities related to BizTalk Server engine:

    - The End Point Manager—Hosts in-process and isolated messaging (but not messages related to orchestrations).

    - **TDDS** service, which implements the tracking and BAM features.

- Although message publication and dequeue processes are implemented with SQL Server stored procedures, host instances are initiating the process.

- Orchestrations—If hosts instances are running orchestrations, a sub service called XLang engine loads into the host instance windows service to provide all the orchestration functionality.

Therefore, you will need to provide high availability for the host instances because if any of those elements are affected, the BizTalk engine will not be able to process messages. As host instances are windows services, the only way to provide redundancy is by deploying at least two BizTalk Servers.

- Enterprise single sign-on service—This service is used in BizTalk Server for the following reasons:

  - To save adapter and ports configuration.

  - To store custom application configuration data.

  - To map a Windows user ID to non-Windows user credentials.

This data is stored in the Single Enterprise sign-on a database that is encrypted in the moment of the BizTalk Server configuration stage. Within the whole BizTalk Server group, one of the Single Enterprise sing-on services is marked as the master secret server. This is the only one that has the encryption key in memory. The rest of the enterprise single sign-on services need to ask for the key to the master.

If the master secret server becomes unavailable, BizTalk Server will stop processing messages, and you will need to set the master secret server to another server manually. Therefore, you will also need to provide high availability to the master secret server.

- Microsoft distributed transaction coordinator (MS DTC)—provides the functionality to ensure complete transactions across a distributed environment. If the distributed transaction coordinators become unavailable, BizTalk Server will fail to enlist a new transaction and it will stop processing messages. Later on, we will look at MSTDC in more detail.

- BizTalk Server databases—BizTalk Server stores a significant amount of information in the databases. If any of the core BizTalk Server databases becomes unavailable, the platform will be able to process service instances. Therefore, you should provide high availability for the databases using one of the following methods:

  - Implementing a Microsoft cluster in the SQL Server

  - Implementing SQL Server Always-On and high availability groups

- BizTalk Server maintenance jobs—When you configure BizTalk Server, the process will create a set of SQL Server agent jobs that are extremely important for the platform as they perform operations such as backing up databases, maintaining integrity within the Message Box and tracking, moving tracking data from the message box to the Tracking database, and purging the Tracking database. Therefore, you will need also to provide high availability to the SQL Server agent service.

Designing a high availability will not cover all the scenarios as there are factors such as the human mistakes and the lack of knowledge, that can cause a production environment to become unavailable. For that reason, you should also consider the following important aspects that will help you to provide an efficient high availability level:

- Application instrumentation—Covered in Chapter 5.

- Side-by-side versioning—Covered in Chapter 7.

- Proactive monitoring—Covered in Chapter 8.

Factors That Are Important for BizTalk Performance

The number of factors that affect BizTalk Server performance is very large. In this section we will review the most important ones, as detailing every specific performance setting will take probably more than 500 pages, and most likely you are not going to face all the situations at the same time.

You will learn about optimizations related to the following areas:

- Tracking

- Host separation policy

- Host performance settings

- Message size

- Message Box database

- Microsoft distributed transaction coordinator

- Windows communication foundation throttling

- Concurrent HTTP connections

Later, in Chapter 6 you learn about how to improve your developments, so the development and administration team can work together to boost the BizTalk Server platform.

Message Size

The message size, along with the number of transactions, have an impact in the following areas:

- Size of the Message Box database—BizTalk Server stores all live messages in the Message Box database and uses a set of queue tables to hold references to those messages. As message size increase, Message Box database increases in size along with the number of live instances.

- Size of the Tracking database—If message body tracking is enabled at any level, Tracking database grows exponentially along with the message size.

- Pipeline CPU consumption—Pipelines use CPU resources to loop through the streamed binary data, therefore as message size increases, the pipeline needs to stream more information, and that increases CPU utilization.

- Map execution—When extracting or setting values with a map the document is loaded into memory and therefore memory consumption increases.

- Orchestration dehydrated size in the Message Box database—Every single time an orchestration dehydrates, it saves all the messages that are part of the actual scope (messages that are not yet used will not be persisted). Therefore, the size of Message Box database is also affected because of the number of dehydrated orchestrations.

- Orchestration memory consumption—As all orchestration messages are stored into the memory, the message size has a direct impact on the server memory consumption. This is especially true if the developer is using XPath expressions or XMLDocument classes because these objects load the message into the memory.

- Orchestration CPU consumption—If the process is looping through a very large message, the host instance is acting as a handler for that orchestration and uses more threads per CPU.

- Overall throughput can be affected if the size of received message increase above the initially defined thresholds.

- XPath and XMLdocument classes—As these objects load the whole message into the memory, memory consumption increases along with the size of the message when XPath or XMLDocument classes are used.

- Number SQL Server locks—The larger the message, the more significant the number fragments that the engine uses to save the binary data into the Message Box. Each fragment creates one or more SQL Server locks within the Message Box database. If the number of messages is quite large, you can experiment with an out-of-lock error in SQL Server.

Note   Keep in mind that if the application receives or sends JSON and flat file messages if you want to use that message for operations such as validation, property promotion, and transformation services, they must be transformed into XML (using a pipeline). The conversion itself can increase the size of the message up to ten times the original size, since XML representation requires element names specification.

While BizTalk Server does not impose any constraint on message size, practical hardware limits might require that you design the BizTalk Server solution in a completely different way to reduce message sizes, because large messages require more processing resources. However, at the group level, you can control how BizTalk Server processes large messages within the Message Box database.

What Is the Large Message Size Setting?

If the size of an incoming message is larger than the number of Kilobytes specified for this setting, the message is split into fragments of that size. If size is not exceeded, then the entire message is committed as one part. In BizTalk Server 2016, the default value is 100 KB.

Let's see this setting in action using an example:

Imagine that BizTalk receives a file of 1089 KB. The engine evaluates the message data size against the large message size setting. In this case, since the setting is set to 100 KB, 11 fragments are inserted in the Fragments table:

- Ten fragments of 100 KB size

- One fragment of 89 KB size

Warning   Changing the large message size could have an adverse/positive impact on the environment and the platform could suffer from one of the following issues:

DTC Locks   Depending on the load, SQL Server could potentially get out of transactions causing DTC Locks and will timeout message publication. If you face this situation, it might be reasonable to increase the size of the large message, as the number of locks decrease exponentially due to fewer fragments inserted in the tables.

Out of Memory   On the other hand, increasing this setting could also raise the amount of memory consumed by BizTalk and SQL Servers, as fragments will be larger. In this case, you should do the opposite: decrease the size until the out-of-memory condition disappears.

This setting is configurable using the BizTalk Administration Console, under the BizTalk group settings, as shown in Figure 4-2.

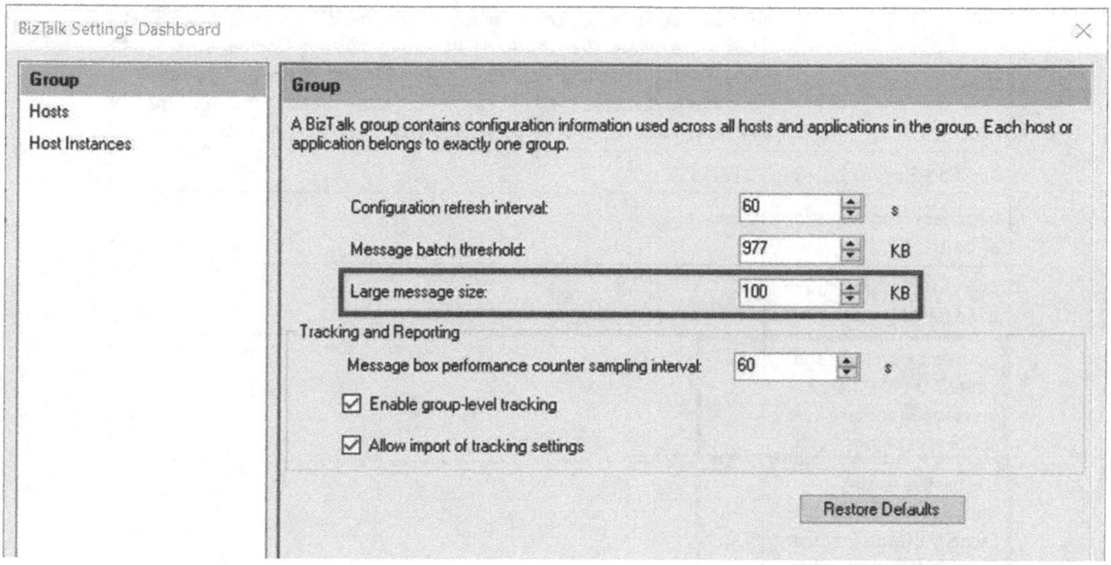

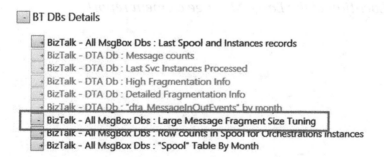

Figure 4-2. Large message size setting

As you can see, there is not a value that fits all scenarios. The recommendation is to start with the default one (100 KB) and, if you experiment any of those issues, you could leverage on the recommendation of an excellent BizTalk Server tool: the health monitor (BHM).

To check the recommendation value for the Large Message Size setting, once BHM tool has generated your report you should navigate to section BT DBs Details and from there locate the element BizTalk - All MsgBox Dbs: Large Message Fragment Size Tuning. See Figure 4-3.

Figure 4-3. Location of the Large Message element report

After you click on the element, you will see a report like the one in Figure 4-4.

Data	value
Title	For Best performance ensure that the Large message fragment size is set to a value greater than the Avg Part Size so that Avg Number of Fragments is close to 1. Use the Suggested fragment size as a guideline in order to decrease the # of fragments. Note increasing this value may increase the amount of memory that is used in a host instance.
Avg Part Size in kb	0.1943359
Avg Num Fragments for all parts	1.00
Avg Num Fragments for large parts	0.00
Current Large Message Size(2010-2013) Large Message Fragment Size (2009 and below) in kb	100
Suggested Large Message Size(2010-2013) Large Message Fragment Size(2009 and below) in kb	100
# Rows in Parts Table	253
Smallest Part in kb	0
Largest Part in kb	1.453125
% Rows with Multiple Fragments	0
Historical Avg Num Fragments in DTA - Relies on MsgBody Tracking	1.00
11 Rows	

Figure 4-4. *Location of the Large Message element report*

Note   To retrieve this information, the BHM tool queries the Tracking database. Therefore, if you want to rely on this recommendation, message body tracking should be enabled while the tool is performing the analysis. As you will learn later, enabling message body tracking is recommended *punctually* over the following scenarios:

1. Troubleshooting issues related to message content.

2. Executing BHM with the objective of getting a large message size recommendation. Ideally, you should do this in a no-production environment by simulating load in a testing server.

When you finish with either of these tasks, you should disable message body tracking again (of course, only if data retention policies allow to do that).

The most important field on the report is the Suggested Large Message Size row, as it gives you the most accurate recommendation based on the message sizes that are currently published in your environment. In this case, the tool is recommending using the default setting of 100 KB.

Tracking

The general best practice for tracking is to not to enable it on production. However, in real-world scenarios, tracking becomes essential when troubleshooting. This is especially true for newly released applications, as they can raise exceptions that were not considered during the design and development stages. The most important considerations for tracking are:

- The size of the message

- The tracking level you want for your BizTalk Server artifacts

- Promoted properties

Additionally, the tracking feature involves a three-step process:

1. Tracked data will be first placed on the tracking data tables into the Message Box database.

2. The `TrackedMessages_Copy_BizTalkMsgBoxDb` job moves message body data to the Tracking database and it runs once per minute by default.

3. The DTA Purge and Archive job will delete old tracking data based on the job configuration. For instance, if you have set the job to keep seven days of data, this is the amount of maximum tracking data that the tracking database will keep for that specific business process.

Therefore, there are two important considerations to size tracking properly:

*   Amount of tracking data per minute—As the `TrackedMessages_Copy_BizTalkMsgBoxDb` runs every minute, the Message Box database will keep tracking data for one minute also. This is the reason; tracking can become a bottleneck that can affect the BizTalk Server runtime. It is crucial that you consider this factor when designing the tracking settings for a specific solution. Therefore, you must calculate the size of the Message Box database based on the message size and the number of instances per minute.

*   Amount of tracking data that the purging job keeps—If you set the purging job to keep seven days of data, you should calculate the size of the Tracking database based on this number, the message size, tracking data points, and the number of instances for those seven days.

Tracking Levels

Tracking can be customized at the following BizTalk Server artifacts:

*   Receive locations

*   Orchestrations

*   Sending ports

*   Schemas

- Pipeline

- Business rules

Orchestrations

At the orchestration level you have the following tracking options:

Tracking Point	Observations	Impact
Events-Orchestration start/end	This will track when the orchestration starts and ends.	It depends on the number of instances.
Events-Message sent/receive	This will track an event every time an orchestration receives or sends a message.	It depends on the number of instances.
Events Shape start/end	Tracks when a orchestrations shape starts and ends.	It depends on the number of instances.
Track message bodies before/after	Saves the message bodies before a and after orchestration processing.	This is the most expensive configuration. Whenever possible, try to avoid it and if you have to save the content of the message, it's better that you enable it at receive or send port only. By doing so, you will have more control because you will save specific messages and not all the messages processed by the orchestration. This setting is only useful when you want to track a message that is not processed by any port.
Track message properties	Will track promoted properties for incoming and outgoing messages	The same principle as the track message body setting, but related to promoted properties.

Receive Ports

The following tracking options are available at the receive port level:

Tracking Point	Observations	Impact
Track message bodies before/after port processing	Saves the message bodies before and after port processing.	This is the most expensive configuration. Whenever possible, try to avoid it.
Track message properties before/after port processing	Will track promoted properties before and after port processing	The same principle as the track message body setting, but related to promoted properties. For the majority of scenarios, you will not need to track properties on the incoming side. Only when you want to troubleshoot based on a promoted property in the incoming message.

Sending Ports

The following tracking options are available at the receive port level:

Tracking Point	Observations	Impact
Track message bodies before/after port processing	Saves the message bodies before and after port processing.	This is the most expensive configuration. Whenever possible, try to avoid it.
Track message properties before/after port processing	Will track promoted properties before and after port processing	The same principle as the track message body setting, but related to promoted properties. For the majority of scenarios, you will not need to track properties in the sending side. Only when you want to troubleshoot based on a promoted property in the sending message.

168

Schemas

For schemas, there is only one tracking configuration setting:

Tracking Point	Observations	Impact
Always track all properties	Will track promoted properties every time a message based on this schema is sent or received.	If you need ever to track properties, it should be explicitly done at orchestration or port level. This should be used only in the development stage where you want to troubleshoot and find bugs in early stages of the project.

Pipelines

At the pipelines level you have the following tracking options:

Tracking Point	Observations	Impact
Events-port start and end	This will track when the pipeline starts and ends.	It depends on the number of instances.
Events-Message sent/receive	This will track an event every time an pipeline receives or sends a message.	It depends on the number of instances.
Track message bodies before/ after	Saves the message bodies before a and after pipeline processing.	This is the most expensive configuration. Whenever possible, try to avoid it and if you must save the content of the message, it's better that you enable it at receive or send port only. By doing so, you will have more control because you will save specific messages and not all the messages processed by the pipeline. Additionally, pipelines can be used in several ports; therefore, if you want to enable a specific pipeline to track information, it's better that you set tracking only at the port level.

Assigning Tracking Configuration Based on the Release Stage (RS) Level

If the business does not require a heavy data retention policy, you use the following guidelines to enable tracking:

RSL	Level	Description
9	First release	Message body tracking at sensible points can be enabled. Orchestration events must be enabled to allow developers to troubleshoot orchestration issues. At this stage, you can enable also tracking for promoted properties if that is used for troubleshooting. All in all, tracking can be enabled in all areas.
8	Unstable release	Applications is now performing for a while but there are still some bugs that are not fixed yet. Partial tracking is enabled to help developers fixing issues.
7	Unstable release (performance)	All known bugs are fixed. Tracking is enabled at orchestration level to find performance bottlenecks *only*. No message body tracking is enabled at this stage.
6	Stable release	The application is now stable and running without known issues for a while now. Tracking is disabled at all artifact levels, and standard host settings are applied.

Dedicate a Host for Tracking

As discussed previously, tracking is a feature that uses many resources of BizTalk and SQL Servers, thus you should isolate the tracking functionality to run in a dedicated host, so that the tracking functionality does not need to compete with the rest of BizTalk Server functionalities (receiving, processing, and sending).

High availability is also essential because if the host instance performing the tracking functionality fails, the following areas of BizTalk Server will be also affected:

- Tracked data will not be moved from the Message Box to the Tracking database.

- BAM tracking data will not be moved to the BAM primary import database, so all your activities will not reflect current data. There is an exception for this situation where developers write BAM data directly to the `BAMPrimaryImport` database using the `DirectEventBuffer` API, and that data is not stored previously in the Tracking database.

As you can see, both situations can cause the Message Box to grow over time, and that could initiate a bottleneck to the message publication and the dequeue processes. Therefore, the tracking host should be running in at least two servers by creating two host instances.

When adding more Message Boxes (see the section Message Box database later in this chapter), the recommendation is to have the same number of tracking host instances plus one more, for high availability reasons. Imagine that you have two Message Boxes, so the total number should be three. If you do not add more tracking host instances, you will have only one that has to move data from the three Message Boxes and, depending on the tracking settings, that could also cause a bottleneck on the Message Box, as the tracking data could not be moved efficiently to the tracking DTA and BAM databases.

Purging the Tracking Database

As BizTalk Server is processing messages, Tracking database grows along with the load (if tracking is enabled for the BizTalk Server artifacts involved in the process) and the maximum sustainable load can be affected, especially if the Tracking and Message Box databases are placed on the same SQL Server instance or if the database files are on the same disk.

The tracking feature is very transactional, and it performs many modification queries to the tracking data files. Thus, the transactional data and log files for the Tracking database can grow very quickly. This is not a good thing from SQL Server performance point of view. The larger the file, the greater the chances of entering into a disk contention issue (along with a high number of write and read operations).

When you configure BizTalk Server for the first time, a SQL Server job called DTA Purge and Archive (`BizTalkDTADb`) is created. This job is used to purge the BizTalk Server database, and as it requires that the user configure all the settings. It is disabled by default.

This job performs the following tasks:

- Purges the Tracking database following specific criteria.

- It can archive the deleted data to an archiving server.

To delete all the data, the job can call on the following stored procedures:

- `dtasp_BackUpAndPurgeTrackingDatabase`: It performs a backup of the data that will be purged.

- Parameters explanation:

  - `@nHours`—All completed instances data, older than the number of hours, will be purged.

  - `@nDays`—all completed instances data, older than the number of days, will be purged.

  - `@nHardDays`—All data (completed or not) older than the number of `@nHardDays` days, will be purged if `@fHardDeleteRunningInstances` is set to 1.

  - `@nvcFolder`—Folder where you want to create the backup files.

  - `@nvcValidatingServer`—Server name that will be used to archive the purged data. This server should be added to the linked servers of the SQL Server instance holding the Tracking database.

  - `@fHardDeleteRunningInstances`—If this parameter is set to 1, the stored procedure will delete all the running service instances older than hard delete days.

- `dtasp_PurgeTrackingDatabase`—Purges the database without performing a backup first. Performance wise, this is the most efficient option as depending on the tracking size, the backup operation can take a long time. if you do not have data retention policies, you should use this option whenever possible.

- Parameters explanation:

    - @nHours—All completed instances data, older than the number of hours, will be purged.

    - @nDays—All completed instances data, older than the number of days, will be purged.

    - @nHardDays—All data (completed or not) older than the number of @nHardDays days, will be purged.

    - @dtLastBackup—The stored procedure uses this date to ensure that the process does not delete data that was not in the last backup. If you pass through the date and time value of the moment of running the job (using getUTCDate()), the stored procedure will delete all the corresponding data. This parameter is used internally to make sure the date of the execution is older than the date calculated by nHardDays, nDays, and nHours.

    - @fHardDeleteRunningInstances—If this parameter is set to 1, the stored procedure will delete all the running service instances older than hard delete days.

Important   The parameter @fHardDeleteRunningInstances for both stored procedures is not exposed by the SQL Server job default call definition. You must manually add it to the call and set it up to 1, as the default value is 0. If you do change it the stored procedure will not delete all the running instances that are older than the @nHardDays parameter.

Editing the job using the SQL Server job interface is usually not clear, as the editing window does not provide IntelliSense. What you can do, though, is to copy the default job step configuration and then, using SQL Server management studio, paste it in a new SQL Server query. Figures 4-5 and 4-6 show you the difference.

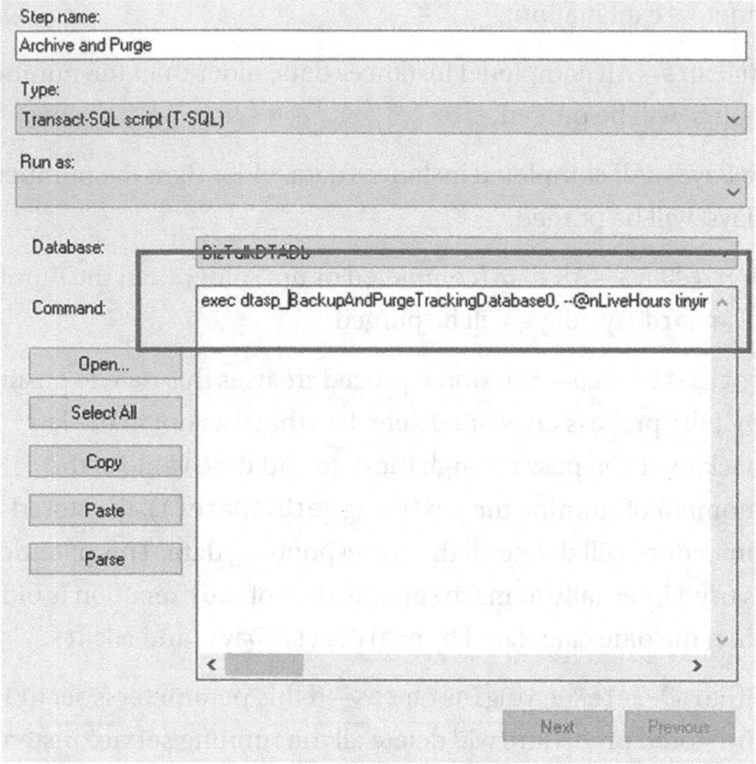
Step name:
Archive and Purge
Type:
Transact-SQL script (T-SQL)
Run as:
Database:
BizTalkDTADb
Command:
exec dtasp_BackupAndPurgeTrackingDatabase0, --@nLiveHours tinyir
Open...
Select All
Copy
Paste
Parse
Next
Previous

Figure 4-5. *Viewing the job configuration using the job properties*

The same code is shown in the SQL Server Management Studio Query Editor in Figure 4-6.

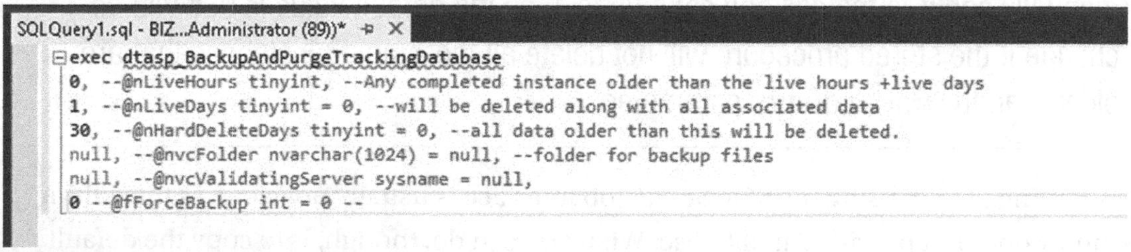
SQLQuery1.sql - BIZ...Administrator (89))*
exec dtasp_BackupAndPurgeTrackingDatabase
0, --@nLiveHours tinyint, --Any completed instance older than the live hours +live days
1, --@nLiveDays tinyint = 0, --will be deleted along with all associated data
30, --@nHardDeleteDays tinyint = 0, --all data older than this will be deleted.
null, --@nvcFolder nvarchar(1024) = null, --folder for backup files
null, --@nvcValidatingServer sysname = null,
0 --@fForceBackup int = 0 --

Figure 4-6. *Viewing the job configuration using the Query Editor*

Host Architecture

As you learned in Chapter 1, host instances are implemented as Windows services. These processes run on the server using their own set of hardware resources such as memory, threads (CPU), and I/O (networking and disk).

By default, the BizTalk Server configuration creates only two hosts: The `BizTalkServerApplication`, which is used as an in-process host, and the `BizTalkServerIsolatedHost`, which controls all the requests received by external processes (IIS in the majority of scenarios of today). With this configuration, you have all that you need to start developing and deploying BizTalk Server solutions to production. However, the initial configuration is not optimum for a real production scenario, as all BizTalk processing artifacts such as receive locations, orchestrations, and send ports will be using the same in-process host configuration (`BizTalkServerApplication`) and that will eventually cause queuing situations into the Message Box database.

For instance, imagine that you have a solution that receives 1,000 large messages. In this scenario, message publication process uses all the available memory and CPU usage before the default throttling condition arises. If the host instance is busy at message publication stage, neither processing nor delivering functionalities will take place, because the host instance does not have resources to start both operations. The same applies to tracking functionality; if the host instance is busy performing the rest of the operations it might not have threads, memory or IO to allocate resources and perform the tracking operation (inserting tracking messages to the Message Box and Tracking databases).

If you decide, however, to separate hosts based on BizTalk Server functionality, even though the publishing host enters in throttling condition, your orchestrations and send ports will still send messages, as they will not be affected by the same throttling condition.

Additionally, as most of the performance settings in BizTalk server are applied at a host level, it is essential that you define a host separation policy that matches the required performance SLA. What does it mean exactly? For example, if you are developing an application that behaves as low latency (performance behavior 9), the best option is to place all the BizTalk Server artifacts to run in a dedicated set of hosts. In other words, you can create three hosts for that application: One for receive locations, another one for orchestrations, and one more for sending ports.

On the other hand, if the application is running only a few transactions per day, you do not need to create additional hosts; you can have a set of standard hosts to run all the low volume applications.

Keep in mind that adding unnecessary hosts can create overhead in the BizTalk and SQL Servers when host instances are started. That is why you have to use common sense when approaching a new BizTalk Server project. Do not just create a new set of receiving, processing, and sending hosts because it is the Microsoft best practice. Instead, create a generic set of hosts that will be used for low volume applications, and then you move forward with the specific cases.

As you can see, choosing the right host separation policy is not easy. Without a doubt, it is one of the most relevant decisions that you will be taking. A good starting point is to leverage on the application priority levels and start from there.

In the following sections, you learn about an optimal initial configuration and general recommendations based on the different application priority levels. The recommendations detailed in the next sections should not be taken as flat recommendations because testing will confirm the best optimum configuration.

Initial Host Separation Policy

As you learned in the previous section, the default BizTalk Server host separation policy is not optimal for the majority of scenarios. You can use the following table as a starting point. Further customization can be applied based on the application priority levels in combination with performance testing.

Host Name	Description
Tracking	Performs the tracking functionality. Also, it is the only host with tracking enabled. It should be 64-bit.
Receiving32	This host is designed to run all the receive locations that handle adapters that only work in a 32-bit mode, such as FTP, POP3, and the old SQL Server adapter (deprecated).
Receiving64	This host is designed to run all of the receive locations that handle adapters that can work in a 64-bit modes, such as File, HTTP, MSMQ, MQSeries, SFTP, SMTP, SOAP, and WCF.
Sending32	This host is designed to run all of the receive locations that handle adapters that only work in a 32-bit mode, such as FTP, POP3, and non-WCF SQL Server adapter (deprecated).
Sending64	This host is designed to run all of the receive locations that handle adapters that can work in a 64-bit mode, such as File, HTTP, MSMQ, MQSeries, SFTP, SMTP, SOAP, and WCF.
Processing32	This host will run orchestrations that for any reason has 32-bit requirements. This is usually required when a custom .NET component can run in 32-bit mode only.
Processing64	The rest of the non 32-bit orchestrations should run under this hosts.

Note   If the BizTalk Server group does not require 32-bit adapters, you should not create 32-bit hosts. Also, you should set the Show Performance Counters to orchestrations if the host is dedicated to orchestrations.

Host Separation Policy Based on Application Priority Levels

In this section you will learn how to use the application priority levels to design an optimal host separation policy.

Host Separation Guidance for Release Stage Level (RSL)

The release stage level reflects how mature is an application from the issues point of view. Because of that, it may be interesting to isolate applications that are not yet stable. You can follow the following suggested recommendations based on the release stage levels:

RSL	Level	Suggested Recommendation
9,8	First or early releases	The application should have its own set of hosts due to the number of deployments required to fix the upcoming issues. By doing so, the rest of the applications will not be affected by deployments, as in the majority of the scenarios you will have to restart host instances or terminate running instances (if no side-by-side version is enabled, of course).
7	Unstable release (performance)	At this stage, application functionality is granted. However, performance is still an issue, and new deployments can occur frequently. Additionally, hosts might have temporary settings to overcome the performance issues caused by inappropriate development decisions.
6	Stable release	The application is now stable and running without known issues for a while now. Tracking is disabled at all artifact levels, and standard host settings are applied. RSL should not be considered as a reason to isolate this application into a different set of hosts.

Host Separation Guidance for Business Priority Level (BPL)

The business priority level reflects the application importance from the business point of view. You can use the following suggested recommendations to apply a host separation policy that matches the business priority level.

BPL	Suggested Recommendation
9–7	Applications must have their own set of dedicated hosts for receiving, processing, and sending functionalities.
6	As business accepts downtime, applications with the same BPL (6) can be assigned to the same set of hosts if they share similar performance requirements. Creating a set of hosts per BizTalk functionality might be required if performance for one of the applications in the BPL level is significant, but the application is not considered mission-critical.
5	Applications should be placed in only one host to handle all operations, but this host cannot be shared with the rest of the applications (no host separation based on BizTalk Server functionality is required).
4	Applications can be running in a shared unique host (no host separation based on BizTalk Server functionality is required).

Host Separation Guidance for Transaction Levels (TL)

The transaction level shows the number of transactions that the application process. You can follow these recommendations for an optimal host separation policy based on this level:

TL	Volume definition	Number of transactions Per Hour	Host Separation Recommended
9	Extremely high	>=3,000,000	Yes
8	Very High	>=1,000,000 and < 3,000,000	Yes
7	High	>= 300,000 and < 1,000,000	Yes

(continued)

TL	Volume definition	Number of transactions Per Hour	Host Separation Recommended
6	Medium	>=100,000 and < 300,000	It depends. You can put in the same set of hosts applications that have similar TL requirements.
6	Common	>= 10,000 and < 100,000	No
7	Low	< 10,000	No

Host Separation Guidance for Performance Behavior Level (PBL)

The performance behavior level reflects the normal behavior of the application regarding latency and throughput. To apply the right host separation policy, you can follow these recommendations.

PBL	Description	Suggested Recommendation
9	Low latency	Yes
8	High throughput	By default, hosts are configured for high throughput. This should suit the majority of the scenarios, but if the application needs unique host settings, then you need to separate hosts per functionality also.
7	Mixed	These are the most challenging one as only testing will give you the right configuration. Use common sense: If you cannot reach your performance SLA using the default settings, then you need to split hosts by functionality.

Host Performance Settings

Especially when I am delivering BizTalk Server performance review services, I frequently hear the following question: How can I give priority to a specific application or even to an artifact within the application?

BizTalk Server has only one setting to control priority at the logical level, and it has been reviewed in Chapter 1, priority at the sending port level. If you adjust this setting, it guarantees that the dequeue process for that send port puts those instances on top of the queue, but not for all of the instances. Even though this feature is there, it does not ensure priority under peak, or high load, as the BizTalk Server engine can eventually rise throttling conditions that can impact priority.

However, it is an excellent practice to decrease priority for all the send ports of the applications that rank higher in the following application priority levels:

- Business priority level (BPL)

- Transaction levels (TL)

- Performance behavior level (PBL)

Keep in mind that if you change priority on all the send ports (or the majority of them), the improvement becomes closer to none because all send ports will have the same priority. Remember that you can adjust this setting to a value that ranges from 1 to 10.

In BizTalk Server, you give priority to applications by allowing them to use more hardware resources. This is a very efficient way to assign priority because, if the host instance takes more "dedicated" resources, it will perform faster than the rest of the host instances as it will not be competing constantly for those resources. Additionally, when the high priority application runs under a high volume of data, it will throttle with specific throttling thresholds that will guarantee its performance SLA, and the rest of applications can still use the common amount of resources without getting impacted. This is another reason that the host separation policy becomes extremely important.

Thanks to the flexibility of the BizTalk Server configuration layer, you can take the host separation policy as far as to dedicate servers to run specific functionalities (receiving, processing, and sending) or even specific orchestrations or ports.

BizTalk Server allows you to change the host performance behavior for the following categories:

- General host settings.

- Resource-based throttling. These settings have been explained in Chapter 2.

- Rate-based throttling. These settings have been explained in Chapter 2.

- Orchestration throttling.

The recommendations in this section should be considered as initial adjustments only. At the end of the day, only performance testing will drive you to the right configuration settings and hardware sizing.

General Host Settings

In this section you will learn about the general host settings and how you can adjust them based on the performance behavior level (PBL). This level reflects the normal behavior of the application in terms of latency and throughput.

You can access the host performance settings using the BizTalk Administration Console and selecting a specific host, as shown in Figure 4-7.

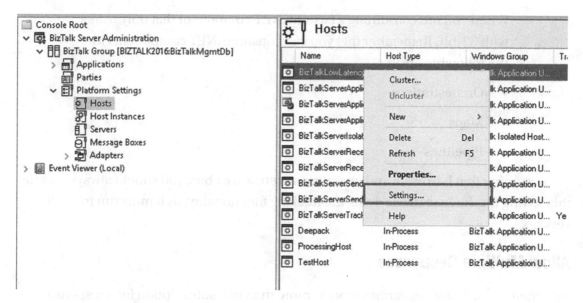

Figure 4-7. *Accessing the host settings*

Move Tracking Data to DTADB

This setting enables the host to move data from the Message Box to the Tracking database. Only the host that is dedicated to tracking functionality should have this setting enabled. If the host is running artifacts that provide application functionality such as orchestrations, the receive and send ports it must be disabled.

32-Bit Only

This setting regulates whether the host is running as a 32-bit or 64-bit process. The only situations where you will be adjusting this setting to 32-bit are:

- 32-bit hardware or 32-bit version of Windows.

- Some adapters, such as FTP, POP3, and the old SQL Server adapter are not supported to run in the 64-bit.

- When you are consuming a custom .NET component that only works with 32-bit. Remember that you can consume .NET components in the following areas:

  - Orchestrations

  - Maps

  - Pipelines

Assuming that hardware and operating system are 64 bits, you should always disable this setting for the host that is doing the tracking functionality, as it must run in the 64 version.

Allow Multiple Responses

By default, host instances cannot process more than one subscription for a response message that is being received through a request/response port. When the engine receives multiple messages, you will get the following error:

Error details: The message found multiple request-response subscriptions.
A message can only be routed to a single request-response subscription

Enable this setting if you want to enable receiving multiple responses in a two-way port scenario.

Response Timeout in Minutes

This is the default timeout for all the ports of this host. Developers can overwrite this setting by code in dynamic ports or by setting the properties at the adapter level in the port configuration. The default configuration is set to 20 minutes, which in most scenarios is very high. As this setting is per host, consider adjusting this setting to more suitable value based on the maximum response time for the consumed service.

Maximum Engine Threads

This setting controls the maximum number of threads per CPU that the host instances of that host will allocate to process messages. The engine load threads based on the current load of messages, up to the maximum engine threads setting.

Note   Do not confuse this setting with the .NET CLR settings at the host instance level, as they control how host instances access CPU resources to perform I/O operations.

For instance, imagine that your server has 16 cores. If you leave the default value, the message engine will allocate a maximum of 20 * 16 (320) threads for that specific host.

Changing this setting can have a negative or positive impact on performance. You can follow this advice:

Situation	Suggested Recommendation
Message Box database servers show high CPU utilization, and it is affecting BizTalk Server performance by increasing latency. Usually, SQL Lock times are higher than 500 milliseconds.	Decrease if scaling SQL Servers is not an option.
SQL Server holding Message Box and BizTalk Servers are under the CPU utilization stated by the maximum sustainable load.	Increase if the system requires more throughput or if you want to make more use of CPU resources.

Show Performance Counters For

This setting controls how BizTalk Server populates the performance counter information. It is more important than it seems because if you do not set it up correctly, performance counters could not be populated with data.

Value	Applicable To
Messaging	Hosts that are not running orchestrations.
Orchestration	Hosts that are dedicated to orchestration processing.
Active service	For hosts that are running more than one functionality (receiving, processing, and sending).

Pooling Intervals

As you learned in Chapter 1, messages are stored in the Message Box. As BizTalk Server creates a set of queue tables related to a specific host, host instances will access those tables to check whether there are new messages associated with that host. While messages exist, the interval settings are ignored, and the host instance starts working on the pending messages at maximum speed using the available host instance resources. When the queue tables are empty, the host instance will access the queues using the interval defined by the polling interval setting.

If the host instances are processing a few service instances a day, you should not decrease the pooling interval because that will increase CPU utilization on SQL Server, as most of the time the host queue tables are empty. Moreover, you should consider increasing it.

Setting	Default Value	Applicable To
Messaging	500ms	Hosts running ports
Orchestrations	500ms	Host running orchestrations

Suggested Pooling Intervals Based on Application Performance Behavior

The performance behavior level reflects the normal behavior of the application regarding latency and throughput. In order to apply the right host pooling interval settings, you can follow these suggested recommendations:

PBL	Description	Suggested Recommendation
9	Low latency	Decrease to the point where MST is granted. A good starting point will be to decrease this setting by 50% for every testing cycle. First, you can decrease it to 250 and test. If performance is improved and MST is still granted, then move to decrease 50% more. Repeat testing until MST is exceeded.
8	High throughput	BizTalk Server is shipped for high throughput scenarios. Therefore, the default 500 milliseconds should fit the majority of needs. If your application needs to deal with a very large number of messages where the load occurs in very specific times (not all along the day), you should test whether increasing this value will have a positive impact. Otherwise, leave the default of 500 milliseconds.

(continued)

PBL	Description	Suggested Recommendation
7	Mixed	These are the most complicated applications to tune. Only testing will give you the actual picture, and proactive changes most likely will not help.
6	No specific	Leave the default 500 milliseconds if the application is running under the performance SLA.

Let's review these recommendations with a few examples.

Scenario 1: High Throughput (I)

A BizTalk Server application receives 1,000 messages through a receive port. Pooling interval settings are set to the default values:

- Messaging interval set to 500

- Orchestrations interval set to 500

1. The host instance is running, and because the load did not start yet (there are zero records in the host queue tables), it will poll the host queue tables every 500 milliseconds (two times per second) to retrieve the new messages when they arrive.

2. A receive location publishes 1,000 messages to that host.

3. The message engine stores those 1,000 messages into the host queue tables of that host after message publication.

4. Now, because there are 1,000 records in the host queue table, the host instance will not poll the tables until the host queue tables become empty. In other words, until the host instance processes all messages.

5. When all queues are empty, if receive locations are not publishing more messages, the host instance will start polling based on the pooling interval period until new messages arrive.

This scenario is a typical high throughput scenario where you are receiving a large number of messages most likely in a batch scenario. When a batch is received, host instances will process everything without checking if there are new messages until the end of the process.

Scenario 2: Low latency

A BizTalk Server application receives 50 messages per second through a receive port. Pooling interval settings are set to these values:

- Messaging interval set to 50

- Orchestrations interval set to 50

    1. The host instance is running, and because the load did not start yet (there are zero records in the host queue tables), it will poll the host queue tables every 50 milliseconds (twenty times per second) to retrieve the new messages when they arrive.

    2. The consumer application starts sending messages one by one but at a rate of 50 messages per second. You can imagine that consumers are retreating money from ATMs and that process will work 24x7.

    3. The message engine stores those 50 messages into the host queue tables of that host.

    4. Now, because there are 50 records in the host queue tables, the host instance will not poll the tables until the host queue tables become empty. In other words, until the host instance process all messages.

    5. The consumer sends another 50 messages while the host instance is still working so the queue increases over time, each time the consumers request new ATM operations.

    6. As consumers can work the whole day, the host queue tables might not become empty again, but if they do, host instances will poll them 20 times per second to ensure new instances are processed extremely fast.

    7. When all queues are empty, if the receive locations are not publishing more messages, the host instance will start polling again until new messages arrive.

Scenario 3: High Throughput (II)

You developed a solution that receives one large file daily at midnight. The file contains a collection of transactions that should be processed during the night. The application can receive up to 10,000 transactions each time.

As this application will be initiated only at midnight, you enable scheduling at receive port just to guarantee that even though new files arrive during the day, it is only at midnight when the process starts.

Additionally, you increase the pooling intervals to 200,000 (200 seconds) for the hosts dedicated to this application, so that the message engine does not continuously polls the Message Box database.

Conclusions:

- Decreasing these values will guarantee that newly published messages are processed faster, as host instances will pool the database more frequently when the queues are empty.

- By Increasing these values, the BizTalk Server engine will not detect new messages with the same frequency. Thus, CPU consumption and IO on SQL Server will improve when there is no load for those host instances. This is ideal for applications that work punctually during the day.

Note As always, keep in mind that changing these settings is intrinsically linked to the type of application and the performance SLA requirements. You should always test the changes— especially this one, because it has a significant impact on SQL Server CPU utilization and I/O.

Orchestration Throttling

You can control the dehydration behavior of orchestrations by accessing the following settings using the BizTalk Administration Console at the host level, as shown in Figure 4-8.

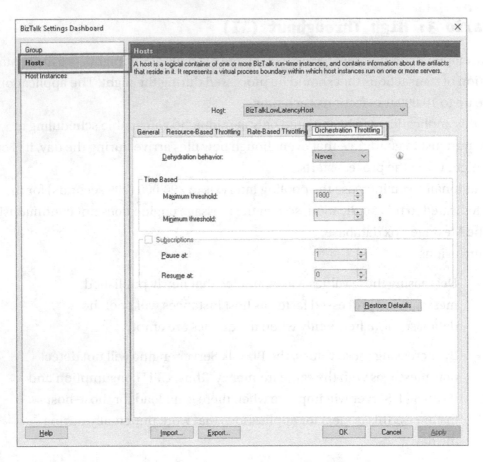

Figure 4-8. Orchestration throttling settings at the host level

- Dehydration Behavior

  - Never—This option disables the dehydration feature for all the
    orchestrations running under that specific host. That means
    that when an orchestration is consuming a service or waiting for
    another event to occur, the orchestration engine will keep the
    orchestration into memory. This option will alleviate SQL Server
    CPU, memory, and IO, as the amount of data that SQL Server has
    to process decreases, and networking usage when SQL Server is
    in a separated box. But it will cause the BizTalk Server machine to
    consume a larger amount of memory, and CPU threads might be
    busy waiting for an activation event to occur.

- Always—Dehydration will always occur. While this option will save memory resources to the BizTalk machine, it can potentially cause an overhead to the SQL Server hosting the Message Box database.

- Custom—Dehydration will take place based on the time based or subscriptions thresholds.

- Time Based

  - Maximum threshold—Idle orchestrations will be held into the host instance memory, for a maximum number of seconds specified by this setting. After that, the orchestration engine forces the dehydration of the orchestration (if it is still idle). The default value is 1800 seconds (30 minutes).

    - Minimum threshold—Orchestrations are considered for dehydration when they are idle for at least the number of seconds specified in this threshold. The default value is 1 second.

For example, if you set the Minimum Threshold to 1 second, and all the orchestrations of that host are completed in less than 1 second, the orchestration engine will never dehydrate those orchestrations. On the other hand, if some orchestrations instances are idle for more than 1 second, the orchestration engine considers those orchestrations for dehydration (depending on the internal algorithm based on elements like number of instances running and resource utilization).

If, for some reason, there are orchestration instances taking longer than the maximum threshold, the orchestration engine will force dehydration if orchestrations are idle.

- Subscriptions

  - Pause At—Orchestrations have subscriptions to messages that are stored to the main host queue tables. When the number of messages in this queue (associated with the orchestration subscription) is equal or higher than the Pause At threshold, the messages are not delivered to orchestrations instances until the number of messages in the host queue decreases to the Resume At threshold.

  - Resume At—As explained in the Pause At setting, this threshold controls whether the message engine starts to deliver new message instances to orchestrations.

For example, if you set the Pause At threshold to 1,000, the message engine will stop delivering messages to the orchestrations running under that host when the number of associated messages to that orchestration reaches 1,000.

If Resume At is set to 600, the message engine will resume delivering messages to those orchestrations when the number of pending messages decreases to 600 or below.

Automating Host Settings

The best way to optimize the BizTalk Server platform, and any other Windows platform, is by automating all settings using PowerShell scripts or the out-of-the-box BizTalk Server features to import and export the settings.

In the previous sections, you learned the most essential BizTalk Server settings. This section focuses on automation, and you will learn how to implement automated scripts to improve the BizTalk Server and the platform environment. As the majority of the techniques detailed in these sections use the PowerShell, this section requires strong PowerShell knowledge.

Since most of the settings are applied at the host level, it is crucial that you understand the WMI classes that BizTalk Server exposes.

What Is WMI?

Windows Management Instrumentation (WMI) is a collection of classes for management data and operations in the Windows world. You can develop your WMI scripts to automate tasks on servers and to access product functionality. At the moment of writing this book, BizTalk Server exposes 31 classes that expose the majority of BizTalk Server administrative actions. These classes are defined in the following table.

Class	Description
MSBTS_AdapterSetting	Registers new adapters
MSBTS_BTSObject	This member supports the BizTalk Server internal infrastructure. You should not be using this in your code, as it is not supported.
MSBTS_DeploymentService	Encapsulates BizTalk assemblies for deployment or undeployment and bindings export or import.
MSBTS_GroupSetting	Represents a BizTalk Server group associated with a specific management database.
MSBTS_Host	Represents a BizTalk server host.
MSBTS_HostInstance	Represents a host instance.
MSBTS_HostInstanceSetting	Used to read and update the host instance settings.
MSBTS_HostQueue	Represents the main queue of a specific host.
MSBTS_HostSetting	Used to represent the settings for a host.
MSBTS_MessageInstance	Represents a message instance.
MSBTS_MessageInstanceSuspendedEvent	Represents a suspended event for a BizTalk message instance.
MSBTS_MsgBoxSetting	Represents a single Message Box setting in the BizTalk Server group.
MSBTS_Orchestration	Represents an instance of an orchestration.
MSBTS_ReceiveHandler	Represents a receive handler.
MSBTS_ReceiveLocation	Represents a receive location.
MSBTS_ReceiveLocationOrchestration	Represents receive locations that are linked to orchestrations.
MSBTS_ReceivePort	Represents a receive port .
MSBTS_SendHandler	Represents a send handler.
MSBTS_SendHandler2	Represents an extended individual send handler.

(continued)

Class	Description
MSBTS_SendPort	Represents a send port.
MSBTS_SendPortGroup	Represents a group of send ports.
MSBTS_SendPortGroup2SendPort (WMI)	Same as the previous one.
MSBTS_Server	Represents computers within a group that have BizTalk Servers installed.
MSBTS_ServerHost	Reflects mappings between BizTalk Servers and BizTalk Hosts.
MSBTS_ServerSetting	Represents specific computers within the same BizTalk group.
MSBTS_Service	This member supports the BizTalk Server internal infrastructure. You should not be using this in your code, as it is not supported.
MSBTS_ServiceInstance	Provides an instance of a service, with a start and stop methods.
MSBTS_ServiceInstanceSuspendedEvent	Represents a suspended event for a service instance.
MSBTS_Setting	Supports the BizTalk Server internal infrastructure. You should not be using this in your code, as it is not supported.
MSBTS_TrackedMessageInstance	Represents a message instance.
MSBTS_TrackedMessageInstance2 (WMI)	Represents a message instance.

Exploring WMI Classes Using WMI Explorer

This open source tool is great tool to explore all of the WMI classes registered in your computer. You can download it from `https://github.com/vinaypamnani/wmie2/releases`.

How to Use WMI Explorer

Executing WMI queries requires administrator privileges. Therefore, you must run the application as an administrator.

1. Type the server name or leave it as the default if you are connecting to a local server. Click the Connect button, as shown in Figure 4-9.

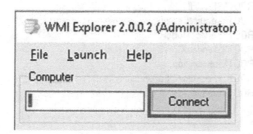

Figure 4-9. *Connecting to a BizTalk Server environment*

If your user has the proper rights, the tool will list all available namespaces, as shown in Figure 4-10.

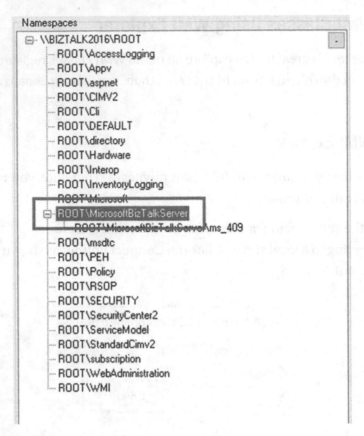

Figure 4-10. *Selecting the BizTalk Server WMI namespace*

2. Double-click the ROOT\MicrosoftBizTalkServer namespace, **not**
ROOT\MicrosoftBizTalkServer\ms_409. The tool will show all
available classes for the BizTalk Server namespace, as shown in
Figure 4-11.

Classes (31)	Search		

Quick Filter:

Classes

Name ˄	Lazy ...	Description	Path
MSBTS_AdapterSetting	False	This class is used to registe...	\\BIZTALK2016\ROOT\M...
MSBTS_BTSObject	False	The CIM_LogicalElement c...	\\BIZTALK2016\ROOT\M...
MSBTS_DeploymentService	False	This class encapsulates Bi...	\\BIZTALK2016\ROOT\M...
MSBTS_GroupSetting	False	This class represents the Bi...	\\BIZTALK2016\ROOT\M...
MSBTS_Host	False	This class represents a Biz...	\\BIZTALK2016\ROOT\M...
MSBTS_HostInstance	False	This class represents a sin...	\\BIZTALK2016\ROOT\M...
MSBTS_HostInstanceSetting	False	This class represents a sin...	\\BIZTALK2016\ROOT\M...
MSBTS_HostQueue	False	The CIM_LogicalElement c...	\\BIZTALK2016\ROOT\M...
MSBTS_HostSetting	False	This class represents the s...	\\BIZTALK2016\ROOT\M...
MSBTS_MessageInstance	False	The CIM_LogicalElement c...	\\BIZTALK2016\ROOT\M...
MSBTS_MessageInstance...	False		\\BIZTALK2016\ROOT\M...
MSBTS_MsgBoxSetting	False	This class represents a sin...	\\BIZTALK2016\ROOT\M...
MSBTS_Orchestration	False	This class represents orche...	\\BIZTALK2016\ROOT\M...
MSBTS_ReceiveHandler	False	This class represents indivi...	\\BIZTALK2016\ROOT\M...
MSBTS_ReceiveLocation	False	This class represents indivi...	\\BIZTALK2016\ROOT\M...
MSBTS_ReceiveLocationO...	False	This class represents all po...	\\BIZTALK2016\ROOT\M...
MSBTS_ReceivePort	False	This class represents indivi...	\\BIZTALK2016\ROOT\M...
MSBTS_SendHandler	False		\\BIZTALK2016\ROOT\M...
MSBTS_SendHandler2	False		\\BIZTALK2016\ROOT\M...
MSBTS_SendPort	False	This class represents indivi...	\\BIZTALK2016\ROOT\M...
MSBTS_SendPortGroup	False	This class represents a gro...	\\BIZTALK2016\ROOT\M...
MSBTS_SendPortGroup2S...	False	This class represents the m...	\\BIZTALK2016\ROOT\M...
MSBTS_Server	False	This class represents speci...	\\BIZTALK2016\ROOT\M...
MSBTS_ServerHost	False	This class reflects mapping...	\\BIZTALK2016\ROOT\M...
MSBTS_ServerSetting	False	This class represents speci...	\\BIZTALK2016\ROOT\M...
MSBTS_Service	False	Classes that derived from t...	\\BIZTALK2016\ROOT\M...
MSBTS_ServiceInstance	False	The CIM_LogicalElement c...	\\BIZTALK2016\ROOT\M...
MSBTS_ServiceInstanceSu...	False		\\BIZTALK2016\ROOT\M...
MSBTS_Setting	False		\\BIZTALK2016\ROOT\M...
MSBTS_TrackedMessageI...	False	This class reflects tracked ...	\\BIZTALK2016\ROOT\M...
MSBTS_TrackedMessageI...	False	This class reflects tracked ...	\\BIZTALK2016\ROOT\M...

Figure 4-11. *Listing the available WMI classes for BizTalk Server*

3. Double-click the `MSBTS_HostSetting` class. The tool will populate the instances.

4. Notice that are several tabs related to the class:

    a. Instances—Lists all instances related to the class, as shown in Figure 4-12.

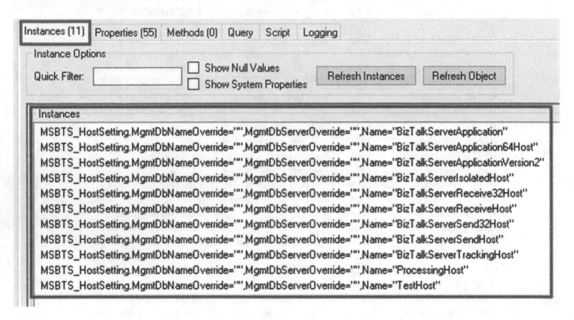

Figure 4-12. *Listing the available instances*

    b. Properties—Lists all available properties for those instances, as shown in Figure 4-13.

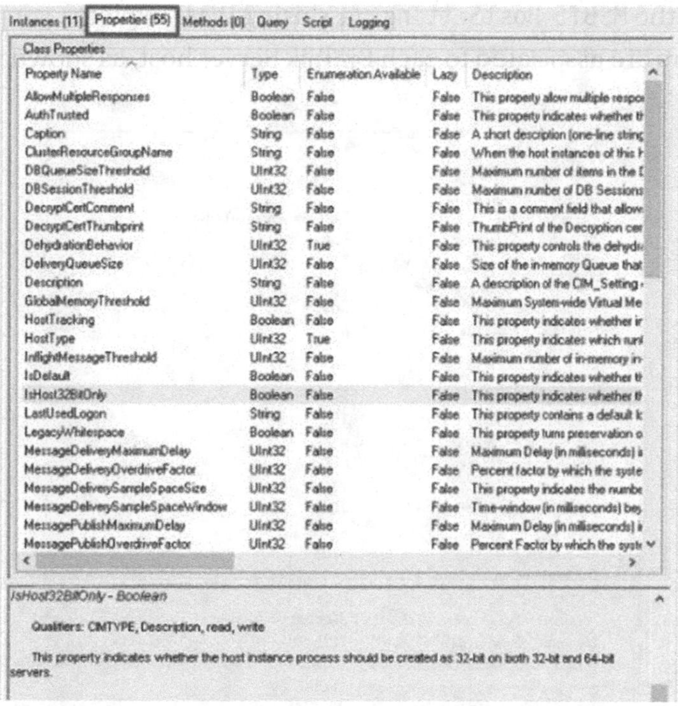

Figure 4-13. *Listing the available properties*

c. Methods—The class MSBTS_HostSetting does not
expose any methods. But if you explore the class MSBTS_
ServiceInstanceSuspendedEvent, you will see that the tool
lists all available methods, as shown in Figure 4-14.

Figure 4-14. *Listing the available methods*

If you explore the MSBTS_HostSetting class using WMI Explorer, you can find that the following members are associated to each BizTalk Server host, as shown in Figure 4-15.

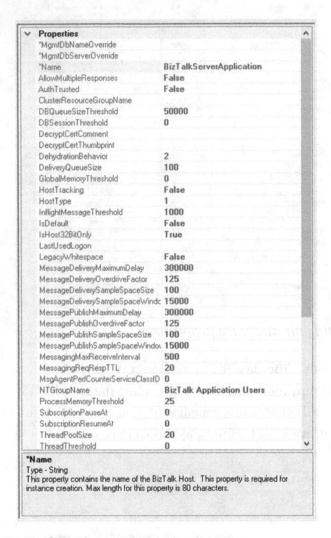

Figure 4-15. *WMI Explorer host setting members*

These members directly represent all of the host settings exposed in the BizTalk Administration Console.

If you explore the MSBTS_HostSetting, you might notice that this class does not have any methods. There is not create, delete, or update so you cannot perform any actions accessing the class directly. However, luckily for us, WMI has standard operations to default actions to all WMI classes. These operations are called PutType options, and the definition is as follows:

```
[-PutType {None | UpdateOnly | CreateOnly }]
```

Where:

- UpdateOnly updates an existing WMI instance.

- CreateOnly creates a new WMI instance.

Using PowerShell to Optimize the Environment

Sandro Pereira, an integration MVP, published a great script to provide the initial BizTalk host separation policy. The script uses the MWI classes presented in this book and PowerShell.

You can download it from here:

```
https://gallery.technet.microsoft.com/PowerShell-to-Configure-0cee83e8
```

In Sandro Pereira's words, the following hosts will be created:

- BizTalkServerTrackingHost—A BizTalk Host that hosts tracking and is responsible for moving the DTA and BAM tracking data from the Message Box database to the BizTalk Tracking (DTA) and BAM Primary Import databases. This movement of tracking data has an impact on the performance of other BizTalk artifacts that are running in the same host that is hosting tracks. Thus, you should use a dedicated host that does nothing but host tracking.

  Only the Allow Host Tracking option must be selected because we only will use this host for tracking.

- BizTalkServerReceiveHost—All options (Allow Host Tracking, 32-bits only, or Make This Default Host in the Group) should be unselected. This host will be responsible for processing messages after they are picked up in a receive location. When a host contains a receiving item, such as a receive location (with a pipeline), the message decoding and decrypting occurs in a pipeline within this host.

All receive handlers, except the isolated ones like SOAP, HTTP, WCF-BasicHttp, WCF-WsHttp, or WCF-CustomIsolated, and the 32-bit adapters (FTP, SQL, and POP3) will be configured for this host. This will mean also that all receive locations will run in this host instance.

- `BizTalkServerReceive32Host`—Has the same goal as the previous one; however, this must have the 32-bits only option selected so that we can run the 23-bits adapters.

  The receive handlers for the FTP, SQL, and POP3 adapters will be configured for this host.

- `BizTalkServerSendHost`—All options (Allow Host Tracking, 32-bits only or Make This Default Host in the Group) should be unselected. This host will be responsible for processing messages before they are sent out to the send port. When a host contains a sending item, such as a send port, the message signing and encryption occurs in a pipeline within this host.

  All send handlers, except 32-bit adapters like native SQL and FTP adapter, will be configured for this host. This will mean also that all send ports will run in this host instance.

- `BizTalkServerSend32Host`—Has the same goal as the previous one; however, this must have the 32-bits only option selected so that we can run the 32-bit adapters.

  The Send handlers for the FTP and SQL adapters will be configured for this host.

- `BizTalkServerApplication`—Only the 32-bits only option should be select in this host. This host will be responsible for processing messages based on the instructions in orchestrations that need to run in 32-bit.

- `BizTalkServerApplication64Host`—Only the Make this Default Host in the Group option should be select in this host. This host will be responsible for processing messages based on the instructions in all or the most common orchestrations.

Using the BizTalk Host Configuration Settings File

The XML BizTalkLowLatencyHostSettings.xml file, located in the Chapter 4 source code file, contains the host configuration and associated host instance that you can reuse in your environment to import this configuration to any of your hosts.

```xml
<?xml version="1.0" encoding="utf-8"?>
<Settings xmlns:xsi="http://www.w3.org/2001/XMLSchema-instance"
xmlns:xsd="http://www.w3.org/2001/XMLSchema">
  <ExportedGroup>BIZTALK2016:BIZTALKMGMTDB</ExportedGroup>
  <GroupSettings>
    <Setting Name="AllowTrackingSettingsImport">True</Setting>
    <Setting Name="ConfigurationCacheRefreshInterval">60</Setting>
    <Setting Name="GlobalTrackingOption">1</Setting>
    <Setting Name="LMSFragmentSize">102400</Setting>
    <Setting Name="LMSThreshold">1000000</Setting>
    <Setting Name="PerfCounterCacheRefreshInterval">60</Setting>
  </GroupSettings>
  <HostSettings>
    <Host Name="BizTalkLowLatencyHost">
      <Setting Name="AllowMultipleResponses">True</Setting>
      <Setting Name="AuthTrusted">False</Setting>
      <Setting Name="DBQueueSizeThreshold">100000</Setting>
      <Setting Name="DBSessionThreshold">0</Setting>
      <Setting Name="DehydrationBehavior">1</Setting>
      <Setting Name="DeliveryQueueSize">1000</Setting>
      <Setting Name="GlobalMemoryThreshold">0</Setting>
      <Setting Name="HostTracking">False</Setting>
      <Setting Name="InflightMessageThreshold">5000</Setting>
      <Setting Name="IsHost32BitOnly">False</Setting>
      <Setting Name="LegacyWhitespace">False</Setting>
      <Setting Name="MessageDeliveryMaximumDelay">300000</Setting>
      <Setting Name="MessageDeliveryOverdriveFactor">125</Setting>
      <Setting Name="MessageDeliverySampleSpaceSize">100</Setting>
      <Setting Name="MessageDeliverySampleSpaceWindow">15000</Setting>
      <Setting Name="MessagePublishMaximumDelay">300000</Setting>
      <Setting Name="MessagePublishOverdriveFactor">125</Setting>
```

```
      <Setting Name="MessagePublishSampleSpaceSize">100</Setting>
      <Setting Name="MessagePublishSampleSpaceWindow">15000</Setting>
      <Setting Name="MessagingMaxReceiveInterval">50</Setting>
      <Setting Name="MessagingReqRespTTL">3</Setting>
      <Setting Name="MsgAgentPerfCounterServiceClassID">0</Setting>
      <Setting Name="ProcessMemoryThreshold">100</Setting>
      <Setting Name="SubscriptionPauseAt">0</Setting>
      <Setting Name="SubscriptionResumeAt">0</Setting>
      <Setting Name="ThreadPoolSize">40</Setting>
      <Setting Name="ThreadThreshold">0</Setting>
      <Setting Name="ThrottlingBatchMemoryThresholdPercent">1</Setting>
      <Setting Name="ThrottlingDeliveryOverride">2</Setting>
      <Setting Name="ThrottlingDeliveryOverrideSeverity">100</Setting>
      <Setting Name="ThrottlingLimitToTriggerGC">80</Setting>
      <Setting Name="ThrottlingPublishOverride">2</Setting>
      <Setting Name="ThrottlingPublishOverrideSeverity">100</Setting>
      <Setting Name="ThrottlingSeverityDatabaseSize">1</Setting>
      <Setting Name="ThrottlingSeverityInflightMessage">75</Setting>
      <Setting Name="ThrottlingSeverityProcessMemory">500</Setting>
      <Setting Name="ThrottlingSpoolMultiplier">10</Setting>
      <Setting Name="ThrottlingTrackingDataMultiplier">10</Setting>
      <Setting Name="TimeBasedMaxThreshold">1800</Setting>
      <Setting Name="TimeBasedMinThreshold">1</Setting>
      <Setting Name="UseDefaultAppDomainForIsolatedAdapter">False</Setting>
      <Setting Name="XlangMaxReceiveInterval">50</Setting>
    </Host>
  </HostSettings>
  <HostInstanceSettings>
    <Host Name="BizTalkLowLatencyHost">
      <Server Name="BizTalk2016">
        <Setting Name="CLRMaxIOThreads">250</Setting>
        <Setting Name="CLRMaxWorkerThreads">250</Setting>
        <Setting Name="CLRMinIOThreads">25</Setting>
        <Setting Name="CLRMinWorkerThreads">25</Setting>
        <Setting Name="PhysicalMemoryMaximalUsage">85</Setting>
        <Setting Name="PhysicalMemoryOptimalUsage">70</Setting>
```

```
    <Setting Name="VirtualMemoryMaximalUsage">85</Setting>
    <Setting Name="VirtualMemoryOptimalUsage">65</Setting>
   </Server>
  </Host>
 </HostInstanceSettings>
</Settings>
```

How to Import a Host Configuration File Using the Administration Console

Follow these steps to import a host setting configuration file:

1. Using the BizTalk Administration Console, access the Settings window of any hosts or by using the right pane of the console and clicking on the Settings option.

2. Click on the Import button, as shown in Figure 4-16.

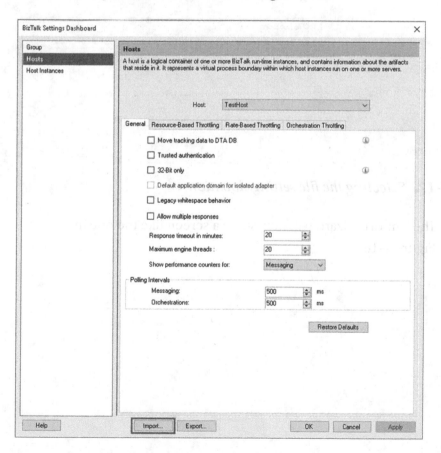

Figure 4-16. *Importing host settings from a file*

3. On the Import Settings Wizard, browse to the template file
BizTalkLowLatencyHost.xml and click Next, as shown in
Figure 4-17.

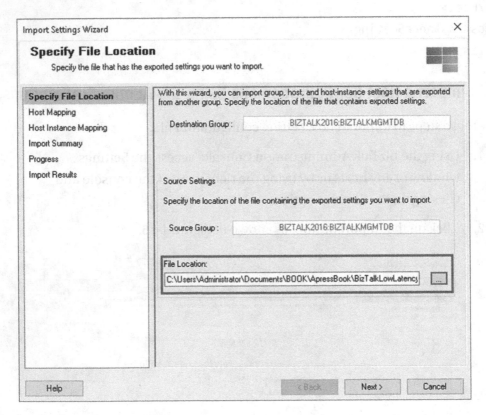

Figure 4-17. *Selecting the file settings location*

4. The Import Wizard will now show a screen like the one in
Figure 4-18.

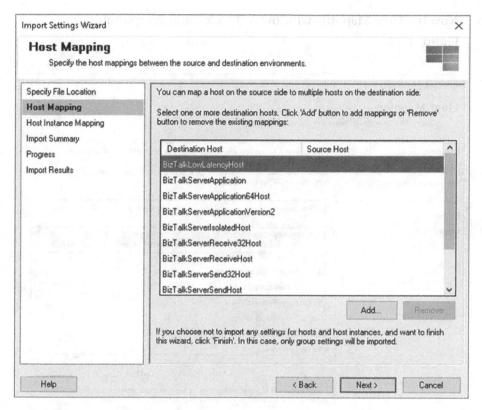

Figure 4-18. *Host mapping window*

5.   The Destination-Host column is showing all the hosts of the
     current environment. The idea here is that you are going to
     select the host configuration for the low latency host contained
     in the configurations file. The BizTalkLowLatencyHost does
     not necessary exist in your environment; you are just using its
     configuration as a template for any other host that needs to
     behave as low latency.

     For instance, imagine that in your case you want to
     apply all the low latency customizations to the host
     BizTalkServerApplicationHost. To do that, select the
     BizTalkServerApplicationHost, then click the Add button and
     select the BizTalkLowLatencyHost configuration host from the
     Select Source Entity window and click OK.

6. Now the Host Mapping window will look something similar to Figure 4-19.

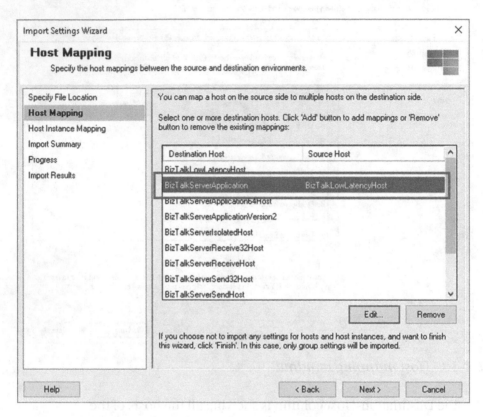

Figure 4-19. *Linking the destination host to the source host*

Here you can see that you are going to assign the low latency settings to the BizTalkServerApplication host only. Click Next.

7. The configuration file also contains low latency settings for host instances, therefore, it's time to do the same for the host instances of the host `BizTalkServerApplication`.

8. On the Host Instance Mapping window, click on Add button
    and select the `BizTalkLowLatencyHost` configuration host from
    the Select Source Entity window. Click OK. The Host Instance
    Mapping window should look something like Figure 4-20.

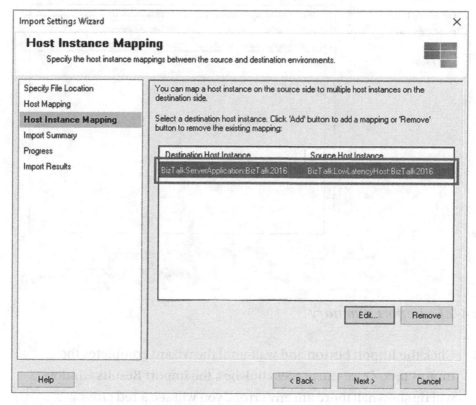

Figure 4-20. *Mapping host instances*

Click Next.

9. Now the wizard shows the Import Summary window where you
    can see all the changes, as shown in Figure 4-21.

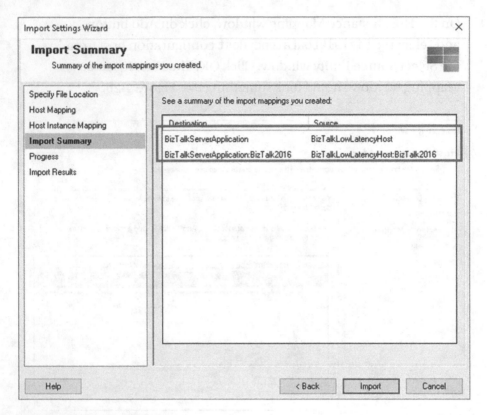

Figure 4-21. *Import summary*

10. Click the Import button and wait until the wizard completes the import task. Once the process finishes, the Import Results window will be shown. If there are any errors, you will see a red cross instead of a green check. See Figure 4-22.

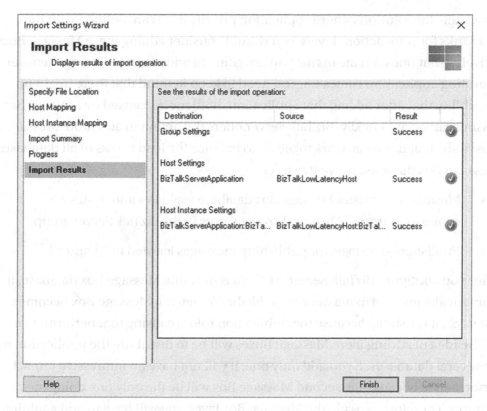

Figure 4-22. *Import results*

11. Now go to the BizTalk Administration Console. Click F5 to
refresh the data and access the host settings window. Locate the
BizTalkServerApplication host and check that the changes are
applied.

Message Box Database

As you learned in Chapter 1, the Message Box is used by the engine to store information
such as messages, host queues, instances, subscription information, promoted
properties, and temporary tracking data. Because of this, it becomes vital when it comes
to performance. Depending on the hardware resources on SQL Server, single Message
Box database environments can impose limitations on the number of transactions that
your BizTalk group can process.

Especially for solutions where application priority levels are defined with the highest ranks for transactions levels, you should consider adding more Message Boxes proactively. That does not mean that you are going to add Message Boxes whenever a demanding application comes up. You need to keep in mind that there might be the possibility that after adding that application, bottlenecks caused by Message Box processing can occur. Luckily, BizTalk Server offers the option to add more Message Box databases so all of them can work together to balance the load across of all databases.

Message Box databases have two roles:

- Master—The master Message Box database evaluates and routes subscriptions to all Message Box databases in the BizTalk Server group.

- Publisher—The logic for publishing messages learned in Chapter 1.

After you configure BizTalk Server, as there is only one Message Box database, it is automatically marked as master and publisher. When the Message Box becomes a bottleneck, it is usually because the publication role is causing that performance issue. The idea of adding more Message Boxes will be to distribute the publication role across several databases. If you add only one, it will not have an impressive impact on performance because the second Message Box will be the only one doing message publication. Therefore, to scale the Message Box layer, you will have to add a minimum of two Message Boxes. You will be disabling message publication to the original one, and now the BizTalk Server engine will distribute the load across the new databases.

Situations to Consider Additional Message Boxes

An essential consideration when planning a BizTalk Server environment should be to determine the maximum sustainable throughput (MST) of the system. The MST of a BizTalk Server system is calculated as the highest load of messages that the BizTalk environment can process. When load exceeds MST, messages are queued in the Message Box and transaction latency can increase.

If the MST is continuously exceeded over time, most likely you will see that the Spool, Host Queue, and Tracking data tables within the Message Box will show increasing trends during the time MST is exceeded. That can eventually raise a throttling condition based on database size and the BizTalk Server engine will put pressure to the message publication and the dequeue process. (Review Chapter 2 to extend the information about BizTalk Server throttling.) It is crucial here to compare the previous indicators along with hardware resource utilization, especially on SQL Server.

If BizTalk Server enters into the throttling state based on database size and CPU and disk utilization in SQL Server are under normal values, this does not mean that MST has been exceeded, as it could be due to an increase in the load that does not cause a bottleneck yet. In this case, you should consider tuning the threshold for message count in the database to allow SQL Server to process more messages. As discussed in Chapter 2, you have three options to update this setting:

- Message count in DB—BizTalk Server will enter the throttling state when any of the host message queues reach this threshold. By default, it is set to 50,000.

- Spool multiplier—If the number of messages in the Spool table reaches the message count DB * the Spool multiplier setting, BizTalk Server will enter the throttling state.

- Tracking multiplier—If the number of messages in the tracking data tables reaches the message count DB * the tracking multiplier setting, BizTalk Server will enter the throttling state.

Keep in mind that by increasing this threshold, the disk usage for Message Box database will also increase. Additionally, the engine will perform slower regarding transaction latency as all the stored procedures that the engine is calling will take longer to retrieve the data (high CPU usage on SQL Server could also be observed).

Performance Indicators of an Exceeded MST

The following performance counters will show increasing trends during the time the Message Box is causing a bottleneck when the MST has been exceeded (or is about to).

- BizTalk: Messaging Latency performance counters—If the Message Box is performing slowly, usually you will also see that all latency performance counters show increasing trends during the same period.

- BizTalk: Message Box: General Counters Spool Size and host queue counters—If the system is not able to keep up with the load, the Spool and Host Queue tables will show increasing trends as well.

- BizTalk: Message Box: General Counters Tracking data size—As tracking information it is first saved to the Message Box, you will see also an increasing trend in this performance counters because messages can be queued up in the Message Box when there is a processing bottleneck.

- Disk: Average Disk Queue Length—When this counter repeatedly shows a value of 3 or more for the Message Box database, it can indicate that there is a bottleneck on the Message Box, as disk contention is most likely to happen.

Adding Two or More Message Box Databases

After you analyze the data and you are sure that the Message Box database is causing a bottleneck, you can follow these steps to add a new database.

Requirements:

- The account used to perform the following steps must be part of the BizTalk Server Administrators groups and SQL Server Administrator role.

- As you should disable message publication in the primary Message Box, no active subscriptions should be present at the moment of adding a message box. You will need to un-enlist all orchestrations and send ports before moving forward so this action requires downtime. For simplification, you can entirely stop all BizTalk Server applications. Keep in mind that stopping host instances does not un-enlist subscribers.

Follow these steps:

1. Open the BizTalk Administration Console.

2. Under Platform Settings, click Message Boxes.

3. Right-click Message Boxes and select New ➤ Message Box, as shown in Figure 4-23.

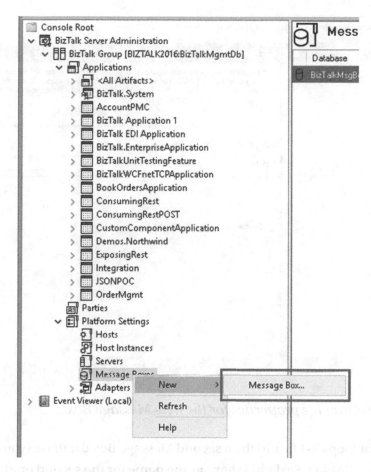

Figure 4-23. *Adding a new Message Box database option*

4.   In the Message Box Properties dialog box, type the Server name
     of the SQL database in the SQL Server field and then type the
     name of the new Message Box in the Database field. You can
     use MessageBoxPublisher1 as these databases will be used for
     publishing role only. See Figure 4-24. Click OK.

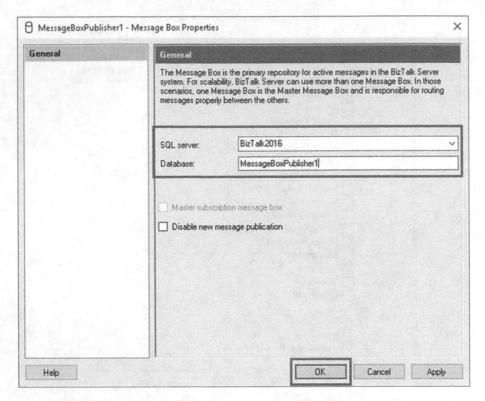

Figure 4-24. *Setting the properties for the new Message Box*

5. Repeat Steps 2-4 to add the a second Message Box database (you
    can use MessageBoxPublisher2 as the name for the second one).

6. Now, go to the original Message Box and disable message
    publication. By doing this, you are distributing the message
    publication feature across the new databases. See Figure 4-25.
    Click OK.

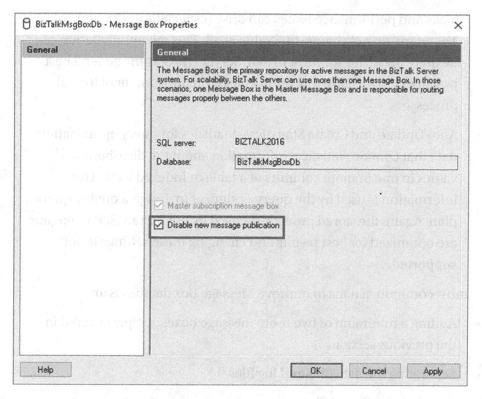

Figure 4-25. *Disable message publication for the original Message Box*

Now the original Message Box will be responsible for routing messages, and the other two will distribute the message publication.

Optimizing Message Box Databases

In previous sections, you learned that BizTalk Server uses Message Box database intensively and how you can add more Message Boxes when there is a processing bottleneck. As this database is the most important one regarding performance, you should proactively optimize it for BizTalk Server.

When you configure BizTalk Server, the configuration wizard will set the Message Box database with the following settings:

- Max Degree of Parallelism—This configuration option controls the number of processors that are used for the execution of a query in a parallel plan. The BizTalk Server engine uses lots of SQL Server stored procedures that are developed in a way that if you change the default max degree of parallelism to a setting different than 1, several locks and performance issues can arise (especially under high load). Therefore, do not change this value at all. This recommendation can be quite deceiving for most of SQL Server DBAs as the general best practice is to increase this setting based on the number of logical processors.

- Auto Update and Create Statistics—Statistics for query optimization data that contain statistical information about the distribution of values in one or more columns of a table or indexed view. This information is used by the query optimizer to design a quality query plan. Again, the stored procedures used by the BizTalk Server engine are optimized for best results and changing these settings is not supported.

The most common actions to improve Message Box databases are:

- Adding a minimum of two more message boxes, a topic covered in the previous section

- Separating the data files and log files

- Creating distributed file groups

- Using 64 KB NTFS allocation unit size

Separating the Message Box Databases Data and Log Files

Note   The recommendation in this section can be also applied to tracking and business activity monitoring databases.

The first time you configure BizTalk Server, using the Configuration Wizard, all the BizTalk Server databases are created with the default settings. Regarding the data and transaction log files, the Configuration Wizard stores them in the same drive. Placing both data and log files on the same drive can cause contention for that drive, resulting in bad performance (especially for BizTalk Server, as it is relaying fully on the Message Box database for processing messages). Placing the files on isolated drives allows the I/O writes and reads to occur in parallel for both the data and the log files. Try to spread the disk I/O across as many LUN as possible so that the storage hardware also performs parallel processing.

Note   To change the file locations, you need to bring the database offline.

You can use this code to move the Message Box database files to a new location:

```
USE master;
GO
-- Return the logical file name.
SELECT name, physical_name AS CurrentLocation, state_desc
FROM sys.master_files
WHERE database_id = DB_ID(N'BizTalkMsgBoxDb')
    AND type_desc = N'LOG';
GO
ALTER DATABASE BizTalkMsgBoxDb SET OFFLINE;
GO
-- Physically move the file to a new location.
-- In the following statement, modify the path specified in FILENAME to
-- the new location of the file on your server.
ALTER DATABASE BizTalkMsgBoxDb
    MODIFY FILE ( NAME = BizTalkMsgBoxDb_Log,
                FILENAME = 'C:\NewLocation\BizTalkMsgBoxDb.ldf');
    MODIFY FILE ( NAME = BizTalkMsgBoxDb_data,
                FILENAME = 'H:\NewLocation\BizTalkMsgBoxDb.mdf');
GO
ALTER DATABASE BizTalkMsgBoxDb SET ONLINE;
GO
--Verify the new location.
SELECT name, physical_name AS CurrentLocation, state_desc
FROM sys.master_files
WHERE database_id = DB_ID(N'BizTalkMsgBoxDb')
    AND type_desc = N'LOG';
```

Creating File Groups

Since the default BizTalk Server configuration creates the Message Box database using a single file in the default file group, if adding additional Message Boxes does not solve the disk contention problem, you should consider improving the file group distribution. You can add more SQL Server files and file groups to improve database performance because this functionality allows splitting database files across different disks. This will enable parallel read and write operations that eventually mean more transactions per second for BizTalk Server. Changing the default file group distribution has the benefit also of dedicating highs speed disks for the Spool table or the Host Queue tables of applications that have higher ranks of transaction priority levels (TL).

Creating File Groups for the Message Box Database

You can follow these steps to create a new file group distribution for the Message Box database:

1. Stop all BizTalk Server host instances, the Internet information server, and the SQL Server agent.

2. Open SQL Server Management Studio and connect to the instance holding the Message Box database.

3. Using the Object Explorer, locate the Message Box database. Right-click it and select Properties.

4. On the Database properties page, select the Filegroups option.

5. Click on the Add Filegroup button. See Figure 4-26.

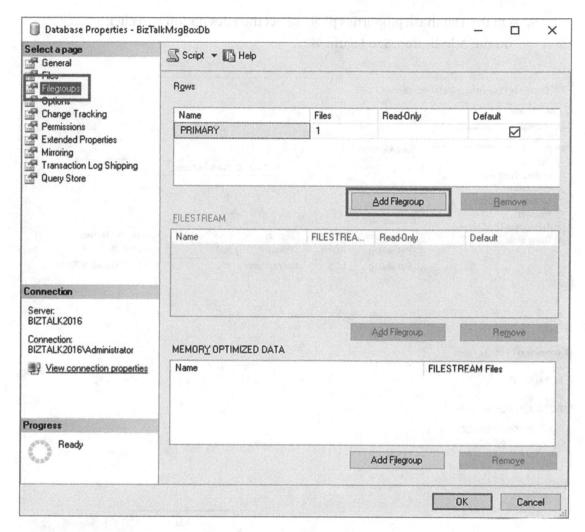

Figure 4-26. *Adding a file group using the Database Properties window*

6. Repeat this operation for the number of files you want to create.

7. Click the OK button.

8. Using the Object Explorer, locate the Message Box database. Right-click it and select Properties.

9. On the Database properties page, select the Files option and click on the Add button. See Figure 4-27.

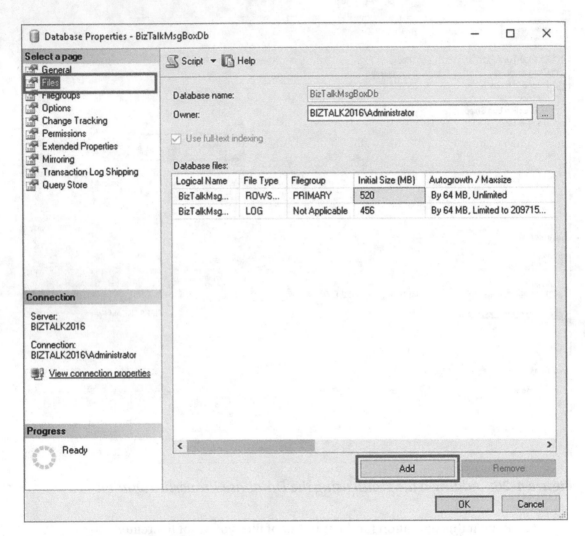

Figure 4-27. *Adding a file using the Database Properties window*

10. Set the logical name to MessageBoxFile1 and select the file group from the Filegroup dropdown box, as shown in Figure 4-28.

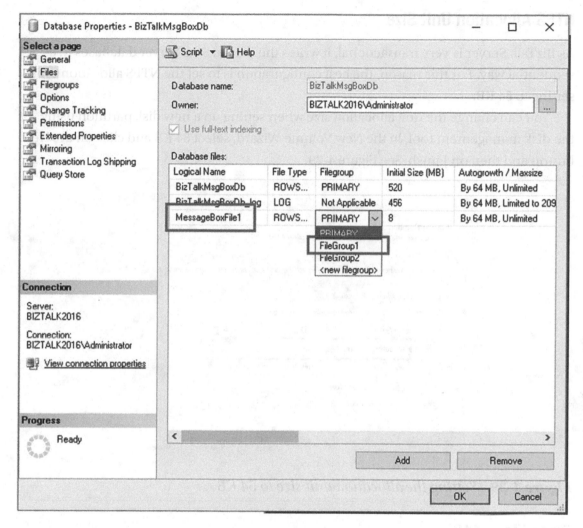

Figure 4-28. *Adding a file and assign the file group*

11. Select and appropriate initial size for the file. You can use 520 (MB).

12. Set the Auto Growth setting to 100 MB.

13. Set the location to a different disk than the primary Message Box database file (whenever possible).

14. Repeat Steps 9-13 to add the second file.

15. Click OK.

NTFS Allocation Unit Size

As BizTalk Server is very transactional, it writes the data to SQL Server databases in a sequential way. For this reason, the best configuration is to set the NTFS allocation unit setting to 64 KB.

You can change the unit allocation size when setting up a new disk partition using the disk management tool. In the New Volume Wizard, select 64 KB and click on the Next button and then on Finish. See Figure 4-29.

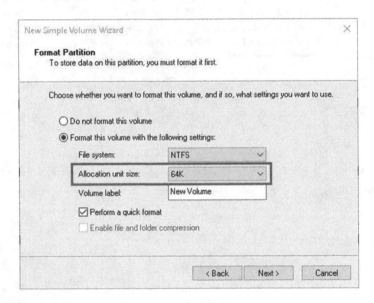

Figure 4-29. *Setting the allocation unit size to 64 KB*

Trace Flag 1118

If your BizTalk Server environment is using SQL Server 2016, you do not need to enable the trace flag 1118, as the new default behavior of SQL Server is to use uniform extent allocation for first eight data pages.

If SQL Server 2014 is used, then you should implement this trace flag, as it helps to reduce data contention, especially for the Message Box and Tracking databases.

To enable the trace flag, open the SQL Server Configuration Manager, select the SQL Server instance, and type the trace flag under the Startup Parameters tab, as shown in Figure 4-30.

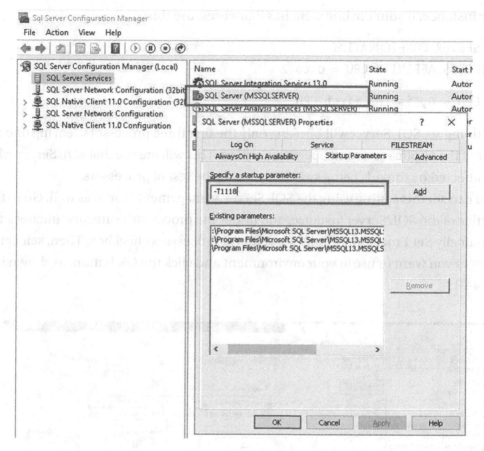

Figure 4-30. *Setting the trace flag 1118*

SQL Server Process Affinity

SQL uses all CPUs available from the operating system. It creates schedulers on all the CPUs to make the best use of the resources for any given workload. When multitasking, the operating system or other apps on the SQL Server can switch process threads from one processor to another. SQL is a resource intensive app and so performance can be impacted when this occurs. To minimize, we can configure the processors in a way that all the SQL load will be directed to a pre-selected group of processors

For instance, if your environment has four cores, use this:

```
ALTER SERVER CONFIGURATION
SET PROCESS AFFINITY CPU = 0 to 2
```

Note: CPU = 0, is the first CPU.

By doing so, SQL Server will be using only the first three processors, leaving one for the rest of the applications and operating system. This will ensure that SQL Server will not be affected by threads being switched among the rest of processors.

You can set this setting using the SQL Server Management Studio as well. Go to the properties of the SQL Server instance, and under the processor's category, uncheck the Automatically Set Processor Affinity Mask for All Processors checkbox. Then, select the processors you want to use in your environment and click the OK button, as shown in Figure 4-31.

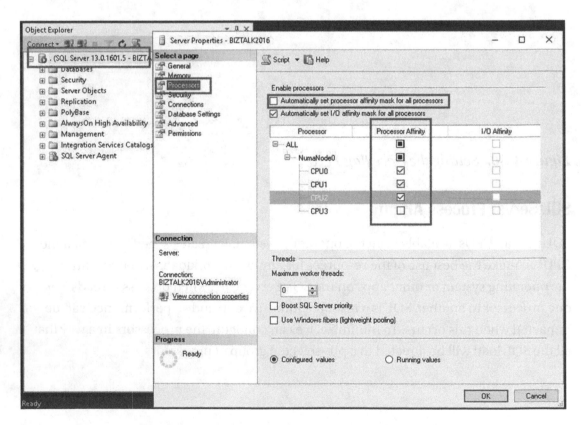

Figure 4-31. Setting the processor affinity

Fixing Database Inconsistencies

Database inconsistencies can occur in BizTalk Server for the following reasons:

- Unknown product bugs

- Known issues

- Convoys leaving zombie messages

When these problems arise, performance can be affected, as internal tables within the Message Box and Tracking databases can grow because the SQL Server management jobs cannot clean messages that are inconsistent.

The Monitor BizTalk Server (`BizTalkMgmtDb`) job alerts you when these inconsistencies occur. This job runs weekly on Sundays and it will generate an error when database inconsistencies are found.

Figure 4-32 shows an example of the output when the job finds database inconsistencies.

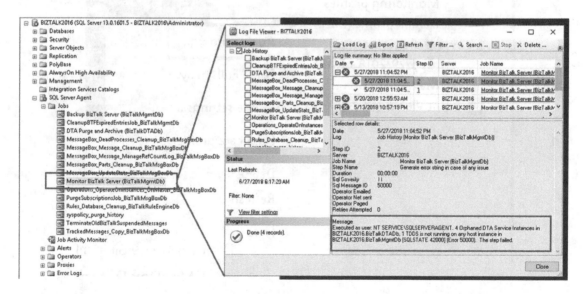

Figure 4-32. *Viewing the monitor job history*

For the latest BizTalk Server versions, you can fix these inconsistencies using the BizTalk health monitor tool.

Follow these steps:

1. Open the BizTalk Health Monitor tool.

2. Right-click at the default profile level (if you do not have a custom profile) and select Analyze Now, as shown in Figure 4-33.

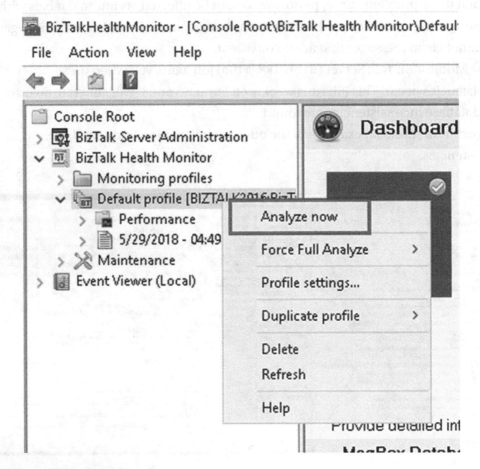

Figure 4-33. *Running the default profile*

3. The tool will check the BizTalk Server environment.

4. Wait until the process finishes.

5. In the dashboard report, click on the Message Box database group and locate the MsgBox database integrity section, as shown in Figure 4-34.

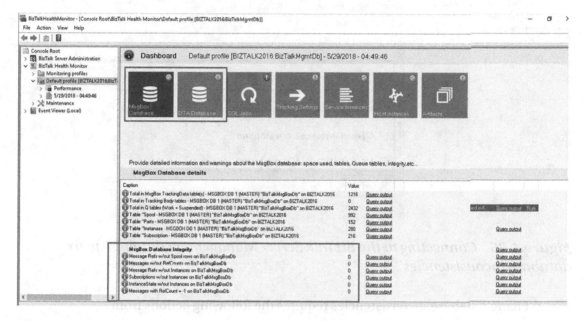

Figure 4-34. *Looking for database inconsistencies Message Box*

6. If the tool finds any inconsistencies, they will be listed here.

7. Click on the Maintenance section on the left pane and select the default profile on the dropdown box, as shown in Figure 4-35.

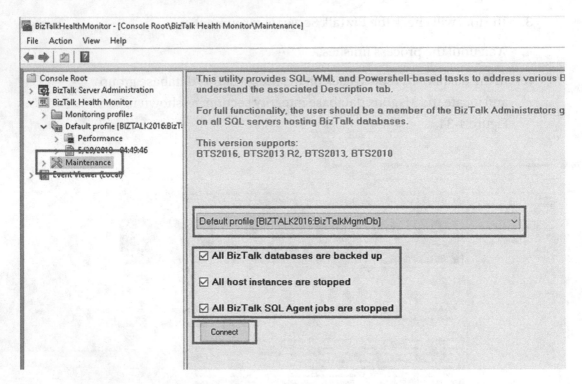

Figure 4-35. *Connecting to the BizTalk Server Management database to fix database inconsistencies*

Fixing database inconsistencies requires the following actions from your side:

- Generate a backup of the BizTalk Server databases.

- Stop all BizTalk Server host instances.

- Stop the SQL Server agent.

8. Once you check all the confirmation checkboxes, click on Connect button and wait until the connection to BizTalk Server is established.

9. From the task type dropdown box, select the From the Latest BHM Report option, as shown in Figure 4-36.

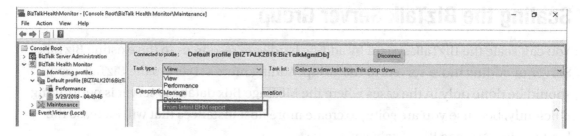

Figure 4-36. *Selecting inconsistencies from the latest BHM Report*

10. The tool will look for all of the inconsistencies found in the previous report and it will populate the Task List dropdown box.

11. Select a task from the Task List dropdown box and click the Execute Task button, as shown in Figure 4-37.

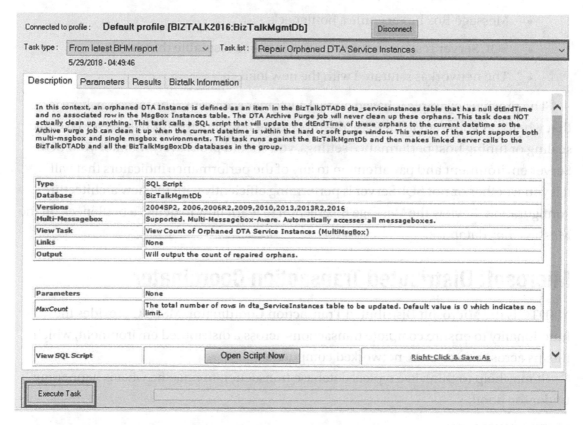

Figure 4-37. *Executing a task list using BHM tool*

12. Repeat the Step 11 until you have fixed all the inconsistencies provided by the BHM tool.

Scaling the BizTalk Server Group

You can scale the BizTalk system by adding hardware resources to the existing BizTalk Server or adding more servers to the group. Adding more servers to the BizTalk group should be done only in the cases where the Message Box database server is performing efficiently, because you are going to create more host instances that will increase the load on the Message Box database.

For instance, imagine that your environment has two BizTalk Server nodes and you decide to add two more to increase the throughput of the system. You perform all the testing and you find out that the throughput has increased by 30%. Your production environment is now able to process more messages. After a while, you have a new requirement and you decide to add two more BizTalk Servers. However, this time you observe that throughput has indeed decreased by 15%. What could be causing this issue?

- Message Box has become a bottleneck.

- SQL Server resources consumption is over acceptable thresholds.

- The network is saturated with the new load.

The previous example is based on real customer scenarios. The takeaway here is that whenever you want to increase the processing power of the BizTalk Server layer by scaling or tuning host performance settings, you should proactively monitor your SQL Server environment and pay attention to any of the performance indicators that will tell you whether or not SQL Server is performing efficiently with the new architecture/ configuration. Review the Message Box section to learn how to detect a bottleneck on the Message Box database.

Microsoft Distributed Transaction Coordinator

MSDTC is the **M**icrosoft **D**istributed **T**ransaction **C**oordinator. MSDTC provides the functionality to ensure complete transactions across a distributed environment, which means across two or more networked computers.

It may help to think in a typical database transaction to imagine what is happening under the hood:

```
BEGIN TRANSACTION

DO SOMETHING across several DIFFERENT MACHINES (MAY USE LOCAL TRANSACTIONS)

COMMIT TRANSACTION (OR ROLLBACK)
```

In this way, database and distributed transactions enforce the ACID properties—
Atomicity, **C**onsistency, **I**solation, and **D**urability.

By default, network DTC access is disabled. Without network DTC access on the
server, applications can only use transactions that stay on the local computer. For
instance, transactions cannot flow from a local computer to a database that runs on a
separate computer. Since BizTalk leverages several different databases, and in most of
the cases spans multiple servers, MSDTC is used extensively to communicate with SQL
Server, especially if using adapters supporting transactions, such as classic SQL Server,
WCF SQL Server, and MQSeries.

How DTC Works

The basic concept is that Server A initiates work in a transactional context (initiates a
transaction). To complete the operation, it must do something in a SQL Server database
running on Server B. It then connects to Server B hosting the SQL Server database
and does some work. Imagine the operation on the SQL Server machine fails due to
a problem so that the transaction initiated on the SQL Server machine must be rolled
back, as well as the operations on Server A.

Each computer, in a distributed transaction, has its resources and participates as
an element in the global transaction that must be committed or aborted across all the
servers involved. MSDTC performs the coordination role for the components (and
machines) and decides if a global transaction is successfully committed or must be
rolled back.

In general, DTC uses a protocol based on two phases:

1. Applications call the transaction manager (DTC) to begin a
   transaction. At this point, the transaction is no longer local, and
   DTC coordinates the state. As BizTalk Server inserts fragments
   in the context of a new DTC transaction, it is imperative that you
   understand this concept because if you increase the number of
   fragments, SQL Server will use more resources to allocate the
   transaction.

2. When the application has prepared its changes, it asks the
   transaction manager to commit the transaction. The transaction
   manager keeps a sequential transaction log, so its commit or
   abort decisions are durable. The transaction log is a physical log
   file on disk.

This log file is more important than it seems since it can become a disk bottleneck in BizTalk Server systems. If your platform is receiving 100 messages per second 24 hours per day, that means 8,640,000 messages per day. Now, imagine that all messages are the same size and that every message is split into 10 fragments. If the disk used to store the DTC log is not dedicated and, for instance, shared with the Windows system drive, the disk could potentially experiment high writing-latency, affecting overall disk performance. In this scenario, the Windows operating system could perform slow IO operations, and that would affect performance globally (especially under a high load scenario).

Note   The DTC log file should be dedicated in an isolated disk to prevent serious performance issues. If DTC fails to enlist a new transaction because of performance issues, it will timeout, and BizTalk Messages will not be published (if fragmentation is in place).

Number of Simultaneous Connections of HTTP Adapters

By default, all the HTTP based adapters will establish only two simultaneous connections from each server with BizTalk Server installed. This specification provides clear limitations, especially for low latency or high throughput applications.

Note   This setting conforms to the IETF RFC for the HTTP 1.1 specification. It is not a BizTalk Server limitation, and although it is suitable for user scenarios, it is not optimized for high load scenarios.

To change the default behavior, you can add the connectionManagement section to the BizTalk Server configuration file:

```
<configuration>
  <system.net>
    <connectionManagement>
      <add address="http://www.YourDestiationServiceURL.com"
      maxconnection="12" />
```

```
    <add address="http://www.YourDestiationServiceURL2.com"
    maxconnection="12" />
    <add address="*" maxconnection="8" />
  </connectionManagement>
 </system.net>
</configuration>
```

You can add the URI of the consumed services that use the HTTP protocol. You can access the adapter configuration at the send port level to retrieve the URI of the service, as shown in Figure 4-38.

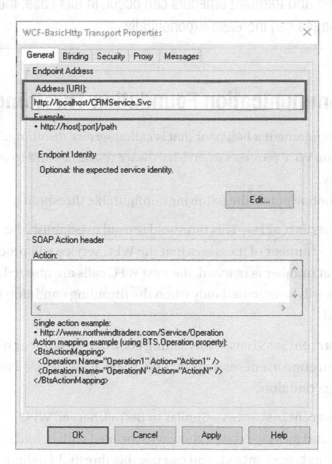

Figure 4-38. *Retrieving the Send port URI*

Note that the setting:

```
<add address="*" maxconnection="8" />
```

Uses an asterisk as the destination URI. You will use this section so that BizTalk Server will use this number of concurrent connections per BizTalk Server to send messages for the rest of the non-specified locations.

Warning   Increasing this setting can flood the destination system. This situation is undesired because the consumed service might not have enough resources to respond on time and frequent timeouts can occur. In this case, the number of suspended messages can increase exponentially.

Windows Communication Foundation Throttling

WCF services can implement a behavior that is called *service throttling*. This behavior allows you to throttle WCF requests to save hardware resources and to avoid flooding destination systems.

The throttling behavior has the following configurable thresholds:

- maxConcurrentCalls—This threshold is used to establish the maximum number of messages that the WFC service will process. When that number is reached, the next WFC calls are queued, and new calls will be executed only when the throttling condition is alleviated.

- maxConcurrentSessions—This setting controls the number of maximum concurrent sessions that WCF will allow before starting a throttling condition.

- maxConcurrentInstances—Similar to BizTalk Server, WFC sessions and messages has a context associated with it, and it is called InstanceContext. You can use this threshold to limit the number of simultaneous InstanceContext objects that the WCF service will process. The default value should be the sum of maxConcurrentSessions and maxConcurrentCalls.

The following table shows the recommended values for BizTalk Server:

Threshold	Recommended Value
maxConcurrentCalls	16*number of cores
maxConcurrentSessions	16*number of cores
maxConcurrentInstances	maxConcurrentCalls + maxConcurrentSessions

To enable this behavior, you need to edit the WFC configuration file and add the serviceThrottling section to the ServiceBehaviors section.

```
<behaviors>
    <serviceBehaviors>
      <behavior name="Throttled">
        <serviceMetadata httpGetEnabled="true"/>
        <serviceDebug includeExceptionDetailInFaults="false"/>
        <serviceThrottling maxConcurrentCalls="200"
        maxConcurrentSessions="200" maxConcurrentInstances ="400"  />
      </behavior>
    </serviceBehaviors>
  </behaviors>
```

Documenting Applications

In this section you learn about documenting your BizTalk Server solutions, which is a topic that provides a framework not only to understand the solution itself but also to size the BizTalk Server databases accordingly.

The idea is that every time you start a new BizTalk Server project, you should have a documentation template that should be fulfilled and maintained throughout all the phases of the project.

A proper BizTalk Server solution documentation should include this information:

- General application information, such as the name, development creation time, documentation version, changes, etc.

- Application priority level definitions

- Performance SLA definitions

- Business flows

- Deployment and troubleshooting instructions

This book uses Excel as an example of how you can document this information. I have chosen Excel, because the document is more of a calculator that will help you size a new BizTalk application properly. The idea is that every time you start a new project you will have to fulfill this document until you completely finish the development. It exposes a clear picture of the application performance requirements, so you can apply specific settings and development techniques in order to achieve the performance SLA. Additionally, it calculates the growth of the Message Box and Tracking databases when you enable tracking for the specific artifacts. Even though calculations are not exact, it will give you a good idea whenever you have to allocate more disk resources to your production SQL Server databases.

The Excel Sheet

The Excel file is divided into the following sheets:

- Application form

- Flows

- Sizing Message Box and Tracking DTA

- Data source

Application Form

This sheet is designed to specify all the application configuration, as shown in Figure 4-39.

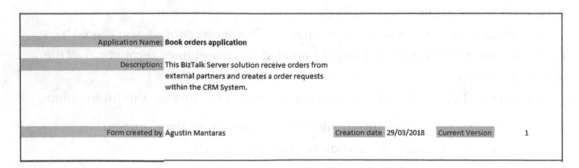

Figure 4-39. *Examining the application general configuration*

Application Priority Levels Section

As discussed in this chapter, application priority levels can be used for sizing and to adjust BizTalk Server performance settings. In this section of the application form, you should classify your application using these concepts, as shown in Figure 4-40.

Application priority levels (APL)	
Release stage (RSL)	9-First Release
Business priority (BPL)	8-Mission critical 2
High availavility (HAL)	9-Required
Transaction (TL)	4-Low priority
Performance Behavior (PBL)	6-No Specific

Figure 4-40. *Examining the application priority levels*

Performance Data Section

This section is designed to document the relevant performance data that has an impact when sizing the BizTalk Server databases.

The following information is included:

- Number of transactions—These definitions should be agreeable to the business decision makers during the initial phases of the project and it is directly related to the performance SLA definitions.

  - Number of incoming business transactions—This value represents the number of incoming business transactions under normal load.

  - Number of outgoing business transactions—This value represents the number of outgoing business transactions under normal load.

  - Max number of live transactions—This value represents the maximum number of incoming business transactions under high load.

- Number of hosts—This definition represents the number of hosts that this BizTalk Server application is using. Refer to the Host Architecture section in this book.

- Number of subscriptions—The number of active subscriptions
  has an impact on the Message Box sizing. This tool calculates the
  maximum size possible per subscription, so you have to provide
  the number of subscriptions that the application is using. The book
  includes a SQL Server script to get this information. Unzip the APRESS
  folder and navigate to Chapter 4\scripts\Number of active
  subscriptions. Then open the Number of Active Subscriptions
  per application.sql file

  Change the application name to the one you want to get the
  number of subscriptions, detailed in bold in the following code:

```
USE BizTalkMsgBoxDb

SELECT count(*)  as [Number of active subscriptions]
FROM Services s WITH(NOLOCK)
LEFT OUTER JOIN Modules m WITH(NOLOCK) ON s.nModuleID =
m.nModuleID
LEFT OUTER JOIN Subscription sub WITH(NOLOCK) ON s.uidServiceID =
sub.uidServiceID
LEFT OUTER JOIN PredicateGroup pg WITH(NOLOCK) ON sub.
uidPredicateGroupID = pg.uidPredicateORGroupID
LEFT OUTER JOIN FirstPassPredicates fp WITH(NOLOCK) ON
pg.uidPredicateANDGroupID = fp.uidPredicateGroupID
LEFT OUTER JOIN EqualsPredicates eq WITH(NOLOCK) ON
pg.uidPredicateANDGroupID = eq.uidPredicateGroupID
LEFT OUTER JOIN EqualsPredicates2ndPass eq2 WITH(NOLOCK) ON
pg.uidPredicateANDGroupID = eq2.uidPredicateGroupID
LEFT OUTER JOIN BizTalkMgmtDb.dbo.bt_DocumentSpec ds WITH(NOLOCK)
ON eq.uidPropID = ds.id
LEFT OUTER JOIN BizTalkMgmtDb.dbo.bts_Orchestration o WITH(NOLOCK)
ON s.uidServiceId = o.uidGUID
where m.nvcName =   'BookOrdersApplication'
```

- Maximum number of scheduled transactions—If the application has
  receive or sending ports with schedules enabled, then you will need
  to specify the maximum number of scheduled message instances.

- Convoy pattern implemented—Convoys have their own set of tables within the Message Box and depending on the size, they can have a significant impact on the database sizing.

- Maximum number of instances of the convoy—This is the maximum number of instances that the convoy will handle.

Figure 4-41 shows an example of the performance data section for the BookOrders application.

Performance Data	
# of Incoming Business transactions	100 Minute
# of Outgoing Business transactions	100 Minute
Max Numer of live transactions	400
Number of hosts	3
Number of Subscriptions	10
Maximum # of scheduled transactions	25
Convoy Pattern implemented	Yes
Max # of instances of the convoy	400

Figure 4-41. *Examining the performance data*

Documented Flows Section

In this section of the application form, you should name all the business flows that the application is dealing with. Later, you will have to add an Excel sheet per business flow so that everything gets document properly. See Figure 4-42.

Documented flows
Call To CRM

Figure 4-42. *Examining the performance message flows*

Flow Forms

You should create detailed documentation of the flows that your BizTalk Server application is using. You have to insert a sheet per every flow documented in the Application Form sheet.

Figure 4-43 shows the flow call to CRM, which is the only flow implemented in the application.

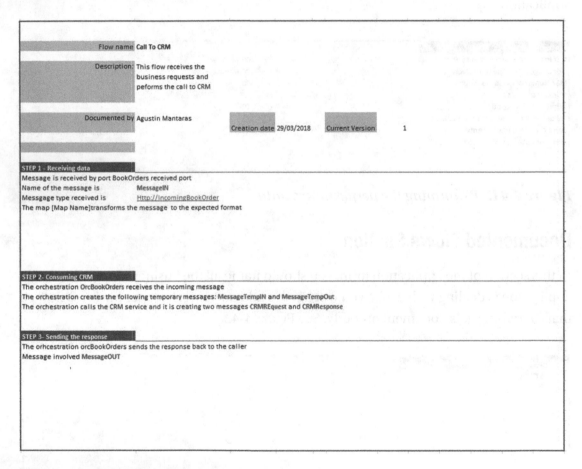

Figure 4-43. *Examining a message flow definition*

Sizing Message Box and DTA

It is very important that you define all messages, with message types and orchestrations, because you will have to populate the Sizing Message Box and DTA sheet with this information.

Configuration Item Section

You can find the configuration item section on the top-left corner of the Excel sheet, as shown in Figure 4-44.

Configuration Item	Value
Purging cycle (days)	7
Size of promoted properties (KB)	0.001
Size of orchestration shapes (KB)	0.0076
Events size (KB)	0.224609375

Figure 4-44. *Examining the configuration item section*

It contains these settings:

- Purging cycle days—This is the number hard days that the purging job is used to keep data. Refer to the Purging Tracking Job section in the book.

- Size of promoted properties—This is the average size in KB of the promoted properties. Do not change this value unless you have very large promoted properties.

- Size of orchestration shapes—This setting should not be changed as it is the internal average size of orchestration shapes within the Message Box.

- Events size—This setting should not be changed as it is the internal average size of pipeline and orchestration events within the Message Box.

Calculated Sizing Data Section

The calculated sizing data section shows the data sizes that your application will use and retrieves this information by calculating all the options specified in the elements table.

Figure 4-45 shows an example of calculated data for the BookOrders application.

Extra size tracking data	Value
MessageBox (MB)	260.25
Tracking DTADB (GB)	43.50
Extra size for messaging (MB)	Value
Max Load for all hosts	8.51
Max Load for subscriptions	9.91
Max Number of suspended	307.50
Max Load for Spool	0.69
Max Load for Instances	1.90
Max Load for Scheduled	0.01
Max load Binary message data	98.83
Max Load Convoy	9.20
Total Extra size for MessageBox (MB)	696.81
Total Extra Size for Tracking(GB)	43.50

Figure 4-45. *Examining the calculated sizing data*

Extra Size Tracking data:

- MessageBox (MB)—This is the number of megabytes required to hold all the tracking data within the Message Box. Remember that the tracking feature inserts first tracking data to the Message Box database and then moves it to the Tracking database.

- Tracking DTADB (GB)—This is the number of gigabytes that your application will generate in the Tracking database (based on the purging cycle specified in the purging job).

Extra Size for messaging (MB)

These fields calculate the maximum size of the following elements when the application is running under the maximum load possible. The maximum load possible is obtained from the application form sheet called Max Number of Live Transactions:

- Max load for all hosts—This is the maximum size of the host queue tables.

- Max load for subscriptions—This is the maximum size of the subscription tables.

- Max number of suspended—This is the maximum size of suspended messages.

- Max load for Spool—The maximum size of the Spool table.

- Max load for instances—The maximum size of the instances table.

- Max load for scheduled—The maximum size of the scheduled instances.

- Max load for binary message data—The maximum binary size of the messages tables.

- Max load convoy—The maximum size of a convoy.

Element Definitions

In this table you define messages, orchestrations, and pipelines per flow.

Steps for Adding Messages

Note that here you have to add messages or send through ports and messages that are processed within the orchestrations.

1. Type the message name in the Element Name field.

2. Specify the transactions per minute.

3. Specify the transactions per purging cycle. By default, this field is calculated by multiplying the number of transactions per minute by the number of purging cycle days (considering that the application will work only eight hours per day). You can overwrite this value with the number you want. For instance, imagine in a particular flow, BizTalk can process 100 instances per minute. Seven days of tracked data, for eight hours of messages processed per day means 336,000 tracked messages for those seven days.

4. Select Message as the type of artifact.

5. Do not fill in the #Receive and #send shapes columns, as those are for orchestrations.

6. Fill in the size of the message in KB.

7. Set the maximum number of suspended messages related to this message.

8. Set the number of promoted properties.

9. Do not fill in the number of shapes, as those are for orchestrations.

10. If the message is received or sent through a receive port, specify if the port has the following tracking properties enabled:

    • Message Body Before

    • Message Body After

    • Properties Before

    • Properties After

11. If the message is used in an orchestration, specify these values when the orchestration is tracking message bodies and properties:

    • Message Body Before ➤ Orchestration tracking settings for track message bodies before orchestration processing.

    • Message Body After ➤ Orchestration tracking settings for track message bodies after orchestration processing.

    • Properties Before ➤ Orchestration tracking settings for track message properties incoming messages.

    • Properties After ➤ Orchestration tracking settings for track message properties outgoing messages.

12. Do not fill in the Events Tracking section, as those are for pipelines and orchestrations.

13. Observe how the calculated data section changes along with the introduced data.

14. Set the name of the flow this message is involved with.

Steps for Adding Orchestrations

Follow these steps to add an orchestration to the documentation:

1. Type the orchestration name in the Element Name field.

2. Specify the transactions per minute.

3. Specify the transactions per purging cycle. By default, this field is calculated multiplying the number of transactions per minute per the number of purging cycle days (considering that the application will work only eight hours per day). You can overwrite this value with the number you want. For instance, imagine in a particular flow, BizTalk can start 100 orchestration instances per minute. Seven days of tracked data, for eight hours of orchestration processed per day means 33,600 tracked orchestrations for those seven days.

4. Select Orchestration as the type of artifact.

5. Fill in the #Receive and #send shapes. These are the number of receive and send shapes executed by the orchestration.

6. Set the maximum number of suspended orchestrations that the application can generate.

7. Do not fill in the number of promoted properties, as this is for messages.

8. Within the orchestration, count the number of shapes and fill in the number of shapes with that value.

9. Do not fill in the Data Tracking section, as those settings are for messages.

10. Set Events Tracking section when the orchestration has tracking enabled for these options:

    - Orchestration start/end

    - Messages send and receive

    - Shape start/end

11. Observe how the calculated data section changes along with the introduced data.

12. Set the name of the flow this orchestration is involved with.

Follow these steps to set up a pipeline:

1. Type the pipeline name in the Element Name field.

2. Specify the transactions per minute.

3. Specify the transactions per purging cycle. By default, this field is calculated multiplying the number of transactions per minute per the number of purging cycle days (considering that the application will work only eight hours per day). You can overwrite this value with the number you want. For instance, imagine in a particular flow, BizTalk can start 100 pipeline instances per minute. Seven days of tracked data, for eight hours of pipeline processed per day means 360,000 tracked pipelines for those seven days.

4. Select Pipeline as the type of artifact.

5. Do not set the #send and #receive shapes, as this is for orchestrations.

6. Do not fill in the size of the message in KB, as this property is only for messages.

7. Ignore the maximum number of suspended.

8. Do not set the number of promoted properties, as those are related to messages.

9. Do not fill in the number of shapes, as those are for orchestrations.

10. Set Events Tracking section when the pipeline has tracking enabled for these options:

    - Port start and event ➤ Start/end

    - Messages send and receive events ➤ Messages send and receive

    - Shape start/end. Not applicable to pipelines, only to orchestrations

11.   Observe how the calculated data section changes along with the introduced data.

12.   Set the name of the flow that this pipeline is involved with.

After you document all the flows, with all messages, orchestrations, and pipelines, Excel will calculate the total extra size required in the Message Box and Tracking databases so that you can size the adequate size for both databases. See Figure 4-46.

Extra size tracking data	Value
MessageBox (MB)	260.25
Tracking DTADB (GB)	43.50
Extra size for messaging (MB)	Value
Max Load for all hosts	8.51
Max Load for subscriptions	9.91
Max Number of suspended	307.50
Max Load for Spool	0.69
Max Load for Instances	1.90
Max Load for Scheduled	0.01
Max load Binary message data	98.83
Max Load Convoy	9.20
Total Extra size for MessageBox (MB)	696.81
Total Extra Size for Tracking(GB)	43.50

Figure 4-46. Examining the required extra size for the databases

Summary

In this chapter you learned how to categorize application based on application priority levels. This action will enable you to decide how the application will behave in terms of business requirements, number of transactions, high availability, performance behavior, and the maturity of the application.

Once you have adjusted the application priority levels to your own needs or based on your experience, you can use this concept to create a solid host separation policy, tracking, and performance settings.

There are hundreds of BizTalk Server performance settings and, in this chapter, you go through the ones that you can certainly use proactively to reduce the chances of running into performance issues within your BizTalk and SQL Server platform.

In the next chapter, you learn how to use the most common techniques to instrument your BizTalk Server solutions. This topic is essential to reducing troubleshooting time and therefore, decreasing application downtime, as you can find bugs faster.

CHAPTER 5

Instrumenting BizTalk Solutions

In software development, instrumentation refers to the ability of an application to monitor business processes, diagnose issues by revealing debugging information, and expose performance indicators.

The BizTalk Server product extensively covers all these requirements by:

- Exposing performance counters

- Revealing debugging information thought ETW Traces

- Writing events to the Event Log

- Creating raw BizTalk Engine traces

- DTA tracking (operational information)

- Custom Business Activity Monitoring (business tracking)

To achieve complex business processes requirements, the majority of BizTalk Server applications of today run custom code that, by default, is not implementing any instrumentation. As detailed in previous chapters, developers can create custom code in any of the following BizTalk elements:

- Custom pipeline components

- Orchestrations

- Custom components

- Maps

- Business rules

© Agustín Mántaras 2019

A. Mántaras, *BizTalk Server 2016*, https://doi.org/10.1007/978-1-4842-3994-0_5

Therefore, you as a developer should instrument your BizTalk applications by inserting trace statements in relevant areas of your custom code.

Efficiently implementing custom tracing mechanisms for BizTalk Server could be very complicated, as the engine might be distributed across several BizTalk Servers and, apart from particular cases like orchestrations with a correlated interchange or order delivery convoys, you will never know in which server a particular service instance is running. Unless your environment has only one BizTalk Server, all tracing and debugging technologies like writing debugging information to local drives, become overly complicated to analyze because the engine is based on a distributed architecture.

Additionally, depending on several factors like BizTalk load, number of issues and concurrent services per second, the cost of implementing custom tracing mechanisms could be potentially remarkably high regarding CPU, memory, and IO consumption.

Luckily for us, BizTalk Server is using already several tracing capabilities from Event Tracing for Windows (ETW) to track what is happening under the hood of most of the BizTalk Server Engine elements, like the End Point manager, the Message Agent, and most of the Transport Adapters.

Instrumenting Using Event Tracing for Windows

Event Tracing for Windows (ETW) is a fabulous, efficient tracing system used by Windows Operating Systems. It exposes an API that is divided into the following components:

- *Controllers* can be custom applications that define the location of the output log file and can also start and stop event tracing sessions.

- *Providers* are the ones providing events to the tracing sessions. There are several types of event providers but, the most important ones for you, as a BizTalk Developer, are TraceLogging providers since BizTalk server implements tracing using this method.

- *Consumers* are the components that read data from memory or the defined log.

Figure 5-1 illustrates the relationship among these three components.

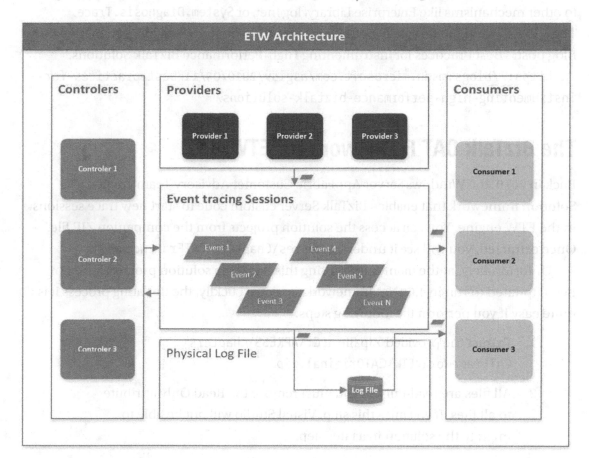

Figure 5-1. Diagram of the ETW architecture

Does this sound familiar to you? If you read the Chapter 1, you can also see that the ETW is based on a publish/subscribe model. The same as BizTalk Server!

BizTalk Server encapsulates the ETW functionality in two assemblies:

- `Microsoft.BizTalk.Diagnostics.dll`

- `Microsoft.BizTalk.Tracing.dll`

It uses the `TraceProvider` class to access most of the methods to interact with the ETW engine.

A long time ago the Microsoft BizTalk CAT Team had tested this solution and compared to other mechanisms like Enterprise Library, log4net, or `System.Diagnosis.Trace`. The ETW showed meaningfully better performance. The study was blogged in the MSDN Blog post: "Best Practices for Instrumenting High-Performance BizTalk Solutions."

`https://blogs.msdn.microsoft.com/asgisv/2010/05/11/best-practices-for-instrumenting-high-performance-biztalk-solutions/`

The BizTalk CAT Framework for ETW

Back in 2010, the Windows Server AppFabric Customer Advisory Team created a Solution framework that enables BizTalk Server custom code to start new trace sessions in the ETW engine. You can access the solution projects from the companion ZIP file. Once extracted, you will see it under `C:\Appres\Chapter5\CATFramework4ETW`.

Unfortunately, at the moment of writing this book, the solution projects have not been updated to run in 4.6x.Net framework versions. Luckily, the updating process it is quite easy if you perform the following steps:

1. Extract the provided Zip file at `C:\APRESS\Chapter5\CATFramework4ETW\CATOriginal.zip`.

2. All files are read-only so you must remove the Read Only attribute to all files. If you miss this step, Visual Studio will not be able to migrate the solution in a later step.

3. Find the solution file `Best Practices for Instrumenting High-Performance BizTalk Solutions.sln` and open it in Notepad.

4. Locate the lines shown in Figure 5-2.

```
Project("{2150E333-8FDC-42A3-9474-1A3956D46DE8}") = "Solution Items", "Solution Items", "{76C16FE4-BD
        ProjectSection(SolutionItems) = preProject
                CreatePackage.cmd = CreatePackage.cmd
                Readme.htm = Readme.htm
        EndProjectSection
EndProject
Global
        GlobalSection(TeamFoundationVersionControl) = preSolution
                SccNumberOfProjects = 4
                SccEnterpriseProvider = {4CA58AB2-18FA-4F8D-95D4-32DDF27D184C}
                SccTeamFoundationServer = http://sqlbuvsts01:8080/
                SccLocalPath0 = .
                SccProjectUniqueName1 = Microsoft.BizTalk.CAT.BestPractices.Samples.Framework\\Micros
                SccProjectName1 = Microsoft.BizTalk.CAT.BestPractices.Samples.Framework
                SccLocalPath1 = Microsoft.BizTalk.CAT.BestPractices.Samples.Framework
                SccProjectUniqueName2 = Microsoft.BizTalk.CAT.BestPractices.Samples.TracingBenchmark\
                SccProjectName2 = Microsoft.BizTalk.CAT.BestPractices.Samples.TracingBenchmark
                SccLocalPath2 = Microsoft.BizTalk.CAT.BestPractices.Samples.TracingBenchmark
                SccProjectUniqueName3 = Microsoft.BizTalk.CAT.BestPractices.Samples.UnitTests\\Micros
                SccProjectName3 = Microsoft.BizTalk.CAT.BestPractices.Samples.UnitTests
                SccLocalPath3 = Microsoft.BizTalk.CAT.BestPractices.Samples.UnitTests
        EndGlobalSection
        GlobalSection(SolutionConfigurationPlatforms) = preSolution
                Debug|Any CPU = Debug|Any CPU
                Release|Any CPU = Release|Any CPU
        EndGlobalSection
```

Figure 5-2. *Locating the TFS settings*

And delete all of it, because if not, the Upgrade Wizard will fail (as the original solution was linked to a local TFS server).

5. Save the file.

6. Now you can open the solution file with Visual Studio 2015.

On the Review project and solution changes screen, check all projects and click OK. See Figure 5-3.

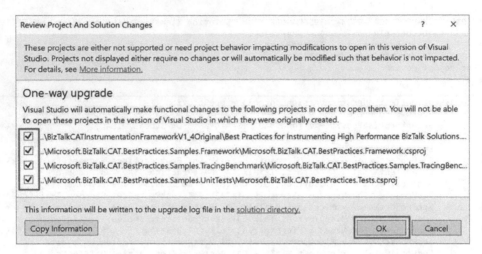

Figure 5-3. Review project and solution changes screen

7.   The Visual Studio migration wizard will update the solution.

Depending on your machine configuration, you could potentially have different issues, as shown in Figure 5-4.

Figure 5-4. Possible migration issues

Projects are pointing to Framework 2.0 and 3.5. If you have these versions installed, you might not get any warnings. However, BizTalk Server 2016 works only with 4.6x versions so we will need to change the target for the three projects.

8.   Remove the `Microsoft.BizTalk.CAT.BestPractices.Samples.UnitTests` project from the solution.

9.   For each project, change the Target Framework property to 4.6, as shown in Figure 5-5.

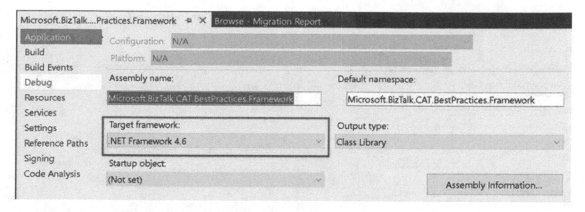

Figure 5-5. *Changing the target framework version*

10. Choose Save All and rebuild the solution.

11. You can get the following error:

    Error CS0535 'ComponentTraceProvider' does not implement interface member 'IComponentTraceProvider. TraceInfo(Func<string>)' (new interface on framework 4.6)

12. Double-click the error. Visual Studio will take you to the ComponentTraceProvider definition.

13. Right-click on ComponentTraceProvider and choose Quick Actions and Refactorings. See Figure 5-6.

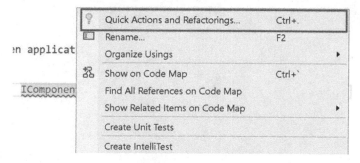

Figure 5-6. *Quick actions and refactorings*

14.   Select the Implement interface option, as shown in Figure 5-7.

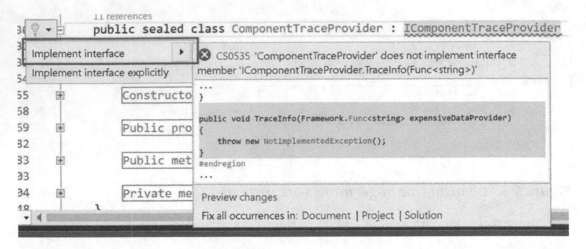

Figure 5-7.   Implementing the missing interface

15.   Choose Save All and rebuild the solution. The rebuild action will succeed now.

16.   At the project level, sign the assembly by creating a strong name key. Access the project properties, go to the signing section, and enable the checkbox Sign the Assembly. Create a new one and set the key file name. Then click OK button, as shown in Figure 5-8.

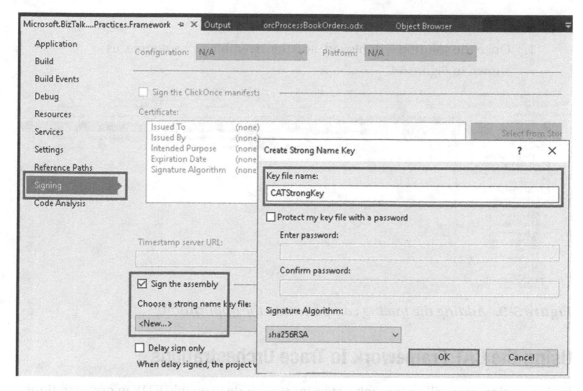

Figure 5-8. Generating a strong file name for the project

Enabling an Existing BizTalk Solution to Work with ETW

Now that you have a compatible version for BizTalk Server 2016, you can use the instrumentation framework by referencing the assembly `Microsoft.BizTalk.CAT.BestPractices.Framework.dll` to your project. As this framework assembly uses `BizTalkTracing.dll`, you must manually deploy it to your BizTalk Server environment also. The BizTalk Server tracing component is installed into the GAC, and you can find a reference to it here:

`C:\Windows\Microsoft.NET\assembly\GAC_MSIL\Microsoft.BizTalk.Tracing`

In this case, we are going to use the `BookOrders` application and it includes a reference to the BizTalk tracking assembly already. For your future projects, remember to reference this assembly also; otherwise, the application will not work.

Follow these steps:

1. Once the solution is deployed, add the assembly as a resource, as shown in Figure 5-9.

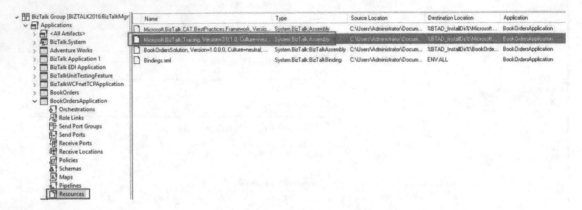

Figure 5-9. *Adding the tracing component to the application*

Using the CAT Framework to Trace Orchestrations

In this section, you will go through a step-by-step guide to enable ETW in orchestrations.

Follow these steps:

1. If you went through previous exercises, you will have a `BookOrdersApplication`. Remove it manually, otherwise you will get unexpected errors.

2. This walkthrough uses the base book order solution contained in the companion source code folder for Chapter 5. Before moving forward, create a back copy of the original file so you can revert the solution to the original state in case something goes wrong. Using Windows Explorer, navigate to `C:\APRESS\Chapter5` and make a copy of the `BookOrdersSolutionBase` folder.

3. Start Visual Studio with elevated privileges (run as Administrator, otherwise the deployment will fail) and open the `C:\APRESS\Chapter5\BookOrdersSolutionBase\BookOrdersSolution.sln` solution.

4. Open and explore the orchestration `orcProcessBookOrders`, located in the `orchestrations` folder. See Figure 5-10.

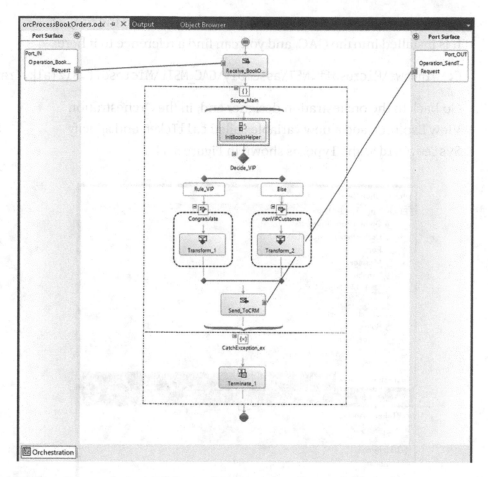

Figure 5-10. *General view of the orchestration ProcessBookOrders*

The orchestration receives a book order and checks whether the customer is a VIP. If affirmative, the process sends a congratulation message.

5. The first thing you have to do is, at project `BookOrdersSolution`, add a reference to the CAT Framework assembly that has been built in the previous section. Add the `Microsoft.BizTalk.CAT.BestPractices.Framework.dll` by navigating to the following location: `C:\Apress \Chapter5\CATFramework4ETW\CATVS2015\BizTalkCATInstrumentationFrameworkV1_4Original\Microsoft.BizTalk.CAT.BestPractices.Samples.Framework\bin\Release` Alternatively, you can add the CAT Framework Visual Studio project to the solution and add a by-project reference.

6. Add the BizTalk Server tracing component reference to the project.
    It is installed into the GAC, and you can find a reference to it here:

    `C:\Windows\Microsoft.NET\assembly\GAC_MSIL\Microsoft.BizTalk.Tracing`

7. Go back to the orchestration designer and, in the Orchestration
    View Explorer, add a new variable called `callToken` and specify
    `System.Guid` as the Type, as shown in Figure 5-11.

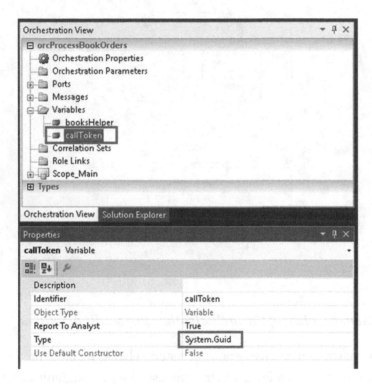

Figure 5-11. *Declaring the callToken variable as System.Guid*

8. Just after the Activation Receive Shape, add a Expression shape and rename it initTrace, as shown in Figure 5-12.

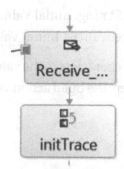

Figure 5-12. Insert the InitTrace expression shape

9. Open the initTrace shape and type the following code to start a new trace session:

```
//trace session starts into the orchestration
//callToken will be used during the orchestration to generate
events associated to that tracing session.
callToken = Microsoft.BizTalk.CAT.BestPractices.
Framework.Instrumentation.TraceManager.WorkflowComponent.
TraceIn("Orchestration starts");
```

10. Just before the End Orchestration shape, add a script shape and name it closeTrace, as shown in Figure 5-13.

Figure 5-13. Insert the closeTrace expression shape

11. Open the closeTrace shape and add the following code:

```
//trace session is closed using the callToken
Microsoft.BizTalk.CAT.BestPractices.Framework.Instrumentation.
TraceManager.WorkflowComponent.TraceOut(callToken,
"Orchestration End");
```

12. Using the orchestration viewer, locate the Scope_Main and add two variables at the local scope level (see Figure 5-14):

    scopeName: Type:System.String. Initial Value: Scope_Main
    scopeStarted: Type: System.int64 Initial Value: 0

    Do not forget to add the "" characters to the value of the scopeName variable! If you miss this step, the build action will fail.

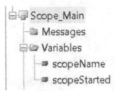

Figure 5-14. *Creating scopeName and scopeStarted variables*

13. Right after the Scope_Main starts, insert a new script shape called TraceMainScopeStart. See Figure 5-15a.

Figure 5-15a. *Creating the traceMain expression shape*

14. Open the TraceMainScopeStart and add the following code:

    ```
    //Sending a new Starting Scope event to the trace.
    Microsoft.BizTalk.CAT.BestPractices.Framework.Instrumentation.
    TraceManager.WorkflowComponent.TraceStartScope(scopeName,
    callToken);
    ```

15. Just before the Scope_Main finishes, insert a new script shape called TraceMainScopeClose, as shown in Figure 5-15b.

Figure 5-15b. *Creating the traceMainClose expression shape*

16. Open the TraceMainScopeClose and add the following code:

```
//Sending a new End Scope event to the trace.
Microsoft.BizTalk.CAT.BestPractices.Framework.Instrumentation.
TraceManager.WorkflowComponent.TraceEndScope(scopeName,
scopeStarted,callToken);
```

17. Now, on the left branch of the decide shape, insert a new script shape called TraceVipCustomer, as shown in Figure 5-16.

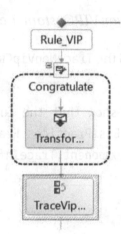

Figure 5-16. *Inserting the traceVIPCustomer expression shape*

18. Add the following code to the TraceVipCustomer script shape:

```
//Send a new event to show that the customer is a VIP Customer
Microsoft.BizTalk.CAT.BestPractices.Framework.Instrumentation.
TraceManager.WorkflowComponent.TraceInfo("Customer has been
detected as VIP");
```

19. Now, on the right branch of the Decide shape, insert a new script shape called TraceNonVipCustomer. See Figure 5-17.

263

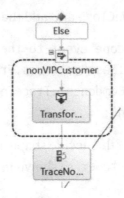

Figure 5-17. *Inserting the traceNonVIPCustomer expression shape*

20. Add the following code to the TraceNonVipCustomer script shape,
     as shown in Figure 5-18.

```
//Send a new event to show that the customer is a not VIP Customer
Microsoft.BizTalk.CAT.BestPractices.Framework.Instrumentation.
TraceManager.WorkflowComponent.TraceInfo("Customer has been
detected as non-VIP");
```

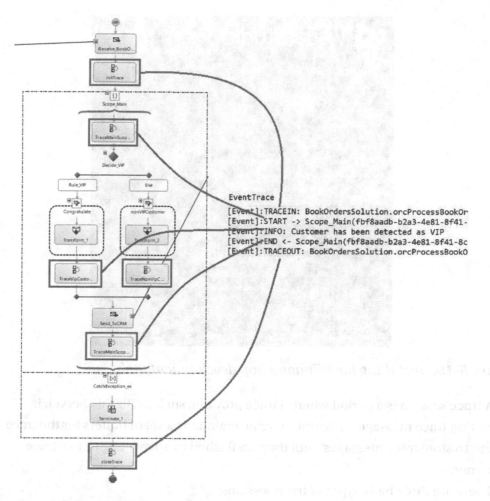

Figure 5-18. *ETW enabled orchestration view*

What would the output trace be if you run the application?

As you can see, each expression shape within the orchestration creates a trace line in the ETL stack. In the next section, you see how to start and read traces. We are not ready yet to test the solution because you need to learn how to control and examine the traces.

Using TraceLog to Control Trace Sessions

TraceLog is a tool designed to start and stop trace sessions. By default, it is not included in any Windows installation. You can install the TraceLog tool from the Visual Studio Installation, as it is included as part of the Windows 10 SDK, as shown in Figure 5-19.

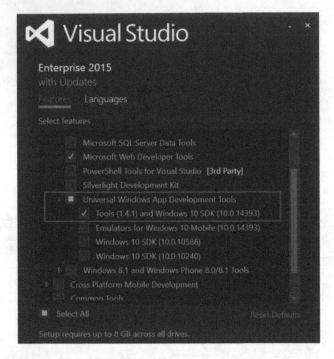

Figure 5-19. *Installing the Windows app development tool*

A trace session is a period where a trace provider, such as BizTalk Server, is generating trace messages. The trace engine maintains a set of buffers for the trace session to store trace messages until they are flushed to a TraceLog or to a trace consumer.

There are three basic types of trace sessions:

- *Non-real time*—Trace messages directly in a log file. This is the default behavior.

- *Real-time*—Instead of using a log file, real-time sessions send trace messages to a trace Consumer like DebugView, TraceView, or TraceFmt tools.

- *Buffered*—Keep messages in memory and does not send messages to any log file or consumer. This is very useful when trying to capture very long running issues as it runs in circular mode, overwriting messages when a maximum size is reached.

With the CAT Framework, our custom BizTalk artifacts will act as providers logging new trace messages to a trace session.

Starting a New Circular Trace Session for BizTalk Server

To start a new BizTalk Server trace session, you can use the following command in the Visual Studio command prompt environment:

```
First, create a folder where you want to save traces. This book uses
C:\BizTalkTraces.TraceLog.exe -cir 100 -start BizTalkServerTrace -flags
0x7FFFFFFF -f c:\BizTalkTraces\BizTalkServer.etl -guid #D2316AFB,414B,42e4,
BB7F,3AA92B96A98A -b 128 -max 100 -rt
```

To see real-time traces, open DebugView.exe after running this traceLog.exe command.

Note   At this stage you do not have any BizTalk solution working with ETL traces, so attempting to run that command will generate nothing. Later, you will deploy the BookOrders solution and you could test it.

Parameters explanation:

- -cir MaxFileSize—Specifies circular logging in the event TraceLog file. It expects a parameter called MaxFileSize that specifies the maximum size of the file in MB. In this case, we are using 100. Therefore, when the size of the TraceLog file reaches 1000 MB, new added trace messages will replace the oldest ones. TraceLog will be captured in this loop until you stop the session.

- -Start SessionName—Starts a new trace session using the SessionName parameter to identify the session. In this case, we call the session BizTalkServerTrace.

- -flags TraceLevel—Used to specify a trace level. At the moment of writing this book, the following trace levels are available:

  - "none" set TraceLevel value =0x0

  - "low" set TraceLevel value =0x1

  - "medium" set TraceLevel value =0x3

  - "high" set TraceLevel value =0x7

  - "all" set TraceLevel value =0x7FFFFFFF

In this example, we are using 0x7FFFFFFF as the trace level (all). Depending on the selected value, the engine will generate more or less data.

- -f LogFile—Used to provide a file in where all trace messages will be stored. In our case, it's c:\BizTalkTraces\BizTalkServer.etl.

- -guid TraceComponentGuid—You can use this parameter to tell the engine to filter for a specific provider. The CAT Framework sends trace messages using the following providers:

  - Pipelines: #691CB4CB,D20C,408e,8CFF,FD8A01CD2F75

  - Workflow (Orchestrations): #D2316AFB,414B,42e4,BB7F, 3AA92B96A98A

  - DataAccess (used internally): #2E5D65D8,71F9,43e9,B477,733EF6212895

  - Transform (BizTalk maps): #226445A8,5AF3,4dbe,86D2, 73E9B965378E

  - Service (used internally): #E67E8346,90F1,408b,AF40,222B6E3C5ED6

  - Rules (Business Rules): #78E2D466,590F,4991,9287,3F00BA62793D

  - Tracking (BAM): #5CBD8BA0,60F8,401b,8FF5,C7F3D5FABE41

  - Custom (custom .NET components): #6A223DEA,F806,4523,BAD0, 312DCC4F63F9

  - In our case we are filtering for Orchestration providers: 2316AFB, 414B,42e4,BB7F,3AA92B96A98A.

- -b BufferSize—Specifies the size, in KB, of each buffer allocated for the trace session. If you do not pass this parameter, a default value will be generated based on system hardware resources.

- -max NumberOfBuffers—Specifies the maximum number of buffers used.

- -rt Starts a real-time trace session—This is very important if we want to use DebugView to see the trace information in real-time mode.

Stopping a BizTalk Server Trace Session

First, you must flush the session using the following command:

```
TraceLog.Exe -flush BizTalkServerTrace
```

When engine receives a flush request, events in the buffers are delivered to the TraceLog or trace consumer immediately (DebugView is an example of a trace consumer).

As flush does not stop the providers, you need to call the -Stop command:

```
TraceLog.exe -stop BizTalkServerTrace
```

Examining the ETL File

You can use the TraceLog format tool to convert the ETL file to flat file.

```
tracefmt.exe TraceLogFileName -o OutputTraceLogFileName -tmf DefaultTMFFile
```

Unfortunately, at the moment of writing this book, the CAT team did not update the ETW Framework, and the tracefmt.exe version has a dependency in a DLL called traceprt.dll. Without it is not possible to format the output ETL file. You can find this DLL in the companion TracingTools folder located here:

```
C:\APRESS\Chapter5\CATFramework4ETW\CATVS2015\BizTalkCATInstrumentationF
rameworkV1_4Original\TracingTools
```

Therefore, change to this path when you want to format the ETL file to TXT.

Using the BizTalk CAT Instrumentation Controller Control Trace Sessions

The BizTalk CAT Instrumentation Framework Controller is an easy-to-use GUI designed for the BizTalk CAT Instrumentation Framework. The tool works as a ETW controller and allows you to start and stop a trace, adjust filter options, log to a file, and/or enable real-time tracing to DebugView. You can download it from here:

```
https://github.com/tfabraham/BizTalkCATIFController.
```

You can install it from the companion folder:

C:\APRESS\Chapter5\CATFramework4ETW\BizTalkCatInstrumentationControllerV1_0_0

Just run the BizTalkCATInstrumentationControllerSetup.msi file and follow the instructions.

Once installed, start the tool from the Windows program menu (or from installation folder, by default at C:\Program Files (x86)\BizTalk CAT Instrumentation Framework Controller 1.0). The user interface is shown in Figure 5-20.

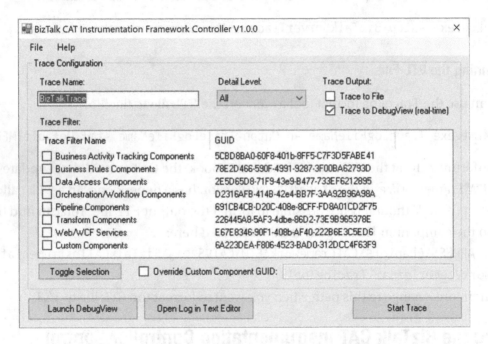

Figure 5-20. *BizTalk Instrumentation Framework controller user interface*

The first thing you should do is to set up the paths for DebugView and the Notepad text editor (consumers of the traces). You can do this by clicking on the File menu and selecting Options, as shown in Figure 5-21.

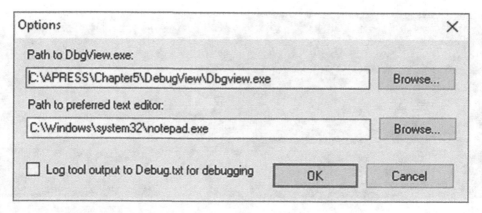

Figure 5-21. *Configuring the trace consumers*

DebugView is included in the companion folder at C:\APRESS\Chapter5\DebugView.

Testing the BookOrdersSolution and Exploring ETL Traces

In this section, you learn how to use the CAT Framework Controller to see the ETL traces generated by the BookOrders solution.

Follow these steps:

1. Remove the BookOrdersSolution using the BizTalk Administration console (if it exists).

2. Using the BizTalk Server administration console, import the BookOrdersSolution MSI file, located here:

    C:\APRESS\Chapter5\BookOrdersSolution\BookOrdersSolution\MSI

3. Install the MSI, either by checking the "Run the Application Installation Wizard to Install the Application at the Local Computer" option at Import MSI wizard (the previous step), or by double-clicking on the .msi file from Windows Explorer.

4. Refresh the BizTalk Server administration console and start the BookOrdersSolution BizTalk application.

5. Locate the CAT Framework Controller application using the Windows Start button, as shown in Figure 5-22.

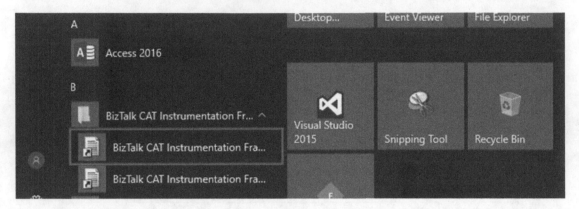

Figure 5-22. *Start the CAT Framework Controller*

6. Once the tool starts, type the trace name. In this case, type
   BizTalktrace.

7. Choose the Select All option from the Detail Level dropdown box.

8. Set the Trace Output by selecting Trace to a File and Trace to
   DebugView (real-time).

9. Select Orchestration/Workflow Component for the Trace Filter.

10. Click the Start Trace button. The screen should look Figure 5-23.

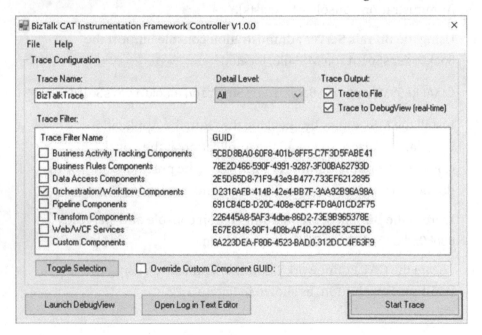

Figure 5-23. *Overview of the tool settings*

11. Click the Launch DebugView button to start the tool. At this stage, all the BizTalk Server ETL trace activity will be captured in real time by the DebugView tool.

12. Now it's time to test the BookOrdersSolution. Using Windows Server Explorer, locate and execute the testing file: C:\APRESS\Chapter5\BookOrdersSolution\BookOrdersSolution\Ports\ Send10VIPBookOrder.bat

13. Observe the DebugView window, as shown in Figure 5-24.

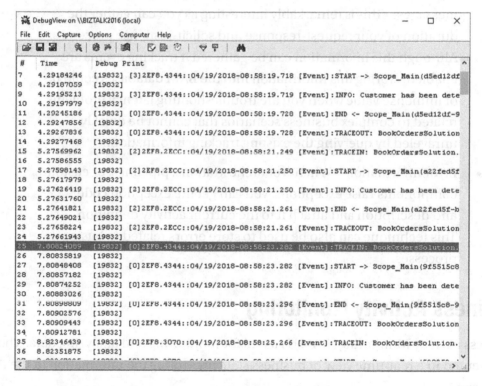

Figure 5-24. *Exploring the DebugView output*

You can see how the tool shows the BizTalk Server trace information.

14. Using the CAT Framework Controller, click the Stop Trace button to finish the capture.

15. Now click on the Open Log in Text Editor button to see the trace information using notepad.exe.

Instrumenting Using Business Activity Monitoring

BAM can also be used to gather and monitor sensitive operations data related to the flow of a business process. The following milestones and data are typically implemented for this objective (among others):

- Starting and finishing times of orchestrations and custom pipeline components—By doing this, you can track the duration of the whole process.

- A point of time when orchestrations send and receive messages—This is remarkably interesting as you can gather the duration of your request-response and solicit-response processes. Although this information can be gathered if tracking events are enabled, storing this information into the BAM databases could be of immense value when you are troubleshooting latency problems related to complex business scenarios that cannot be quickly unraveled by querying the existing tracking information.

- Error information—Whenever orchestrations, pipelines, or custom components raise exceptions, you can get the exception code and description and attach it to the current activity definition. This technique can also be used to store errors related to business processes.

Business Activity Monitoring

Business Activity Monitoring (BAM) is a tool for monitoring and analyzing data. The data is presented in a real-time view of business state presenting the information in the BAM portal site.

The BAM portal provides users with a web interface for viewing the data collected by BAM, as shown in Figure 5-25.

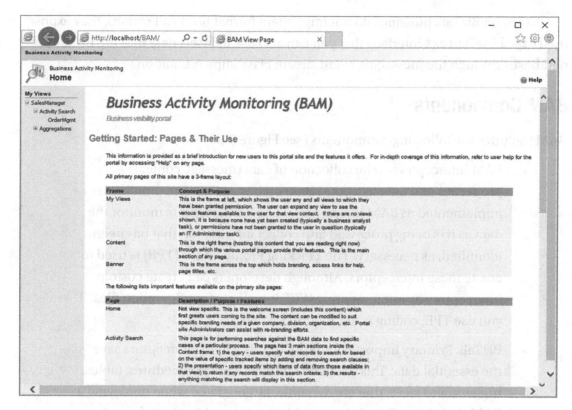

Figure 5-25. *BAM portal view*

BAM exposes a .NET API that can be used to gain visibility into data external to BizTalk processes, such as .NET Windows Form applications, ASP.NET, Workflow Foundation, and more. At the moment of writing this book, the following interfaces were available:

- OES: `OrchestrationEventStream`—Insert data into the BAM tables asynchronously, and as it participates in orchestration transactions, it should be called from an orchestration.

- DES: `DirectEventStream`—This class inserts data synchronously. This is typically used when real-time data is required, as it does not introduce latency. On the other hand, it could affect throughput, as it consumes more resources.

- BES: `BufferedEventStream`—Designed for high-throughput scenarios, it buffers the information and asynchronously inserts the data into the BAM databases.

Although BizTalk pipelines do not implement formal BAM API classes, they expose the `IPipelineContext` interface that you can also use to insert data into the BAM databases through the messaging event stream class implementation.

BAM Components

BAM includes the following components (see Figure 5-26):

- BAM interceptors—The collection of data (message context properties and message data) from orchestrations and pipelines is implemented as BAM interceptors. These interceptors monitor the data as it is being processed and collect information that has been identified, as necessary. The Tracking Profile Editor (TPE) is used to create these interceptors. Although developers can create custom interceptors by implementing WCF interceptor configuration files, if you use TPE, coding is not required.

- BizTalk Primary Import database—This is where interceptors save the essential data. This database contains stored procedures, tables, triggers, and views that are dynamically generated when deploying a BAM Definition. Data is kept in this database while the information is within defined Windows time and is then moved to the BAM Archiving database by the BAM Archiving Job.

- BAM activity aggregations and OLAP cubes—Developers and business analysts can generate aggregations to present the information in a grouped way. These aggregations are maintained represented by cubes within the SQL Server Analysis Service and generated by integration packages run under the control of the SQL Server Integration services.

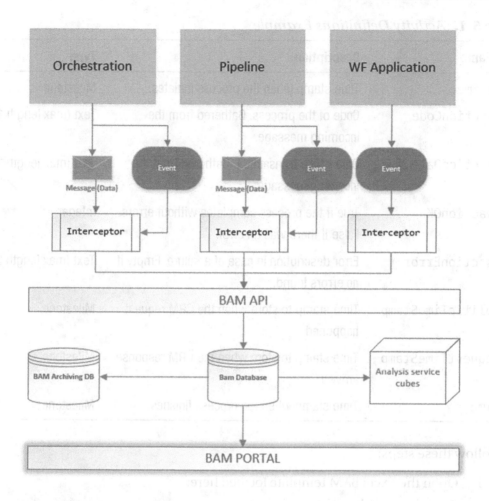

Figure 5-26. *BAM portal components view*

Designing the Instrumentation Activities for a BizTalk Server Solution

The first step to implement successful instrumentation using the BAM feature is to review the business process and design the BAM activity definitions based on that. You can use Table 5-1 for guidance.

Creating the Book Orders Approvals Activity Definition

In this step-by-step guide, you will create an activity that will generate all the elements detailed in the previous section (see Table 5-1).

Table 5-1. *Activity Definitions Example*

Item Name	Description	Type
StartTime	Time stamp when the process initiates.	Milestone
TransactionCode	Code of the process. Gathered from the incoming message.	Text (max length 10)
TransactionDate	Date of the transaction. Gathered from the incoming message.	Text (max length 10)
TransactionOK	True if the process completes without errors. False if there was an error.	Integer
TransactionError	Error description in case of a failure. Empty if no errors found.	Text (max length 255)
CRMSoliticTimeStamp	Time stamp to store when the CRM request happened.	Milestone
CRMRequestTimeStamp	Time stamp to store when the CRM response arrived.	Milestone
EndTime	Time stamp when the process finishes.	Milestone

Follow these steps:

1. Open the Excel BAM template located here:

   `C:\Program Files (x86)\Microsoft BizTalk Server 2016\ExcelDir\Bam.xla`

2. Once Excel opens the sheet, go to the Add-ins toolbar option and select the BAM ➤ BAM Activity option.

3. The BAM activity wizard will load.

4. On the Business Activity definition window, click the New Activity button, as shown in Figure 5-27.

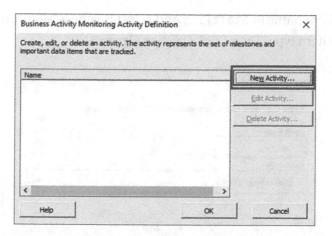

Figure 5-27. *Creating a new business activity definition*

5. In the new activity window, type BookOrdersApprovals and click
    on the New Item button, as shown in Figure 5-28.

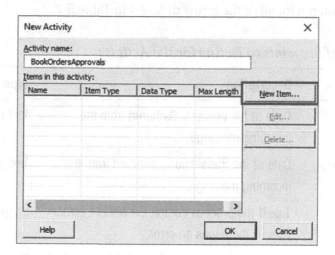

Figure 5-28. *Creating a new activity Item*

6. Set the Item name to StartTime and select Business Milestones as the type item type. Then Click OK. See Figure 5-29.

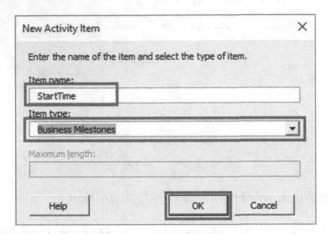

Figure 5-29. *Creating a new activity Item*

7. Repeat Step 6 for all of the items detailed in Table 5-2.

Table 5-2. *List of Elements to Define for the Activity*

Item Name	Description	Type
TransactionCode	Code of the process. Gathered from the incoming message.	Text (max length 10)
TransactionDate	Date of the transaction. Gathered from the incoming message.	Text (max length 10)
TransactionOK	True if the process completes without errors. False if there was an error.	Integer
TransactionError	Error description in case of a failure. Empty if no errors found.	Text (max length 255)
CRMSoliticTimeStamp	Time stamp to store when the CRM request happened.	Milestone
CRMRequestTimeStamp	Time stamp to store when the CRM response arrived.	Milestone
EndTime	Time stamp when the process finishes.	Milestone

Once you finish adding the elements, your screen should look Figure 5-30.

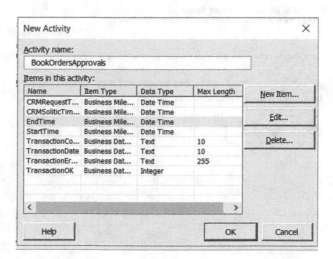

Figure 5-30. *List of the items of the activity*

8. Click OK to close the New Activity dialog box.

9. Click OK in the Activity Definition dialog box.

10. Now that the activity definition has been created, it's time to create the BAM view that will be used to populate the BAM portal. The wizard for view creation will load the welcome screen. Click Next.

11. On the View Creation dialog box, select Create a New View and click Next.

12. In the New View Creation window, type `BookOrdersView` as the view name and select the previously created activity, `BookOrdersApprovals`. See Figure 5-31. Click Next

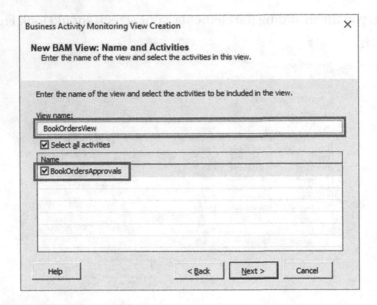

Figure 5-31. *Creating a new BAM view*

13. In the View Items dialog box, select All Items and click Next.
    See Figure 5-32.

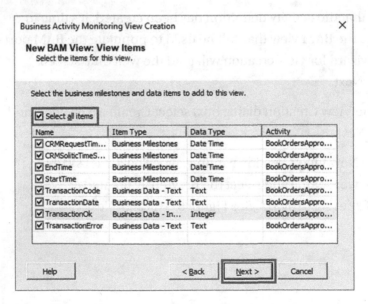

Figure 5-32. *Selecting all view items from the activity definition*

14. Take a moment to review the Monitoring View Creation dialog box. You have three main option buttons here:

  • New Alias—You use this option to provide an alias to an item view. This is useful when the activity elements have a nondescriptive name. In this scenario, you will not create an alias as the activity elements are quite clear.

  • New Duration—This option will enable you to create duration fields in the view. You will use two milestones, and the BAM feature will calculate the duration by subtracting both values. This is very useful if you want to know the duration of activities.

  • New Group—You can use a milestone group to set related milestones together; for example, the beginning and end milestones that define how long a book order is valid.

15. Click on the New Duration button and set following properties (see Figure 5-33):

Duration Name: `OrchestrationDuration`

Start Business milestone: `StartTime` (BookOrdersApproval)

End Business milestone: `EndTime` (BookOrdersApprovals)

Time Resolution: Second

Click OK.

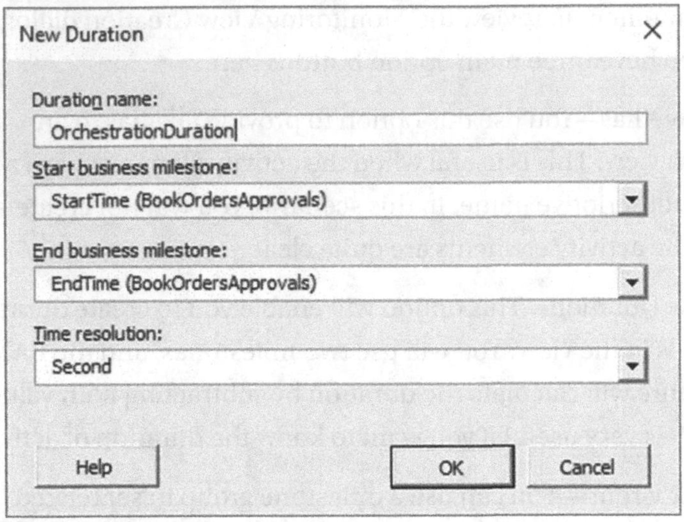

New Duration   ✕

Duration name:

OrchestrationDuration|

Start business milestone:

StartTime (BookOrdersApprovals)   ▼

End business milestone:

EndTime (BookOrdersApprovals)   ▼

Time resolution:

Second   ▼

Help   OK   Cancel

Figure 5-33. Setting the duration properties

16. Repeat Step 15 to create a duration name called CRMCallDuration:

    Duration Name: CRMCallDuration

    Start Business milestone: CRMSolicitTimeStamp
    (BookOrdersApproval)

    End Business milestone: CRMRequestTimeStamp
    (BookOrdersApprovals)

    Time Resolution: Second

17. On the NewBAM View:View items window, click Next. In this
    scenario, you will not create dimensions and measures. This
    option is very interesting to create aggregation data in the BAM
    reports.

18. Click Next on the View Summary window.

19. Click the Finish button to finish the process.

20. The wizard will show the Excel view of the activity.

21. Go to the BAM menu and select the Export XML option.

22. Choose a folder location and set the file name to
    BookOrdersActivityDefinition.xml.

Deploying the BAM Definition XML File

BizTalk Server administrators and developers use the Deploy All BAM Management utility command to deploy a BAM definition from the XML definitions file exported from the Excel sheet.

The BAM utility creates the necessary elements within the SQL Server databases so the BAM feature can populate the business data associated with the activity definition.

Follow these steps:

1. Open a command prompt as follows: Click Start, click Run, type cmd, and then click OK.

2. Navigate to the tracking folder by typing C:\Program Files (x86)\Microsoft BizTalk Server 2016\Tracking and at the command prompt. Press Enter.

3. Type the following instruction:

   bm.EXE deploy-all -DefinitionFile:"C:\APRESS\Chapter5\ BookOrdersSolutionBAM\BookOrdersSolution\BAM\ BookOrdersActivityDefinition.xml"

4. Press Enter.

5. If everything runs successfully, you will see the screen in Figure 5-34.

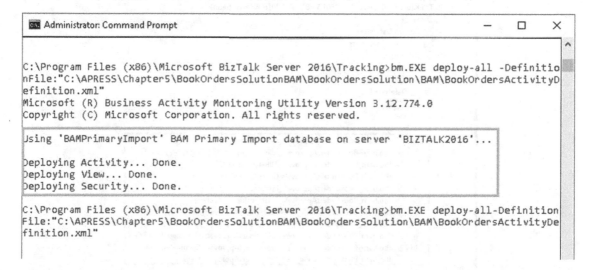

Figure 5-34. *Viewing the BAM.exe output*

Now if you explore the BAMPrimaryImport database, you will see that the BAM.exe tool created the tables shown in Figure 5-35.

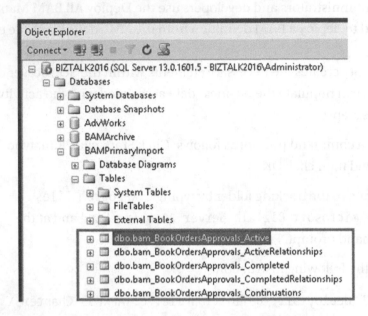

Figure 5-35. *Exploring the BAMPrimaryImport created tables*

As well as the views shown in Figure 5-36.

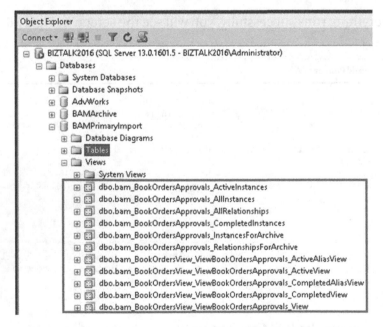

Figure 5-36. *Exploring the BAMPrimaryImport created views*

Configuring and Deploying the Tracking Profile

Now that everything is ready from an infrastructure point of view, it's time to define how the activity tables are going to be populated. For that purpose, you will use the tracking profile editor tool (TPE) that will link orchestration interesting points and data to the BAM activity definition.

Follow these steps:

1. **Remove** the BookOrdersSolution using the BizTalk Administration console (if it exists).

2. Using the BizTalk Server administration console, import the BookOrdersSolution MSI file, located here: C:\APRESS\Chapter5\BookOrdersSolutionBAM\BookOrdersSolution\msi\

3. Install the MSI, either by checking Run the Application Installation Wizard To Install The Application At The Local Computer at the Import MSI wizard (previous step), or by double-clicking on the .msi file from Windows Explorer.

4. Refresh the BizTalk Server administration console and start the BookOrdersSolution BizTalk application.

5. Locate and launch the Tracking Profile Editor tool (TPE) in the BizTalk Server 2016 Windows Start menu.

6. Click on the link Click Here to Import a BAM Activity Definition, as shown in Figure 5-37.

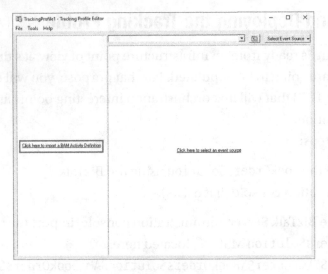

Figure 5-37. *Importing a BAM activity definition*

7. In the Import Activity Definition window, locate
    BookOrdersApprovals and click OK. See Figure 5-38.

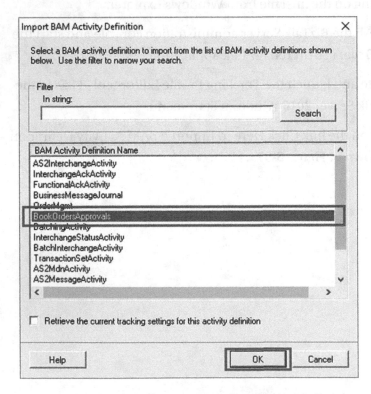

Figure 5-38. *Selecting the BookOrdersApprovals activity definition*

8. TPE will now show all the item definitions created for the activity
    BookOrdersApprovals, as shown in Figure 5-39.

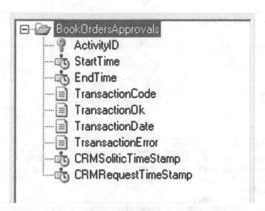

Figure 5-39. *Exploring the BookOrdersApprovals activity*

9. Click on the Select an Event Source link, as shown in Figure 5-40.

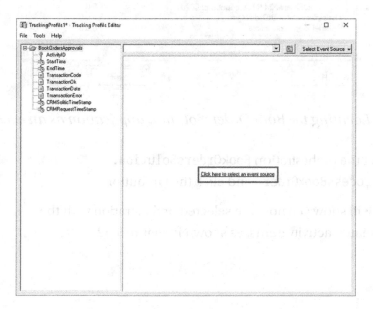

Figure 5-40. *Selecting an event source*

10.   Locate the orchestration BookOrdersSolution and click the Next
      button. See Figure 5-41.

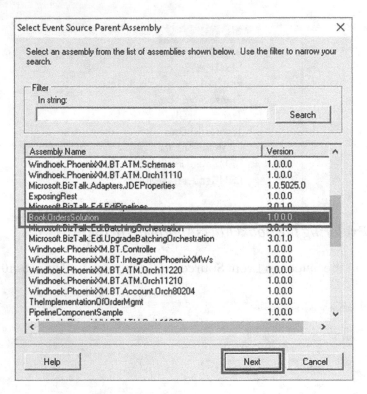

Figure 5-41. *Locating the BookOrdersSolution application as an event source*

11.   Select the orchestration BookOrdersSolution.
      orcProcessBookOrders and click the OK button.

12.   TPE will show you now the selected orchestration with the
      associated activity items, as shown in Figure 5-42.

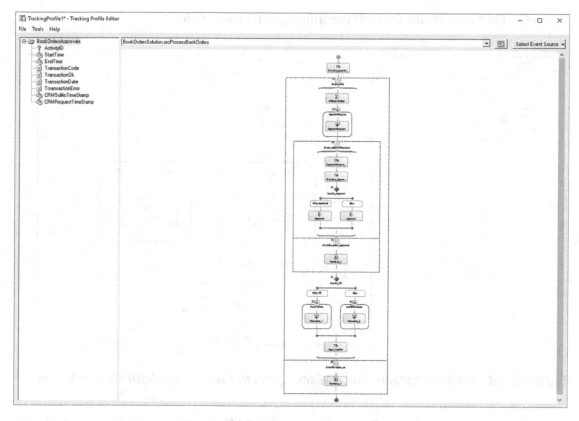

Figure 5-42. *Exploring the whole TPE profile*

It's time to link the events of the orchestration to the activity definition.

13. Drag and drop the receive shape `Receive_BookOrders` to the `StartTime` milestone of the activity definition, as shown in Figure 5-43.

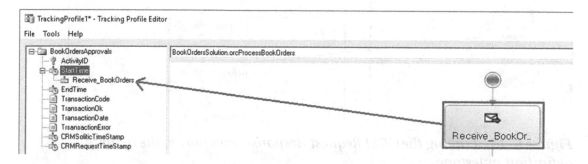

Figure 5-43. *Linking orchestration events to the activity definition milestones*

14. Do the same for the EndTime milestone (see Figure 5-44).

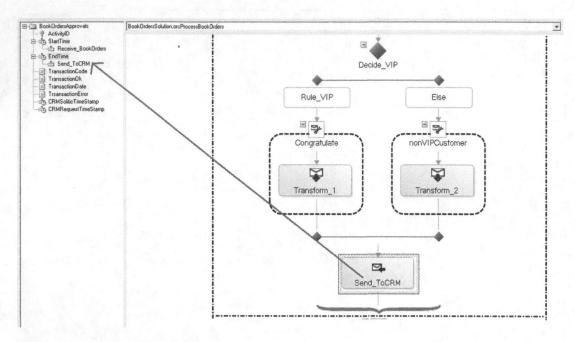

Figure 5-44. *Linking the sendToCRM send port to the activity definition milestone*

15. Do the same for the Request Response CRM activities, as shown in Figure 5-45.

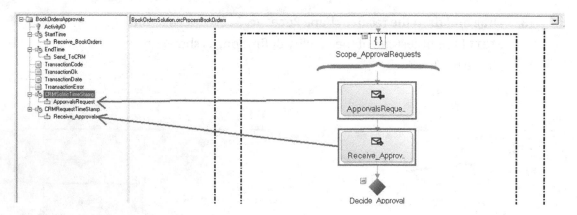

Figure 5-45. *Linking the CRM Request Response send port to the activity definition milestone*

With these actions, the BAM feature will be able to track orchestration events to the BAM activity and insert the right data to the BAM Primary Import tables.

It's time now to assign the data elements to the activity definition

16. Right-click the first receive shape of the orchestration and select the option Message Payload schema, as shown in Figure 5-46.

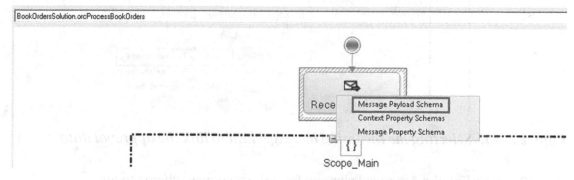

Figure 5-46. *Selecting the Incoming message data to link items to the activity definition*

TPE will show you the list of available fields.

17. Now drag and drop the `OrderId` and `OrderDate` fields corresponding to the activity definitions, as shown in Figure 5-47.

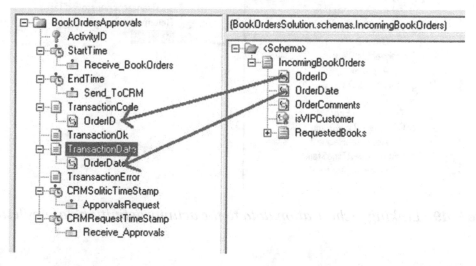

Figure 5-47. *Linking orchestration data to the activity definition data milestones*

18. Right-click the `receive_Approvals` receive shape of the orchestration and select the Message Payload Schema option, as shown in Figure 5-48.

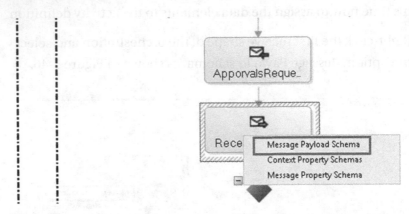

Figure 5-48. *Selecting the incoming message data to link the approval data*

19. Now link the Approved element from the response schema to the activity definition, as shown in Figure 5-49.

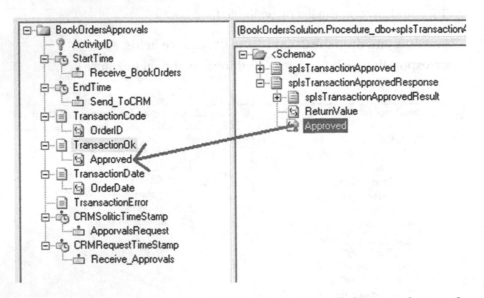

Figure 5-49. *Linking orchestration data to the activity definition data milestones*

20. Save the tracking profile using the File menu.

21. Go to the Tools menu and select the Apply Tracking Profile option.

22. TPE will inform you that the profile was successfully applied.

The binding between the business process and BAM is applied, which will make BAM events be triggered when the message arrives in the orchestration and populate the proper data in BAM Primary Import database.

Now you can test the solution and check if the BAM primary import table for book orders contains the BAM data, as shown in Figure 5-50.

	RecordID	ActivityID	StartTime	EndTime	TransactionCo...	TransactionOk	TransactionDate	TransactionEr...	CRMSoliticTimeStamp	CRMRequestTimeStamp	LastModified
▶	1	070977d5-f5b7-...	2018-04-20 10:2...	2018-04-20 10:2...	0000000003	1	21/12/2016	Ok	2018-04-20 10:27:48.917	2018-04-20 10:27:51.573	2018-04-20 10:2...
	2	8b675493-b5ad...	2018-04-20 10:2...	2018-04-20 10:2...	0000000003	1	21/12/2016	Ok	2018-04-20 10:28:39.007	2018-04-20 10:27:51.573	2018-04-20 10:2...
	3	aa9d1ef6-0ca1-...	2018-04-20 10:2...	2018-04-20 10:2...	0000000003	1	21/12/2016	Ok	2018-04-20 10:28:40.247	2010-04-20 10:27:51.573	2018-04-20 10:2...
	4	6331aae8-f7d9-...	2018-04-20 10:2...	2018-04-20 10:2...	0000000003	1	21/12/2016	Ok	2018-04-20 10:28:42.247	2018-04-20 10:27:51.573	2018-04-20 10:2...
	5	494dafac-1c5d-...	2018-04-20 10:2...	2018-04-20 10:2...	0000000003	1	21/12/2016	Ok	2018-04-20 10:28:44.263	2018-04-20 10:27:51.573	2018-04-20 10:2...
	6	52167372-3f4f-...	2018-04-20 10:2...	2018-04-20 10:2...	0000000003	1	21/12/2016	Ok	2018-04-20 10:28:46.247	2018-04-20 10:27:51.573	2018-04-20 10:2...
	7	aea41ecb-a86d...	2018-04-20 10:2...	2018-04-20 10:2...	0000000003	1	21/12/2016	Ok	2010-04-20 10:28:48.247	2018-04-20 10:27:51.573	2019-04-20 10:2
	8	addf978d-a1c7-...	2018-04-20 10:2...	2018-04-20 10:2...	0000000003	1	21/12/2016	Ok	2018-04-20 10:28:50.247	2018-04-20 10:27:51.573	2018-04-20 10:2...
	9	d6268f5f-1401-...	2018-04-20 10:2...	2018-04-20 10:2...	0000000003	1	21/12/2016	Ok	2018-04-20 10:28:52.187	2018-04-20 10:27:51.573	2018-04-20 10:2...
	10	402c2f24-cd94-...	2018-04-20 10:2...	2018-04-20 10:2...	0000000003	1	21/12/2016	Ok	2018-04-20 10:28:54.187	2018-04-20 10:27:51.573	2018-04-20 10:2...
	11	c07030df-483d-...	2018-04-20 10:2...	2018-04-20 10:2...	0000000003	1	21/12/2016	Ok	2018-04-20 10:28:56.187	2018-04-20 10:27:51.573	2018-04-20 10:2...

Figure 5-50. *Observing the associated BAM data*

Alternatively, you can log in to the BAM portal and perform a query in the activity search section, as shown in Figure 5-51.

Figure 5-51. *Observing the associated BAM data using the BAM portal*

Instrumenting Creating Custom Performance Counters

As most of the out-of-box BizTalk Server counters are at host level, it might be very interesting to create your own performance counters from business or operational point of views. You could develop performance counters in the following BizTalk Server elements:

- Custom pipeline components

- Custom components (BizTalk and external assemblies)

- Orchestrations

- Custom adapters

For example, if you create custom performance counters for a specific orchestration, counter data will be fulfilled only when that orchestration executes. Ideally, all performance counters should be reset when host instances start and stop.

You could use these counter information later in performance reports. It will save you a huge amount of time. Examples of useful performance counters are:

- Messages received by an orchestration

- Messages sent by an orchestration

- Number of errors by orchestration

- Number of errors at pipeline level

In addition, you could also use this technique to monitor your BizTalk Server platform because if those counters remain static for long period of time, that usually means that BizTalk Server is not processing messages (for that particular orchestration application, of course).

Developing Custom Performance Counters

In this scenario, you have an orchestration called orcProcessBookOrders that will receive book orders requests. This orchestration is bound to the host BizTalkServerApplication and, therefore, will run under the context of BizTalkServerApplication host instance process.

When the orchestration receives a new message, it will use the component PerformanceCounterHelper in an attempt to create the following Performance Counter Category, BizTalkOrchestrations_ProcessBookOrders, with these performance counters:

- #Received Messages

- #Sent messages

If the category already exists, it will not be created. This is very useful because you do not have to create counters manually as the component will check it for you every time the BizTalk Server engine is creating a new orchestration instance (it implements a constructor to overwrite categories upon creation though).

The component has an overload method for categories creation. If the orchestration is using side-by-side versioning, you have the option to create the category with the following format:

BizTalkOrchestrations_VersionNumber_ProcessBookOrders

Figure 5-52 shows that the component is creating a performance counter category called BizTalk Orchestrations_2.0_ProcessBookOrders. The number 2.0 identifies the orchestration version. In this way we could have counters associated to specific orchestration versions.

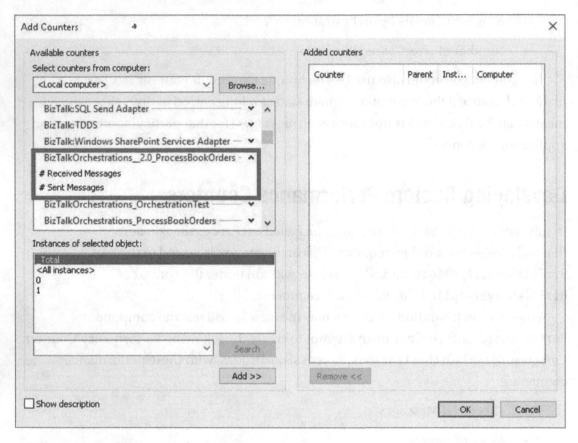

Figure 5-52. *Observing the custom performance counters*

How Does It Work?

When the orchestration has been activated by a specific host instance, the component will attach both performance counters to the HostInstance process by creating a new performance counter instance called BizTalkServerApplication:BizTalkMsgBoxDb: BizTalk2016. This information is automatically gathered by the component using the following BizTalk Server WMI classes:

- MSBTS_Orchestration. To get the HostName.

- MSBTS_MsgBoxSetting. To get the MsgBoxDb database name.

By picking up the current process server name. This is very important as the Orchestration can potentially run in all of your servers. For example, if you have two BizTalk Servers, ServerA and ServerB, and the host for that orchestration has host instances running in all of them, counters will be generated locally in both servers by creating the following counter instances:

- `BizTalkServerApplication:BizTalkMsgBoxDb:ServerA`

- `BizTalkServerApplication:BizTalkMsgBoxDb:ServerB`

You might be wondering why counters instances are attached to the BizTalk Server process. Well, if you do not attach counters to a process, they will be gathering data until the server reboots and you will need to implement a mechanism to reset counter instances values somehow.

After testing the BizTalk Server application, you can see counter values by opening Windows perfmon tool, as shown in Figures 5-53 and 5-54.

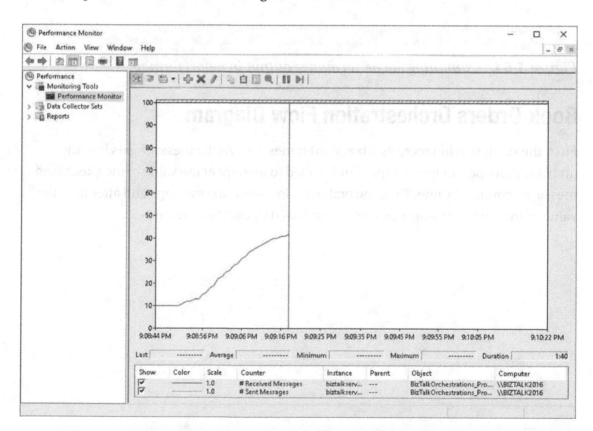

Figure 5-53. *Examining the performance output using perfmon tool*

Figure 5-54 shows the report view.

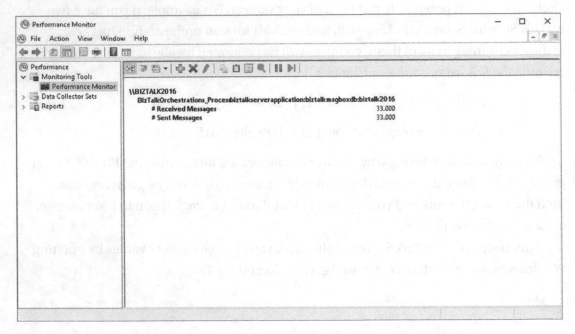

Figure 5-54. *Examining the performance output in report format*

Book Orders Orchestration Flow Diagram

First, the orchestration receives a book order message. As the message gets into the orchestration, perf helper component is called to increment the value of the #Received messages counter by one. Then the orchestration sends the message and after that, the value of the #Sent messages counter is increased by one. See Figure 5-55.

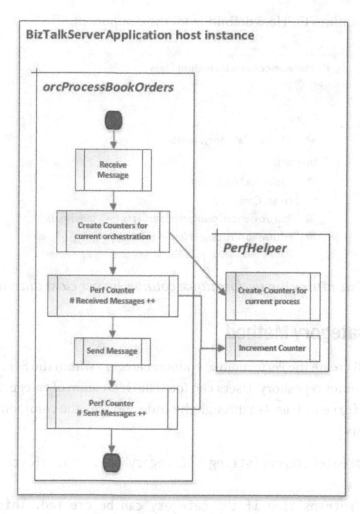

Figure 5-55. *Book orders orchestration diagram*

Examining PerformanceCounterHelper Component

This is the component that implements all the performance counter logic. You can find the Visual Studio solution in the companion code file at C:\APRESS\Chapter5\ PerformanceCounters\BookOrdersSolution\PerformanceCounterHelper.

Figure 5-56 outlines the class definition for the component.

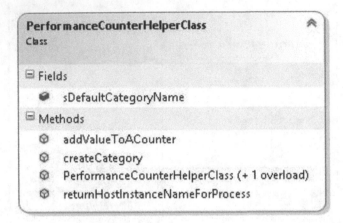

Figure 5-56. *Examining the performance counter helper class diagram*

The createCategory Method

This method will create the Performance counter category within the Server performance counter repository. Users can force the recreation of categories by setting the parameter bforce to True. Go through the code and read the comments as the code is self-explanatory.

```
public bool  createCategory(string slCategoryName, bool bforce = false)
        {
            //returns true if the category can be created. This is just
            creating the category and the draft counters.
            //as Counters are declared as multiInstance, they will be
            created and assigned every time a BizTalk HostInstance
            //process an orchestration of this type.
            //if force, the category will be deleted first and then recreated
            Boolean r = false;

            try
            {
                if (bforce) //if user is forcing re-creation
                {
                    //we delete the category first
```

```
    if (PerformanceCounterCategory.Exists(slCategoryName))
    {
        PerformanceCounterCategory.Delete(slCategoryName);
        //we delete the category
    }
}
if (!PerformanceCounterCategory.Exists(slCategoryName))
{
    //this is creating a collection of data counters.
    //We will use it at the end of the If to create Counter
    metadata configuration associated with the category.
    CounterCreationDataCollection counters = new
    CounterCreationDataCollection();
    //we create the counter #received messages
    CounterCreationData receivedMessages = new
    CounterCreationData();
    receivedMessages.CounterName = "# Received Messages";
    receivedMessages.CounterHelp = "Total number of
    received messages";
    receivedMessages.CounterType = PerformanceCounterType.
    NumberOfItems64;
    counters.Add(receivedMessages);
    //we create the counter #sent messages
    CounterCreationData sendMessages = new
    CounterCreationData();
    sendMessages.CounterName = "# Sent Messages";
    sendMessages.CounterHelp = "Total number of sent
    messages";
    sendMessages.CounterType = PerformanceCounterType.
    NumberOfItems64;

    counters.Add(sendMessages);

    //Create a new category with the new orchestration
    performancecounters
    //We set up the counters as multiInstances
    (PerformanceCounterCategoryType.MultiInstance)
```

```
                        //so we could add them later to the Host instance
                        PerformanceCounterCategory.Create(slCategoryName,
                        slCategoryName + " counters",
                        PerformanceCounterCategoryType.MultiInstance, counters);
            }
            r = true;
        }
        catch (Exception)
        {
            r = false;
            throw;
        }
        return r;
    }
```

When this method completes, if you open the perfmon tool, you will see that the category BIzTalkOrchestrations_ProcessBookOrders has been created, with their respective performance counters attached to it. See Figure 5-57.

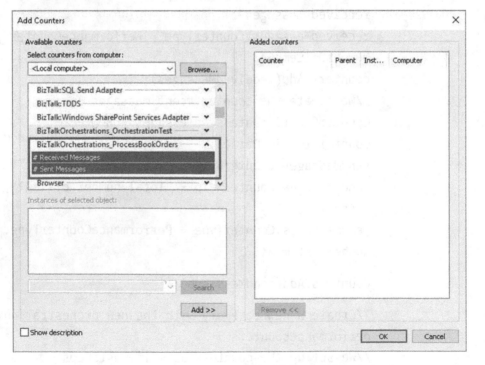

Figure 5-57. *Examining the expected output using perfmon tool*

There is an override with the following definition:

```
public bool  createCategory(string slCategoryName, string sVersion,bool
bforce = false)
```

This override will add a version token to the category (if you are using
side-by-side versioning, you should have different performance counters per version of
orchestration).

The addValueToACounter Method

This method performs the following actions:

- Creates counter instances.

- Attaches that counter instance to the BizTalk process. By doing this,
  counter data will be reset when host instances stop.

- Increments by 1 the value of counter (received or sent messages).

Here is the code:

```
public  bool addValueToACounter(string sCounterFamilyName,string
counterName,string realOrchestrationName)
        {
            bool r = false;
            string sCounterFullName = "";

            try
            {
                sCounterFullName = sCategoryName + sCounterFamilyName;
                System.Diagnostics.PerformanceCounter p = new
                PerformanceCounter();
                p.CategoryName = sCategoryName;
                p.CounterName = counterName;
                //we build the instance name.
                p.InstanceName = returnHostInstanceNameForProcess(realOrche
                strationName);
                //the following line will attach the counter to the BizTalk
                Process. If you want the counters to be independent of the
                host instance,
```

```
            //Choose PerformanceCounterInstanceLifetime.Global.
            p.InstanceLifetime = PerformanceCounterInstanceLifetime.
            Process;
            p.ReadOnly = false;
            p.Increment(); //we increment the counter by 1.
            r = true;
        }
        catch (Exception ex)
        {
            r = false;
            throw ex;
        }
        return r;
}
```

After the method execution, the performance monitor tool will show the associated instances as well, as shown in Figure 5-58.

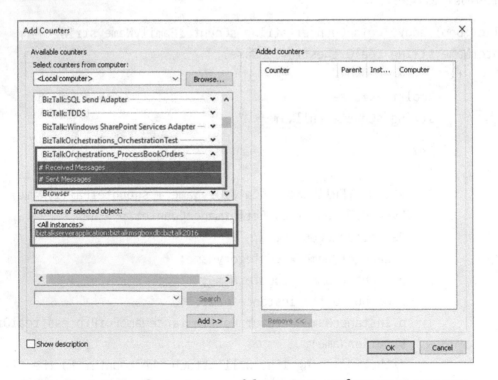

Figure 5-58. *Examining the instances of the custom performance counters*

Consuming the Component in an Orchestration

The orchestration orcProcessBookOrders receives orders and verifies if the customer is a VIP customer. If that is the case, the component creates the output message inserting a congratulations message.

Follow these steps:

1. Using Visual Studio Open the Solution BookOrdersSolution, located here: C:\APRESS\Chapter5\PerformanceCounters\ BookOrdersSolution\BookOrdersSolution.sln\.

2. Once loaded, open the Orchestration orcProcessBookOrders.

The orchestration has two main scripting shapes that call the PerformanceCounter Helper, as shown in Figure 5-59.

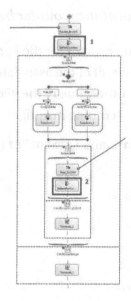

Figure 5-59. *Points where the component is called to populate the custom counters*

3. Double-click the first script shape SetPerfCounters. See Figure 5-60.

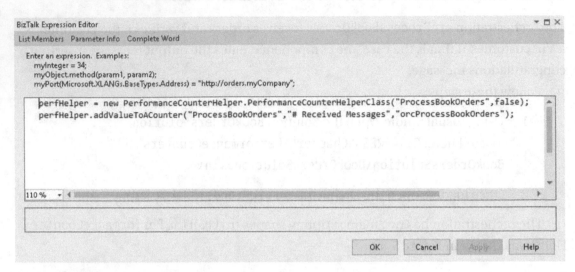

Figure 5-60. *Setting up the performance counter helper component*

The first line calls the default constructor for the PerformanceCounterHelper to create the performance category with all of the associated counters.

The second one increments by 1 the value of the #Received Messages Counter, as the orchestration has just received the incoming message.

4. Now open the Expression shape SetSentPerfCounter. See Figure 5-61.

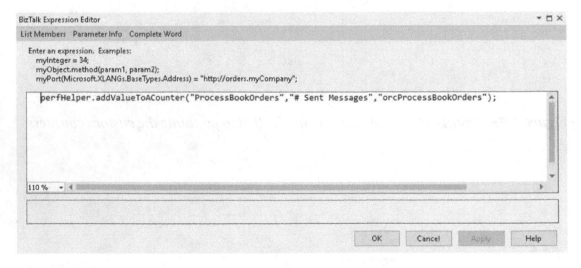

Figure 5-61. *Incrementing the sent messages counter to 1*

This script block increments by 1 the value of the #Sent Messages Counter since the orchestration has just sent the output message in the previous step.

5. Using the File Explorer, navigate to the folder: `C:\APRESS\`
    `Chapter5\PerformanceCounters\BookOrdersSolution\Setup`.

6. Run the `SetUp.cmd` command file as an administrator. This will deploy and test the solution by dropping 10 messages in the input folder.

7. Open perfmon and add the following performance counters `BizTalkOrchestrations_ProcessBookOrders` (see Figure 5-62):

    a. #Recevied messages

    b. #Sent messages

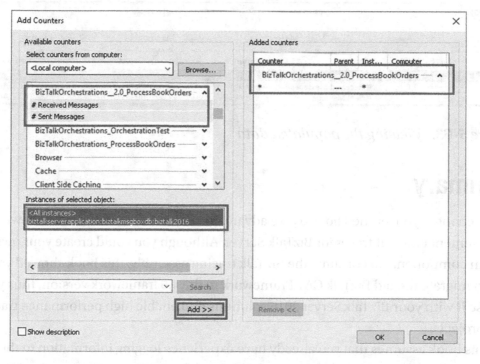

Figure 5-62. *Adding the custom performance counters to a perfmon view*

8. Open the perfmon console and explore the results. You should get something similar to Figure 5-63.

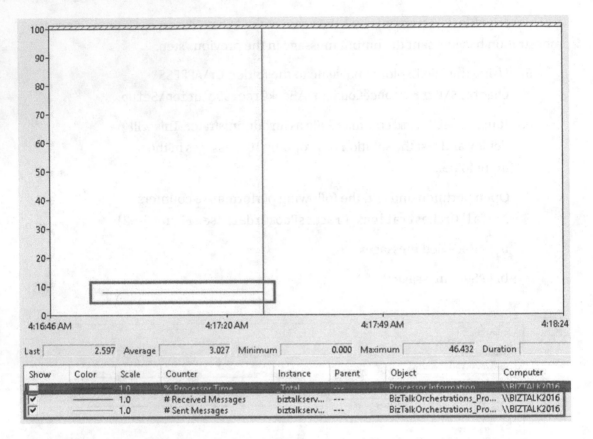

Figure 5-63. *Viewing the populated data*

Summary

In this chapter, you learned how to take advantage of the event traces for Windows
to implement efficient traces for BizTalk Server. Although you could create your own
custom components to consume the BizTalk tracing assembly, this book showed you
how to migrate the old BizTalk CAT Framework to the 4.6 framework version, thus you
can use it with your BizTalk Server 2016 solutions and enable high performance traces in
your projects.

This book assumes that you already have experience logging information to the
Windows event log and extends that capability by using BAM to instrument business
and system important milestones. All of this can be enriched by creating custom
performance counters that can populate business or system data.

In the next chapter, you learn how to use development techniques to proactively
improve how BizTalk Server applications run in production.

CHAPTER 6

Developing High-Performance Solutions

In previous chapters, you learned how to optimize the BizTalk Server environment based on application priority levels and performance SLA definitions. Additionally, in Chapter 5, you learned how to instrument your BizTalk Server solutions using ETW, customer performance counters, and BAM to enhance system monitoring. Now it's time to discuss the most common optimizations that you, as a developer, will need to know to develop robust BizTalk Server solutions.

You can improve the performance of a BizTalk Server solution by using the following elements:

- Schemas
- Orchestrations
- Maps
- Pipelines

Improving Schema Definitions

In this section, you learn how to improve the schema definitions. This topic is more important than it seems as BizTalk Server engine uses schema definitions to represent messages, and as you have learned previously, messages are the center of all the information that goes through BizTalk Server. Follow the recommendations detailed in this section to simplify schemas because as the complexity increases, overall performance decreases. This is especially true for large files and unclear schemas with several optional elements and nodes.

The idea for schema optimization is to reduce the time that the BizTalk Server engine takes to retrieve messages for further processing.

© Agustín Mántaras 2019

A. Mántaras, *BizTalk Server 2016*, https://doi.org/10.1007/978-1-4842-3994-0_6

Length of the Element Names

If you ever worked with the swift adapter, EDI, or HL7 specifications, you probably noticed that the element names look like weird codes. Most of those schemas definitions have a huge number of elements and nodes, and if they were using very descriptive names, the size of the final message instance would be very large.

When you are developing a new solution, especially for applications that rank high on the application transaction levels, you should consider reducing the length of the name for the nodes and elements, because the final size of the message will be also decreased. This is especially true for the nodes that have repeating records or for very large messages.

Note   Keep in mind also that using deceptive names can complicate troubleshooting and developing, especially in maps, where non-specific names can become quite deceiving. Therefore, you need to find a balance between performance and clarity. Use common sense. For instance, if you are working with a schema that has an element name called `CustomerCode`, consider reducing it to `CxId`. If the root node name is called `CustomerInformation`, rename it `CxData` or `CxInfo`.

Do not reach a point where maps or code become a nightmare to understand.

Message Properties Performance Recommendations

Whenever using promoted or distinguished properties, you should keep in mind the following performance factors and recommendations:

- Reduce the number of written and promoted properties and eliminate those that are not needed.

- Warning using XPath expressions. XPath expressions can be very long, primarily when the element is located very deep in the message. Therefore, the more distinguished fields you have, the larger the context size. This situation affects the overall performance of the platform. Whenever possible, consider moving the deep elements at the beginning of the schema.

- Property name length. In the same way that reducing the size of the element names also reduces the size of the message, it is recommended to reduce the length of the properties as much as possible. Shorter names ensure that the engine consumes less memory and still provides business functionality. This fact is especially true for distinguished fields as they do not have 256-character limitation.

- Routing. If you are not planning to use the property for routing or correlation, do not promote it! Just distinguish it. Promoted properties consume more resources as the engine inserts them into the subscriptions table, while distinguished properties are not. Also, if you enable property tracking, SQL Server process consumes more memory, processor, and IO resources, as it must insert the tracking information into the tracking data tables within the Message Box and then to the tracking database. These two facts might not be relevant while you are coding, but when the solution goes live and must process millions of instances per day, believe me: it matters!

- Promoted property location. Especially for flat file scenarios, performance is affected by the position of the promoted property within the schema definition. Promoted properties are found faster if you position them at the beginning of the schema.

- Extremely Low latency environments. If messages are small (fewer than 100 kilobytes), you can de-serialize the message into a .NET class object and access the public static fields and properties (instead of using XPath). If the message needs complex business rules, accessing data using the properties exposed by an instance of a .NET object is faster than using XPath expressions because XPath loads the full message into the memory every time it executes.

The following code shows an example of a serialized message that exposes distinguished properties:

```
using System;
using Microsoft.XLANGs.BaseTypes;
```

```
namespace NetClass
{
    [Serializable]
    public class MyBookNameSpace
    {
        public MyBook()
        {
            iSBN = "101928818910111";
            bookTitle = "BizTalk Server 2016 book";
        }

        [DistinguishedFieldAttribute()]
        public String iSBN;

        [DistinguishedFieldAttribute()]
        public int bookTitle;
    }
}
```

The code to create an instance of this object should be implemented within the context of a construct shape because the properties are implementing the `DistinguishedField` attribute (defined in `Microsoft.XLANGs.BaseTypes`). The following code checks if the ISBN property equals `"101928818910111"` and, if yes, it changes the `bookTitle` property to `"BizTalk 2016, performance tuning and optimization"`.

```
msgMessageIn = new MyBookNameSpace.MyBook();
if (msgMessageIn.iSBN== "101928818910111"}
{
    msgMessageIn.bookTitle ="BizTalk 2016, performance tuning and optimization"
}
```

Canonical Schemas

Canonical schemas are message definitions used to encapsulate the internal logic of your processes. The idea is to decouple the schema definitions of the integrated parties from the ones used by the BizTalk application. They are extremely powerful, especially when receiving information from entirely different sources.

As an example, imagine that you are developing a BizTalk application that consolidates customer data to a CRM application. Customer information can be received from four different systems and it must be sent to three CRM solutions. As the solution requires advanced business process and granular exception handling, you develop an orchestration that will receive and send canonical messages. By implementing it in this way, you avoid the creation of one orchestration per source system. See Figure 6-1.

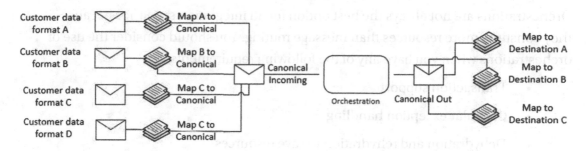

Figure 6-1. *Canonical integration example*

In the previous example, customer data is received through four different receive locations. Receive port executes then the corresponding map that transforms the incoming message into the canonical message used by the orchestration. After the business rules are executed within the orchestration, send port will transform the canonical message to the right destination system format.

Benefits of canonical schemas include:

- Schema changes from the source and destination systems will not affect orchestration received/sent messages, as these will use canonical schemas from receiving and sending information. This will reduce the number of deployments.

- New parties can be added to the solution without implementing global changes at the orchestration level, by creating new receive location/send ports and developing new maps.

- Performance increases. As complexity of the solution is reduced, this approach can have a positive impact on performance (depending on the number of instances). In the previous example, instead of having four dedicated orchestrations per source system, you develop only one that interacts directly with canonical messages.

Improving Orchestrations

The following sections discuss relevant techniques and topics related to orchestrations that you should consider at early stages of the project.

To Orchestrate or Not To Orchestrate, That Is the Question

Orchestrations are not always the best option for all integration scenarios because they consume more resources than message routing. You should consider the use of orchestrations when you have any of the following requirements:

- Transaction support

- Granular exception handling

- Dehydration and rehydration to save resources

- Persistent points to recover from failures

- Correlation

- Convoy patterns

- Business activity monitoring at the business process level

If none of these techniques and features are required, then consider avoiding orchestrations and move business logic using a combination of custom pipeline components and ports. This technique diminishes the overhead to the Message Box database and consequently reduces latency.

Using Orchestrations When Transaction Support Is Required

BizTalk orchestrations offer a transactional programming model that includes support for recovery from failed transactions using compensation and exception handling. All orchestrations expose a property called Transaction Type that can have the following values:

- *Atomic*—Enables a transaction to automatically roll back to a previous state in case the transaction does not successfully complete.

- *Long running*—You use this type of transaction when the implemented business process can span longer time durations (years even), contain nested transactions, and use exception handling to recover from error scenarios.

- *None*—If you just want to catch exceptions without transaction support, you should set the scope or the whole orchestration to None.

You can set the transaction type property using the orchestration viewer and accessing the orchestration properties, as shown in Figure 6-2.

Figure 6-2. Available transaction types for orchestrations

Using Orchestrations to Benefit from Dehydration

Especially for applications where application priority levels or performance behavior rank higher, the use of hardware resources can increase exponentially. Orchestrations typically consume services that take some time to deliver the response. The BizTalk Server engine will not ever know when the response is going to get back to the flow because what is happening under the hood of the service is completely out of the scope of the BizTalk Server engine. Now, imagine that at some point an application has an orchestration that executes 1000 instances simultaneously. If the total in-memory representation of that orchestration is 300 KB, the 1.000 instances will consume 300.000 KB (292 MB) of the process memory.

While orchestrations are idle, ready to run or waiting for something to happen, the BizTalk Server engine will store the orchestration state to the Message Box database to save hardware resources related to the BizTalk Server machine. In the previous example, if all orchestrations wait for the response at the same time, 292 MB of memory will be released as all orchestration states are stored into the Message Box database.

When orchestrations get activated again, the orchestration loads the orchestration state from the latest point and resumes the flow of the orchestration. This process is formally called *rehydration*.

Note   Dehydration may take place whenever the engine estimates that an orchestration is idle for an extended period. The only exception to this rule is when the flow of an orchestration enters an atomic scope. Actions taken within an atomic scope do to initiate a dehydration situation because these types of transactions persist the orchestration state only once, at the end of the scope.

While the orchestration engine oversees the dehydration feature, you can control its behavior by changing the orchestration throttling settings at the host level.

Orchestration Throttling Settings Related to Dehydration at the Host Level

You can control the dehydration behavior of orchestrations by accessing the settings shown in Figure 6-3 using the BizTalk Administration console at the host level.

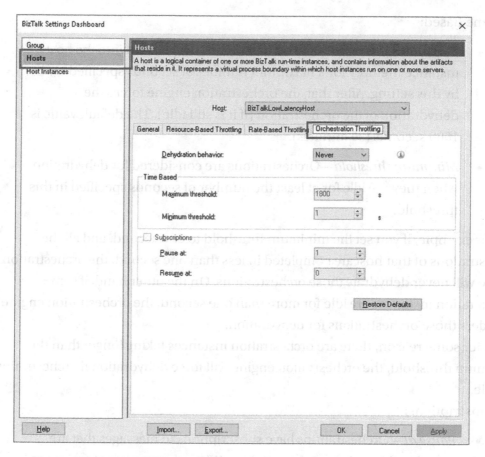

Figure 6-3. Accessing orchestrations throttling settings at the host level

Dehydration behavior:

- *Never*—This option is disabling the dehydration feature for all the orchestrations running under that specific host. That means that when an orchestration is consuming a service or waiting for another event to occur, the orchestration engine will keep the orchestration into memory. This option will alleviate SQL Server CPU, memory and IO, but puts strain on memory consumption.

- *Always*—Dehydration will occur always. While this option will save memory resources to the BizTalk machine, it can potentially cause an overhead to the SQL Server hosting the Message Box database.

- *Custom*—Dehydration will take place based on the Time Based or Subscriptions thresholds.

Time Based:

- *Maximum threshold*—Idle orchestrations will be held into the host instance memory for a maximum number of seconds specified by this setting. After that, the orchestration engine forces the dehydration of the orchestration (if it is still idle). The default value is 1800 seconds (30 minutes).

- *Minimum threshold*—Orchestrations are considered for dehydration when they are idle for at least the number of seconds specified in this threshold.

For example, if you set the minimum threshold to one second, and all the orchestrations of that host are completed in less than one second, the orchestration engine will never dehydrate those orchestrations. On the other hand, if some orchestration instances are idle for more than one second, the orchestration engine considers those orchestrations for dehydration.

If, for some reason, there are orchestration instances taking longer than the maximum threshold, the orchestration engine will force dehydration if orchestrations are idle.

Subscriptions:

- *Pause at*—Orchestrations have subscriptions to messages that are stored to the main host queue tables. When the number of messages in this queue (associated with the orchestration subscription) is equal or higher that the Pause at threshold, the messages are not delivered to orchestrations instances until the number of messages in the host queue decreases to the Resume At threshold.

- *Resume at*—As explained in the Pause At setting, this threshold controls whether the message engine starts to deliver new message instances to orchestrations.

For example, if you set the Pause At threshold to 1.000, the message engine stops delivering messages to the orchestrations, running under that host, when the number of associated messages to that orchestration, reaches 1.000.

If the resume at is set the Resume At threshold to 600, the message engine will resume delivering messages to those orchestrations when the number of pending messages decreases to 600 or below.

Reducing the Impact of Persisted Data

BizTalk Server engine stores the orchestration state within the Message Box in the following situations:

- End of a transactional scope (atomic or long running)

- At debugging breakpoints

- At a Start Orchestration shape

- At the Send shape (except in an atomic transaction)

- When an orchestration is suspended

- When the system shuts down in a controlled manner

- When dehydration occurs

- When an orchestration completes

Therefore, reducing the number of persistent points is all about making the right use of transactional scopes and send shapes because the rest of situations are out of reach (the engine controls orchestration events that cannot be modified).

Reduce the Number of Persistent Points in Exception handling

If in a section of your orchestration you want to catch exceptions, but compensation or timeout control is not required, then set the transaction type of that scope to none. This technique will eliminate a persistent point from the whole process as the BizTalk Server engine will not save the state of the orchestration when that scope finishes.

Reduce the Number of Persistent Points in Sending Operations

If an orchestration needs to send multiple messages using a send shape per operation, try these approaches instead:

- Encapsulate all the send operations with a send port group when the outgoing message is the same one. With this action the engine will persist the information only once because you are using only one send shape.

- If the first option is not possible, then try to wrap up all the send shapes within an atomic scope because atomic scopes generate only one persistent point at the end of the scope.

For instance, imagine that you have an orchestration that has to send three messages to three different destination systems, as shown in Figure 6-4.

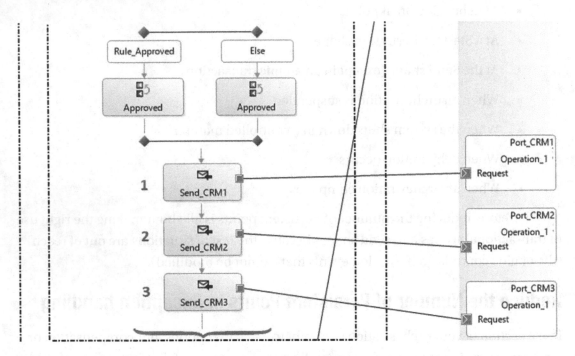

Figure 6-4. *Orchestration with three persistent points*

If you develop the orchestration by adding three subsequent send shapes, the orchestration engine will persist the orchestration state three times. If the application ranks high in the application priority levels for the number of transactions, the amount of persisted data per second will be large.

Therefore, as discussed, you can decrease the number of persistent points by wrapping up all the send shapes within an atomic scope, as shown in Figure 6-5.

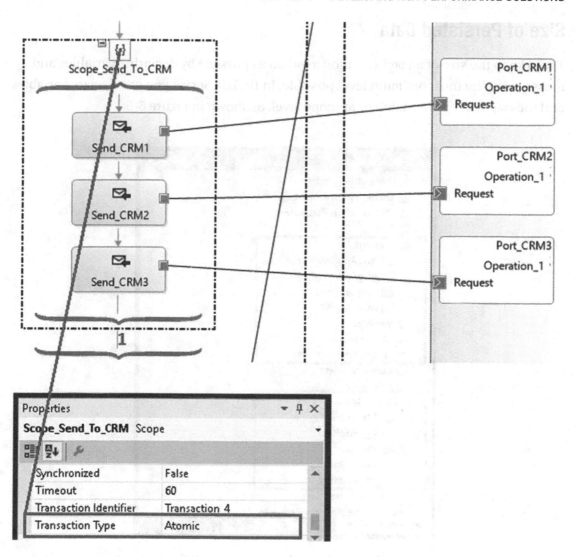

Figure 6-5. *Orchestration with one persistent point using an atomic scope*

Size of Persisted Data

Try to keep the size of an orchestration as small as possible by declaring variables and messages at the most optimum level possible. In BizTalk Server you can declare variables and messages at orchestration or at scope level, as shown in Figure 6-6.

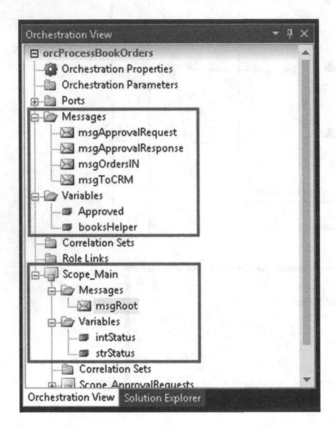

Figure 6-6. *Declaration of variable and messages at different levels*

Variables and messages declared at orchestration level are always stored in the Message Box in each persistent point, while the ones declared at scope level will be only stored if the scope has not been completed yet. This small action will reduce the time spent by the host instance when storing and retrieving persisted data from the Message Box database. This is essential for all BizTalk Server applications, but it is especially crucial for solutions where application priority levels rank higher for the transaction levels.

For instance, imagine that an orchestration needs to process 100 transactions per second and it is using a message of 10 KB size that is declared at orchestration level.

Making some quick calculations, you get the following data: 100 KB * 100 = 10.000 KB per second to store that message per orchestration persistent point.

If the orchestration has 10 persistent points, you get a total size of 100.000 KB (around 97 MB) of persisted information, and only for that message!

Declaring that message at scope level, if only two persistent points are occurring at that scope, that will reduce the size of the persisted data to 20% because now, only two persistent points out of 10 will store that message.

Improving Orchestration Latency

The following sections discuss the most common techniques to reduce orchestration latency.

Loading and Unloading Assemblies Into Memory

When host instances start, they load all the assemblies into the memory associated to the host instance process. The first request can take up to 15 seconds to start processing messages. If an orchestration is idle for a long time (ready to run or dehydrated) or if The BizTalk host instances has not process a new orchestration instance for more than 30 minutes, assemblies will be unloaded from the host instance until a new request arrives.

You can control the way host instances load and unload assemblies by adding a configuration setting to the BizTalk configuration file that is called AppDomain.

This setting allows you to define profiles with shared settings so that you can assign BizTalk Server assemblies to load with those profile configuration settings. If you do not specify custom profiles, in other words if you do not want specific settings per BizTalk Server assembly, there is a default profile called DefaultSpec that will be used to load all the configuration.

```
<AppDomains AssembliesPerDomain ="10">
<DefaultSpec SecondsIdleBeforeShutdown="-1"
SecondsEmptyBeforeShutdown="1800">
</AppDomains>
```

- SecondsIdleBeforeShutdown—BizTalk Server host instances will
  unload all the assemblies in this domain when all orchestrations are
  idle for a period of time specified by the SecondsIdleBeforeShutdown
  setting. Idle orchestrations are the ones that have the status as ready
  to run or dehydrated. Specify -1 to when a domain should never
  unload when idle.

- SecondsEmptyBeforeShutdown—BizTalk Server host instances will
  unload all the assemblies in this domain when it is empty for a period
  of time specified by the SecondsEmptyBeforeShutdown setting. This
  is the number of seconds that an app domain is empty (does not
  contain any orchestration instances) before being unloaded. Setting
  it to -1 will cause the AppDomain to never unload, even when it's
  empty.

In the previous example, SecondsIdleBeforeShutdown is set to -1. Therefore,
BizTalk host instances will not unload assemblies that have idle orchestrations.
SecondsEmptyBeforeShutdown is set to 1800, and that means that when a domain gets
empty, the BizTalk Server engine will wait 30 minutes to unload all the assemblies
within the host instance and it will not load them until a new orchestration instance is
activated.

Note   When an idle but non-empty domain is unloaded, all the contained
orchestration instances are dehydrated first.

If you want to create a custom profile based on specific assemblies, with different
configuration than the default one, you have to add the AppDomainSpec section to the
AppDomainSpecs section.

For instance, imagine that you have a mission-critical application called
BookOrdersApplication and you want the BizTalk host instance processes to not unload
the BookOrders application assemblies (even when they are empty for an extended
period).

First, you have to create the custom AppDomain by adding the AppDomainSpec section to the AppDomainSpecs section:

```
<AppDomainSpecs>
        <AppDomainSpec Name="DomainForBookOrdersAppplication"
        SecondsIdleBeforeShutdown="-1" SecondsEmptyBeforeShutdown="-1">
        </AppDomainSpec>
</AppDomainSpecs>
```

And now you just need to tell the BizTalk Server engine which assemblies should be considered as part of the custom domain "DomainForBookOrdersAppplication". To do that, you need to create an ExactAssignmentRules and include all the assemblies for the custom domain:

```
<ExactAssignmentRules>
        <ExactAssignmentRule AssemblyName="BookOrdersSolution,
        Version=1.0.0.0, Culture=neutral, PublicKeyToken=9c7731c5584592ad"
        AssemblyName_0="""  AppDomainName="
DomainForBookOrdersAppplication ="""  />AppDomainName_1" />
```

Replacing Send Shapes by Custom Code

Especially for applications where application transaction or performance behavior levels rank higher, consider removing the send shapes and implementing the send operation using a custom .NET component.

This technique will reduce latency of the orchestration, because the custom code evades the BizTalk messaging engine, and provides the following benefits:

- It will reduce the number of round trips to the Message Box database.

- As you are eliminating a send shape, the orchestration will have a persistent point less.

However, by implementing a custom send operation, you are not accessing the following BizTalk Server features:

- Pipeline features such as recovery interchange, message validation, disassembling and decoding/encoding, party resolution

- Send port retries

- Send port scheduling options

- Correlation

- Backup transports

- Tracking

- Integrated monitoring and troubleshooting using the BizTalk administration console

Creating Static Classes

Whenever you are developing a custom .NET component to provide additional functionality to orchestrations, consider creating them as static because they provide the following benefits:

- *Hardware resources*—Since static classes have no internal state, the host instance will reduce hardware resources such as memory and CPU.

- *Decreasing the orchestration state size*—This is very important because the orchestration engine will not have to save the status of the component on every persistent point or whenever it needs to dehydrate.

- *Avoiding atomic scopes*—Since components that require serialization must me placed under an atomic scope, .NET components exposing static classes or methods will not require to implement the serializable attribute and can be consumed everywhere in the orchestration without the need of using an atomic scope. This will reduce the number of persistent points per orchestration because atomic scopes generate a persistent point at the end of the scope.

To create a class or method as static, you just need to add the static modifier to the declaration. The following example outlines how to achieve this:

```
public static class BizTalkServerHelper
{
    public static string GetConnectionString(string connectionString)
    {

        return _connectionString;
    }
```

```
public static GetProperty (string itemProperty)
{
    return _itemProperty;
}
}
```

Controlling Orchestration Memory Consumption

Especially for large messages scenarios where orchestrations consume large amounts of memory, you might have the need of tuning the default throttling behavior of memory consumption at the host instance level.

You can access these settings using the BizTalk Administration console at the host instance level, as shown in Figure 6-7.

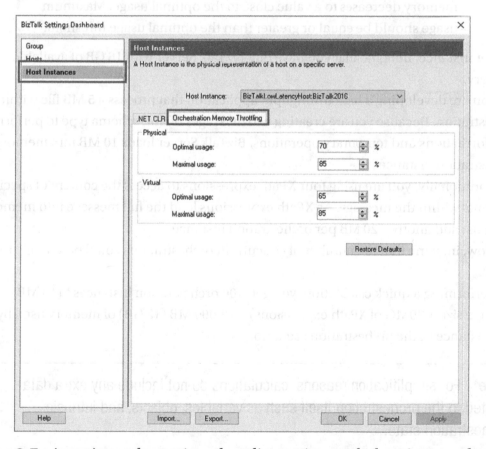

Figure 6-7. *Accessing orchestrations throttling settings at the host instance level*

As you can see, there are two sections—Physical and Virtual. The first one refers thresholds related to physical memory consumption while the second one refers to virtual process memory consumption. Both sections have Optimal and Maximal usage thresholds that behave the same way, but specifically dedicated for the type of memory that they are related to. The threshold explanation is as follows:

- Optimal usage—When the consumed physical/virtual memory for that host instance is below this threshold, the engine does not throttle orchestrations. On the other hand, if it reaches this threshold, the orchestration engine will start throttling orchestrations instances to save physical/virtual memory resources.

- Maximal usage—If the consumed physical/virtual memory reaches this value, the throttling condition becomes very aggressive and the host instance will not load new orchestrations until the consumed memory decreases to a value close to the optimal usage. Maximum usage should be equal or greater than the optimal usage threshold.

For instance, imagine that you have one BizTalk Server with 16 GB of available memory.

You are developing a high throughput application that process a 5 MB file within an orchestration. Because you are creating two messages of that schema type to perform transformations and temporary operations, BizTalk Server loads 10 MB into memory per orchestration instance.

Additionally, you are using four XPath expressions to access the content of specific elements within the message. As XPath expressions load the full message into memory, you must add another 20 MB per orchestration instance.

Now, imagine that the number of concurrent orchestrations could potentially reach to 400.

Performing a quick calculation, you get: 400 orchestration instances * (10 MB message size + 20MG of XPath expressions) = 12.000 MB (12 GB) of memory used by the host instance in the orchestration scenario.

Note   For simplification reasons, calculations do not include any extra data related to the orchestration itself such as variables, objects, and intrinsic orchestration state.

As the server has 16 GB, a consumption of 12 GB means a 75%. In this scenario the orchestration engine will start throttling orchestrations because the consumed memory exceeds the default 70% for the Optimal Usage threshold.

Reducing Orchestration Complexity

As orchestration complexity increases, performance decreases, as most likely the following elements will also increase:

- Number of shapes that the orchestration executes

- Number of persistent points

- Number of messages and variables

- Dehydration cycles

- Consumed memory

- Access to I/O (network and disk)

- CPU resources

Try to design business processes using a modular style by using the same concept of canonical schemas but applied to orchestrations. Create orchestrations that you can reuse for several scenarios or try to segment orchestrations to isolate functionalities into different orchestrations.

For example, imagine that you have developed several Web API services that exposes business functionality through REST. You have an orchestration that is calling those REST services seven times during the flow. To consume those REST services within the orchestration, you have inserted seven request/response ports. The solution works fine, but the orchestration looks huge and complex. Deployment is also complicated as you must bind seven extra logical ports to physical ports. This is a perfect situation to isolate the REST service call in a separated orchestration. The new orchestration will use the canonical schema technique, so that changes at REST services level will not affect the business orchestration. The business orchestration will call the nested orchestration, providing the name of the service and the operation to execute, and it will do that sending and receiving canonical messages through the child orchestration.

Improving Maps Execution

Adjusting the temp folder location and using the XslCompiledTransform class will speed up map processing, especially if a fast disk is deployed in the local server.

BizTalk Host Instance Temp Folder Location

BizTalk Server engine uses the host instance account temp folder to stream files to disk when maps are executed. You should consider placing the temp folder in a separated disk to reduce the chances of disk contention. This is especially true when maps are executed under the following conditions:

- Processing large messages or complex schemas.

- Complex maps with hundreds of links or more.

Using the XslCompiledTransform Class

BizTalk 2016 introduces the use of the XslCompiledTransform class. This class is used to compile and execute XSLT transformations. In most cases, the XslCompiledTransform class significantly outperforms the XslTransform class in terms of the time needed to execute the same XSLT against the same inbound XML document.

There is only one performance limitation with this new class: Because the XSLT is compiled to MSIL, the first time the transform is executed, there is a performance delay because the map need to be compiled first. However, following executions are much faster than using XslTransform.

You can decide whether to use the XslCompiledTransform class by accessing the map property called Use XSL Transform, as shown in Figure 6-8.

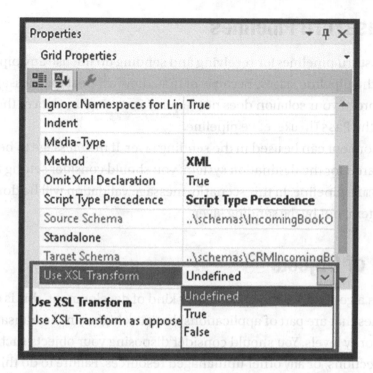

Figure 6-8. Examining the Use XSL Transform property

When you create a new map, the property is set to Undefined by default (same as true). That means that the map will be executed using the old non-compiled version. If you want to use the compiled version, you must set the property to false.

Note The recommendation is that you test the application with both settings and choose the one that gives you the best performance.

Improving Pipelines

There are several techniques to improve custom pipeline processing, but probably the most relevant ones are related to efficient memory management. In this section, you learn about using passthru pipelines, disposing objects efficiently, and how to avoid loading the full message into memory using streaming technology.

Use the PassThru Pipelines

The default passthru pipelines for receiving and sending do not use any pipeline component in the pipeline stages. Because of that, they just treat the message as a chunk of data. Therefore, if your solution does not require accessing the data of the message, you can set up the `PassThruReceive` pipeline.

The same concept can be used in the sending layer. If the message to be sent is already prepared for the destination system, you should consider setting up the `PassThruTransmit` pipeline. In this scenario, message validation will be done by the destination system, not by the sending layer.

Disposing of Objects

Although this is a general best practice for any kind of development, this is especially true for pipelines that are part of applications that rank higher in the transaction application priority levels. You should consider disposing your objects such as helpers, database connections, or any other unmanaged resources. Failure to do this could cause a memory leak in the server, preventing BizTalk Server host instances from accessing memory resources that could have been released before.

In your .NET custom components, you can provide explicit control by implementing the `IDisposable` interface and override the declaration by adding custom code that will release external resources such as database connections, network drives, and so on. Then, you can call this method to make sure everything is released.

BizTalk Server message engine uses the concept of resource tracker to add to it references of objects that must be released at a specific moment of time. Custom pipeline components can add objects to this tracker through an instance of an `IPipelineContext` object and then the engine will release them just when the pipeline execution has completed successfully.

For instance, in the `Execute` method of a custom pipeline component (explained deeply in further sections), you can load the message into a memory stream object and then add this instance to the resource tracker so that the message engine will terminate it when the pipeline completes.

```
public IBaseMessage Execute(IPipelineContext pContext, IBaseMessage pInMsg)
{

      MemoryStream messageData = new MemoryStream();

      //code to load the content of the message into the memoryStream
      . . .

      //We add the memory stream to the resource so it gets disposed by the
        message engine.

      pContext.ResourceTracker.AddResource(messageData);

      //rest of the code
      . . .

      return outMessage;

}
```

Avoid Using XMLDocument Objects

Frequently, once a custom pipeline component receives a message, the application has
a requirement to read the receiving message to act based on the content by creating
context properties, validate the message or any custom activity. In such scenarios you
should avoid loading the message into an XMLDocument object because it will load the full
message into memory and its representation will cost up to 10 times the original data.

Instead of using the XMLDocument, consider creating an XMLTextReader that can
retrieve data from one of the following classes exposed by the Microsoft.BizTalk.
Streaming.dll assembly:

- VirtualStream

- ReadOnlySeekableStream

- SeekAbleReadOnlyStream

You can find an implementation of these techniques in the SDK installation folder of
BizTalk Server:

C:\Program Files (x86)\Microsoft BizTalk Server 2016\SDK\Samples\
Pipelines\ArbitraryXPathPropertyHandler.

An explanation of the scenario is detailed here:

https://docs.microsoft.com/en-us/biztalk/core/arbitrary-xpath-property-handler-biztalk-server-sample?redirectedfrom=MSDN

Developing Pipeline Components to Improve Performance

When orchestrations are not required or can be avoided, consider implementing advance processing at the pipeline level. This will improve performance as there will not be added latency due to the orchestration engine (persistent points, dehydration, and hardware resources).

Pipeline components are used in the pipeline phases to perform the following tasks:

- *In receive pipelines*—Decode, disassemble, validate, and party resolution.

- *In send pipelines*—Pre-assemble, assemble, and encode.

Custom pipeline components can be dragged and dropped to pipeline stages using the Visual Studio toolbox. By default, BizTalk Server includes the pipeline components outlined in Figure 6-9.

Figure 6-9. *Examining the BizTalk pipeline components in the toolbox*

You can create custom pipeline components to provide extended capabilities that are not provided by all default pipelines. For example, you might have business requirements to:

- Receive messages that are zipped.

- Send zipped messages.

- Look for a database setting and insert it into the message context before the message gets published to the Message Box database.

- Improve the performance of the application by implementing the orchestration functionality within the pipeline.

This section guides you through the process of custom pipeline component creation.

Types of Pipeline Components

You can develop the following pipeline components:

- *General*—Designed to get one message (no batch), execute relevant code, and return to BizTalk Server. See Figure 6-10.

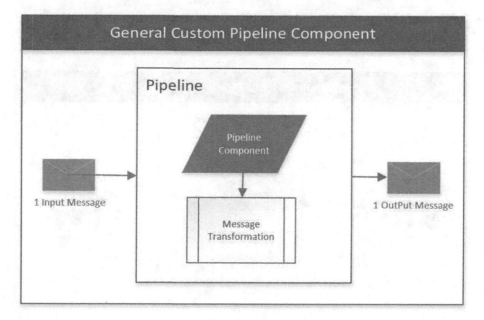

Figure 6-10. General custom pipeline component

- *Assembling*—Designed to receive several messages and send one message to the engine. See Figure 6-11.

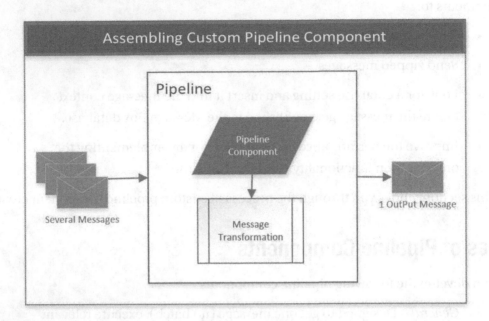

Figure 6-11. *Assembling custom pipeline component*

- *Disassembling*—Designed to receive several messages and send one message to the engine. See Figure 6-12.

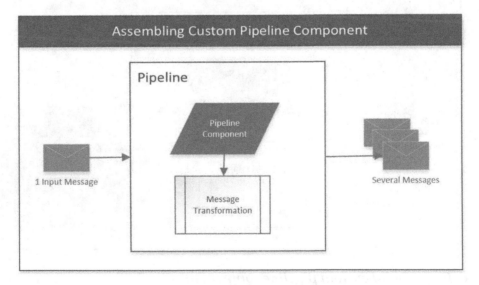

Figure 6-12. *Disassembling custom pipeline component*

Custom Pipeline Interfaces

At the pipeline stage, the BizTalk Server engine executes several specific methods to access the data stream that is going through the pipeline. Thus, your pipeline components should implement those methods so that the BizTalk Server engine can receive or send messages. The way to provide those methods is to implement several interfaces that will help you send and receive messages to the BizTalk Messaging Engine. Depending on the type of component you want to create (general, assembling, or disassembling), you need to implement different interfaces.

Available interfaces:

- IBaseComponent—Provides standard information to the BizTalk Engine and to the designer like Description, Name, and Version. It is shared across the three types of components (general, assembling and disassembling).

- IComponent—This interface is implemented only in general pipeline components. It is exposing a method called Execute that is used to:

  - Receive messages from the engine.

  - Send processed messages back to the engine.

- IPipelineContext—Implements all document processing related interfaces by providing the following main functionalities (among others).

  - Retrieves pipeline and stage configuration settings.

  - Provides the mechanism to interpret XSD schemas and BizTalk Server annotations.

- IPropertyBag—Used to store custom settings for the pipeline. Developers will use them to regulate how a pipeline process documents. It is exposes two methods:

  - Read, which reads a custom setting.

  - Write, which saves a custom setting.

- IPersistPropertyBag—Provides a mechanism to persist the properties identified by the IpropertyBag interface.

- `IDisassemblerComponent`—Used only in disassembling custom components and can be associated only with receive pipelines. It will receive only one document and will produce one or more messages. It is the typical scenario in which a batch message is received and contains one or more child messages with the same structure. It exposes two methods:

  - `Disassemble`—It will disassemble the incoming message.

  - `GetNext`—The disassemble method will create a set of messages. You need call the `GetNext` method to loop through them. When this method returns null, that means that you have reached the end of the set.

- `IAssemblerComponent`—Used only in assembling custom components. Therefore, it can be used only in sending pipelines. it will receive multiple messages and will generate only one output message. It exposes two methods:

  - `AddDocument`—Creates a lest of messages that will be included in the process of creating the individual output batching file.

  - `Assemble`—Takes all the messages included in the previous list and creates the batch message.

- `IDocumentSpec`—Used to perform actions to the message content, such as:

  - Writing properties into the message context.

  - Removing properties from the message context.

  - Changing the message body part.

  - Adding or changing the target `nameSpace` property.

- `IComponentUI`—Used to display the icon in the Visual Studio toolbox and to validate configuration properties.

- `ICustomTypeDescriptor`—Used to provide user friendly names and descriptions of properties used in pipelines.

Attributes of Pipeline Components

All custom pipeline components can behave in many ways. You can define custom attributes to specify how the pipeline should be interpreted by the BizTalk Server engine and use it in the right pipeline stage.

Here, you can see all the available attributes:

CATID_Any—Specifies a component with no specific category. Like general components.

CATID_AssemblingSerializer—The component is an assembling serializer.

CATID_Decoder—The component is a decoder.

CATID_DisassemblingParser—The component is a disassembling parser.

CATID_Encoder—The component is an encoder.

CATID_Parser—The component is a parser.

CATID_PartyResolver—The component is a party resolver.

CATID_PipelineComponent—The component is a pipeline.

CATID_Receiver—The component is a receiver.

CATID_Serializer—The component is a serializer.

CATID_Streamer—The component is a streamer.

CATID_Transmitter—The component is a transmitter.

Developing a General Custom Pipeline Component

As an example on how to use pipeline components to avoid orchestration scenarios, in this section you are going to learn how to develop a general custom pipeline component that writes a custom promoted property into the message context. The application uses that promoted property later for a message routing scenario.

Figure 6-13 outlines what will you achieve.

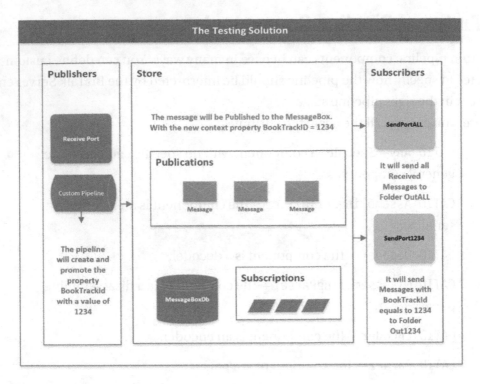

Figure 6-13. Understanding the scenario

Solution Overview

The solution will be implemented by developing three BizTalk Server projects:

- The BizTalk project that will contain the schema used for property promotion

- The Custom pipeline component

- The Testing BizTalk project

Developing the Property Schema Project

This project will contain a schema file that implements the promoted property.
    Follow these steps:

1. Using Visual Studio, create a new BizTalk project called BookPromotedPropertiesSchema.

2.   Add a new schema file called `BookPromotedProperties`.

3.   Rename the main root name to `PromotedProperties`.

4.   Go to the property schema file. Examine the Target Namespace property. You use this schema to promote the properties later in the pipeline code. `https://BookPromotedProperties.PropertySchema`

5.   Add the following Child Field elements:

   - `BookTrackId`

   - `BookSystemId`

6.   Right-click the `BookTrackId` element and select Quick Promotion. With this action, the BizTalk Editor creates the `PropertySchema` schema that will be used to store all of the promoted properties.

7.   Right-click the `BookSystemId` element and select Shows Promotions.

8.   Select the Property Fields tab.

9.   In the Promote Properties dialog box, select `BookSystemID` and click on the Add button. Click OK.

10.   Choose Save All.

11.   Sign the output assembly by accessing the project properties. Right-click at the Project level and choose to deploy. The schemas will be deployed on the default application. Using Visual Studio, create a new BizTalk project called `BookPromotedPropertiesSchema`.

Developing the Custom Pipeline Component Project

In this section, you create a fully functional general custom pipeline component that will be used to write the properties created previously to the message context.

The idea is that the pipeline will expose the properties outlined in Figure 6-14 in the pipeline user interface.

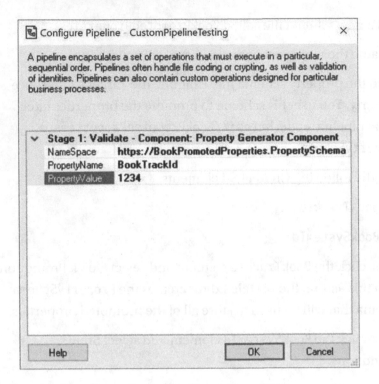

Figure 6-14. *Examining the custom pipeline properties*

So that whenever a message goes through the pipeline, the BookTrackId property will be filled with the custom PropertyValue 1234.

Creating the Visual Studio Project for the Custom Pipeline Component

All general custom pipelines components should implement the following interfaces:

- IBaseComponent

- IComponent

- IComponentUI

- IPersistPropertyBag

Follow these steps:

1. Open Visual Studio as an administrator and create a new Visual Studio project.

2. From the Templates menu, choose Visual C#, select Class Library, and navigate to the location where you want to save it.

3. Type `PropertyGeneratorPipeline` in the Name and click OK.

4. Rename the default CS class file to `PropertyGeneratorPipeline.cs`.

5. Add the following references to the project as they will be used by the BizTalk Server Engine:

   - `Microsoft.BizTalk.Pipeline`, located in `C:\Program Files (x86)\Microsoft BizTalk Server 2016\Microsoft.BizTalk.Pipeline.dll`

   - `Microsoft.XLANG.BaseTypes`, located in `C:\Program Files (x86)\Microsoft BizTalk Server 2016\Microsoft.XLANGs.BaseTypes.dll`

   - `Microsoft.XLANG.BizTalk.Engine`, located in `C:\Program Files (x86)\Microsoft BizTalk Server 2016\Microsoft.XLANGs.BizTalk.Engine.dll`

   - `Microsoft.XLANG.BizTalk.ProcessInterface`, located in `C:\Program Files (x86)\Microsoft BizTalk Server 2016\Microsoft.XLANGs.BizTalk.ProcessInterface.dll`

   - `Microsoft.XLANG.Engine`, located in `C:\Program Files (x86)\Microsoft BizTalk Server 2016\Microsoft.XLANGs.Engine.dll`

   - `System.Drawing`, located in `C:\Program Files (x86)\Reference Assemblies\Microsoft\Framework\.NETFramework\v4.5\System.Drawing.dll`

6. Once you've added these, set the Copy Local property to True for all references but `System.Drawing` (it should be done by default).

7. Go to the project settings and sign the assembly with a new strong name key file.

8. Go to the Application category under the project settings and change the target Framework to point to .NET Framework 4.6.

9. In the Application Category, click the AssemblyInformation button.

10. Enable the Make Assembly COM Visible setting.

11. Save all your changes.

12. Open the `PropertyGeneratorPipeline` file and add the following using statements to the namespace:

```
namespace PropertyGeneratorPipeline
{
    using System;
    using System.Resources;
    using System.Drawing;
    using System.Collections;
    using System.Reflection;
    using System.ComponentModel;
    using System.Text;
    using System.IO;
    using Microsoft.BizTalk.Message.Interop;
    using Microsoft.BizTalk.Component.Interop;
```

13. Now it's time to tell to the BizTalk engine that our component is a general custom pipeline component. You do that by adding the `ComponentCategory` attribute and setting it to `CATID_PipelineComponent` so that it can be used in the Validate stage of the pipeline (it could act as a validator).

14. Type the following code just before the `PropertyGeneratorPipeline` class definition:

```
//the component is a pipeline
[ComponentCategory(CategoryTypes.CATID_PipelineComponent)]
//the component is a general component
[ComponentCategory(CategoryTypes.CATID_Any)]
//it can be used in the validate stage at the pipeline component.
[ComponentCategory(CategoryTypes.CATID_Validate)]
```

15. Navigate to the `PropertyGeneratorPipeline` class definition and insert the following private variable declarations:

```
public class PropertyGeneratorPipeline
    {
        private string customPromotedPropertyName = null;
        private string customPromotedPropertyNameSpace = null;
        private string customPromotedPropertyValue = null;
```

You use these variables to save the local properties defined in the pipeline user interface.

Namespaces Warning!   As with every .NET application, custom pipeline components elements (methods, properties, interfaces, and so on) are accessible through namespaces. It is very important that you set up the namespaces properly. If you do not, you cannot add the pipeline component to Visual Studio toolbox and you will get the following error:

```
"You have selected an invalid pipeline component assembly.
Please check security settings for the assembly if you are
loading it from an UNC path"
```

To prevent this issue, you must check that your class namespace specification is the same as the project nameSpace.

In this scenario, the class namespace is:

```
namespace Microsoft.BizTalk.Pipelines.CustomComponent.
PropertyGeneratorPipeline
{
```

Go to the project settings and verify that the default namespace property is identical.

Adding a Resource File

You use resources to save the literal strings you use in the pipeline user interface and to store pipeline properties (such as Namespace, Name, and Value). See Figure 6-15.

Figure 6-15. *Examining the custom pipeline properties*

Follow these steps:

1. In Visual Studio, right-click at the project level, choose Select New Item, Navigate to the Visual C# Items, and go to the General section. Select Resource File and type the following name: PropertyGeneratorResourceFile.rex

2. Add the following string resources:

   a. Containers for user settings:

   - customPromotedPropertyNameProp

   - customPromotedPropertyNameSpaceProp

   - CustomPromotedPropertyValueProp

Leave the three of them with empty values, as they will be filled in later by the user using the pipeline user interface.

    b.   Containers to show the caption that the pipeline interface shows:

- `customPromotedPropertyNameSpaceText`. Value: Custom namespace

- `customPromotedPropertyNameText`. Value: Name of the property to promote

- `customPromotedPropertyValueText`. Value: Value of the promoted Property

3.   Now you are going to create the icon that will be shown in the Visual Studio toolbox. Click the Add Resource menu, go to New Image, and select BMP Image, as shown in Figure 6-16.

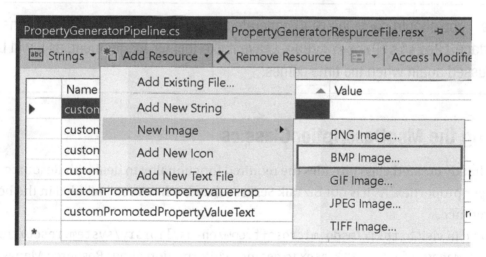

Figure 6-16. *Adding a new image to a resource file*

The Image designer tool will now load. Create your own icon; be creative!

4. Go back to the `PropertyGeneratorPipeline` class and below the local variables declarations, add a resource manager object to access the pipeline design properties:

```
private string customPromotedPropertyName = null;
private string customPromotedPropertyNameSpace = null;
private string customPromotedPropertyValue = null;

static ResourceManager resManager = new
ResourceManager("Microsoft.BizTalk.Pipelines.CustomComponent.
PropertyGeneratorPipeline", Assembly.GetExecutingAssembly());
[System.Runtime.InteropServices.Guid("48BEC85A-20EE-40ad-
BFD0-319B59A0DDBC")]
```

Note   You should paste the GUID generated in the `GetClassID` method of the Interface `IPersistPropertyBag`. Leave it like this for the moment, as it will be discussed again when the time comes.

Adding the MsgDescriptionClass.cs

This already created class provides the required functionality to deal with Resource Manager properties. As it is not BizTalk Server related, it has been included in the book for reference.

You can visit `https://msdn.microsoft.com/en-us/library/system.resources.` `resourcemanager(v=vs.110).aspx` to get more Information about Resource Manager implementations.

1. Right-click the Visual Studio Project and choose Add Exiting Item. Navigate to Module 6 source code folder and locate the class file called `MsgDescription.cs`.

2. Choose Save All.

Implementing the custom Interface BaseCustomTypeDescriptor

The `MsgDescriptionClass.cs` class defines a custom interface called
`BaseCustomTypeDescriptor`. It contains all the logic to access the Resource Manager
Information and retrieve and set properties in the resource file. In this section, you
enable this implementation in the `PropertyGeneratorPipeline` class so that the custom
pipeline component can access the user interface properties.

1. Add the implement `BaseCustomTypeDescriptor` to the the
    `PropertyGeneratorPipeline` class:

    ```
    public class PropertyGeneratorPipeline : BaseCustomTypeDescriptor
    ```

2. Select the `BaseCustomTypeDescriptor` statement and auto-
    generate the constructor by selecting the Implement Interface
    Code Generator.

    Notice that Visual Studio will generate all the implementation
    code for us. It is recommended that you use regions, so the code
    will be clearer later. Change the constructor and adapt it to the
    following, assigning the already created `resManager` object:

    ```
    public PropertyGeneratorPipeline() : base(resManager)
        {
        }
    ```

    Let's define now all the properties that will help us to interact with
    the user defined properties in the pipeline:

3. Add the implementation for the `PropertyName` property.

    ```
    [MsgPropertyName("customPromotedPropertyNameProp"),
     MsgDescription("customPromotedPropertyNamePropText")]
        public string PropertyName
    {
        get { return customPromotedPropertyName; }
        set { customPromotedPropertyName = value; }
    }
    ```

4. Add the implementation for the NameSpace property.

```
[
MsgPropertyName("customPromotedPropertyNameSpaceProp"),
MsgDescription("customPromotedPropertyNameSpaceText")
]
    public string NameSpace
    {
        get { return customPromotedPropertyNameSpace; }
        set { customPromotedPropertyNameSpace = value; }
    }
```

5. Add the implementation for the PropertyValue property.

```
[   MsgPropertyName("customPromotedPropertyValueProp"),
    MsgDescription("customPromotedPropertyValueText ")
    ]
        public string PropertyValue
        {
            get { return customPromotedPropertyValue; }
            set { customPromotedPropertyValue = value; }
        }
```

Implementing the IBaseComponent Interface

The IBaseComponent interface provides standard information to the BizTalk Engine and to the designer like Description, Name, and Version. It is shared across the three types of components (general, assembling, and disassembling).

Follow these steps:

1. Add the implement IBaseComponent to the class
    PropertyGeneratorPipeline:

    ```
    public class PropertyGeneratorPipeline : IBaseComponent
    ```

2. Select the IBaseComponent statement and auto-generate the implementation by selecting the Implement Interface Code Generator. See Figure 6-17.

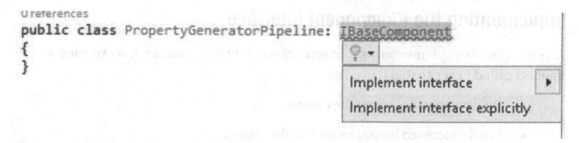

```
0 references
public class PropertyGeneratorPipeline: IBaseComponent
{
}
```

Implement interface

Implement interface explicitly

Figure 6-17. *Implementing the interface declaration*

3. Notice that Visual Studio will generate all the implementation code for us. In this case, we will be using a region called #region IBaseComponent.

Let's write the code to implement all the interface properties.

4. Navigate to the property Name and type the following code:

```
get { return "Property Generator Component"; }
```

This property will be used to show the name of the component in the Visual Studio toolbox.

5. Navigate to the Description property and type the following code:

```
get { return "This pipeline will insert a custom promoted property"; }
```

This property will be used to show the description of the component in the Visual Studio toolbox.

6. Navigate to the Version property and type the following code

```
get { return "0.99"; }
```

This property will be used to show the version of the component in the Visual Studio toolbox.

7. Choose Save All.

Implementing the IComponent Interface

This interface is implemented only in general pipeline components. It is exposing a method called Execute that is used to:

- Receive messages from the engine

- Send processed messages back to the engine

Follow these steps:

1. Add the Microsoft.BizTalk.Component.Interop.IComponent interface. We need the full BizTalk Server namespace notation here because if not, Visual Studio will interpret we are trying to use the System.ComponentModel.IComponent interface and not the one provided by BizTalk Server.

   ```
   public class PropertyGeneratorPipeline : IBaseComponent,
   Microsoft.BizTalk.Component.Interop.IComponent
       {
   ```

2. As you did for the IBaseComponent interface, auto-generate the implementation. Notice that Visual Studio will generate all the implementation code for us. It is recommended that you use regions, so the code will be clearer later. In this case, we will be using a region called #region IComponent.

3. Navigate to the method InitNew and delete all the generated code inside the method.

   ```
   public void InitNew()
           {
           }
   ```

Note   If you do not delete the code, the pipeline properties will not be populated because, by default, the code is throwing an exception.

---

4. Navigate to the Execute method and type the following code:

```
try
{
        IBaseMessageContext msgContext = pInMsg.Context;
        msgContext.Write(customPromotedProperty
        Name, customPromotedPropertyNameSpace,
        customPromotedPropertyValue);

        msgContext.Promote(customPromotedPropert
        yName, customPromotedPropertyNameSpace,
        customPromotedPropertyValue);
}
catch (Exception ex)
{
    if (pInMsg != null)
    {
        pInMsg.SetErrorInfo(ex);
    }
    throw ex;
}

        return pInMsg;
```

The Execute method will be called by the BizTalk Engine to get the full incoming message and publish it later to the Message Box database. As we want to write a new promoted property to the context, we have first to get the context itself. The object IBaseMessageContext has two methods to interact with the message context:

- Write—Used to write properties into the context.

- Promote—Used to promote a property into the context. Basically it is changing the type from non-promoted to promoted.

Both methods are expecting the following parameters:

- NameSpace—Namespace in which the property will be written to the context (customPromotedPropertyNameSpace)

- Name—Name of the promoted property (customPromotedPropertyName)

- Value—Value of the promoted property (customPromotedPropertyValue)

    In this pipeline, these properties are assigned by the user using the pipeline user interface.

5. Choose Save All.

Implementing the IPersistPropertyBag Interface

This interface is used to store custom settings for the pipeline. Developers use them to regulate how a pipeline processes documents. It is exposes two methods:

- Read, which reads a custom setting.

- Write, which saves a custom setting.

Follow these steps:

1. Add the Microsoft.BizTalk.Component.Interop. IPersistPropertyBag interface. We need the full BizTalk Server namespace notation here because if not, Visual Studio will interpret we are trying to use the System.ComponentModel. IPersistPropertyBag interface.

    ```
    public class PropertyGeneratorPipeline : IBaseComponent,
        Microsoft.BizTalk.Component.Interop.IComponent,
        Microsoft.BizTalk.Component.Interop.IPersistPropertyBag
    ```

2. As we did for the IBaseComponent Interface, auto-generate the implementation. Notice that Visual Studio will generate all the implementation code for us. It is recommended that you use regions, so the code will be clearer later. In this case, we will be using a region called #region IPersistPropertyBag.

3. We need no to create two methods for writing and reading values from the properties assigned to the pipeline (in the user interface).

4. Create a new static method in the region IPersistPropertyBag called ReadPropertyBag and type the following code:

```
private static object ReadPropertyBag(Microsoft.BizTalk.Component.
Interop.IPropertyBag pb, string propName)
        {
            object val = null;
            try
            {
                pb.Read(propName, out val, 0);
            }
            catch (ArgumentException)
            {
                return val;
            }
            catch (Exception ex)
            {
                throw new ApplicationException(ex.Message);
            }
            return val;
        }
```

5. Create a new static method in the region IPersistPropertyBag
   called WritePropertyBag and type the following code:

```
private static void WritePropertyBag(Microsoft.BizTalk.Component.
Interop.IPropertyBag pb, string propName, object val)
        {
            try
            {
                pb.Write(propName, ref val);
            }
            catch (Exception ex)
            {
                throw new ApplicationException(ex.Message);
            }
        }
```

6. Navigate to the GetClassID method and type the following code:

```
classID = new System.Guid("48BEC85A-20EE-40ad-BFD0-319B59A0DDBC");
```

Generate a new GUID with the Visual Studio and paste it there. This GUID will be referenced at the beginning of the class definition.

The method GetClassID will return the class ID of the component for usage from unmanaged code.

7. Navigate to the Load method and type the following code:

```
string val = (string)ReadPropertyBag(propertyBag, "NameSpace");
if (val != null) NameSpace = val;

val = (string)ReadPropertyBag(propertyBag, "PropertyName");
if (val != null) PropertyName = val;

val = (string)ReadPropertyBag(propertyBag, "PropertyValue");
if (val != null) PropertyValue = val;
```

This method reads all property bags from the store. The BizTalk Engine will call the Load method in two phases:

- When the pipeline initializes

- When the pipeline reads the data from a specific pipeline instance

8. Navigate to the Save method and type the following code:

```
object val = (object)customPromotedPropertyNameSpace;
WritePropertyBag(propertyBag, "NameSpace", val);

val = (object)customPromotedPropertyName;
WritePropertyBag(propertyBag, "PropertyName", val);

val = (object)customPromotedPropertyNameSpace;
WritePropertyBag(propertyBag, "PropertyValue", val);
```

This method writes all values to the property bag's store. The administration console will invoke the Save method when the user changes the values in the pipeline user interface.

Implementing the IComponentUI Interface

This interface is used to display the icon in the Visual Studio toolbox and to validate configuration properties.

Follow these steps:

1. Add the IComponentUI Interface.

    ```
    public class PropertyGeneratorPipeline : IBaseComponent,
        Microsoft.BizTalk.Component.Interop.IComponent,
        Microsoft.BizTalk.Component.Interop.IPersistPropertyBag,
        IComponentUI
    ```

2. As we did for the IBaseComponent Interface, auto-generate the implementation. Notice that Visual Studio will generate all the implementation code for us. It is recommended that you use regions, so the code will be clearer later. In this case, we will be using a region called #region IComponentUI.

3. Navigate to the Validate method and type the following code:

    ```
    IEnumerator enumerator = null;
    ArrayList strList = new ArrayList();

    if ((customPromotedPropertyNameSpace != null) &&
    (customPromotedPropertyNameSpace.Length >= 256))
    {
        strList.Add("Invalid Name Space");
    }

    if ((customPromotedPropertyName != null) &&
    (customPromotedPropertyName.Length >= 100))
    {
        strList.Add("Invalid property Name");
    }

      if ((customPromotedPropertyValue != null) &&
      (customPromotedPropertyValue.Length >= 256))
      {
    ```

```
        strList.Add("Invalid property value");
    }
    if (strList.Count > 0)
    {
        enumerator = strList.GetEnumerator();
    }

    return enumerator;
```

This method will validate that the pipeline properties are not null and have the appropriate size. If not, the user will get validation messages.

Installing the Custom Pipeline Component

1. Deploy the assembly into the global assembly cache. Use the Gacutil /I tool or any other preferred method.

2. Copy the output assembly to the BizTalk Server pipelines folder, located by default in:

   ```
   C:\Program Files (x86)\Microsoft BizTalk Server 2016\
   Pipeline Components
   ```

   BizTalk Server uses this folder to load all the pipeline components.

3. Using Visual Studio, right-click over the toolbox and select the Choose Items option. Visual studio will show the component loader tool.

4. Select BizTalk Pipeline Components tab and click on the Browse button, as shown in Figure 6-18.

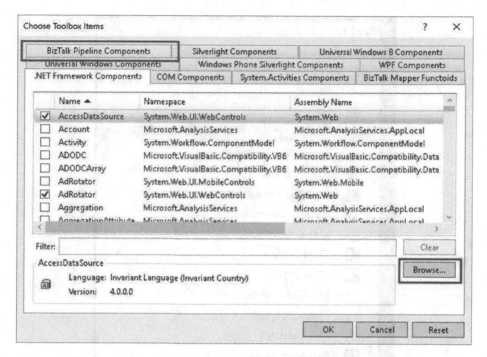

Figure 6-18. *Adding the custom pipeline component to the toolbox*

5. Navigate to `C:\Program Files (x86)\Microsoft BizTalk Server 2016\Pipeline Components` and select the `PropertyGeneratorPipeline.dll` file.

If everything went well, you should see now your brand new pipeline component available in the toolbox when designing new pipelines. See Figure 6-19.

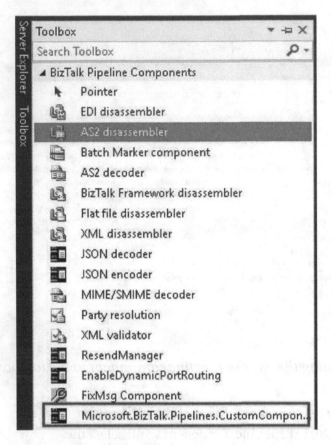

Figure 6-19. *Adding the custom pipeline component to the toolbox*

Creating the Test Routing Application

Follow these steps to create a test routing application:

1. Using Visual Studio, create a new BizTalk Server project and call it
    CustomPipelineTesting.

2. Add to the project a new receive pipeline.

3. Visual Studio will open the Pipeline Designer, as shown in
    Figure 6-20.

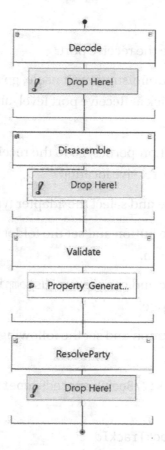

Figure 6-20.   Examining the pipeline designer

4. Now, using the toolbox, drag and drop the new custom pipeline
    component into the validate stage of the pipeline and choose Save All.

5. Add a new Schema file and call it TestSchema.xsd.

6. Rename the main root name Book.

7. Add the following two field elements:

    - ISBN

    - Title

8. Choose Save All.

9. Sign the assembly using the Project properties.

10. Deploy the solution.

11. Ignore all warnings.

12. It is time now to create the receive port.

13. Open to the BizTalk Administration Console, go to BizTalk Application 1, right-click at Receive port level, and select add new One-way Receive Port.

14. Under the receive port properties, go to the receive locations section and add a new receive location.

15. Type the desired name and select the adapter type to FILE.

16. Click on the Configure button and set the folder you want BizTalk to receive messages from.

17. Go to Receive pipeline and choose our `custompipelineTesting` pipeline from the dropbox.

18. Click on the ellipsis button and set the following values for the custom properties:

    - NameSpace: `https://BookPromotedProperties. PropertySchema`

    - PropertyName: `BookTrackId`

    - PropertyValue: `1234`

    - It should look similar to Figure 6-21.

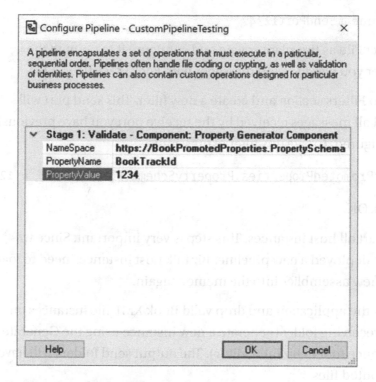

Figure 6-21. Examining the pipeline properties

19. Now we will create Send ports. Using the BizTalk Administration Console, go to the Send ports section of BizTalk Server Application 1.

20. Create a new static one-way send port.

21. Rename it SendPortALL.

22. Select File as the adapter type and configure it to point to the folder you want to Send All messages.

23. Go to the Filters section and create a new filter. This send port will send all messages received by the receive port you have previously configured. Create this filter expression:

    BTS.ReceivePortName = ReceivePort1 (Go to step 19 and verify the port name)

24. Click OK.

25. Create a new static one-way send port.

26.   Rename it `SendPort1234`.

27.   Select File as the adapter type and configure it to point to the folder you want to send messages with `BookTrackID = 1234`.

28.   Go to Filters section and create a new filter. This send port will send all messages received by the receive port you have previously configured. Create this filter expression:

`BookPromotedProperties.PropertySchema.BookTrackId  = 1234`

29.   Click OK.

30.   Restart all host instances. This step is very important. Since we have deployed a new pipeline, BizTalk host instances need to load the new assemblies into the memory again.

31.   Start the application and drop valid Book XML file instances on the receiving folder (generate a new instance using the Generate Instance tool in BizTalk Editor). The output send folders will have all routed files.

Summary

In this chapter you learned how to improve your BizTalk Server solutions from the basic building blocks of the schemas to maps, orchestrations, and pipelines.

In general, you should develop your solutions to avoid or reduce the complexity of the orchestrations involved. This is when the use of custom pipeline components can boost your solution. In this scenario, pipelines can become crucial, especially for applications that rank higher in the application priority levels.

In the next chapter, you learn two techniques that will enable you to reduce application downtime.

CHAPTER 7

Decreasing Downtime

In the previous chapter, you have learned how to develop solutions to improve schemas definitions, orchestrations, and pipelines.

Another important factor of developing robust BizTalk Server solutions is to reduce application downtime. If the application has a high availability level (HAL) of 9, high availability is required. You will have to think of a strategy to provide high availability with zero downtime (especially for long-running processes that cannot be stopped).

This chapter covers two techniques that help you reduce the downtime of BizTalk Server applications:

- Side-by-side versioning

- Business rules

Although security is not a performance requirement, you will also learn how to secure data using the Enterprise Single Sing-On database to protect application configuration settings in a secured store.

Side-by-Side Versioning

Most BizTalk Server applications provide functionality to mission-critical solutions that must run 24x7 with no downtime. The complexity of these applications is usually tremendous, as they interact with lots of different components and could potentially be involved in long-running processes, that can remain active for days, months, or even years. As you can guess, the deployment process of such applications becomes a very delicate task, since you cannot stop them while they are processing instances.

Frequently, BizTalk developers and administrators deploy applications using the BizTalk Administration Console or PowerShell scripts. If new installation binary files include changes to orchestrations that are already running and processing instances, the BizTalk administration console will not update the orchestration until the person

© Agustín Mántaras 2019
A. Mántaras, *BizTalk Server 2016*, https://doi.org/10.1007/978-1-4842-3994-0_7

performing the change terminates/suspends active instances. The same will happen to pipelines and schemas. Because of this, it is very important to develop a robust deployment procedure.

How Can You Solve this Problem?

There is a technique in .NET Framework called side-by-side versioning and it applies to any kind of .NET assembly. Luckily for us, all BizTalk Server Solutions create .NET assemblies, which means BizTalk Server is fully compatible with this technique, at the application level only.

Side-by-side execution is the ability to run multiple versions of an application on the same computer. You can have multiple versions of the CLR, and multiple versions of applications that use a specific version of the runtime, all on the same computer at the same time. See Figure 7-1.

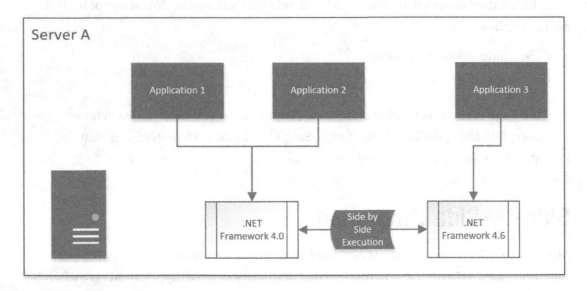

Figure 7-1. *CLR side-by-side execution diagram*

The .NET Framework extensively uses this feature to allow a server to run different versions of the CLR engine. In most scenarios today, servers can run different .NET Framework versions, such as 2.0, 3.5, 4.0, and 4.6x, and consumer applications decide which engine the version will use by pointing to the right Global Assembly Cache store.

Note BizTalk Server 2016 does not support side-by-side execution at the CLR Engine level, as Microsoft has tested the product in 4.6x versions of the .NET Framework only.

Component Version Side-by-Side Execution

This is the when BizTalk Server uses its full potential. Since the BizTalk Server leverages the .NET Framework to execute applications at runtime, it uses assemblies to encapsulate all BizTalk artifacts. Therefore, you could have different assembly versions where orchestrations, pipelines, custom code, and whatever you want to include, also have different versions.

In the diagram shown in Figure 7-2, Application 1 is using component Version 1 only. Applications 2 and 3 are using the same component but with Version 2. That will allow BizTalk Server to simultaneously run different artifact versions within the same BizTalk Server application. The idea is that you will be adding new functionalities to the new version, while the old version will be still up and running and processing old version flows.

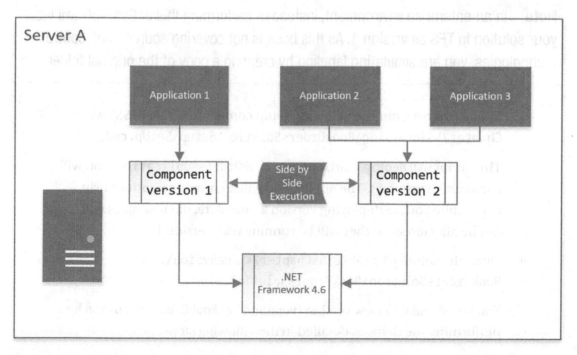

Figure 7-2. *Component side-by-side execution diagram*

And there is more! By applying versioning to your BizTalk solutions, you can deploy side-by-side without having to stop the old version. Therefore, old subscribers will be still processing instances. It is recommended though that you create a new host for all the new deployments because you will not have to restart the old host instances. As soon as the old systems are no longer using the old version, you can un-deploy the previous version of the orchestration.

Applying Side-by-Side Versioning to a BizTalk Server Project

In this section you learn how to apply side-by-side versioning to the book orders solution.

Follow these steps:

1. Open File Explorer and go to `C:\APRESS\Chapter7\SideBySide\`.

2. Copy and paste the `BookOrdersSolution` to folder the same location and rename it to `BookOrdersSolutionVersion1`.

Note   In an enterprise environment, instead of performing this action, you will label your solution in TFS as version 1. As this book is not covering source code control technologies, you are simulating labeling by creating a copy of the original folder.

---

3. In File Explorer, run the following setup command: `C:\APRESS\Chapter7\SideBySide\BookOrdersSolution\Setup\SetUp.cmd`.

    This script will deploy, start, and test `BookOrdersApplication` (you will consider it version 1). The application will be running continuously, even while you are deploying version 2; therefore, old instances will not be affected since they will be running with version 1.

4. Open the solution `C:\APRESS\Chapter7\SideBySide\BookOrdersSolution\BookOrdersSolution.sln`.

    You will simulate a new version (version 2) of `BookOrdersSolution` by performing the changes detailed in the following steps.

5. Open the schema `IncomingBookOrders.xsd` and add a new Element Field called `OrderStatus`. The idea here is that you are forcing a change in the incoming message so that original consumers can still send the old messages and new consumers will initiate the process by sending the new format of the message. See Figure 7-3.

Figure 7-3. *Examining the OrderStatus element*

6. Change the `minOccurs` and `MaxOccurs` properties of `Orderstatus` to 1. By implementing this change, this field must be present in the incoming message; otherwise, message validation at pipeline level will fail.

7. Open the schema `CRMIncomingBookOrders.xsd` and add new Element field called `CRMOrderState`. This action will wrap the `OrderStatus` into the simulated CRM application. See Figure 7-4.

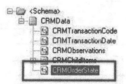

Figure 7-4. *Examining the CRMOrderState element*

8. Change the `minOccurs` and `MaxOccurs` properties to 1. Now the field is mandatory.

9. Open the map `Map_IncomingMessage_To_CRM_CongratulationMessage.btm` and create a new link button for the two new Element fields. See Figure 7-5.

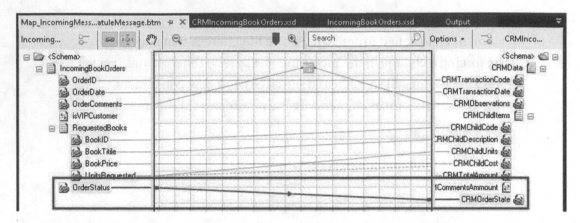

Figure 7-5. *Examining the OrderStatus map link*

10. Open the `Map_IncomingBookOrders_To_CRMFormat.btm` map and create a new link button for the two new Element fields. See Figure 7-6.

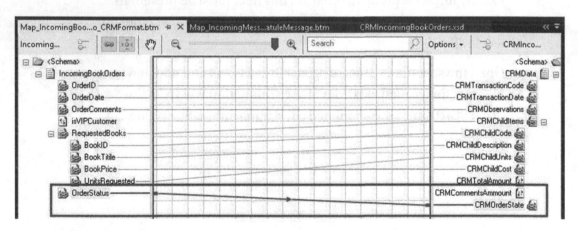

Figure 7-6. *Examining the Order status new map link*

11. Open the orchestration and, just after the script shape `SetPerfCounters`, add a new script shape and name it `WriteLog`. Add the following code:

```
System.Diagnostics.EventLog.WriteEntry("Orchestration
Version 2", "new Message Received in orchestration version 2")
```

This action will add a new log entry in the Windows Application Event log so you can later see that the orchestration version 2 is processing messages.

12. It is time to change the assembly version. Go to Project properties, select the Application tab, and click on Assembly Information button. Choose version 2 for the assembly and file versions and click OK. See Figure 7-7.

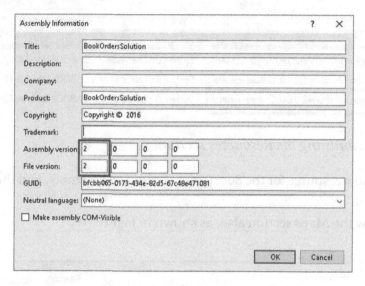

Figure 7-7. *Examining the assembly and file versions*

13. Choose Save All.

14. Build the solution.

15. Deploy the solution without stopping the old `BookOrdersSolution`.

Observing Both Versions

To understand how BizTalk Server side-by-side execution works, let's examine the differences after deploying application version 2.

Open the BizTalk Server Administration Console and refresh. As a result, you still have only one `BookOrdersApplication`. However, if you explore all the application sections you will notice some differences. Go to the Resources section and observe the changes shown in Figure 7-8.

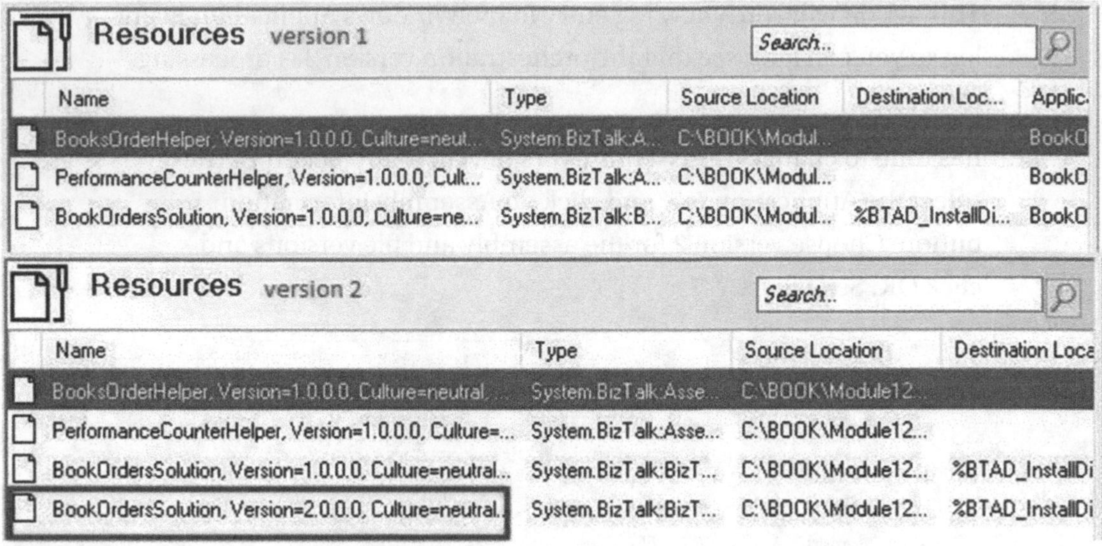

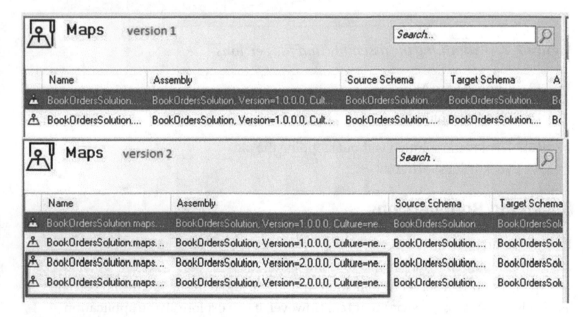

Figure 7-8. *Examining the Resources section*

There is a new resource for the BookOrdersSolution assembly, and the version is 2.0.0.0.

Explore now the Maps section also, as shown in Figure 7-9.

Figure 7-9. *Examining the maps section*

You can see now version 1.0.0.0 and 2.0.0.0 in the same application. Explore the schemas section, as shown in Figure 7-10.

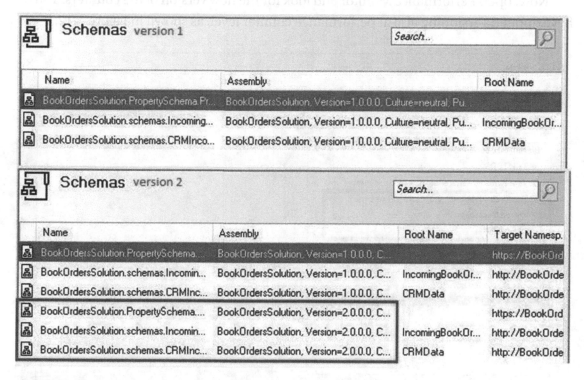

Figure 7-10. *Examining the Schemas section*

The Property schema and the two business schemas have a new version deployed. Next, explore the Orchestrations section, as shown in Figure 7-11.

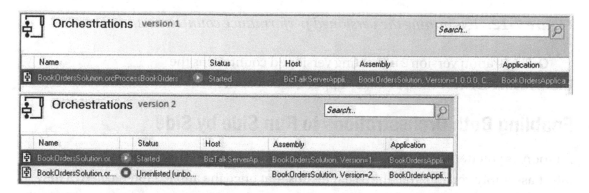

Figure 7-11. *Examining the Orchestrations section*

There is a new version of the orchestration. Notice that the version 1 is still up and running. That means that existing running instances will not be affected by the changes.

Now, open Performance Monitor and look for the new version of the counters. You have applied versioning also at performance counter level, as shown in Figure 7-12.

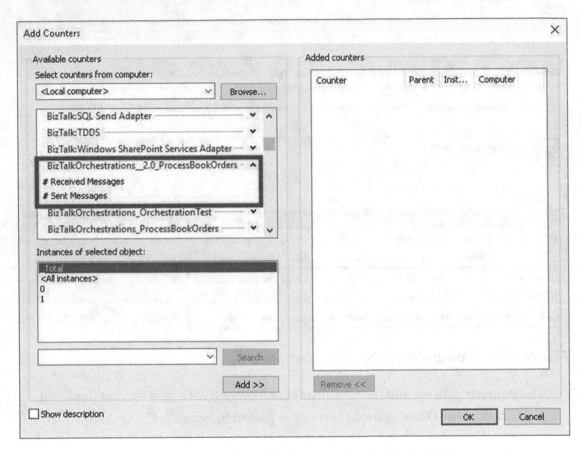

Figure 7-12. *Examining the versioned performance counters section*

Orchestration version 2 is creating versioned counters, as the PerformanceCountersHelper class supports that feature.

Enabling Both Orchestrations to Run Side by Side

As soon as you deploy the new version, like business rules, BizTalk Server will invoke the latest assembly version available. That means that once the application receives a new transaction, the BizTalk Server engine will parse the message as version 2.0.0.0. This will be a problem for the old orchestration, as it is linked to use version 1 of the assembly.

At first glance, this behavior might look wrong, but it makes all the sense of the world, as the idea is that new instances will be redirected to the new version only. If you need the old version to work with new instances, you must adjust the documentSpecNames property of the receiving pipeline.

Follow these steps to change the documentSpecNames property. First, set the DocumentSpecNames property of the receiving pipeline to the old schema version. Then, to generate a valid documentSpecNames property, do the following:

1. Using the BizTalk Administration console, go to the application schema section and locate the assembly containing version 1. See Figure 7-13.

Schemas					Search..
Name		Assembly	Root Name	Target Namespace	Schema Type
BookOrdersSolution.PropertySchema...		BookOrdersSolution, Version=1.0.0.0, Culture=neutral, PublicKeyToken=e82b5e911d58f5b		http://BookOrdersSolution.Property...	Property
BookOrdersSolution.schemas.Incom...		BookOrdersSolution, Version=1.0.0.0, Culture=neutral, PublicKeyToken=e82b5e911d58f5b	IncomingBookOrders	http://BookOrdersSolution.Incoming	Document
BookOrdersSolution.schemas.CRMIn...		BookOrdersSolution, Version=1.0.0.0, Culture=neutral, PublicKeyToken=e82b5e911d58f5b	CRMData	http://BookOrdersSolution.CRMInco...	Document
BookOrdersSolution.PropertySchema...		BookOrdersSolution, Version=2.0.0.0, Culture=neutral, PublicKeyToken=e82b5e911d58f5b		http://BookOrdersSolution.Property...	Property
BookOrdersSolution.schemas.Incomi...		BookOrdersSolution, Version=2.0.0.0, Culture=neutral, PublicKeyToken=e82b5e911d58f5b	IncomingBookOrders	http://BookOrdersSolution.Incoming...	Document
BookOrdersSolution.schemas.CRMIn...		BookOrdersSolution, Version=2.0.0.0, Culture=neutral, PublicKeyToken=e82b5e911d58f5b	CRMData	http://BookOrdersSolution.CRMInco...	Document

Figure 7-13. *Locating the assembly with the older version*

2. Right-click the schema and choose Properties.

3. Copy the content of name and assembly information into a notepad, as shown in Figure 7-14.

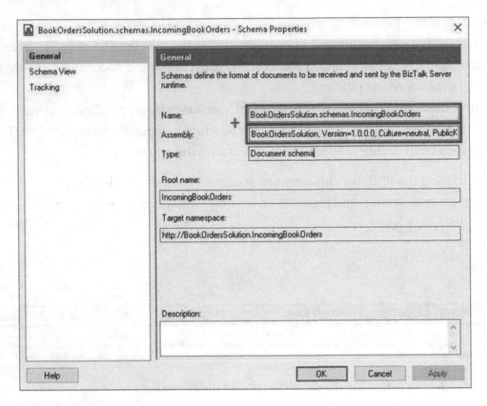

Figure 7-14. *Obtaining the schema and assembly names*

4. Concatenate both values into one, separated by a coma, like this:

   BookOrdersSolution.schemas.IncomingBookOrders,BookOrders
   Solution, Version=1.0.0.0, Culture=neutral, PublicKey
   Token=e82fb5e911d58f5b

5. Using the BizTalkAdministration console, go to
   BookOrdersApplication, locate the receive location
   rlBookOrdersApp, and access the properties.

6. Go to the receive pipeline section and click on the ellipsis button.

7. Set the DocumentSpecNames property to the content you created
   using Notepad (see Figure 7-15):

   BookOrdersSolution.schemas.IncomingBookOrders,BookOrders
   Solution, Version=1.0.0.0, Culture=neutral, PublicKeyTok
   en=e82fb5e911d58f5b

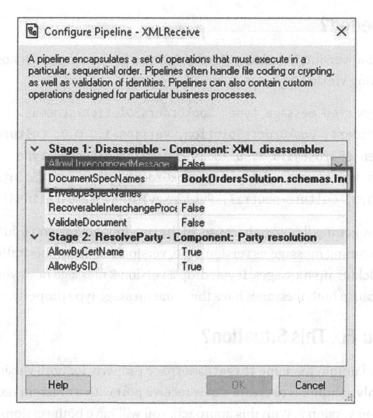

Figure 7-15. *Setting the DocumentSpecNames property*

8. Click OK.

Note   If the OK button is not enabled, change the cursor to any other property and the button will be enabled again.

---

9. Test the solution, now dropping a file for version 1. To do it,
    run this BAT file: C:\APRESS\Chapter7\BookOrdersSolution\
    BookOrdersSolution\Ports\Send1VIPBookOrder.bat

What Happened?

The orchestration version 1 worked perfectly, but you get an error in version 2 saying that it is expecting version 2:

```
Received unexpected message type 'BookOrdersSolution.schemas.
IncomingBookOrders, BookOrdersSolution, Version=1.0.0.0, Culture=neutral,
PublicKeyToken=e82fb5e911d58f5b' does not match expected type
'BookOrdersSolution.schemas.IncomingBookOrders, BookOrdersSolution,
Version=2.0.0.0, Culture=neutral, PublicKeyToken=e82fb5e911d58f5b'.
```

You are now getting this error because, in the previous action, you told BizTalk Server to parse the incoming message as version 1. So, version 1 of the orchestration can still be running and picking up messages. If you drop a version 2 message now, you will get the same error because both messages have the same message type property.

How Do You Fix This Situation?

If you want to maintain the same `targetnamespace` property for both versions of the schema, the only solution is to create a new receive port with a different receive location for orchestration version 2. With this approach, you will have both versions running in parallel. Therefore, you will need to inform your source systems that the old version of the application will be available until a certain point of time only. After that, you will disable the original receive location and the system will only work with version 2.

Using Business Rules to Reduce Deployment

To reduce the number of deployments, you can always consider using the Business Rules Engine to separate certain business functionalities from orchestration processing. The Business Rules Engine allows policies to be changed in real time. That means that any orchestrations that consume those business rules do not need to be adjusted when the business policy changes. Developers will change business rules by creating new versions, and orchestrations, by default, will consume the latest version available without the need to redeploy the application again.

Developers can create business rules using a tool called the Business Rules Composer (or using Business Rule APIs). Once published, the policy cannot be modified directly. To perform a change, a new version of the policy must be created.

Once deployed, the policy can be called from a BizTalk orchestration and all the policy evaluations will take place.

Business rules are put together into a single *policy definition*. That means that a policy can have one or more rules. A rule is composed of a condition and an action. Conditions are evaluated, and if they return true, a collection of actions are considered for later execution.

Note   Keep in mind that in business rules there is no `else` option available. Therefore, if you want to also perform an action when the condition is not met, you have to add a new rule and create a new condition that encapsulates the else situation.

Actions are not executed immediately after the condition is evaluated. Instead, the Business Rules Engine will add that action to a temporary agenda and, when all rules are evaluated, all actions within the agenda are executed based on priority.

Important   Priority is designed to sort the actions by priority, not by the condition.

The source of information for a business rule is called a *fact* and developers define them into vocabulary definitions. Using the Business Rules Composer, you can create the following types of facts:

- A constant value, a range of values, or a set of values

- A .NET class or class member

- An XML document element or attribute

- A database table or column

Policy Execution Steps

The Business Rules Engine follows these steps to execute a policy.

1. All facts are obtained.

2. All rules are evaluated.

3. Actions of the rules that evaluate to true are added to the list of actions to execute.

4. Actions are executed in descending order by priority. That means that the higher-priority actions are executed first.

5. Facts are disposed.

Note   If an action changes a fact that is used as a condition of a rule, the rule will be evaluated again.

Business Rules Performance Recommendations

There are several recommendations and best practices that you should be aware of to implement business rules successfully.

Fact Types

The Business Rules Engine uses more resources to access XML and database facts. Therefore, whenever possible, use .NET facts to improve performance.

Database Types

To access a data from a database, developers usually create database facts within a vocabulary by adding a new database definition to it.

You can follow these steps to create a fact that accesses database information:

1. Using the Facts Explorer, select the Add New Definition option, as shown in Figure 7-16.

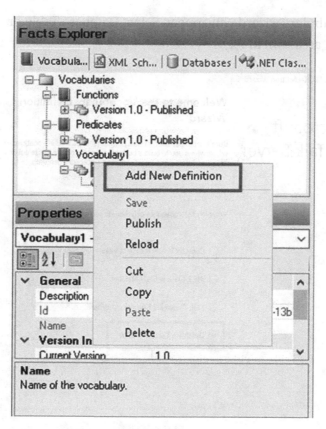

Figure 7-16. Adding a new vocabulary definition

2. The Vocabulary wizard will appear. Select Database Table or Column, as shown in Figure 7-17.

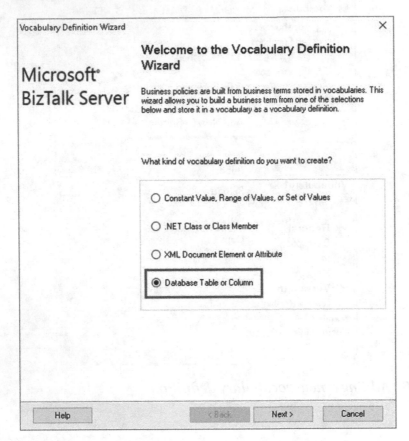

Figure 7-17. *Adding database vocabulary definitions*

3. The wizard will now show the data Binding Type options, as shown in Figure 7-18.

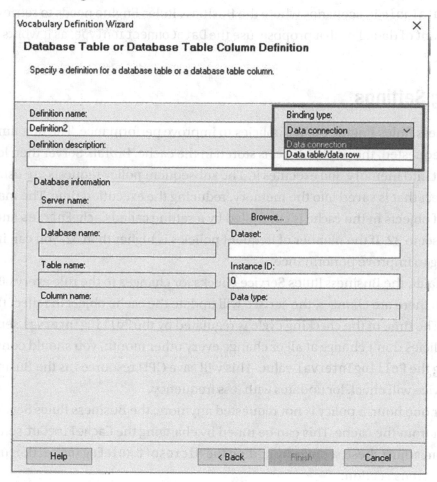

Figure 7-18. Setting the binding type

4. To access a database to retrieve data, the Business Rules Engine provides the following database types:

- DataConnection—Represents a table in a database accessed through a database connection.

- TypedDataRow—This type is based on the ADO.NET DataRow object.

- TypedDataTable—Represents a collection of TypedDataRow objects.

The `TypedDataTable` type loads all data into the memory of the server, which can cause a memory problem if the polled data is large. Therefore, you should avoid the use of `TypedDataTable` in scenarios where the Business Rules Engine needs to retrieve a large amount of data. For that propose, use the `DataConnectionType`, as it works more efficiently.

Caching Settings

The Business Rules Engine caches policies to improve performance. The first time a policy is requested, the policy object is stored in the cache. BizTalk Server then loads that object into memory and executes it. The subsequent policy requests are using the cache object that is saved into the memory, reducing the execution time. The maximum number of objects in the cache is controlled by a setting called `CacheEntries` and by default is set to 32. If the number of frequent policies is higher than 32, you can increase this setting to improve performance.

By default, the Business Rules Service checks for changes to the rule every 60 seconds. If there are changes, the service will update the cache object to reflect the changes. The time of the checking cycle is regulated by the `PollingInterval` setting. If your policies don't change at all or change every other month, you should consider increasing the `PollingInterval` value. This will save CPU resources as the Business Rules Service will check for updates with less frequency.

If after one hour, a policy is not requested anymore, the Business Rules Service removes it from the cache. This can be tuned by changing the `CacheTimeOut` setting.

You can adjust these settings by adding the `Microsoft.RuleEngine` section under the `configSections` section:

```
<configuration>
    <configSections>
        <section name="Microsoft.RuleEngine" type="System.Configuration.
        SingleTagSectionHandler" />
    </configSections>
    <Microsoft.RuleEngine
        CacheEntries="120"
        CacheTimeout="1860"
        PollingInterval="30"
    />
</configuration>
```

Securing Application Configuration Settings

Enterprise applications usually have to access configuration data that, in most cases, is very sensitive. Eventually, you will need to store connection strings, user information, passwords, and settings that change the behavior of your applications like debugging modes, performance analysis, and things like that. In today's world, protecting this information in a secure storage system decreases the chances of undesired attacks. BizTalk Server relies on the Enterprise single sign-on database to store all the sensitive data related to the engine configuration, such as adapters, ports, and application-related settings. This database is already encrypted with a very strong key, and the good news is that you can use it to store applications settings.

Figure 7-19 illustrates the Enterprise single sign-on database and shows how you can use it by developing a custom .NET component that will access the store.

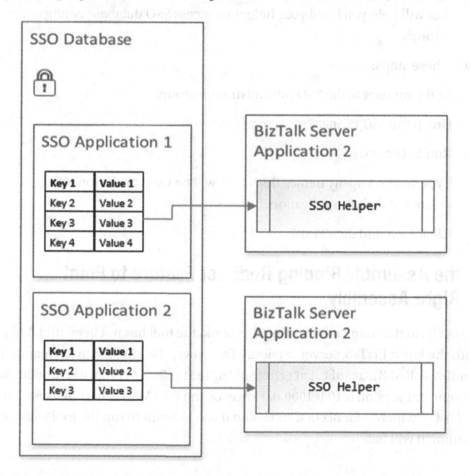

Figure 7-19. *Understanding the SSO database to store settings*

The SSO MMC Snap-In Tool

Around 2009, the BizTalk Server product group team released an SSO Configuration Application MMC snap-In that can be used to create the configuration values within the store. You can download it at `https://www.microsoft.com/en-us/download/confirmation.aspx?id=14524`.

Once you have downloaded it, you will see the following files:

- `SSOMMCSnapInSetup.zip`—Contains the installation files.

- `SSOConfigurationApplicationMSBuildImportTask`—If you want to integrate the tool with MSBuild, you could reuse the script and the DLL provided.

- `SSOConfigurationApplicationClientHelper`—It contains a C# class that will help you build your helper to access SSO database config settings.

Follow these steps:

1. Add your user to the SSO Administrators group.

2. Unzip the `SSOMMCSnapInSetup.zip` file.

3. Run `Setup.exe`.

4. Type your company name. This value will be used by the tool to create the default application.

5. Click Next and then Finish.

Using the Assembly Binding Redirect Feature to Point to the Right Assembly

Unfortunately, at the moment of writing this book, the tool has not been updated to work with the latest BizTalk Server versions. The Enterprise single sign-on feature uses the assembly called `Microsoft.EnterpriseSingleSignOn.Interop.dll`, and for BizTalk 2016, the current version is 10.0.1000.0. However, the SSO MMC Snap-in uses an old version 5.0.1.0, which is for BizTalk 2009, and if you attempt to run the tool without any modification, it will fail.

Luckily there is a .NET Framework feature called Assembly Binding Redirect. By using this option, you can redirect an assembly to a different version. You can change the MMC snap-in config file to use the latest `Microsoft.EnterpriseSingleSignOn.Interop.dll` version.

Follow these steps to do so:

1. Using the File Explorer, go to `C:\Program Files (x86)\Microsoft Services\SSO Application Configuration` and edit the `SSOMMCSnapIn.dll.config` file.

2. Under the Configuration setting, add the setting shown in Figure 7-20.

```
<configuration>
  <appSettings>
    <add key="CompanyName" value="DevelopingBizTalkSolutions" />
  </appSettings>

  <runtime>
    <assemblyBinding xmlns="urn:schemas-microsoft-com:asm.v1"
appliesTo="v4.0.30319">
      <dependentAssembly>
        <assemblyIdentity name="Microsoft.EnterpriseSingleSignOn.Interop"
publicKeyToken="31bf3856ad364e35" culture="neutral" />
        <bindingRedirect oldVersion="5.0.1.0" newVersion="10.0.1000.0"/>
      </dependentAssembly>
    </assemblyBinding>
  </runtime>

</configuration>
```

Figure 7-20. *Enabling the assembly redirect option*

3. Save the file.

Adding New Keys to the SSO Store

This section shows you how to add new keys to the SSO store. The key concept is very similar to C# hash tables, where elements are defined with a key and a value.

Follow these steps:

1. Open the SSO Application Configuration Tool, located by default here:
   `C:\Program Files (x86)\Microsoft Services\SSO Application`
   `Configuration\SSO Application Configuration.msc`.

2. Right-click at the main root level, in our case that's
   `DevelopingBizTalk2016Solutions`, and choose Add Application,
   as shown in Figure 7-21.

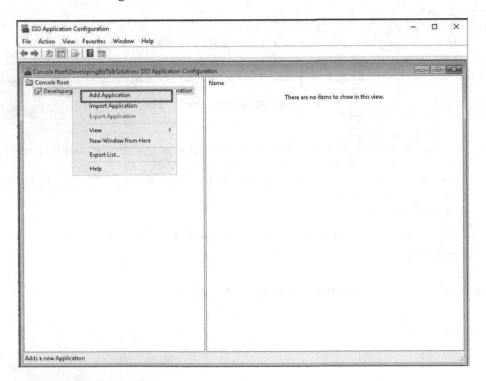

Figure 7-21. *Adding an SSO application*

3. The tool will set the default name to `newApplication`. Right-click it
   and choose Rename. Set the name to `BookOrdersApplication`.

4. Right-click at BookOrdersApplication level and select the Add
    Key Value Pair option, as shown in Figure 7-22.

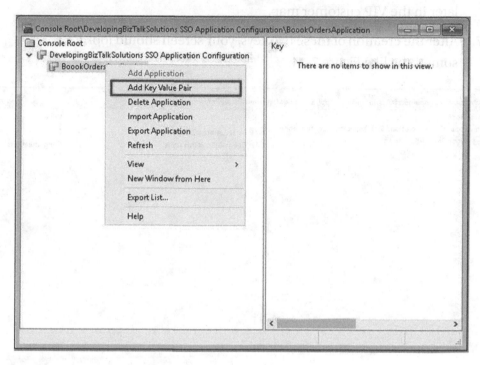

Figure 7-22. *Adding a key value pair*

5. Set the key to ForceCountersCreation and the value to 0, as
    shown in Figure 7-23. Click OK.

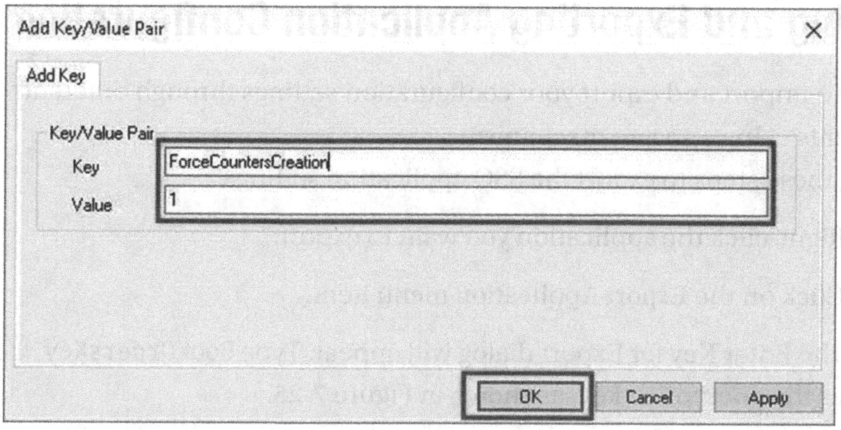

Figure 7-23. *Setting the value for the key*

6. Create a new key called `CongratulationMessage` and set the value to "Congratulations, you are a VIP Customer". You will use this later in the VIP customer map.

7. After the creation of these two keys, your screen should look something like Figure 7-24.

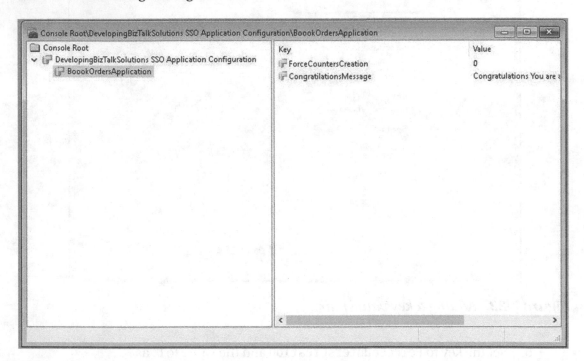

Figure 7-24. *Examining the SSO application with the related values*

Importing and Exporting Application Configuration

You can also import and export your configuration settings through different environments using a secure mechanism.

Follow these steps to export the SSO application settings:

1. Right-click the application you want to export.

2. Click on the Export Application menu item.

3. The Enter Key for Export dialog will appear. Type `BookOrdersKey` as the encryption key, as shown in Figure 7-25.

Figure 7-25. Examining the SSO application with the related values

This key is used to encrypt the configuration data that is written to the hard drive. You must use this same key when you import this application.

4. Choose a location for the export file. If you open it, you will see the encrypted data.

Follow these steps to import the SSO application settings:

1. Right-click at the root level.

2. Choose Import Application.

3. Locate the SSO file that contains the application settings you want to import.

4. Type the key used when exporting the settings (see Figure 7-26).

5. Click OK.

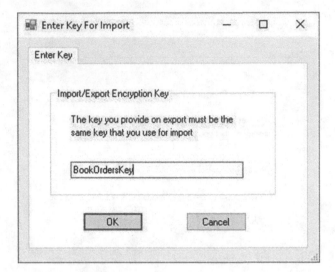

Figure 7-26. *Importing the encryption key*

Note   If that application already exists, you will see new key/pairs added to the
existing application.

Creating an SSO Helper Component

The tool comes with a C# class that you can reuse to create your own custom SSO helper
component. In this section, you learn how to incorporate this component in your BizTalk
Server solutions to access secure configuration data.

Follow these steps:

1. Open the BookOrders solution located at C:\APRESS\Chapter7\
    SSOConfigStore\BookOrdersSolution\BookOrdersSolution.sln.

2. Add a new class library Visual C# project called SSOClientHelper.

3. Using File Explorer, locate the SSOClientHelper class file that
    comes with the tool you downloaded previously.

4. Copy the class implementation from the SSOClientHelper class
    and replace it in the default class1.cs file in the new solution.

5. Rename the class1.cs file to SSOClientHelper.

6. Add the following references to the project:

   - C:\Program Files\Common Files\Enterprise Single Sign-On\Microsoft.BizTalk.Interop.SSOClient.dll

   - C:\Program Files\Common Files\Enterprise Single Sign-On\Microsoft.EnterpriseSingleSignOn.Interop.dll

7. Add the following using statements to the SSOClientHelper class file:

   ```
   using System;
   using System.Collections.Specialized;
   using Microsoft.BizTalk.SSOClient.Interop;
   ```

8. Locate the SSOClientHelper class definition, add the serializable attribute, and remove the static statement so you can use it in a BizTalk Sever map:

   ```
   Serializable]
       public class SSOClientHelper
       {
   ```

9. Sign the assembly using the project properties.

10. Choose Save All.

11. Build the project.

Using the SSO Client Helper Component to Access SSO Data

In this example, you are going change BookOrdersApplication so the map will use the SSOClientHelper component to access the BookOrders application SSO keys. This will fill the Observations Element field with the text specified by the CongratulationMessage key.

1. Open the BookOrders solution located at C:\APRESS\Chapter7\SSOConfigStore\BookOrdersSolution\BookOrdersSolution.sln.

2. Add a reference to the SSOClientHelper project created in the previous section.

3. Open the orchestration called orcProcessBookOrders.

4. Open the Map_IncomingMessage_To_CRM_CongratulationMessage.btm map.

5. Delete all the existing links and functoids related to the
    CRMObservations element field. See Figure 7-27.

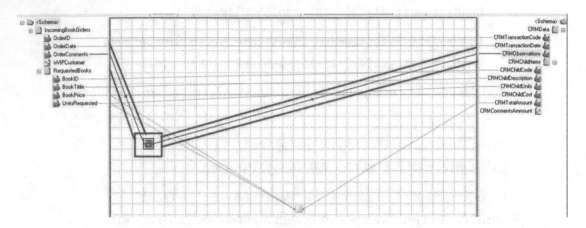

Figure 7-27. *Changing the map to retrieve the SSO configuration values*

6. Add a new scripting functoid and set up and configure it as follows.

    In the Functoid Inputs tab, add two Input parameters (see
    Figure 7-28):

    a. Input[0]: Value BookOrdersApplication

    b. Input[1]: Value CongratulationMessage

    In the Script Functoid Configuration tab, set the following values:

    a. Script Assembly: SSOClientHelper, version=1.0.0.0

    b. ScriptClass: SSOClientHelper.SSOClientHelper

    c. ScriptMethod: Read.

7. Choose Save All.

8. Choose Build All.

9. Run the command file C:\APRESS\Chapter7\SSOConfigStore\
    BookOrdersSolution\Setup\SetUp.cmd to deploy and test the
    application. If you did not go through all the previous steps, this
    CMD file will just deploy the book orders base solution, which
    does not contain SSO functionality. Additionally, if your solution
    does not compile, this CMD file will also fail.

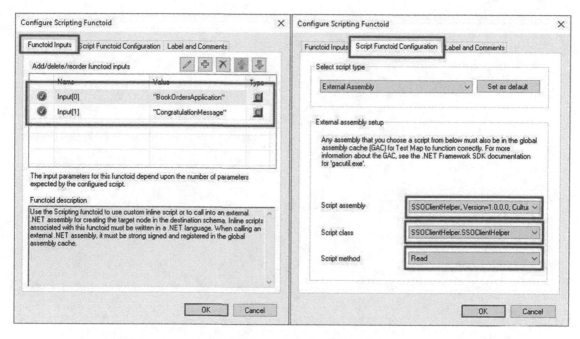

Figure 7-28. *Calling the SSO helper component in a map*

Summary

Decreasing downtime is a major issue when developing mission-critical solutions that require processing messages 24x7, 365 days a year. In this chapter, you learned how to decrease application downtime using side-by-side versioning and business rules to derive the business flow from orchestration to the rule's engine.

Even though this book does not focus on security, this topic is a recurrent requirement for the majority of BizTalk Server applications that rank higher on the application priority levels, thus I decided to include the topic about storing configuration data in the SSO database.

In the next chapter, you learn how to test your BizTalk Server solutions.

CHAPTER 8

Monitoring Using BizTalk 360

This chapter is focused on using the BizTalk 360 tool to monitor the BizTalk Server platform. Once your BizTalk solutions are deployed into the production environment, it is important that the BizTalk Server team be aware of the issues that are occurring on a daily basis to proactively increase the health of the platform. For instance, you need to be notified if a receive location or host is down.

The BizTalk experts at BizTalk 360 have identified challenges that customers have faced in the past 10+ years. BizTalk Server customers usually build custom management solutions on top of BizTalk to address all these challenges. Well, in this case, you do not have to reinvent the wheel, as BizTalk 360 extends BizTalk Server monitoring to a point where most scenarios are efficiently covered.

Understanding Monitoring in BizTalk 360

In this section, you learn which types of monitoring exist in BizTalk 360 and how they can be set up.

Different Types of Monitoring

There are several different ways to monitor using BizTalk 360 and they are discussed in this section. These possibilities are:

- *Threshold monitoring*—Used when a condition is violated, for example, a receive location that's expected to be enabled is disabled due to a temporary failure.

© Agustín Mántaras 2019
A. Mántaras, *BizTalk Server 2016*, https://doi.org/10.1007/978-1-4842-3994-0_8

- *Health Check monitoring*—Used, for example, to perform a daily check at 9AM every business day.

- *Data monitoring*—Used, for example, to set up monitoring whether specific workloads are really being processed, BAM milestones are achieved, or alarms are raised based on suspended messages.

Threshold Monitoring

When a threshold parameter is exceeded, BizTalk 360 can be configured to redirect immediate alerts. If you want to monitor only during business hours, you can tell BizTalk 360 to send alerts only during a specific time of the day. When the situation comes back to normal, you can set up the alert so that you will receive notification stating that the original condition has been solved. If the issue happens frequently, it might overload your inbox, so BizTalk 360 provides a mechanism to limit the number of notifications that will be sent.

Health Check Monitoring

It is common practice in supporting a BizTalk environment for support people to maintain daily/weekly routines to check the health of the environment. You can use BizTalk 360 to automate the daily health check process by creating a health check/status alarm that checks at specific times (for example, Mon-Fri, 7AM).

Data Monitoring

BizTalk 360 provides you with query builders that will help you access special BizTalk Server information, such as the message box database to look for suspended service instances, latency information, and active instances. If your solution is implementing the business activity-monitoring feature, you can create queries to monitor BAM activities to create specific alerts when a certain condition is met.

Setting Up an Alarm

To configure an alarm, you need to follow these steps:

- Basic settings: Provide information such as name, email recipients, and template email to use.

- Set the alarm type: The following options are available:

  - Threshold,

  - Health

  - Data Monitoring

- Alarm mappings: Define the elements to monitor in this alarm.

Configuring the Basic Settings

Follow these steps to configure the basic settings for an alarm.

1. Log in to the BizTalk 360 application as a Super User.

2. Access the Navigation panel on the left side of the screen and click the Monitoring tab.

3. Click the Manage Alarms tab.

4. In the toolbar, click New Alarm and select the alarm type from the drop-down.

   - Threshold

   - Health

   - Data Monitoring

   The Alarm - Basic section appears, as shown in Figure 8-1.

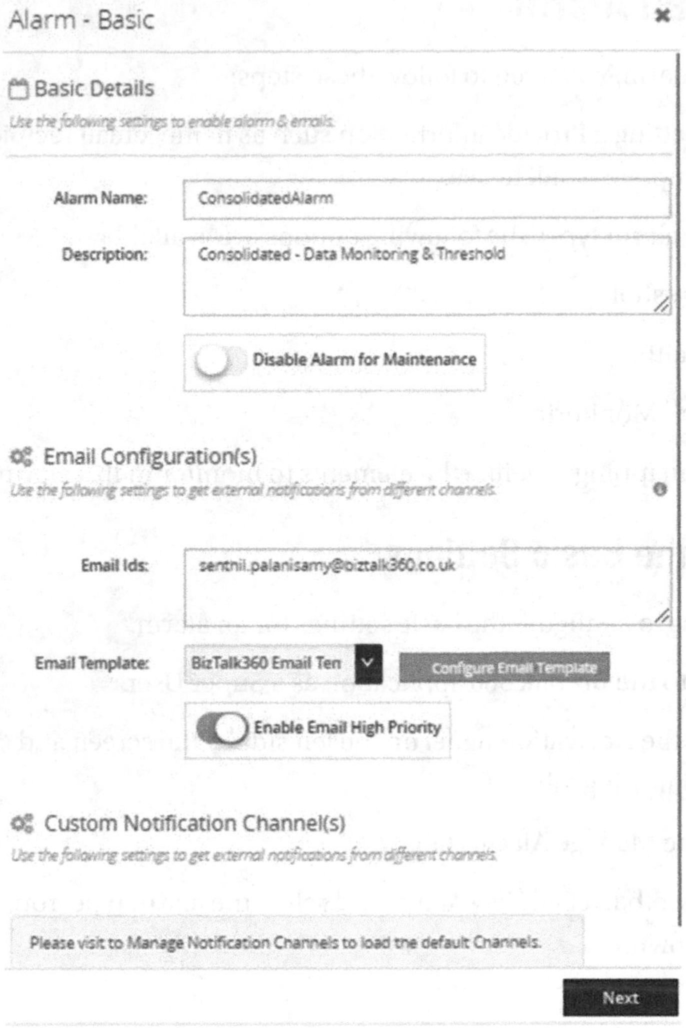

Figure 8-1. *Basic alarm settings*

Fill in these fields:

- Alarm Name (required): A descriptive name of the alarm.

- Description: A detailed description on the purpose of this alarm.

- Disable Alarm for Maintenance: This allows you to temporarily disable the alarm. As long as the alarm is disabled, you won't receive notifications

- Email IDs (required): The email addresses of the people who need to receive the email notifications.

- Email Template: Select one of the available templates.

- Enable Email High Priority: This option allows you to enable/disable high-priority emails. Based on this configuration, the email notification priority is set. By default, high priority is enabled.

- Configure Email Template: By clicking on this button, you will be redirected to a screen where you can create new templates, make changes to a template, or delete existing email templates.

- Custom Notification Channels: Besides receiving notifications by email, you can receive notifications by other channels. Configure them here to receive notifications from this alarm.

5. The Next button navigates you to the next screen. Click Next twice until you reach the Alarm – Advanced pane (see Figure 8-2). The Alert - Threshold and Alert - Health panes are discussed in later sections.

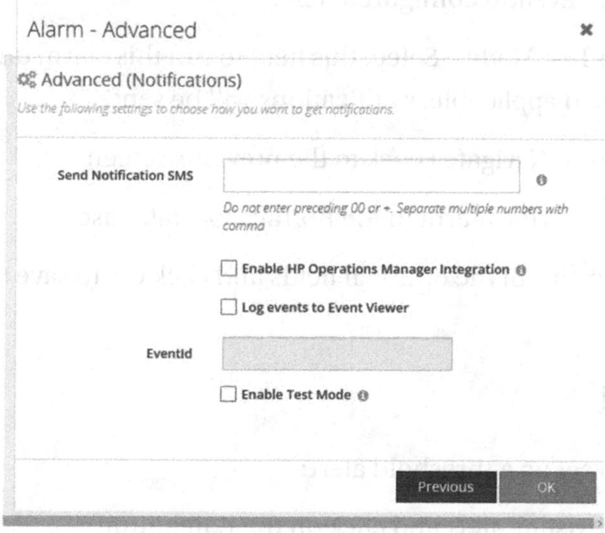

Figure 8-2. *Examining the advanced options for an alarm*

The Alarm – Advanced pane has the following fields:

- Send Notification SMS—Enter a mobile number (without 00 or the +- sign to receive SMS Notifications). Note: BizTalk 360 uses the Azure Gateway for sending SMS messages. If you want to receive more than five (free) messages per day, you need a subscription to that gateway.

- Enable HP Operations Manager Integration—Select this field if you have an HP Operations Manager and want to receive notifications there. Note: HP Operations Manager Integration has to be configured under Settings/Monitoring and Notification/HP Operations Manager.

- Log Events to Event Viewer—Select this if you want to write events from this alarm to the Event Log. If the Event Log option is enabled, down and up alert notifications are written to the BizTalk 360 Monitor source in the application log.

- EventId—Once the previous field is selected, this field is enabled and a numeric value is required. When a notification from the alarm is sent, an event log entry is written in the Application log, with the EventId configured here.

- Enable Test Mode—Select this field to run this alarm once per minute. If applicable, notifications will be sent.

- Previous—Navigates back to the previous screen.

- OK—Stores the alarm in the BizTalk 360 database.

6. Enter/select any of the optional fields and click OK to save the alarm.

Threshold Alert

Follow these steps to set up a threshold alert:

1. Locate an existing alert and click on the Edit button.

2. Enable the Alert on Threshold Violation option. Otherwise, the threshold options are not enabled.

3. Use the Violation Persist Duration setting to tell BizTalk 360 that you want to receive notifications only when the issue has been happening for a period of time. For instance, you can receive notifications if the violation persists for 10 minutes.

4. The Limit Alerts per Violation parameter limits the alerts sent about a specific violation. For instance, if you set it to 3, BizTalk 360 will send a maximum of three notifications per violation persist duration period.

5. The Notification When Situation Becomes Normal setting tells you when the situation becomes normal after a violation is over.

6. Set alerts on set day(s) and time(s) only to restrict the threshold violation alerts.

7. Save the alarm information. See Figure 8-3.

Figure 8-3. *Examining the threshold alarm options*

Health Monitoring Alert

To set up a Health Monitoring alert, follow these steps:

1. Follow the steps as mentioned in the Basic Settings section.

2. On the Alarm - Health page, you have option to choose the days and times you want to receive periodic update about the health of your environment.

3. You can click OK or Next to move to the last screen to add some Advanced Settings like SMS configuration and advanced configuration.

Once you finish, the alarm will be set, and the BizTalk 360 user interface will take you to the Manage Alarms page. This page lists all the alarms that you have created in your environment. See Figure 8-4.

Figure 8-4. *Examining the health monitoring alarm options*

Data Monitoring Alert

Follow these steps to create an alert for Data Monitoring:

1. Follow the steps mentioned in the Basic Settings section.

2. On the Alarm - Data Monitoring section, enable the Use This Alarm for Data Monitor Alerts checkbox.

3. Select the Notify on Success As Well checkbox if you want BizTalk 360 to send a notification when the query runs successfully.

What Do You Monitor?

As you are now aware what kinds of monitoring exist, you can start thinking about what kind of artifacts you want to monitor. At a high level, this can be separated into a few areas:

- BizTalk Platform monitoring

- BizTalk Application monitoring

- Data monitoring

- Endpoint monitoring

For each of these categories, BizTalk 360 contains multiple capabilities, most of which are explained in the following sections.

BizTalk Platform Monitoring

Your BizTalk solutions run on the BizTalk Server platform. So, when something is wrong with the BizTalk platform, that might affect how your BizTalk solutions run and, as a result, damage your business processes. Therefore, it is important to constantly have a good understanding of the health of your BizTalk Server platform.

When you want to monitor your BizTalk environment, there are several things you should be aware of, and you can use monitoring to watch these things. Consider these examples:

- BizTalk host instances

- BizTalk Server's SQL Server jobs

- Availability of the BizTalk Servers

- Certain Windows NT services

- Host throttling

BizTalk 360 can help you monitor all these different artifacts and of course, when something is wrong with any of these components, you can become notified. In many cases, BizTalk 360 will try to automatically bring the components back to the expected state.

Monitoring Host Instances

As you learned in the previous chapters, host instances are the Windows services that encapsulate most of the BizTalk Server functionality. Providing a proactive monitoring mechanism to ensure that all relevant host instances are started becomes crucial to the health of the platform. BizTalk 360 enables you to monitor host instances by creating monitoring rules that check whether the service is started, stopped, or disabled.

Additionally, if you have clustered host instances, BizTalk 360 can check if the host instance is active in more than one server.

Setting Up Monitoring for Host Instances

To set up monitoring for host instances, follow these steps:

1. Log in to the BizTalk 360 application.

2. Click Monitoring in the navigation panel.

3. Click the expand button of the Manage Mapping tab and select the BizTalk Environment link.

4. Select an Alarm name from the drop-down for which you would like to associate the alerts.

5. Select the Host Instances tab.

6. Select the host instances you want to monitor.

7. Set the value of Expected State. For instance, if you want to receive a notification when a specific host instance starts (because it should be always stopped, like a FTP host instance), you need to set the value to Started. See Figure 8-5.

Figure 8-5. *Creating a host instance alarm*

Note   From the Platform Health alarm, the BizTalkServerApplication host instance needs to be monitored to be in the Started state. In case the host instance is stopped, BizTalk 360 should automatically try to start the host instance, so Auto Correct needs to be Enabled.

The Auto Correct Feature

This is a very useful feature, as it will allow you to set a specific state when the artifact current state differs from the expected state.

For instance, imagine that you have a host instance monitor that checks whether the status of the host instance is started or stopped. If you created the monitor to expect a Started state, and if you enable the auto-correct functionality, BizTalk 360 will attempt to start the host instance if the current state is Stopped.

To enable auto-correct for a host instance, just follow these steps:

1. Select the desired host instances.

2. Select Started in the Auto Correct drop-down.

3. Save your changes.

Monitoring Host Instances That Are Clustered

To provide high availability for FTP adapters, for instance, Microsoft recommends clustering them. BizTalk 360 has the capability to monitor clustered host instances. The difference with non-cluster host instances from BizTalk 360's point of view is that a clustered host instance should be marked with a state of `AtleastOneActive`. BizTalk 360 will check if the host instance is started in only one instance. See Figure 8-6.

Figure 8-6. *Monitoring clustered host instances*

Monitoring SQL Server Jobs

As you have learned in the book, BizTalk Server uses SQL Server jobs to make sure tables within the Message Box and Tracking DTA databases are consistent. If any of these jobs fail, the engine will start behaving unexpectedly and most likely performance will decline, as internal tables will grow over the time.

Luckily, BizTalk 360 enables you monitor all SQL jobs by paying attention to two important thresholds:

- The Job State, which is used to check if a job is running or not.

- The Last Run State, which is used to diagnose the latest execution state.

All BizTalk Server jobs must run successfully but these:

- `MessageBox_Message_Cleanup_BizTalkMsgBoxDb`—This job should be disabled because is being called from within the `MessageBox_Message_ManageRefCountLog_BizTalkMsgBoxDb` logic.

- `MessageBox_Message_ManageRefCountLog_BizTalkMsgBoxDb`—Can show an execution error if the job or SQL Server Agent has been manually or unexpectedly stopped. The job calls a stored procedure that runs in an infinite loop. This behavior is by design and cannot be changed. Because of this, DBAs usually disable this job so it does not raise any errors, which is a practice not supported in the BizTalk product support information.

Therefore, keep this in mind when creating monitoring for these jobs and act accordingly:

- The Expected Job state for the **MessageBox_Message_Cleanup_BizTalkMsgBoxDb** job should be disabled.

- The Last Run state for the job `MessageBox_Message_ManageRefCountLog_BizTalkMsgBoxDb` should be error.

Establishing Monitoring for SQL Jobs

Follow these steps:

1. Select SQL Server Instances in the Manage Mapping section.

2. Select the SQL Server instance that runs the SQL Server job you want to monitor.

3. Select an educated alarm.

4. Select the desired SQL jobs.

5. Set the value of the Expected Job state and the Expected Last Run state.

Monitoring the Availability of the BizTalk Servers

In a real-world scenario, large enterprises will typically have one or more sets of deployed BizTalk environments. To handle such scenarios with BizTalk 360, you can set up monitoring on specific components of BizTalk Server such as BizTalk applications and their associated Send Ports, Receive Locations, Orchestrations, Service Instances, Disks, Event Logs, NT Services, System Resources (CPU, Memory), SQL Jobs, Web Endpoints, BizTalk Health Monitor Errors, and Warnings and Host instances (normal, clustered). See Figure 8-7. In addition to these existing monitoring features, BizTalk 360 has the capability to monitor the BizTalk Server availability.

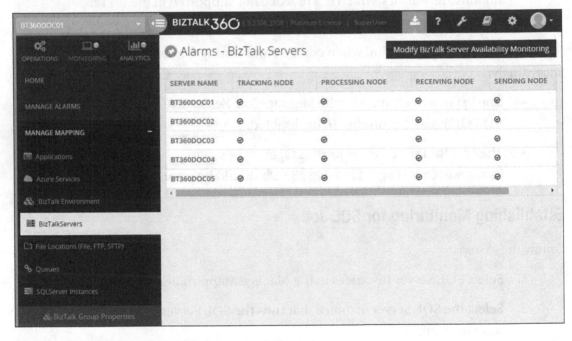

Figure 8-7. *Monitoring the servers of the group*

Why BizTalk Server Availability Monitoring in BizTalk 360?

Say that ACME Corp has a highly complex BizTalk Server group with five BizTalk Servers running 24/7 operations. Typically, these complex BizTalk Server groups are configured for high availability and scalability, keeping in mind the high volume of traffic. With such a setup, administrators will be under a lot of pressure to make sure all the BizTalk Servers are up and running and can process all the messages at the expected level. In any complex BizTalk Server group configuration, there is a high likelihood that, for various reasons, one or more servers will go down. It becomes a daunting task for the BizTalk administrators to continuously monitor the server availability and react to downtime quickly. To help administrators overcome this challenge, BizTalk 360 provides the BizTalk Server Availability Monitoring functionality. See Figure 8-8.

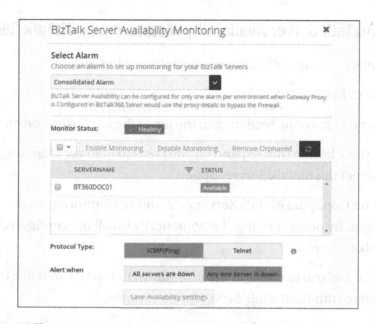

Figure 8-8. *BizTalk Server Availability Monitoring*

Important Points to Remember in BizTalk Server Availability Monitoring

While setting up BizTalk Server Availability Monitoring, there are a few things to be aware of:

- Choose the ICMP or Telnet protocol. To check the BizTalk Server availability, administrators need to reach (ping) the servers. BizTalk 360 supports Ping and Telnet; therefore, one of these protocols needs to be enabled on the BizTalk Servers.

- BizTalk administrators can choose when to receive the alert—when one of the BizTalk servers in the group has gone down or only when all the servers in the group have gone down.

- In BizTalk 360, BizTalk Server availability can be configured for only one alarm per environment.

413

- When a gateway proxy is configured in BizTalk 360 (under BizTalk 360 Settings), Telnet uses the proxy details to bypass the firewall.

- BizTalk 360 also gives you the option to modify the existing configured server availability monitoring at any time,

Configuring BizTalk Server Availability Monitoring in BizTalk 360

Follow these steps to set up BizTalk Server Availability Monitoring:

1. Log in to BizTalk 360.

2. Click the Monitoring section from the top of the left Navigation menu.

3. Click the + button (the Expand button) next to Manage Mapping and select the BizTalk Servers option.

4. Click on Configure BizTalk Server Availability Monitoring on the top right. By doing this, it will automatically list all the configured BizTalk Servers.

5. Select the alarm name from the drop-down that you would like to associate with the BizTalk Server for monitoring.

6. When there is no BizTalk Server configured for monitoring, the value of Monitor Status will be be to Not Configured.

7. By default, the ICMP protocol and Any One Server Are Down options will be selected.

8. Select the BizTalk Server that you want to monitor and click Enable Monitoring to start monitoring the BizTalk Server.

When the settings are configured, BizTalk 360 will start monitoring the BizTalk Servers for any state-based violations. Once a violation occurs for the configured alarm, BizTalk 360 will notify the users via the configured notification channels.

Monitoring Windows NT Services

As you have seen throughout the book, BizTalk Server uses these Windows services:

- The Enterprise single sign-on service

- The BAM Alerts service, if BAM alerts are enabled

- The Rule Engine Update service, if business rules are installed and implemented

- Internet information server service to expose and consume services

You can monitor those NT services for the following two different states:

- Running

- Stopped

Follow these steps to set up monitoring for your Windows NT services:

1. Log in to the BizTalk 360 application.

2. Click Monitoring in the navigation panel.

3. Click the expand button next to the Manage Mapping tab and, depending on your requirement, select the BizTalk Servers or the SQL Servers link.

4. Select the BizTalk or SQL Server for which you want to set up monitoring on NT services.

5. Select the alarm name you want to use.

6. Select NT Services tab at the top of the page.

7. Select the relevant NT services.

8. Select the checkbox on the NT services to activate the alert.

9. Set the expected state (started or stopped) by selecting the value from the drop-down.

Viewing and Monitoring Host Throttling

The idea behind the BizTalk 360 Throttling Analyzer is to simplify the complexity in understanding the BizTalk Throttling mechanism and provide a simple dashboard view. The purpose of host throttling monitoring is to notify the customers if there is any throttling happening in their environment.

The BizTalk 360 Throttling Analyzer

The BizTalk 360 helps solve the following problems:

- As you learned in Chapters 2 and 4, throttling situations can become complicated to analyze even for seasoned BizTalk Server professionals.

- BizTalk Server only provides performance counter data. You have to use external tools, such as performance monitor or PAL, to analyze the raw information.

The objective of BizTalk 360 is to provide a visual representation of what is occurring in the environment in a near real-time situation.

The Throttling Performance Counters Collection Service

BizTalk 360 provides a monitoring service that collects throttling performance counter data and stores it into the BizTalk 360 database. The default collection interval is 15 seconds. The data is persisted for seven days, and users cannot modify it.

The throttling analyzer is in the Analytics tab. The service status of the Throttling Analyzer can be accessed from Settings ➤ Analytics Health ➤ Analytics Service Status.

Setting Up Monitoring for Host Throttling

Follow these instructions to set up monitoring for host throttling (see Figure 8-9):

1. Log in to the BizTalk 360 application

2. Click Monitoring in the navigation panel.

3. Expand the Manage Mapping tab and select BizTalk Environment.

4. Select an alarm name.

5. Select the relevant hosts. For instance, if you want to monitor `BizTalkServerApplication`, select the `BizTalkServerApplication` checkbox and click Enable Monitoring.

6. BizTalk 360 will automatically start monitoring the host and looking for throttling events.

7. Click the Edit button and configure the threshold alert for publishing and delivery throttling.

8. Click the Save Configuration button.

Figure 8-9. *Setting up monitoring for host throttling*

Note From the Platform Health alarm, the BizTalkServerApplication Host needs to be monitored for throttling. In case of throttling due to publishing, a warning should be sent if the duration of the throttling condition is longer than 60 seconds.

BizTalk Application Monitoring

A BizTalk environment usually contains several BizTalk applications that use most of the BizTalk Server artifacts and elements, such as receive locations, orchestrations, ports, and business rules. At any given time, an issue related to these artifacts can occur, which leads to business process interruptions.

To prevent you from monitoring all these elements reactively and manually, BizTalk 360 allows you to monitor all these artifacts in a proactive way. The following sections guide you through the process of enabling monitoring for all these BizTalk Server elements.

Receive Locations, Orchestrations, and Send Ports

In BizTalk 360, you can monitor these BizTalk Server artifacts by checking whether the status is disabled or enabled. You also can choose to not monitor the artifact at all.

Configuring Alerts for BizTalk Artifacts

Follow these steps to monitor BizTalk Server artifacts:

1. Click on the Monitoring panel.

2. Expand the Manage Mapping tab and select the Applications link

3. Select the application that owns the artifact.

4. Select an alarm name.

5. Select all relevant artifacts, such as orchestrations, receive locations, or send ports.

6. Set the value of the Expected State.

7. Enable the Auto Correct functionality for the receive location if you want BizTalk 360 to change the status of the receive location when they are in a state that's different than the expected one.

Figure 8-10 shows how the interface looks when setting receive locations.

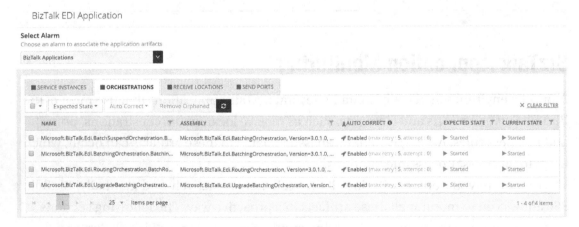

Figure 8-10. *Monitoring receive locations view*

Figure 8-11 shows the Orchestrations alarm view.

Figure 8-11. *Monitoring orchestrations view*

Figure 8-12 shows the Send Ports Alarm view.

Figure 8-12. *Monitoring send ports view*

Service Instances

For a healthy BizTalk environment, it is important to keep an eye on the number of service instances in the environment. As you have seen in previous chapters, service instances and messages are stored in the Message Box database with a specific state that can vary along the life of the instance.

The BizTalk administration console will display the following service states:

- Ready to Run

- Scheduled

- Dehydrated

- Suspended, Resumable

- Suspended, Non-resumable

- Active

- In Breakpoint

Using BizTalk 360, you can monitor those states and set up different threshold levels based on the instances count.

Setting Up Alerts for Service Instances

Follow these steps to set up monitoring of service instances:

1. Click Monitoring in the navigation panel.

2. Expand the Manage Mapping tab and select the Applications link.

3. Select the application that work with the service instances you want to monitor.

4. Select an alarm name.

5. Select the service instance states that you want to receive notifications.

6. You can edit the warning and the error thresholds level by clicking the Edit link, as shown in Figure 8-13.

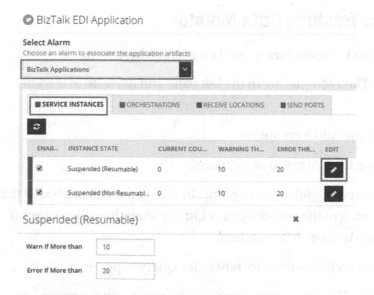

Figure 8-13. Monitoring services instances view

What Is Data Monitoring?

The best way to understand this feature is to go through an example. Imagine that every day, early in the morning, you expect a batch of at least 100 messages from a specific location. If the messages do not arrive, business operations are adversely affected. If you have tracking enabled for that receive location, BizTalk 360 can access the tracking database to check whether the messages have arrived to your BizTalk Server or not.

BizTalk 360 can access data from the following integration layer elements:

- Tracking Data

- Message Box

- Business Activity Monitoring

- Electronic Data Interchange (out of the scope of the book)

- Enterprise Service Bus (out of the scope of the book)

- Logic Apps (out of the scope of the book)

- Event Log

Setting Up a Tracking Data Monitor

Follow these steps to create a tracking-data monitoring alarm:

1. Go to Data Monitoring in the left pane and navigate to tracking data.

2. Select the Add New option.

3. Choose the alarm you want to use.

4. Use a meaningful monitor name. In the scenario described at the beginning of the section, you could use something like: *Check if the 100 Message batch arrived*.

5. Select Tracked Service Instances for Query Type.

6. You can filter the tracked service instances to get a specific instance as you can do using the BizTalk Server administration console. The following options are available:

   - Assembly name

   - Assembly version

   - Error code

   - Error description

   - Host name

   - Service class

   - Service instance ID

   - Service name

   - State

7. The Warning Threshold setting configures when BizTalk 360 should send the notification as a warning. For instance, if the number of tracked service instances is greater than 100, throw a warning.

8. The Error Threshold setting is similar to the warning section, but it sends an Error notification.

9. In terms of frequency, decide if you want to monitor the host instances daily, weekly, or monthly.

10. Select the time to execute the alarm.

11. Set an specific time of the day (detailed frequency option) or the end of the business day (end of business day option).

12. Review all the advanced scheduling options available in this tool. This book does not cover the advanced section because it is very specific and designed for more complex scenarios.

13. Decide how do you want BizTalk 360 to validate the output data. You can base the analysis using the following options:

    • Query result count (no date/time filter): The query will return a record count that you can use to set up the thresholds.

    • Query result with date/time range: You can filter the output data to check if the records are generated on a specific time frame.

14. Review the summary information just in case you missed something.

15. Click Save and Close.

Message Box

As you learned in Chapters 1 and 4, the number of suspended messages can impact negatively the performance of your BizTalk Server group. You can use BizTalk Server 360 to automatically archive and/or terminate suspended instances.

Archive and Terminate Suspended Service Instances

If you want to archive suspended messages for further investigation or just as a backup before automatic termination occurs, you have to configure the Archiving folder.

Follow these steps to set up the Archiving folder:

1. Navigate to BizTalk 360 Settings.

2. Choose the System Settings option from the left menu.

3. Edit the Archive Location for data monitoring setting to specify the Archiving folder.

4. Click Save.

   You can now create a Message Box Data Monitor to terminate the suspended messages. Follow these steps:

5. Go to Data Monitoring in the left pane and navigate to the Message Box.

6. Select the Add New option.

7. In the Set Actions section, select the Is Action Required checkbox.

8. Depending on the requirement, select the When To Action option.

9. In the What Action option, choose Terminate.

10. Click Save and Close.

Business Activity Monitoring (BAM)

The BAM portal in BizTalk 360 allows business users to query BAM views and perform activity searches. The concept of this feature is similar to BAM alerts, as you can create advanced filters based on the content of the BAM activity. This is extremely helpful if you want to receive alerts based on certain criteria when the Activity Completed table is populated within the BAM primary import database. For instance, you can create a data monitor alert when a book order has been denied or when an error occurred during the whole business flow (of course, only if the BAM activity is tracking errors).

Event Log

BizTalk 360 can monitor the event logs of your BizTalk and SQL Server boxes. This feature is useful not only to detect undesired BizTalk errors, but also to monitor custom event logs raised by applications.

Endpoint Monitoring

Besides monitoring BizTalk artifacts, server resources, Azure services, and so on, you can also monitor resources like web services and FTP sites, which are part of your integration. BizTalk 360 allows you to monitor the following endpoints:

- Folder locations

- FTP, FTPS, and SFTP sites

- HTTP web endpoints

- MSMQ

- IBM MQ

- Azure services

Refer to the BizTalk 360 documentation to get more information about these topics.

How Are You Notified?

When a threshold is exceeded, the tool will rise a notification. BizTalk 360 exposes several functionalities to notify you when these situations arise. Let's look at the different options:

- Dashboards

  - Operations Dashboard

  - Monitoring Dashboard

  - Data Monitoring Dashboard

- Notification channels

  - Email

  - Other Notification channels

  - Custom Notification channels

Dashboards

BizTalk 360 has dashboards that show an overview of the platform's health. These dashboards are:

- Operations Dashboard
- Monitoring Dashboard
- Data Monitoring Dashboard

Operations Dashboard

The Operations Dashboard provides access to key functionalities of the product that you will be using more frequently (see Figure 8-14). When the Dashboard loads, it shows a set of default widgets that will give you important insights on the environment.

Figure 8-14. *The Operations Dashboard view*

Dashboards are customizable and you can add your custom widgets to redirect how users see the information.

Monitoring Dashboard

The Monitoring Dashboard is used to populate all the alarms of the platform. The information displayed on this dashboard can be abundant, so it is recommended to have a big monitor to deal with the alerts efficiently. To access the monitoring dashboard, follow the steps below:

1. Click the Monitoring tab in the Navigation panel.

2. Select the relevant alarm.

3. Examine the alerts.

Graphical Hierarchy View Structure

The Monitoring Dashboard provides a tree view representation of all the configured sections within an alarm and implements the following functionalities (see Figure 8-15):

- Clicking on element of the tree representation takes you to the associated element.

- You can click on the Toggle Fit to Screen option to adjust the visualization to your screen size. If you have many alerts set up, it might be handy to display the information on a large monitor.

- The tool draws the information using these colored patterns:

    - Red: The monitor returned an error.

    - Amber: The monitor returned a warning.

    - Green: The monitor did not find any error or warning.

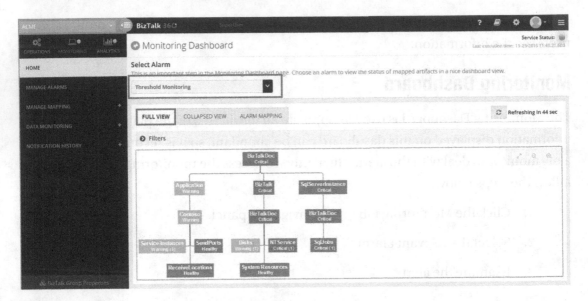

Figure 8-15. *The graphical tree view*

Data Monitoring Dashboard

The Data Monitoring Dashboard populates the monitoring elements using a calendar view that helps you to understand which data monitoring took place and when. It's shown in Figure 8-16.

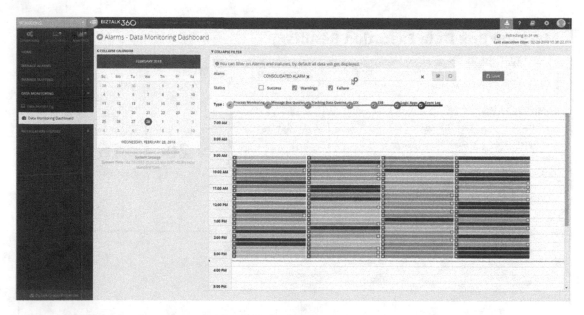

Figure 8-16. *The monitoring dashboard view*

The tool will draw the information using the following color pattern:

- Red: A data monitor returned an error.

- Amber: A data monitor returned a warning.

- Green: All data monitors ran successfully during that period.

Viewing Execution Details

If you want to extend information on a particular day and time, you can click on any area of the calendar and you will see what happened with much more detail, as shown in Figure 8-17.

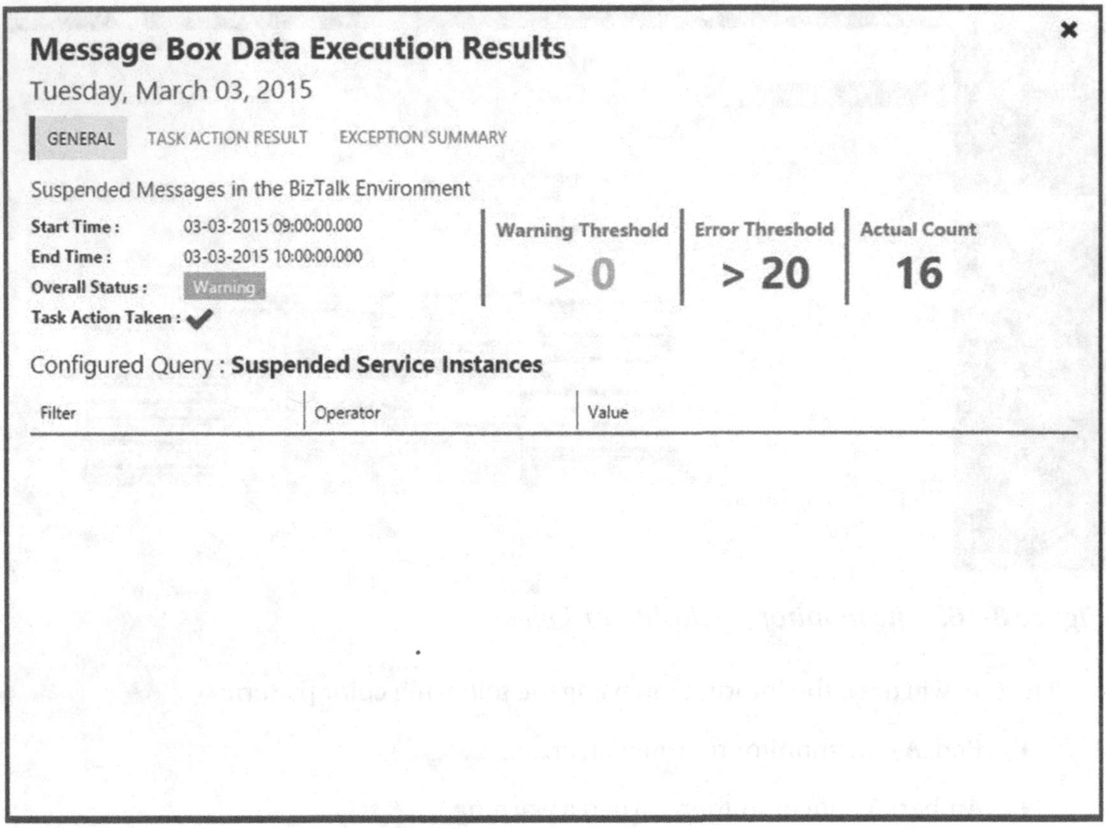

Message Box Data Execution Results   ✕

Tuesday, March 03, 2015

| GENERAL | TASK ACTION RESULT | EXCEPTION SUMMARY |

Suspended Messages in the BizTalk Environment

Start Time :	03-03-2015 09:00:00.000		Warning Threshold	Error Threshold	Actual Count
End Time :	03-03-2015 10:00:00.000		**> 0**	**> 20**	**16**
Overall Status :	Warning				
Task Action Taken : ✔					

Configured Query : **Suspended Service Instances**

Filter	Operator	Value

Figure 8-17. *Execution detail view*

Automated Recovery

BizTalk 360 has quite an extended set of artifacts that can be monitored and that can send notifications. Besides that, it also has a number of automated recovery features. These features are:

- Auto-correct state bound artifacts: For example, bringing a Host Instance, which did not start after a reboot, back to the Started state

- Auto-resume: For example, resuming service instances that were suspended due to a network glitch.

- Auto-terminate: For example, terminating routing failure reports.

Summary

In this chapter, you learned how to use the BizTalk Server 360 tool to extend the out-of-the-box monitoring features of BizTalk Server, not only from the availability and health points of view, but also by creating custom alerts that will help you monitor tracking, live, or even external data sources.

In the next chapter, you read a BizTalk Server tale about a company that starts with BizTalk Server and evolves to a mature architecture by facing and solving problems.

CHAPTER 9

Testing BizTalk Server Solutions

BizTalk Server solutions frequently integrate highly critical business processes where the integrated parties define very restricted service level agreements. Most of these applications rank high on the application priority level and must run 24x7 with downtime. In this situation, developing a successful testing architecture will make a huge difference in finding application bugs, performance bottlenecks, issues with new application versions, and in detecting problems when scaling the BizTalk Server platform.

In this chapter, you learn the performance methodology required to assess a BizTalk Server environment and how to include unit and performance testing as part of your application development cycle.

Unit Testing

Unit testing is used to develop and execute testing applications to verify that your code is running as expected. It is called unit testing because the idea is that you break down the functionality of the BizTalk Server solution into discrete testable pieces of code that you can test as separate units. In BizTalk Server, those units are usually identified by an individual message flow.

If you include unit testing as part of your development strategy, the quality of the application can increase by reducing the chances of bugs. Once you finish the development of a business flow, you should create unit tests to verify that the behavior of the application, with all the possible messages involved, is expected in terms of the business functionality. Furthermore, unit tests can be used later for performance testing.

© Agustín Mántaras 2019

A. Mántaras, *BizTalk Server 2016*, https://doi.org/10.1007/978-1-4842-3994-0_9

When developing .NET custom components, you can quickly produce test projects and test methods from your code, or you manually create the tests as required.

You can leverage the following technologies to perform BizTalk unit testing:

- Using the Unit Testing feature—At the moment of writing this book, only the following BizTalk artifacts are available for unit testing:

  - Schemas

  - Pipelines

  - Maps

Unfortunately, orchestrations cannot be unit tested using the Unit Testing feature because they require the BizTalk Server engine to be executed. However, you could test the end-to-end process by creating a general Visual Studio unit testing project, a topic that will be covered in the section "Assessing the Performance of a BizTalk Application" later in this chapter.

- General Visual Studio Unit Testing Project—If you have Visual Studio Unit and Load Testing experience, this is probably the most convenient way to automate BizTalk Server Solutions testing.

- BizUnit—BizTalk BizUnit it is a declarative XML framework designed to create unit tests for BizTalk Server projects. BizUnit Test Cases have three phases: Stage, Execution, and CleanUp. Every test is defined in a typed XML document that the BizUnit Engine will execute. BizUnit has been used frequently over the past few years and it will not be covered in this book. You can review BizUnit documentation in the MSDN Microsoft page here: `https://docs.microsoft.com/en-us/biztalk/technical-guides/using-bizunit-to-facilitate-automated-testing`.

Creating Unit Testing for a .NET Component

The fastest way to create unit testing for .NET components is generate the unit test project from your code. This action creates the blueprint for the testing project and accelerates your development.

Note   The following sections provide a step-by-step guide to implement unit testing to a .NET component. You can locate the full generated code in this location if you do not want to go through the guide:

`C:\APRESS\Chapter9\BooksOrderHelperCompleted`

Follow these steps:

1. Using Visual Studio, open the project located here: `C:\APRESS\Chapter9\BooksOrderHelper\BooksOrderHelper.sln`

2. **Open** the class file `BooksOrderHelper.cs`.

3. Right-click at the `BooksOrderHelper` class level and select the Create Unit Tests option, as shown in Figure 9-1.

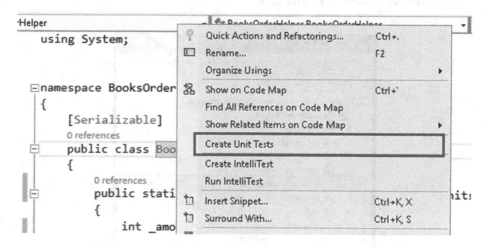

Figure 9-1. *Creating the unit tests option*

4. Visual Studio shows the default properties for the unit tests. You can change these values if you want to create the unit test cases with specific names and output folders. Leave the default values for now. See Figure 9-2.

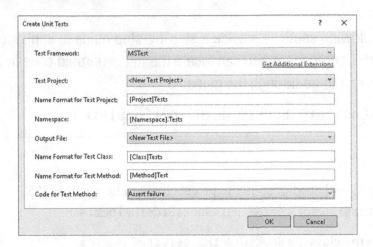

Figure 9-2. *The Create Unit Tests dialog box*

5.   Visual Studio generates a unit testing project and adds it to the
     solution, as shown in Figure 9-3.

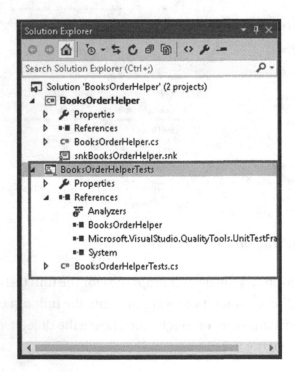

Figure 9-3. *Examining the generated test project*

6. Open the BooksOrderHelperTests.cs file and observe that Visual
    Studio has created the BooksOrdersHelperTests class and added
    the [TestClass()] attribute:

    ```
    namespace BooksOrderHelper.Tests
    {
        [TestClass()]
        public class BooksOrderHelperTests
        {
            [TestMethod()]
            public void returnTotalAmountTest()
            {
                Assert.Fail();
            }
        }
    }
    ```

7. Additionally, the test method returnTotalAmountTest() has been
    added using the [TestMethod()] attribute.

Note   The Add New Unit Test feature creates a sample test method for each
method in the custom .Net component.

Adding Testing Code

The generated code for the testing methods is Assert.Fail():

```
{
    [TestClass()]
    public class BooksOrderHelperTests
    {
        [TestMethod()]
        public void returnTotalAmountTest()
        {
            Assert.Fail();
```

```
        }
    }
}
```

The fail method forces the test method to fail, so you will need to write the custom code to test this method.

To help developing clean and structured code, the AAA (Arrange-Act-Assert) pattern has become a standard across the development industry when it comes to testing projects. It recommends that you divide your test method into three sections: arrange, act, and assert. Each section is responsible for a small part:

- The Arrange section initializes variables used during the method.

- The **Act** section invokes the method with the variables initialized in the Arrange section.

- The Assert section verifies that the method under the Act section test behaves predictably.

To test the returnTotalAmount method of the BooksOrdersHelper component, you can write two tests:

- One that verifies a valid amount (<=10.000)

- One that sets the amount to a value bigger than 10.000. The objective of this test will be to evaluate the returnTotalAmount when the price is bigger than 10.000.

Follow these steps to create the valid amount test:

1. **Open** the BooksOrderHelperTests.cs file of the BooksOrderHelperTests.csproj project.

2. Add a reference to the BooksOrderHelper solution.

3. Locate the test method returnTotalAmountTest(). You are going to use this method to validate the amount.

4. Replace the content of the function with the following code:

```
#region Arrange
    int price = 1000;
    int units = 9;
```

```
    int expectedValue = 9000;
    int iReturn = 0;

#endregion Arrange
#region act
    iReturn = BooksOrderHelper.returnTotalAmount(price, units);
#endregion act
#region Assert
    Assert.AreEqual(expectedValue, iReturn);
#endregion Assert
```

As you can see in the code:

- The Arrange region sets the price, units, and the expected output of the method returnTotalAmount.

- The Act region calls the method returnTotalAmount() using the price and units set in the Arrange region.

- The Assert region evaluates whether the output of the returnTotalAmount method returns the expectedValue using the static method AreEqual of the assert object.

Note   The assert object is available for use in all testing projects. It contains a set of static methods that evaluate a logical condition. If this condition evaluates to true, the assertion passes. Otherwise, it fails. To learn about all the static methods that this class provides, visit https://msdn.microsoft.com/en-us/library/microsoft.visualstudio.testtools.unittesting.assert.aspx?f=255&MSPPError=-2147217396.

Follow these steps to create the invalid amount test:

1. Copy the returnTotalAmountTest and paste it later in the BooksOrderHelperTests class.

2. Name the new method returnTotalAmountTestHighAmount().

3. Add the [TestMethod()] attribute to the method if you did not copy it.

4. Examine the BooksOrdersHelper.returnTotalAmount method:

```
if (_amount >= 10000)

    {

        throw new ArgumentException(_amount.ToString(),
        "amount not valid!");
    }
```

5. In the code, if the total amount is greater than 10.000, the component will throw an argument exception. Therefore, to assert the output of the method instead of calling the Assert object, you are going to add the attribute [ExpectedException(typeof(Arg umentException))] to the returnTotalAmountTestHighAmount testing method and Visual Studio will automatically assert the output using this ExpectedException attribute.

6. Insert the following code for the returnTotalAmountTestHighAmount method.

```
[TestMethod()]
  [ExpectedException(typeof(ArgumentException))]
  public void returnTotalAmountTestHighAmount()
  {
      #region Arrange
      int price = 1000;
      int units = 20;
      int iReturn = 0;

      #endregion Arrange
      #region act
      iReturn = BooksOrderHelper.returnTotalAmount(price, units);
      #endregion act
      #region Assert
      //assertion is managed by the ExpectedException attribute.
      #endregion Assert

  }
```

As you can see in the code:

- The Arrange region sets the price, units, and the expected output of the method `returnTotalAmount`.

- The Act region calls the method `returnTotalAmount()` using the price and units set in the Arrange region.

- The Assert region is managed by the `ExpectedException` attribute.

7. **Choose** Save All.

8. Build the solution.

9. Install the `BooksOrdersHelper` assembly into the GAC.

Running the Tests

When you build the test project, the tests will appear in Test Explorer. If Test Explorer is not shown, choose Test from the Visual Studio menu, select Windows, and then click on Test Explorer. See Figure 9-4.

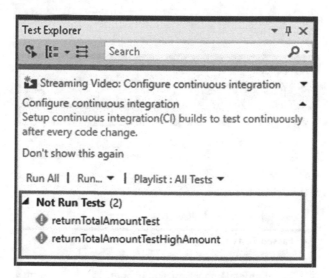

Figure 9-4. Examining the tests using the Test Explorer

To run all the tests, click the Run All command, as shown in Figure 9-5.

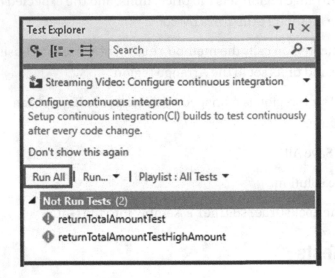

Figure 9-5. *Running all tests using the Test Explorer*

Once the tests are complete, the Test Explorer will show the output, as shown in Figure 9-6.

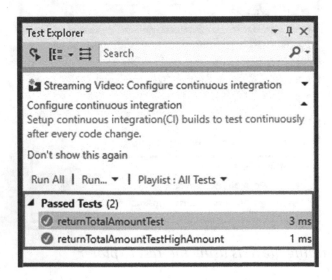

Figure 9-6. *Examining the output of the test*

Creating Unit Testing for a BizTalk Project

In this section, you are going to use the Visual Studio Unit Testing feature to enable unit testing for the following BizTalk server elements:

- Maps
- Schemas
- Pipelines

Note   The following sections provide a step-by-step guide to implement unit testing to BizTalk Server projects. You can locate the full generated code in this location:

`C:\APRESS\Chapter9\BizTalkUnitTestingFeatureCompleted`

Adding a Unit Testing Project to the Book Orders Solution

Follow these steps to add a unit testing project to the BookOrders solution:

1. Using Visual Studio, open the sample solution located here:
   `C:\APRESS\Chapter9\BizTalkUnitTestingFeature\`
   `BizTalkUnitTestingFeatureProject\`
   `BizTalkUnitTestingFeatureProject.sln`

2. Go to Project properties and, in the Deployment section, verify that Enable Unit Testing is set to True. See Figure 9-7.

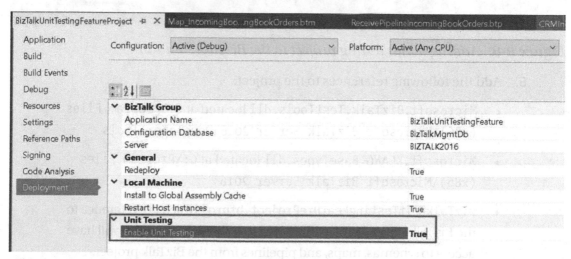

Figure 9-7. Enabling unit testing at the project level

3. Choose Save All and rebuild the solution. As you enabled unit
    testing, now you have to rebuild the solution in order to tell Visual
    Studio to call the unit testing interfaces. If you miss this step, you
    cannot add new testing projects to the solution.

4. Right-click at the solution level and add a new unit test project
    (under Visual c#\Test). Double-check that :Net Framework 4.6
    is selected. See Figure 9-8.

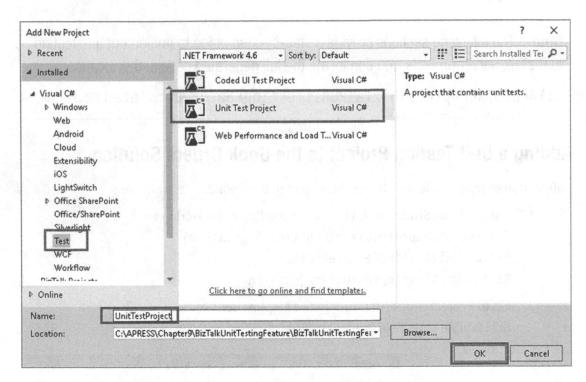

Figure 9-8. *Adding a unit testing project to the BizTalk solution*

5. Add the following references to the project:

    - Microsoft.BizTalk.TestTools.dll located at C:\Program Files
      (x86)\Microsoft BizTalk Server 2016\Developer Tools

    - Microsoft.XLANG.BaseTypes.dll located at C:\Program Files
      (x86)\Microsoft BizTalk Server 2016

    - BizTalkUnitTestingFeatureProject.btproj which is a reference to
      the BizTalk Sample project. By doing this, the testing project will have
      access to schemas, maps, and pipelines from the BizTalk project.

- Microsoft.BizTalk.Pipeline.dll located at C:\Program Files
  (x86)\Microsoft BizTalk Server 2016\Microsoft.BizTalk.
  Pipeline.dll

6. Open the UnitTest1.cs class and add the following using
    statements, so you will be able to create objects based on the
    BizTalk project and use the Visual Studio testing features:

```
using System;
using Microsoft.VisualStudio.TestTools.UnitTesting;
using BizTalkUnitTestingFeatureProject;
using System.IO;
using System.Collections.Specialized;
using System.Collections.Generic;
```

Note   All the test methods detailed in the following sections use the AAA
(Arrange-Act-Assert) pattern, so you will see this reflected by #region statements.

Creating Test Methods to Validate Schemas

BizTalk Server schemas have a method called ValidateInstance that behaves in the
same way as when you right-click the schema at design time and select the Validate
Instance option. In this section, you are going to create two test methods:

- One to validate a valid instance.

- One to validate an invalid instance.

Follow these steps:

1. Open the UnitTest1.cs class and declare a string variable called
    IncomingBookOrdersInstance that will be used to save the path of
    the incoming message instance.

```
public class UnitTest1
{
    //Used to save the message example instances
    public string IncomingBookOrdersInstance = "";
```

2. Open the UnitTest1.cs class and add a Test method to test a
    valid message instance. Delete the default TestMethod and add
    this one:

```
[TestMethod]
public void ValidTestIncomingBookOrderSchema()
{
    //example test method that provides a valid message
    #region Arrange
    bool boolTestOK = false;
    BizTalkUnitTestingFeatureProject.IncomingBookOrders
    IncomingBookOrdersSchema = new IncomingBookOrders();
    //replace the IncomingBookOrdersInstance with your instance file
    IncomingBookOrdersInstance = @"C:\APRESS\Chapter9\
    BizTalkUnitTestingFeature\BizTalkUnitTestingFeatureProject\
    BizTalkUnitTestingFeatureProject\MessageInstances\
    IncomingBookOrders\ValidMessages\ValidIncomingBookOrders_1_
    Book.xml";
    #endregion Arrange

    #region Act
    boolTestOK = IncomingBookOrdersSchema.ValidateInstance(Inco
    mingBookOrdersInstance, Microsoft.BizTalk.TestTools.Schema.
    OutputInstanceType.XML);
    #endregion Act

    #region Assert
    Assert.IsTrue(boolTestOK);
    #endregion Assert
}
```

This TestMethod will evaluate the IncomingBookOrders schema against a valid
message instance.

3. Add a Test method to test for a wrong message instance:

```
[TestMethod]
public void WrongTestIncomingBookOrderSchema()
    {
```

```
//example test method that provides a wrong message
#region Arrange
bool boolTestOK = false;
BizTalkUnitTestingFeatureProject.IncomingBookOrders
IncomingBookOrdersSchema = new IncomingBookOrders();
//replace the IncomingBookOrdersInstance with your
instance file
IncomingBookOrdersInstance = @"C:\APRESS\
Chapter9\BizTalkUnitTestingFeature\
BizTalkUnitTestingFeatureProject\
BizTalkUnitTestingFeatureProject\MessageInstances\
IncomingBookOrders\WrongMessages\
WrongIncomingBookOrders_1_Book.xml";
#endregion Arrange

#region Act
boolTestOK = IncomingBookOrdersSchema.ValidateInsta
nce(IncomingBookOrdersInstance, Microsoft.BizTalk.
TestTools.Schema.OutputInstanceType.XML);
#endregion Act

#region Assert
Assert.IsTrue(boolTestOK);
#endregion Assert

}
```

This `TestMethod` will evaluate the `IncomingBookOrders` schema against a wrong message instance.

4. Choose Save All.

Creating Test Methods to Validate Maps

BizTalk Server maps have a method called `TestMap` that behaves the same way that right-clicking the map at design time and selecting the Validate Map option does. In this section you are going to create two test methods:

- One to validate a map that receives a valid message instance.

- One to validate a map that receives an invalid instance.

The testMap method is different from the ValidateInstance of schemas:

- When the testMap method executes, an output file is generated.

- The test method does not return True or False, so you have to evaluate whether the output file exists. If it does exist, that means that the map executed without raising exceptions. (The map could still be executed incorrectly from business point of view.)

- Checking the existence might not be enough, so you also check if the output file is empty. In that case, that means that the map worked from a validation point of view but it did not generate any output because something went wrong at the transformation level that did not raise an exception.

Let's now implement our test method to test the Map_IncomingBookOrders_To_CRMIncomingBookOrders map.

Follow these steps:

1. Add a new test method called ValidInstanceMap and type the following code:

```
[TestMethod]
public void ValidInstanceMap()
{
    //example test method that provides a wrong message
    #region Arrange
    bool boolTestOK = false;
    //replace the sOuputInstance with your output instance file
    string sOuputInstance = @"C:\APRESS\Chapter9\
    BizTalkUnitTestingFeature\BizTalkUnitTestingFeatureProject\
    BizTalkUnitTestingFeatureProject\MessageInstances\
    OutputInstances\ValidatedMapMessage.xml";
    //deleting the output instance
    if (File.Exists(sOuputInstance)) { File.
    Delete(sOuputInstance);}

    BizTalkUnitTestingFeatureProject.Map_IncomingBookOrders_To_
    CRMIncomingBookOrders map = new Map_IncomingBookOrders_To_
    CRMIncomingBookOrders();
```

```
//replace the IncomingBookOrdersInstance with your instance file
IncomingBookOrdersInstance = @"C:\APRESS\Chapter9\
BizTalkUnitTestingFeature\BizTalkUnitTestingFeatureProject\
BizTalkUnitTestingFeatureProject\MessageInstances\
IncomingBookOrders\ValidMessages\ValidIncomingBookOrders_1_
Book.xml";
#endregion Arrange

#region Act
map.TestMap(IncomingBookOrdersInstance, Microsoft.BizTalk.
TestTools.Schema.InputInstanceType.Xml, sOuputInstance,
Microsoft.BizTalk.TestTools.Schema.OutputInstanceType.XML);
//in this case we will check if the out put file exists:
var vFileInfo = new FileInfo(sOuputInstance);
if (vFileInfo.Exists ) { boolTestOK = true; }
#endregion Act

#region Assert
Assert.IsTrue(boolTestOK);
#endregion Assert
}
```

2. Add a new test method called WrongInstanceMap and type the
    following code:

```
[TestMethod]
        public void WrongInstanceMap()
        {
            //example test method that provides a wrong message
            #region Arrange
            bool boolTestOK = false;
            //replace the sOuputInstance with your output instance file
            string sOuputInstance = @"C:\APRESS\
            Chapter9\BizTalkUnitTestingFeature\
            BizTalkUnitTestingFeatureProject\
            BizTalkUnitTestingFeatureProject\MessageInstances\
            OutputInstances\ValidatedMapMessage.xml";
```

```
//deleting the output instance
if (File.Exists(sOuputInstance)) { File.
Delete(sOuputInstance); }
BizTalkUnitTestingFeatureProject.Map_
IncomingBookOrders_To_CRMIncomingBookOrders map = new
Map_IncomingBookOrders_To_CRMIncomingBookOrders();
//replace the IncomingBookOrdersInstance with your
wrong instance file
IncomingBookOrdersInstance = @"C:\APRESS\
Chapter9\BizTalkUnitTestingFeature\
BizTalkUnitTestingFeatureProject\
BizTalkUnitTestingFeatureProject\
MessageInstances\IncomingBookOrders\WrongMessages\
WrongIncomingBookOrders_1_Book.xml";
#endregion Arrange

#region Act
map.TestMap(IncomingBookOrdersInstance, Microsoft.
BizTalk.TestTools.Schema.InputInstanceType.Xml,
sOuputInstance, Microsoft.BizTalk.TestTools.Schema.
OutputInstanceType.XML);
//in this case we will check if the out put file
exists or if the File is empty
var vFileInfo= new FileInfo(sOuputInstance);
if (!vFileInfo.Exists || vFileInfo.Length < 4) {
boolTestOK = false; }

#endregion Act

#region Assert
Assert.IsTrue(boolTestOK);
#endregion Assert

        }
```

3. Choose Save All.

Creating Test Methods to Validate Pipelines

BizTalk Server pipelines have a method called TestPipeline that behaves the same way that executing the Pipeline.Exe tool does. In this section you are going to create a test method that executes a pipeline that receives a valid message instance.

Follow these steps:

1. Add a new test method called FFReceivePipelineUnitTest() and type the following code:

```
[TestMethod()]
        public void FFReceivePipelineUnitTest()
        {

            #region Arrange
            //loading the flat file pipeline rcvPipBookOrdersFF
            from the BizTalk server project
            BizTalkUnitTestingFeatureProject.rcvPipBookOrdersFF
            target = new rcvPipBookOrdersFF();

            //the testpipeline method is expecting the incoming
            message as a stringCollection//
            StringCollection documents = new StringCollection();
            IncomingBookOrdersInstance = @"C:\APRESS\
            Chapter9\BizTalkUnitTestingFeature\
            BizTalkUnitTestingFeatureProject\
            BizTalkUnitTestingFeatureProject\MessageInstances\
            IncomingBookOrders\ValidMessages\FFBooksOrder.txt";
            Assert.IsTrue(File.Exists(IncomingBookOrdersInstance));
            documents.Add(IncomingBookOrdersInstance);

            //Only a body part for this test
            message so an empty collection will be
            passed.             ===//
            StringCollection parts = new StringCollection();

            //The testpipeline method expects the schemas in a
            dictionary.
```

```
Dictionary<string, string> schemas = new
Dictionary<string, string>();
string SchemaFile = @"C:\APRESS\
Chapter9\BizTalkUnitTestingFeature\
BizTalkUnitTestingFeatureProject\
BizTalkUnitTestingFeatureProject\BookOrdersCompleted.
xsd";
Assert.IsTrue(File.Exists(SchemaFile));
schemas.Add("BizTalkUnitTestingFeatureProject.
BookOrdersCompleted", SchemaFile);
#endregion Arrange

#region Act
//=== Test the execution of the pipeline using the
inputs ===//
target.TestPipeline(documents, parts, schemas);
//=== Validate that the pipeline test produced the
message ===//
//=== which conforms to the
schema.                        ===//
#endregion Act

#region Assert
//Checking for the output file existence. If it exists
that means that the pipeline executed successfully
string[] strMessages = Directory.GetFiles(@"C:\
APRESS\Chapter9\BizTalkUnitTestingFeature\
BizTalkUnitTestingFeatureProject\UnitTestProject\bin\
Debug", "Message*.out");
Assert.IsTrue(strMessages.Length > 0);
BizTalkUnitTestingFeatureProject.BookOrdersCompleted
BookOrdersValidationSchema = new BookOrdersCompleted();
foreach (string outFile in strMessages)
{
    //for every output file we check if the message is
    valid calling the validateInstance method.
```

```
Assert.IsTrue(BookOrdersValidationSchema.
ValidateInstance(outFile, Microsoft.BizTalk.
TestTools.Schema.OutputInstanceType.XML));
    }
    #endregion Assert
}
```

2. Click on Save All.

Running the Tests

To run the tests cases you created previously, just follow these steps:

1. In the Visual Studio menu, navigate to the Test menu, select Run, and click on All Tests. See Figure 9-9.

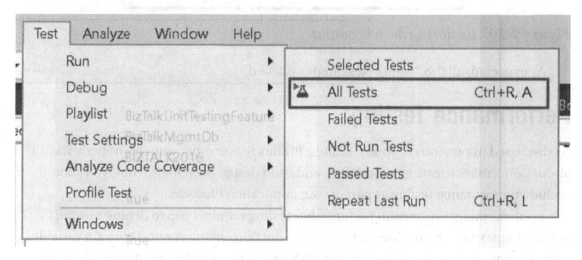

Figure 9-9. *Running all tests using the Test menu*

2. All unit tests will be executed. When it's finished, Visual Studio will show the output window shown in Figure 9-10 with the test results.

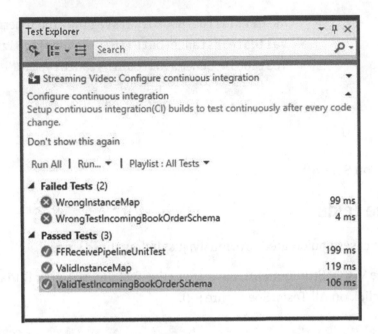

Figure 9-10. Exploring the test output

As expected, all the "wrong" test methods failed.

Performance Testing

As discussed in previous chapters, sizing a BizTalk Server environment properly it is all about performance testing, experience, and good design principles. Thus, you should include performance testing as part of your application lifecycle.

Implementing a successful performance testing requires you to deploy a testing environment that is nearly identical to the production environment. There are variables such as network, storage, Server IP, and DNS names that would be different, of course, but hardware sizing and components should be very similar. This fact must be a priority at the architecting phase because if production and testing environments are not nearly identical, you will have to extrapolate the gathered performance data in an attempt to represent that the test scenarios have run with production hardware resources, and that, at the end of the day, you will generate output that is not based on real sizing.

Additionally, there are two actions that you should consider when testing BizTalk Server:

- Assessing the production environment.

- Assessing the performance of individual BizTalk Server applications.

Performance Testing Methodology

Every single time you plan to deploy a new application to production you should follow this process:

1. Assessing the performance status of the production environment.

2. If the production performance assessment does not reveal a bottleneck, you can move to the stage of performing individual performance test for the new BizTalk application (in the testing environment).

3. Evaluate the performance of the application against the defined SLA.

4. If the individual performance tests show that the new application does not reach the target SLA, you have the following options:

    a. Whenever possible, try to identify the elements within the application that cause prevents the application to run under the agreed performance SLA. Evaluate whether the application will improve its behavior by applying the optimizations discussed in Chapter 4.

    b. Improve orchestration processing by applying the techniques explained in Chapter 6.

    c. Scale the production environment to fix the performance problem by adding more resources.

5. If the application performs under the defined SLA, you need to analyze the output test data to decide whether or not the application will impact production performance negatively.

6. If that analysis reveals that the application can impact the production environment to a point of exceeding the Maximum Sustainable Throughput (MST), then you should again evaluate whether or not to scale the production platform.

7. If the analysis reveals that the application will not impact the production environment, you can go ahead and deploy the application. Figure 9-11 shows this whole process.

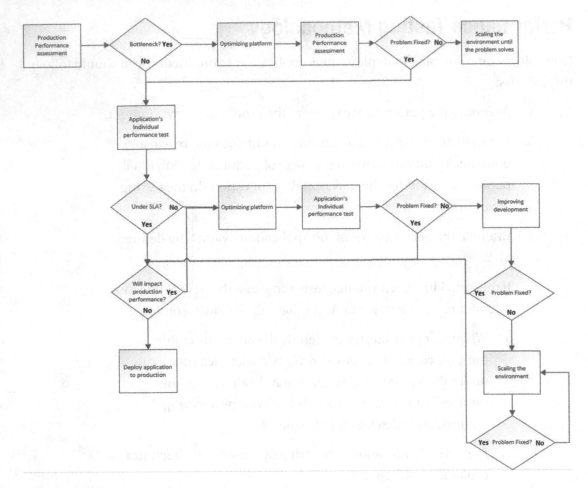

Figure 9-11. *Performance methodology flow*

Assessing the Production Environment

If your production environment is already running applications, it is essential that you
know how it's performing before you test a new solution. This information is crucial to
know the current status of the system regarding resource utilization.

In Chapters 1 and 2, you learned how to interpret the most important BizTalk Server
performance counters and, in Chapter 3, you learned how to use the performance
monitor and PAL tools to analyze the performance of a BizTalk Server platform.

As you learned in Chapter 6, an essential consideration when planning a BizTalk
Server environment should be to determine the maximum sustainable throughput
(MST) of the system. The MST of a BizTalk Server system is calculated as the highest

load of messages that the BizTalk environment can process. When load exceeds MST, messages are queued in the Message Box and transaction latency can increase.

Now is the time to apply all these concepts and techniques to assess the production environment and to evaluate whether the system is running under an optimum MST. By doing this you will know if there is enough room to add a new application based on the performance data gathered for that solution on the testing environment.

To assess the production environment, follow these steps:

1. Set up a 24 hour performance log. This topic is detailed in Chapter 3.

2. Process the captured data using PAL tool. This topic is detailed in Chapter 3.

3. Analyze the PAL report using the thresholds and techniques detailed in Chapter 2 as a guide.

4. Pay special attention to the analysis combination of the following performance counters:

   - BizTalk: MessageBox: General Counters: Spool Size

   - BizTalk: Messaging: Documents received-processed-sent /sec

   - Processor: %Processor Time

   - Physical Disk: Idle Time

   - Processor: %Processor time has been covered extensively in Chapter 2, but we need at this time to analyze all of them together.

BizTalk: Message Box: General Counters: Spool Size

This is probably the most important one. As you learned in Chapter 1, this performance counter gives you an idea of how the system is processing messages. If during the analyzed period there are increasing trends for this performance counter, there is a processing bottleneck that prevents the system from processing messages under the MST.

In the other hand, if the Spool Size counter shows no increasing trends, that means that the system is performing efficiently and is keeping up with the current load (of course, if performance degradation is not observed).

Physical Disk: Idle Time

If the Physical disk: Idle Time performance counter is high, especially for the SQL Server hosting the Message Box database, it is a good indicator that disks are processing writes and reads very efficiently. The disk is not busy most of the time and the loads that enter are being processed very quickly. On the other hand, if disks are not idle frequently means that they are busy and disk contention can appear. This condition can have a negative impact on the Message Box database. Review the section about the Message Box database in Chapter 4.

BizTalk: Messaging: Documents Received-Processed-Sent/Sec

Under the BizTalk Messaging category, you can find these performance counters:

- Documents received/sec
- Documents processed/sec
- Documents sent/sec

These performance counters by themselves do not provide any information related to the MST. However, if you analyze them in combination with the Spool Size performance counter, you can discover the area of the engine causing the performance bottleneck. If the BizTalk: MessageBox: General Counters: Spool Size performance counter shows increasing trends during the evaluating period, check whether any of the messaging counters show increasing trends also. You can experiment the following scenarios, individually or combined:

- Documents Received/sec increase—That means that your production system is receiving more messages than usual. If spool increases along with this counter but Documents Sent and Documents Processed/sec remain stable, that could means that the bottleneck is at the receiving layer.

- Documents Processed/sec increase—That means that your production system is processing more messages in orchestrations than usual. If the spool increases along with this counter but Documents Received/s and Documents Sent/sec remain stable, that could mean that the bottleneck is more likely at the processing layer.

- Documents Sent/sec increase—That means that your production
  system is sending more messages than usual. If the spool increases
  along with this counter, but Documents Received/s and Documents
  Processed/sec remain stable, that could mean that the bottleneck is
  at the sending layer because sent messages are getting suspended or
  they are retrying ports.

Example Scenarios of Evaluating the MST

Let's review a few examples to understand spool counters versus the messaging
performance counters and CPU usage. This topic is crucial when assessing the
production environment.

Scenario (I) Processing Messages Under the MST

Figure 9-12 shows a performance diagram for a 24-hour capture period.

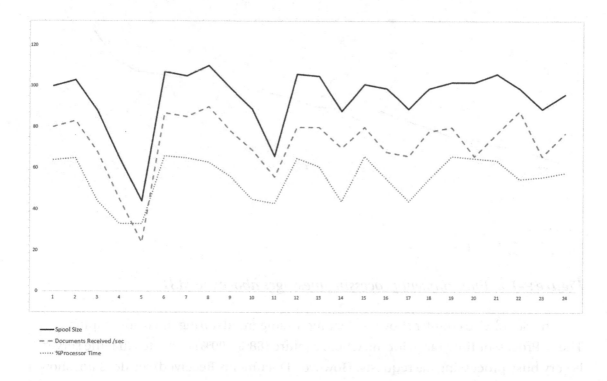

Figure 9-12. *Environment processing messages under the MST*

The Spool Size counter does not show increasing trends during the whole capture and Documents Received/sec does not show extreme peaks. When the number of received messages increases, the spool table also grows, but then it gets decreased quickly, indicating that the system is processing messages efficiently and that it can keep up with the current load.

The % Processor time range for the whole capture (36%-67%) indicates that there is still room for receiving more messages.

In this situation, you could add a new application if the load test in the testing environment does not show an excessive processor usage for that application.

Scenario (II) Processing Messages Above the MST

Figure 9-13 shows a different performance diagram for a 24-hour capture period.

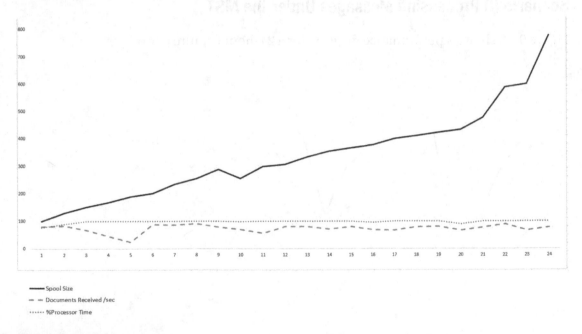

Figure 9-13. *Environment processing messages above the MST*

The Spool Size counter shows a clear increasing trend during the whole capture. The % Processor time range for the whole capture (88%-100%) indicates that the server is very busy processing the requests. However, Documents Received/sec does not show extreme peaks.

What could be happening in this scenario? Most likely there is a processing bottleneck caused by orchestration processing (assuming that the sending layer is processing smoothly), as the documents received per second do not provide a clue. Now you can analyze the Documents Processed/second along with the spool size and %Processor time, as shown in Figure 9-14.

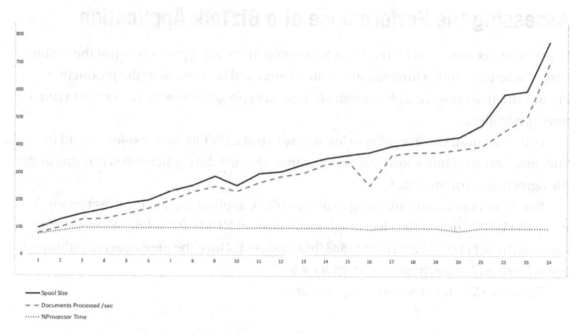

Figure 9-14. Environment processing messages above the MST due to messages processed by orchestrations

In situation outlined here, when the number of processed messages increases, the spool table also grows, and it increases exponentially along with the processed messages. This indicates that the system is not processing messages efficiently and it cannot keep up with the load caused by messages processed by orchestrations.

Under this circumstance you cannot add a new application to the environment because it is already a processing bottleneck. It is time to evaluate the following options:

- Whenever possible, try to locate the application that causes the issue and evaluate whether the application will improve its behavior by applying the optimizations discussed in Chapter 4.

461

- Scale the production environment to fix the performance problem by adding more resources.

- Improve orchestration processing by applying the techniques explained in Chapter 6.

Assessing the Performance of a BizTalk Application

In previous sections, you learned how to develop unit testing projects to test the BizTalk Server solutions from a functionality point of view and how to assess the production environment, so you will now consider if there are enough hardware resources to run the new application.

In this section, you are going to learn how to test a BizTalk Server solution end to end, and how to create a load test, so you can evaluate if the application is running under the agreed performance SLA.

For this example, you are going to use a BizTalk application that receives messages using the WCF-Custom Receive Adapter with custom NETTCP binding. A receive port is listening to `net.tcp//localhost:8888/btsloadtest`. Once the messages are published, a send port will write them to an output folder.

Figure 9-15 illustrates the testing scenario.

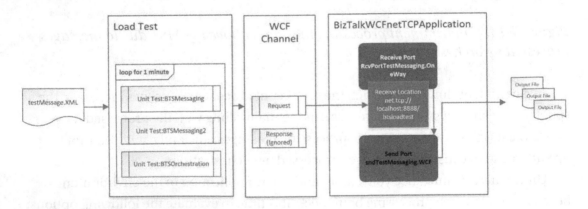

Figure 9-15. *The testing scenario diagram*

1. The Load Test Visual Studio project will execute, in a loop for one minute, the following BizTalk Unit tests:

   - `BTSMessaging`

   - `BTSMessaging2`

   - `BTSOrchestration`

2. Each loop iteration creates a new WFC message that is sent to a `netTcp` WCF Channel.

3. A BizTalk Server Receive Port is listening to that URI, `net.tcp://localhost:8888`, and receives the WCF request through the receive location.

4. The Send port `sndTestMessaging` is subscribed with a filter expression to the `ReceivePort` and sends all received messages to the output folder.

5. To simplify the scenario, the BizTalk application will not send a response back to the original WCF request.

Prerequisites

The coded solutions have the following requirements.

1. Visual Studio load tests requires Visual Studio Enterprise.

2. TCP Activation. The example uses WCF Net TCP bindings and because of that you need a Windows service called Net TCP Listener Adapter.

3. In Windows Server 2016, you can add the TCP Listener Adapter by adding the Tcp Activation feature, as shown in Figure 9-16.

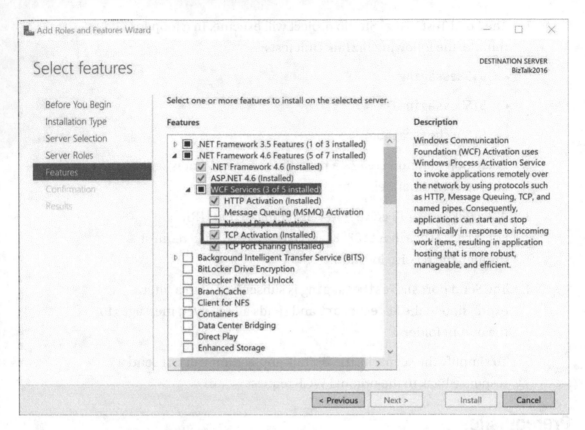

Figure 9-16. *Adding the TCP Activation feature using the Add Roles and Features wizard*

Once it's installed, make sure the following Net TCP services are running:

- Net.Tcp Listener Adapter

- Net.Tcp Port Sharing Service

Installing the BizTalkWCFnetTCP Sample Application

BizTalkWCFnetTCP receives the messages from the WFC channel and sends the messages to an output folder. Follow these steps to install it:

1. Using the File Explorer, navigate to: `C:\APRESS\Chapter9\BizTalkWCFnetTCPApplication`

2. Locate the following MSI file: `C:\APRESS\Chapter9\BizTalkWCFnetTCPApplication\MSI\BizTalkWCFnetTCPApplication.msi`

3. Install the MSI.

4. Import the MSI to the BizTalk Server database using the BizTalk Administration Console.

5. Start the `BizTalkWCFnetTCPApplication` application.

Creating a New Visual C# Test Project

Follow these steps to create a new test project:

1. Using Visual Studio, create a new project. Click to expand Visual C#, and click Test. At the bottom of the New Project dialog box, specify the following options:

   - Template: Visual C# -Test - Unit Test Project (.Net 4.6)

   - Name: BizTalkUnitTest

   - Location: Choose a location

   - Solution name: BizTalkUnitTest

2. Click OK.

3. Once the project loads, add the following references:

   - `System.XML`

   - `System.ServiceModel`

   - `System.ServiceModel.Channels`

   - `System.Configuration`

   - `System.RunTime.Serialization`

4. Add a new item to the project. Go to Visual C# Items, navigate to General, and choose Application Configuration File.

5. Double-click the `App.Config` file and replace the content with the following code. The original file is located in `C:\Apress\Chapter9\BizTalkUnitTest\BizTalkUnitTest\BizTalkUnitTest`.

```xml
<?xml version="1.0" encoding="utf-8"?>
<configuration>
  <system.serviceModel>
    <!-- Bindings used by client endpoints -->
    <bindings>
      <netTcpBinding>
        <binding name="netTcpBinding" closeTimeout="01:10:00"
        openTimeout="01:10:00" receiveTimeout="01:10:00"
        sendTimeout="01:10:00" transactionFlow="false"
        transferMode="Buffered" transactionProtocol="OleT
        ransactions" hostNameComparisonMode="StrongWildca
        rd" listenBacklog="100" maxBufferPoolSize="1048576"
        maxBufferSize="10485760" maxConnections="400"
        maxReceivedMessageSize="10485760">
          <readerQuotas maxDepth="32" maxStringContentLength="8192"
          maxArrayLength="16384" maxBytesPerRead="4096"
          maxNameTableCharCount="16384" />
          <reliableSession ordered="true"
          inactivityTimeout="00:10:00" enabled="false" />
          <security mode="None">
            <transport clientCredentialType="Windows" protectionLe
            vel="EncryptAndSign" />
            <message clientCredentialType="Windows" />
          </security>
        </binding>
      </netTcpBinding>
    </bindings>
    <client>
      <!-- Client endpoints used to exchange messages with WCF
      Receive Locations -->

      <!-- BTSMessagingEP -->
      <endpoint address="net.tcp://<BizTalk Server Name>:8888/
      btsloadtest" binding="netTcpBinding" bindingConfiguratio
      n="netTcpBinding" contract="System.ServiceModel.Channels.
      IRequestChannel" name="BTSMessagingEP" />
```

```
<endpoint address="net.tcp://<BizTalk Server Name>:8888/
btsloadtest" binding="netTcpBinding" bindingConfiguration
="netTcpBinding" contract="System.ServiceModel.Channels.
IRequestChannel" name="BTSMessagingEP2" />

<!-- BTSOrchestrationEP -->
<endpoint address="net.tcp://<BizTalk Server Name>:9999/
btsloadtest" binding="netTcpBinding" bindingConfiguration
="netTcpBinding" contract="System.ServiceModel.Channels.
IRequestChannel" name="BTSOrchestrationEP" />
    </client>
  </system.serviceModel>
  <appSettings>
    <!-- Folder containing test messages -->
    <add key="testMessageFolder" value="C:\APRESS\Chapter9\
    BizTalkTestingSolution\TestMessages" />
    <add key="ClientSettingsProvider.ServiceUri" value="" />
  </appSettings>
</configuration>
```

This is the configuration file where you set the netTcpBinding properties and the location of the test messages used by the test case:

- netTcpBinding properties—Send messages through using the netTCPbinding on ports 8888 and 9999. Since our receive locations will be listening on those ports, BizTalk Server will pick up messages from there.

- Location of the test messages—Locate the test message folder using the TestMessageFolder key.

6. Visual Studio created an empty UnitTest1.cs file. Open it and replace the content with the already generated class, located here:

```
C:\APRESS\Chapter9\BizTalkUnitTest\BizTalkUnitTest\
BizTalkUnitTest\UnitTest1.cs
```

This class implements the load test interfaces that will be called by Visual Studio test engine.

7. In the Visual Studio menu, navigate to the Test menu, select Run, and click on All Tests. See Figure 9-17.

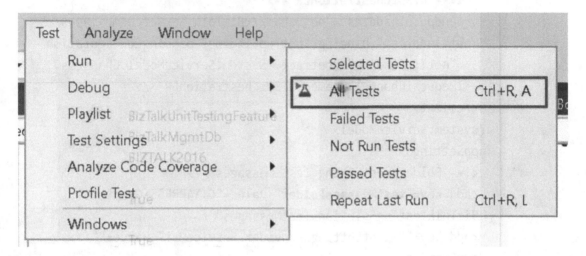

Figure 9-17. *Running all tests using the Test menu*

8. Choose Save All.

Adding a Load Test to the Project

Now it's time to simulate a load against the united test you created previously. Follow these steps to add a load test to the project:

1. Create a new folder called LoadTests. You will use this folder to save the LoadTest cases data.

2. Right-click at the LoadTests folder level, select Add ➤ New Item, and choose the Load Test option under Visual c# items\Test. The Create New Load Test Wizard window will be shown. See Figure 9-18.

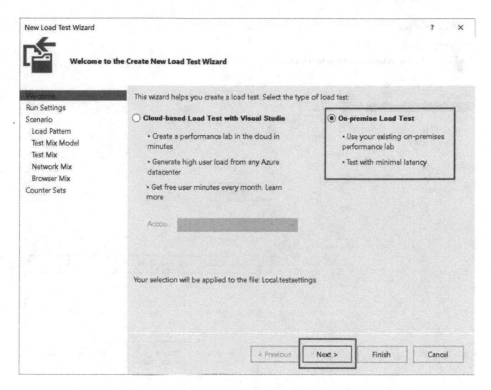

Figure 9-18. *Selecting the on-premise version of the load test*

3. From the welcome screen, select On-Premise Load Test and click Next.

4. On the Review and Edit Run settings for a load test window, take the following actions (see Figure 9-19):

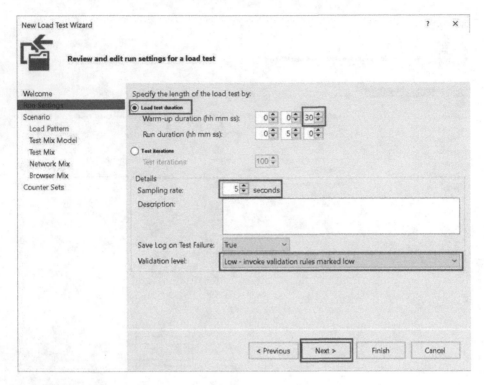

Figure 9-19. *Selecting the load test duration mode*

- Select the Load Test duration option.

- Specify 30 seconds for the Warm-Up Duration setting.

- Change the Run Duration to 1 minute or leave it at 5 (five minutes will load more than 4.000 instances into BizTalk Server).

- Set the Sampling Rate setting to 5 seconds.

- Invoke validation rules marked Low as the Validation level.

5. Click Next.

6. On the Edit Settings for a load test scenario, type `TestWCFNetTcp` as the name of the scenario and choose the Do Not Use Think Times option. See Figure 9-20.

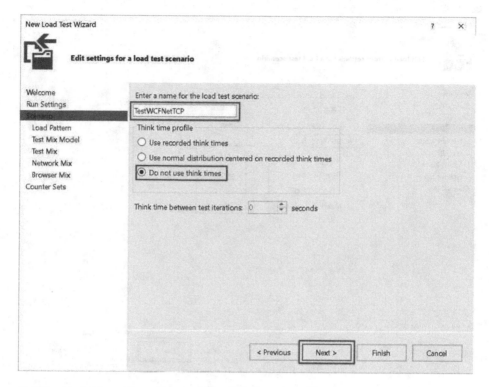

Figure 9-20. *Entering the name of the load test scenario*

7. Click Next.

8. From the Edit Load Pattern settings window, choose Step Load and assign the following values to configuration step settings (see Figure 9-21a):

   - Start user count: 10 users

   - Step duration: 60 seconds

   - Step user count: 10 users

   - Maximum user count: 80

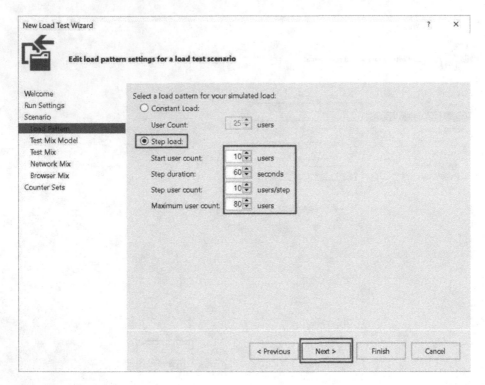

Figure 9-21a. *Setting the load pattern for the load test*

9.   Click Next.

10. From the Test Mix Model window, select Based on the Total Number Of Tests and click Next, as shown in Figure 9-21b.

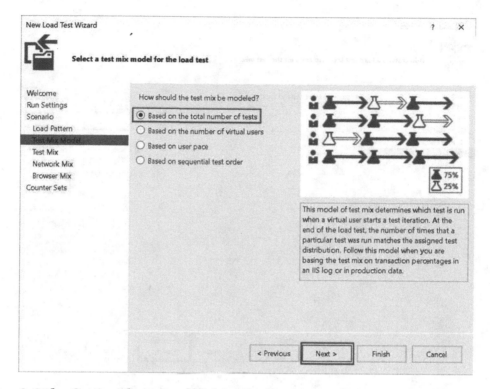

Figure 9-21b. *Setting the mix model for the load test*

11. You now select the unit test cases you created previously. From the Add Tests window, click Add. Then add the following test cases to the scenario:

    • BTSMessaging

    • BTSMessaging2

    • BTSOrchestration

12. Use the sliders to set the BTSMessaging unit test to a 60% distribution. See Figure 9-22.

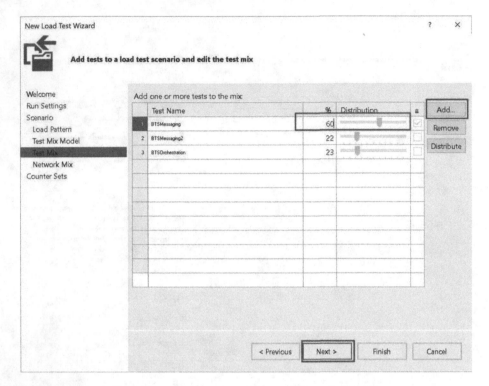

Figure 9-22. *Selecting the unit test scenarios and load distribution*

13. Click Next.

14. Leave the LAN settings at the defaults and click Next.

15. From the Specify Computers to Monitor window, add Localhost. In the next section you will be adding BizTalk Server performance counters, so you do not need to add counters at this stage.

16. Click Finish.

Create a BizTalk Server Counter Set

While the load test runs, you should capture all the BizTalk Server relevant counters for that scenario. Visual Studio does not come with a counter set for BizTalk Server. Therefore, you will have to create one. Use the counters referenced throughout all the book, especially in Chapter 2.

Follow these steps:

1. Using the Visual Studio Solution Explorer, double-click the
   LoadTest1.loadtest file. See Figure 9-23.

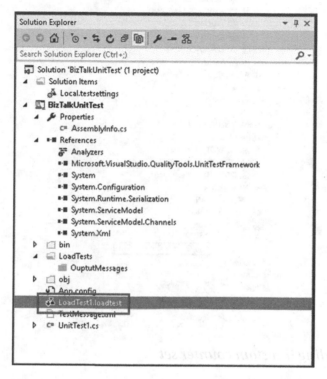

Figure 9-23. *Opening the load test file*

2. Locate the Counter Sets node. Right-click and select the option
   Add Custom Counter Set. See Figure 9-24.

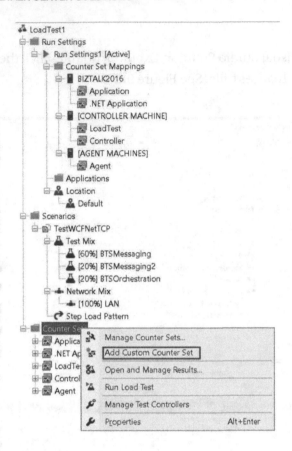

Figure 9-24. *Adding a custom counter set*

3. Notice that an empty Custom1 CounterSet is created.

4. Right-click the Custom1 counter set, select the Properties option, and change the name to BizTalk Server.

5. Locate the new BizTalk Server counter set, then right-click and select the Add Counters option. See Figure 9-25.

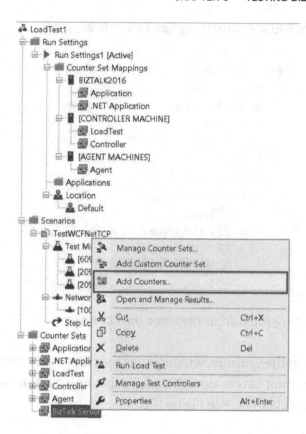

Figure 9-25. *Adding counters to a counter set*

6. Add the following BizTalk Server performance counters:

    - Processor: Select only %Privileged Time and %Processor Time

    - BizTalk: Message Box: General Counters: Select all counters, all instances

    - BizTalk: Messaging: Select all counters, all instances

    - BizTalk: Message Agent: Select all counters, all instances

    - XLANG/s Orchestrations: Select all counters, all instances

As a result, you should see something like Figure 9-26.

Figure 9-26. *Exploring the added performance counters*

7. Right-click at the Counter Set Mappings root level and select the
    Manage Counter Sets option. Make sure that only BizTalk Server is
    selected and click OK. See Figure 9-27.

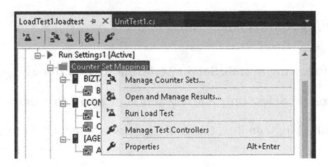

Figure 9-27. *Accessing the counter set mappings*

8. Check the BizTalk Server Counters checkbox and click OK. See Figure 9-28.

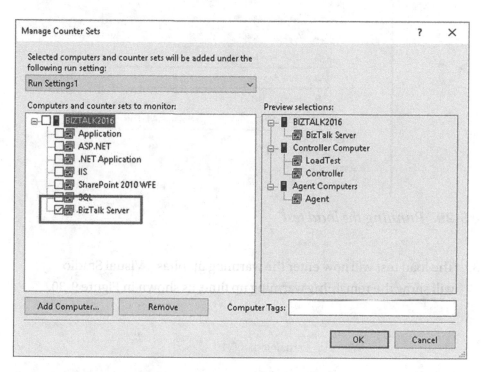

Figure 9-28. *Selecting BizTalk Server performance counter set*

9. Choose Save All.

Running the Load Test

Let's run the load test:

1. Open the LoadTest1.loadtest file.

2. Right-click at the root level and choose Run Load Test. See Figure 9-29.

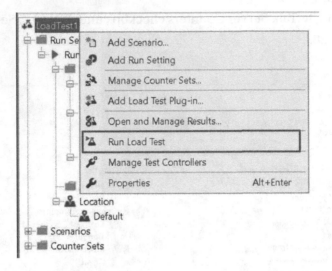

Figure 9-29. *Running the load test*

3.   The load test will now enter the warming up phase. Visual Studio
     will show the remaining warming up time, as shown in Figure 9-30.

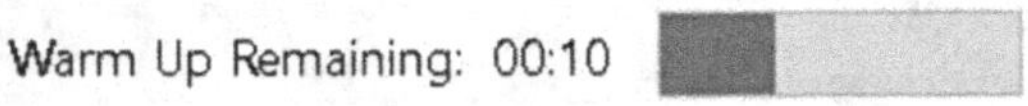

Warm Up Remaining: 00:10

Figure 9-30. *Showing the warming up progress*

4.   Wait until warming up time finishes. Visual Studio will run the
     load test scenario. It will show you the remaining time, as shown
     in Figure 9-31.

Remaining: 00:08

Figure 9-31. *Showing the remaining time for the load test*

5.   Once it's finished, Visual Studio will show the Load Test Summary
     screen.

Examining the Load Test Results

Let's now review all the data generated by the load test. This information is crucial to understanding whether the new application will affect production performance.

Note   Keep in mind that, along with the load test output data, you could also set up a performance log using the performance monitor tool and then analyze the data by running the PAL tool. You can then include the PAL report as part of the load test result by copying the PAL output files to the test folder.

Load Test Summary Dashboard

The Summary dashboard is accessible from the Load test menu, as shown in Figure 9-32.

Figure 9-32. *Accessing the load test summary section*

Generated data:

1. General information: Overall Test Run Information, Max User Load forced, Tests Run Per Second, Number of Failed Tests, and the Top 5 slowest tests. See Figure 9-33.

Load Test Summary

Test Run Information

Load test name	LoadTest1
Description	
Start time	12/15/2016 8:02:48 AM
End time	12/15/2016 8:03:48 AM
Warm-up duration	00:00:15
Duration	00:01:00
Controller	Local run
Number of agents	1
Run settings used	Run Settings1

Key Statistic: Top 5 Slowest Tests

Name	95% Test Time (sec)
BTSMessaging2	1.33
BTSOrchestration	1.32
BTSMessaging	1.08

Figure 9-33. *Examining the load test summary data*

2. The overall results are shown in Figure 9-34.

Overall Results

Max User Load	10
Tests/Sec	33.5
Tests Failed	2
Avg. Test Time (sec)	0.30
Transactions/Sec	0
Avg. Transaction Time (sec)	0
Pages/Sec	-
Avg. Page Time (sec)	-
Requests/Sec	-
Requests Failed	-
Requests Cached Percentage	-
Avg. Response Time (sec)	-
Avg. Content Length (bytes)	-

Figure 9-34. *Examining the overall results data*

3. For each unit test, Visual Studio shows the number of executed tests, number of failed tests, and the average individual test time in seconds, as shown in Figure 9-35.

▾ **Test Results**

Name	Scenario	Total Tests	Failed Tests (% of total)	Avg. Test Time (sec)
BTSMessaging2	TestWCFNetTCP	393	0 (0)	0.31
BTSOrchestration	TestWCFNetTCP	425	2 (0.47)	0.31
BTSMessaging	TestWCFNetTCP	1,192	0 (0)	0.29

Figure 9-35. *Examining test results data*

4. It also shows overall physical resource consumption—Processor Time and Available Memory—as shown in Figure 9-36.

▾ **System Under Test Resources**

Machine Name	% Processor Time	Available Memory at Test Completion (Mb)
BIZTALK2016	36.1	1,849

Figure 9-36. *Examining the resource utilization*

5. It also shows the errors that occurred during the load test execution, grouped by error type, as shown in Figure 9-37.

▼ Errors

Type	Subtype	Count	Last Message
Test Error	TestError	8	Test method Microsoft.BizTalk.Samples.BTSLoadTest.BTSOrchestration threw exception: System.ServiceModel.E
Exception	LoadTestCounterNotFoundException	2	The performance counter 'Documents transmitted/Batch Base' in category 'BizTalk:Messaging' on computer 'BIZ
Test Error	LoadGeneratorLocationError	1	Geo locations configured with load test will only be honored with load test runs using Visual Studio Team Service

Figure 9-37. *Exploring the list of errors generated during the test*

Graphs Dashboard

Graphs view is accessible from the Load Test menu, as shown in Figure 9-38.

Figure 9-38. *Accessing the graph summary section*

Generated data:

1. In the Default Graph view, there is a pane on the left that shows all the counter categories you have access to, as shown in Figure 9-39.

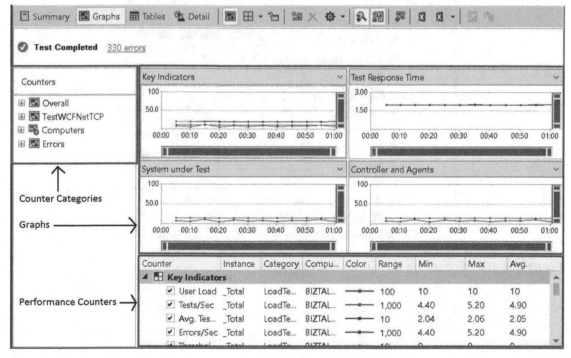

Figure 9-39. *Exploring the graph information*

This view is dynamic, so if you select a different category, the graphs and performance counters views will change accordingly.

Note   Notice the Error symbol at the Counters Category Computers. This icon appears when any of the studied performance counters are not within the default thresholds.

---

2. Navigate to Computers\<BizTalk Server Name>\MessageBox General Counters. Locate the Spool Size counter, right-click, and select Show Counters on Graph option. See Figure 9-40.

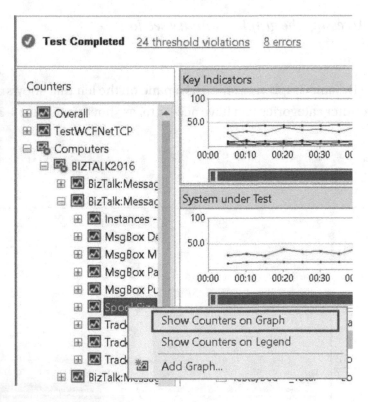

Figure 9-40. *Accessing the Spool counter data*

The graph view will change to display the Spool Size performance counter data, as shown in Figure 9-41.

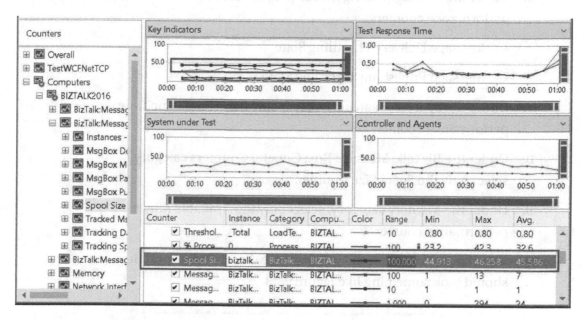

Figure 9-41. *Examining the Spool counter data*

Generating an Excel Report

This feature allows you to crate Excel reports with the analyzed data, so you will be able to share the output results. This feature requires Microsoft Excel installed in your computer. Otherwise, it will not be available.

Follow these steps to create an Excel report.

1. At the Load Test results, click on the Generate Excel Report toolbox icon, as shown in Figure 9-42.

Figure 9-42. *Accessing the Excel exporting tool*

2. The generate report wizard will start.

3. Choose Create a Trend Report and click Next.

4. Type the following name for the report: `BizTalk Trend Report`. Click Next.

5. Select the latest load test results. Click Next.

6. Under the Message Box Agent category, select only the following performance counters:

    - Message Delivery Throttling State

    - Message Publishing Throttling State

7. Under the Processor category, select only the %Processor Time performance counter.

8. Under the BizTalk: Message Box: General Counters category, select only the Spool Size Counter.

9. Under the Memory category, select only the Available Mbytes performance counter.

10. Click Finish. Visual Studio will generate the Output Report. It should look something like Figure 9-43.

Name: BizTalk Trend Report				
Table of Contents				
Runs in report				
Runs				
Reports				
BizTalk:Message Agent				
	Message delivery throttling state			
	Message publishing throttling state			
BizTalk:Message Box:General Counters				
	Spool Size			
Memory				
	Available MBytes			
Processor				
	% Processor Time			

Figure 9-43. *Examining the Excel report*

11. Navigate through the report to access the performance data.

Creating a Web Test for BizTalk WCF Service HTTP Binding

In this section, you are going to learn how to test a BizTalk Server application that has an orchestration exposed as a WCF service, so you can evaluate if the application is running under the agreed performance SLA.

In this example, a BizTalk application called WebServiceBookOrders receives messages using the WCF-BasicHttp receive adapter.

Follow these steps:

1. Install and import the WebServiceBookOrders MSI file located here:
    C:\APRESS\Chapter9\WebServiceBookOrders\MSI

2. The MSI file will create a WCF service called WebServiceBookOrders and a BizTalk Server application with the same name.

3. Using Internet Information Server, change the application pool to BAMAppPool.

4. Start the BizTalk application called WebServiceBookOrders. Otherwise, the WCF service will fail.

5. Once it's installed, use your preferred Internet browser to navigate to the following URI: http://localhost/WebServiceBookOrders/ WebServiceBookOrders_orcBookOrders_Port_WebBookOrders.svc

---

Warning   Note that troubleshooting IIS and WCF services are out of the scope of the book. If you do not see the service description and the WSDL, the steps will fail. Troubleshoot your local Internet information server until you are able to see the service definition.

---

6. Using Visual Studio, create a new web load test project. See Figure 9-44.

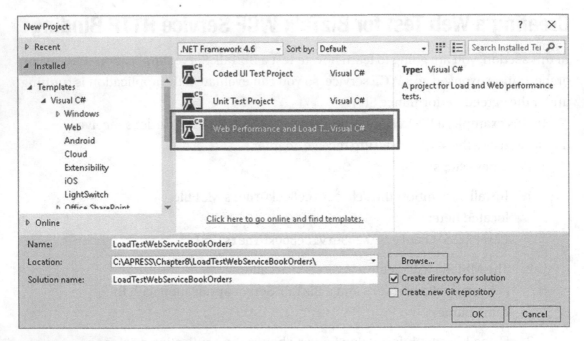

Figure 9-44. *Adding a web performance and load testing Visual C# project*

7. Visual Studio creates the test project and adds an empty web test.

8. Double-click the Webtest1.webtest file.

9. Right-click at the web test level and select the Add Web Service
    Request option. See Figure 9-45.

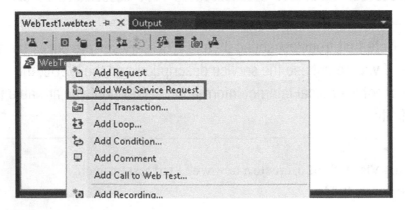

Figure 9-45. *Adding a web service request*

10. Visual Studio creates a default local host request.

11. Click on the default local host request and, in the Properties window, set the URL property to `http://localhost/WebServiceBookOrders/WebServiceBookOrders_orcBookOrders_Port_WebBookOrders.svc`. See Figure 9-46.

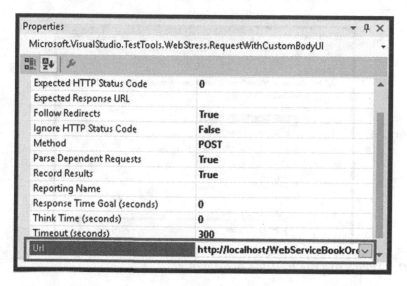

Figure 9-46. *Setting the destination URL property of the web test*

12. Right-click at the test level and select the Add Header option, as shown in Figure 9-47.

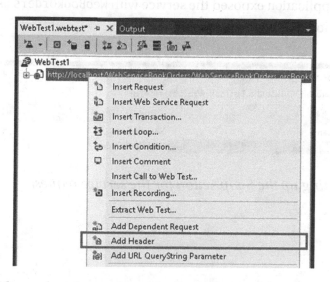

Figure 9-47. *Adding a header to the web request*

13. Visual Studio adds a header section and a body string parameter that will be used to send the request to the service.

14. Expand the Headers folder, select the default header, and right-click and select Properties. See Figure 9-48.

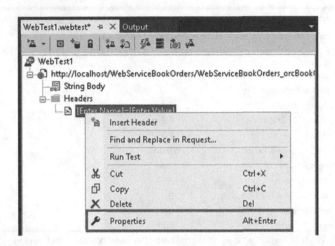

Figure 9-48. *Accessing the header properties*

15. Set the Name field to SoapAction. Set the **Value** field based on your web service action name. The SoapAction value can be obtained from your web service's WSDL. In this case the BizTalk Server application exposed the service with WebBookOrders as the SoapAction. See Figure 9-49.

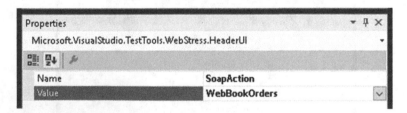

Figure 9-49. *Setting up the SoapAction for the service request*

16. Right-click on String Body and choose Properties. See Figure 9-50.

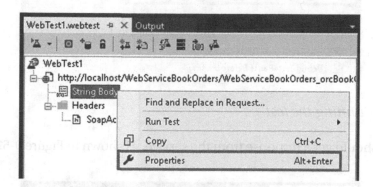

Figure 9-50. *Accessing the properties of the body string request parameter*

17. Set text/xml to Content Type. Set a valid request XML into the string body. In this case, I generated the request using the Soap UI, but you can leverage any other software for that objective:

```
<soapenv:Envelope xmlns:soapenv="http://schemas.xmlsoap.
org/soap/envelope/" xmlns:web="http://WebServiceBookOrders.
BookOrderRequest">
    <soapenv:Header/>
    <soapenv:Body>
        <web:BookOrderRequest>
            <OrderDate>21/04/1977</OrderDate>
            <CustomerId>777888</CustomerId>
            <TotalAmount>345666</TotalAmount>
            <Description>test</Description>
            <isVIP>0</isVIP>
            <OrderId>453453433</OrderId>
        </web:BookOrderRequest>
    </soapenv:Body>
</soapenv:Envelope>
```

18. Choose Save All.

19. Click the Run Test button (see Figure 9-51) to test your service call. Make sure that it is successful and fix it if the test failed.

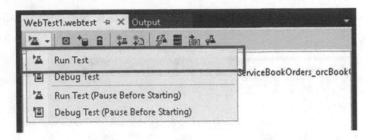

Figure 9-51. *Running the test*

20.   You should get a response from the service, as shown in Figure 9-52.

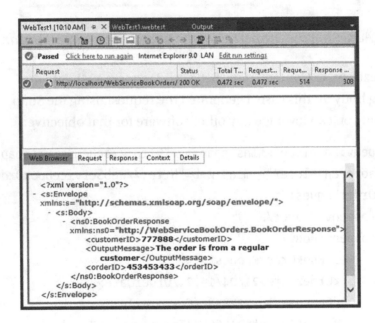

Figure 9-52. *Examining the response from the service*

21.   Now you can add a load test to run the web test. Follow the steps
      detailed in the previous section, entitled "Adding a Load Test to
      the Project".

Providing a Dynamic Data Source

For most of the performance testing labs, you should include dynamic data sources that
will help you test all possible scenarios for the business flow.

At the moment of writing this book, Visual Studio provides the following options to retrieve data from a dynamic data source:

- Database

- CSV file

- XML file

Follow these steps to add a CSV file as the data source for a load test project:

1. Select the web test and click the Add Data Source button. See Figure 9-53.

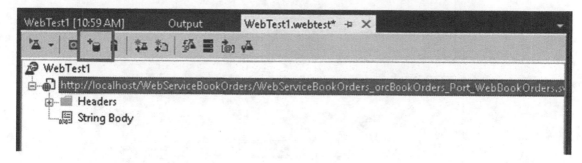

Figure 9-53. *Adding a data source to the web test project*

2. Visual Studio will load the wizard for data source selection. Type
    BookOrders as the data source name, select CSV file as the data
    source type, and click Next. See Figure 9-54.

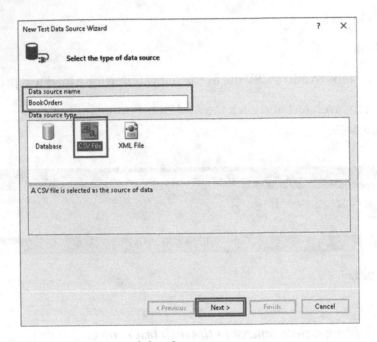

Figure 9-54. *Selecting the type of the data source*

3. Select C:\APRESS\Chapter9\LoadTestWebServiceBookOrders\
   DataSource\WebServiceBookOrdersRequests.csv as the CSV file
   and click Finish. See Figure 9-55.

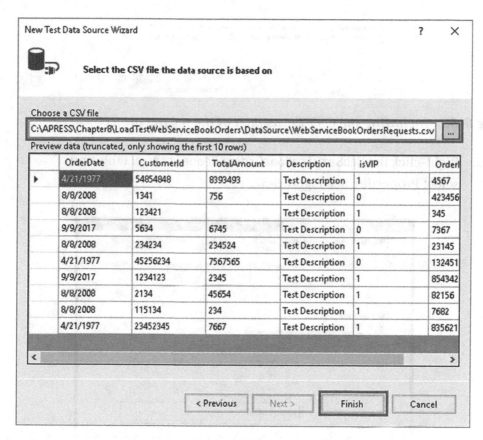

Figure 9-55. Selecting the CSV file and exploring the data

4. Click Yes if Visual Studio asks you if you want to include the CSV file as part of the project. See Figure 9-56.

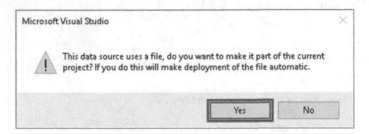

Figure 9-56. *Including the CSV file as part of the testing project*

5. Right-click the `WebServiceBookOrdersRequests#csv` table and select Properties. See Figure 9-57.

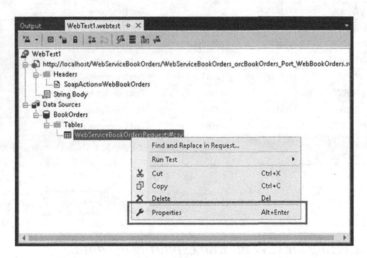

Figure 9-57. *Selecting the table properties*

6. Change the Access Method to Random so that Visual Studio will randomly access the CSV file. See Figure 9-58.

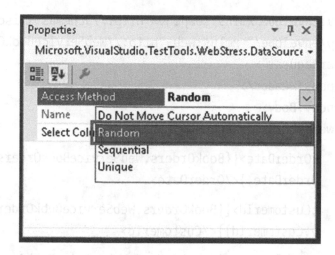

Figure 9-58. *Selecting the Access Method*

7. Right-click at the String Body section of the web test request and click on Properties. See Figure 9-59.

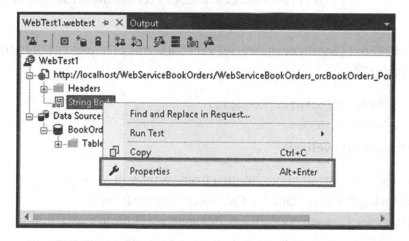

Figure 9-59. *Accessing the properties of the string body request property*

8. Edit the string body property to the following and replace it with the following text:

```
<soapenv:Envelope xmlns:soapenv="http://schemas.xmlsoap.
org/soap/envelope/" xmlns:web="http://WebServiceBookOrders.
BookOrderRequest">
    <soapenv:Header/>
    <soapenv:Body>
        <web:BookOrderRequest>

            <OrderDate>{{BookOrders.WebServiceBookOrdersRequests#csv.
            OrderDate}}</OrderDate>

            <CustomerId>{{BookOrders.WebServiceBookOrdersRequests#cs
            v.CustomerId}}</CustomerId>

            <TotalAmount>{{BookOrders.WebServiceBookOrdersRequests#cs
            v.TotalAmount}}</TotalAmount>

            <Description>TestDescription</Description>

            <isVIP>{{BookOrders.WebServiceBookOrdersRequests#csv.
            isVIP}}</isVIP>

<OrderId>{{BookOrders.WebServiceBookOrdersRequests#csv.OrderIs}}
</OrderId>

        </web:BookOrderRequest>
    </soapenv:Body>
</soapenv:Envelope>
```

9. Notice that instead of providing a fixed value, you are now retrieving the data from the CSV file, using the format `{{DataSourceName.TableName.ColumnName}}` for instance in our example. If you want to provide the CustomerId parameter, you should use this format:

```
{{BookOrders.WebServiceBookOrdersRequests#csv.CustomerId}}
```

Now run the test several times and you will see how Visual Studio is using data from the CSV file.

498

Summary

In this chapter, you learned how to use all the knowledge acquired in previous chapters of the book to include testing procedures as part of your normal application development lifecycle.

Performance testing is very important for BizTalk Server environments as usually, BizTalk Server integrates applications that are part of the core business within the organization. That is why implementing the unit and performance testing techniques discussed in this chapter will increase the quality of the code you write. It does this by reducing the chances of bugs and ensuring that the production environment will be able to keep up with the load that new applications will generate.

You also learned about the preferred performance methodology that mature customers are applying to their mission-critical BizTalk Server environments.

In Chapter 9, you read a BizTalk Server tale that will help you put into practice several advanced topics discussed in this book.

CHAPTER 10

A BizTalk Server Tale

In this chapter, I am going to tell you a story. This is the story about a fictitious customer (ACME corporation) that decides to start with BizTalk Server as its integration system. Because at the beginning they start only with one non-mission critical application, the sizing of the initial environment is small. Gradually, they add more and more applications, so they have to figure out a way to improve the platform. Even though this is an imaginary exercise, the situations described here are quite common with each evolving BizTalk server customer.

Additionally, you will learn about the most common architectures that customers are using all over the world and how they provide high availability to the single point of failure areas.

Chapter 1: The One with the Baby BizTalk Server

ACME corporation started using BizTalk Server to move customer data from an Excel file to the internal CRM application. If this solution fails, business operations will not be affected, as this application is mainly used for internal reporting; the core solutions are currently operated by custom .NET services and applications.

Because of the light availability and performance requirements, they decided to start with a small BizTalk Server deployment using BizTalk Server Standard edition, which has the following limitations:

- Access to CPU is restricted by two cores

- Only one BizTalk Server is possible

- Maximum of five BizTalk Server applications

As they do not need high availability, BizTalk and SQL Server are on the same box to reduce hardware and licensing costs.

© Agustín Mántaras 2019
A. Mántaras, *BizTalk Server 2016*, https://doi.org/10.1007/978-1-4842-3994-0_10

Architecture:

- Number of total servers: 1

- Number of SQL Servers: 1

    - Standard edition, 2 CPU, 8 GB of memory

- Number of BizTalk Servers: 1

    - Standard edition, 2 CPU, 8 GB of memory

Chapter 2: The One with New Applications

After using BizTalk Server for a while, the team saw the great value of the mapping feature and how BizTalk Server could convert flat files to XML. The development team wanted to create more applications and deploy them to BizTalk Server. However, they realized that they would need to upgrade the BizTalk Server version to the Enterprise edition because now they would need eight applications to provide the business functionality. Additionally, upon testing, they realized that the CPU was above 70% most of the time, so they decided to scale up the server to four cores. SQL and BizTalk are still on the same standalone server.

New Architecture:

- Number of Total servers: 1

- Number of SQL Servers: 1

    - Standard edition, 4 CPU, 8 GB of memory

- Number of BizTalk Servers: 1

    - Enterprise edition, 4 CPU, 8 GB of memory

Chapter 3: The One with Performance Problems (I)

After a few months, the DBA observes that the SQL Server process is using high CPU and is preventing the `BizTalkServerApplication` host instance from accessing CPU resources. Applications are slow. To fix this problem, the team decides to move SQL Server to a dedicated server.

After some testing in the testing environment, they observe that the SQL Server process CPU consumption is still high, but the BizTalk Server host instance performs smoothly, so they decide to apply this new architecture to production.

The team will now monitor CPU consumption in both servers.

New Architecture:

- Number of total servers: 2

- Number of SQL Servers: 1

  - Standard edition, 4 CPU, 16 GB of memory

- Number of BizTalk Servers: 1

  - Enterprise edition, 4 CPU, 8 GB of memory

Chapter 4: The One with Performance Problems (II)

One of the most commonly used applications starts processing more messages than the original performance definition. BizTalk Server administrators now observe that CPU consumption during business hours increases to 90%, so they decide to add more CPU resources to the BizTalk Server.

Upon testing, they realize that even by adding more CPU to the BizTalk Server, they are not able to increase the rate. After further investigations they observe that SQL Server CPU usage is also increasing, so they decide to increase the number of CPUs that SQL Server utilizes. After this change, the platform runs efficiently.

The team will now monitor CPU consumption in both servers.

New Architecture:

- Number of total servers: 2

- Number of SQL Servers: 1

  - Standard edition, 8 CPU, 8 GB of memory

- Number of BizTalk Servers: 1

  - Enterprise edition, 8 CPU, 8 GB of memory

Chapter 5: The One with the Disaster (I)

Over a weekend, for some unknown reason, the SQL Server stops working. This causes one of the most important BizTalk Server applications, which is preparing data for the working week, to not process files on time. The business operations were therefore delayed until the DBA could fix the issue on Monday. The SQL Server was down due to a failure related to the local disks.

The DBA suggests to the project manager that if this application had become that important, it might be time to add a second server and provide high availability to the SQL Server layer by implementing a Microsoft cluster.

The project manager approves the budget and the team implements a cluster in an active/ passive configuration with only one SQL Server instance.

New Architecture:

- Number of total servers: 3

- Number of SQL Servers: 2 in a cluster configuration

  - Standard edition, 8 CPU, 8 GB of memory

- Number of BizTalk Servers: 1

  - Enterprise edition, 8 CPU, 8 GB of memory

Chapter 6: The One with the Disaster (II)

This time, around 2AM during a normal work week, BizTalk administrators receive alerts because the environment is not processing anything. They go onsite, and they detect that the BizTalk Server is down. Upon investigation, they notice the same disk issue that caused SQL Server to stop the previous month is happening again, but this time in the local BizTalk Server disk.

As there is an application that, during the night, processes important information for the business, the BizTalk Server administrator suggests that providing high availability to the BizTalk Server layer will ensure that this issue will not happen again.

The project is approved again by the project manager and the team adds another BizTalk Server box.

Upon testing, they realize that the platform can process even more messages than before, and that BizTalk Server CPU consumption has decreased by 20%.

The DBA raises a warning, because overall SQL Server CPU usage has increased by 15%. This is because there are now two host instances polling the databases.

New Architecture:

- Number of total servers: 4

- Number of SQL Servers: 2 in a cluster configuration

  - Standard edition, 8 CPU, 8 GB of memory

- Number of BizTalk Servers: 2

  - Enterprise edition, 8 CPU, 8 GB of memory

Chapter 7: The One with the Big File that Changes Everything

A new application comes onto the scene. This application needs to process a 1 GB flat file daily, apply some transformations to it, and send the output to the CRM application.

Developers start coding the solution with a small sample file that contains all the possible message definitions.

When they test the solution with a real file, BizTalk Server starts processing messages extremely slow, to the point that it takes more than five hours to complete the whole process. Additionally, while the system is busy processing the flat file, the rest of applications are processing extremely slowly.

As they do not know what is happening, they decide to open a Microsoft Support case. After a few days of investigation, the support engineer comes back with the following explanation:

- BizTalk is entering a throttling state due to memory pressure and that is most likely the reason why the process is taking so long to complete.

- The rest of the applications do not have enough resources to process messages at an acceptable rate, because orchestrations and receive and send ports are running under the same host, and when the large file comes, the host instance is busy (consuming most of the server resources) in the disassembling stage.

- The XML representation of the flat file allocates around 8 GB of memory to the BizTalk Server process.

To fix this problem, the engineer recommends the following plan:

- Create a set of hosts for receiving, processing, and sending, and have the non-large flat file applications run under these new hosts.

- Create a new set of hosts dedicated exclusively to process the large file and increase the process virtual memory threshold to 50% so that all the host instances of this application can take up to 50% of available memory on the server.

- Increase the BizTalk Server memory so it will have enough resources to process the large file.

- Isolate the DTC log file into a dedicated disk (BizTalk and SQL Server).

The BizTalk team at ACME corporation implements all the suggested changes and, upon testing, they realize that the process completes in a reasonable period, from the business point of view. Additionally, the rest of the applications are still processing messages without entering a throttling state.

From now on, the team will consider the host separation policy as an important subject.

New Architecture:

- Number of total servers: 4

- Number of SQL Servers: 2 in a cluster configuration

  - Standard edition, 8 CPU, 32 GB of memory

- Number of BizTalk Servers: 2

  - Enterprise edition, 8 CPU, 32 GB of memory

- There is now a new set of hosts (receiving, processing, and sending) that process the large-file application.

- There is also a new set of hosts split by BizTalk Server functionalities to deal with the rest of applications.

Chapter 8: The One with Web Service

At this point, BizTalk Server applications were receiving messages only from shared folders over the network. ACME corporation was changing fast, though, and was evolving to a more service-oriented architecture. Part of this transformation creates the need to expose several applications as rest services.

Developers attend a Microsoft course and they learn the right steps to publish orchestrations as Web Services. However, when they test the solution, they realize that only one BizTalk Server is receiving all the requests. The CPU on that server rises to 80%, while the other one stays stable with an average consumption of 20%. They contact the networking team and together they come to the conclusion that they need to implement a network load-balancing mechanism that will distribute the load across both BizTalk Servers.

New Architecture:

- Number of total servers: 4

- Number of SQL Servers: 2 in a cluster configuration

  - Standard edition, 8 CPU, 32 GB of memory

- Number of BizTalk Servers: 2 implemented using a Hardware NLB solution to distribute the load

  - Enterprise edition, 8 CPU, 32 GB of memory

- There is now a new set of hosts (receiving, processing, and sending) that are processing the large-file application.

- There is also a new set of hosts split by BizTalk Server functionalities to deal with the rest of applications.

Chapter 9: The One with the Disk Performance Issue

Developers are creating applications and deploying them into production on a monthly basis. With the new architecture, no performance issues have been detected and the platform is up and running efficiently.

One afternoon, the DBA observed that SQL Server disks are performing very slow and that the read and write latency for the disk holding all of the BizTalk Server databases has increased to the point that, on average, write and reads operations are taking more than 25 milliseconds. The DBA contacts the storage team and they discard configuration problems on SAN level, as they are following the vendor best practices. It just seems that the disks holding the BizTalk Server databases are quite busy.

At this stage, several business areas start complaining about the performance of the BizTalk Server applications because they observe that overall throughput is affected.

The DBA raises the issue and recommends that they separate data and transaction files into different LUNs in the SAN. The storage team then dedicates several LUNs to allocate all the required disks to BizTalk Server.

They come up with the recommendation outlined in Table 10-1.

Table 10-1. *Data Files Distribution*

Database File	Drive
MessageBox data	F
MessageBox log	G
BizTalk tracking data	H
BizTalk Tracking log	I
BizTalk BAM primary import data	J
BizTalk BAM primary import log	K
Business application data	L
Business application log	M
Rest of databases data	N
Rest of databases log	O

After the team applies the changes, the disks performance turn back to acceptable values. New Architecture:

- Number of total servers: 4

- Number of SQL Servers: 2 in a cluster configuration

    - Standard edition, 8 CPU, 32 GB of memory

- Number of BizTalk Servers: 2 implemented using a Hardware NLB solution to distribute the load

    - Enterprise edition, 8 CPU, 32 GB of memory

- There is now a new set of hosts (receiving, processing, and sending) that are processing the large-file application.

- There is also a new set of hosts split by BizTalk Server functionalities to deal with the rest of applications.

- A new disk infrastructure is provided that guarantees BizTalk Server database isolation.

Chapter 10: The One with the New Application (I)

A new business application comes that requires processing 500 messages per second during the entire day. Developers develop the application and when they test it in the testing servers, they realize that they are not getting even close to that number and the available memory on BizTalk and SQL Server decreases into the danger zone.

To fix the issue, the BizTalk administrator recommends they create a new set of hosts for receiving, processing, and sending and dedicate them to the new application so the team can test this separately and adjust all of the required performance values.

After several days of testing, the team comes to the following conclusions:

- **Pooling intervals**—Reduce to 50 milliseconds for all of the application hosts. By doing so, new messages and orchestrations are processed earlier by the engine (almost as soon as they are assigned to the host queues).

- **Disabling orchestration dehydration**—If a failure occurs in the middle of a Web Service call, the consumer of the service will send the request again so there is no need to dehydrate orchestrations.

- As dehydration is disabled, orchestrations will not be stored in the MessageBox while they are consuming a service; they will be held on memory. BizTalk Servers now have to have more memory to keep up with the load.

509

- **Maximum engine threads**—By increasing this setting to 40 it seems that the BizTalk engine can increase the rate of documents processed per second. However, SQL Server CPU rises exponentially, so they decided that they have to scale up SQL Server by adding more CPUs.

- **.NET CLR host instance settings**—They also observed that the receiving and sending host instances are processing more messages if they decrease the value of the maximum IO threads to 100.

With all these customizations, they reach a rate of 400 messages per second, but the platform enters in throttling state because of the database size.

They tune then the Message Count in Database setting to 100.000 so that the engine enters the throttling condition later. As SQL Server needs to process more messages, they contact the DBA team to ensure there is enough backlog for the drives that hold BizTalk Server databases. The DBA evaluates the new situation and changes the SAN distribution to add more space to the BizTalk Server database drives.

Developers now test the solution and they get very close to the performance requirement of 500 messages per second. However, DBA detects that the MessageBox database is growing very fast and disk latency increases exponentially over 30 milliseconds.

After several hours of investigation, they do not find root cause of the issue, so they decide to open a support case.

Once the engineer reviews all the data, analyzes all the BizTalk traces, and runs several troubleshooting tools, he delivers an explanation and an action plan:

- The reason that the platform is slow is because the MessageBox database has become a bottleneck. To fix this situation, you should test the solution with the following changes:

  - Add two more message boxes to distribute the message publication between them.

  - Isolate all MessageBoxes to run in a separated SQL Server instance in a dedicated server.

The team implements all the suggested changes in the testing environment. The solution can now achieve the performance target of 500 messages per second while the latency is stable for the rest of the applications. SQL disk performance is not an issue anymore.

New Architecture:

- Number of total servers: 4

- Number of SQL Servers: 2 in a cluster configuration. MessageBoxes are running on server A and server B has the rest of databases.

  - Standard edition, 12 CPU, 64 GB of memory

- Number of BizTalk Servers: 2 implemented using a Hardware NLB solution to distribute the load.

  - Enterprise edition, 12 CPU, 64 GB of memory

- There is now a new set of hosts (receiving, processing, and sending) that are processing the large-file application.

- There is also a new set of hosts split by BizTalk Server functionalities to deal with the rest of applications.

Chapter 11: The One with FTP Server

A new application that needs to retrieve files from a FTP server arrives. Developers create the application and test it. Everything looks fine, so the solution goes live. A few months later, the business responsible for that application complains that from time to time they receive duplicated requests.

Developers analyze the code, looking for bugs, but they cannot find anything. Using the BizTalk administration console, they detect those duplicated message instances by enabling message body tracking, but they cannot still figure out why the duplicated messages are being generated. They seriously consider that there might be a bug in the product. They install the latest BizTalk Server 2016 service pack, but as the issue is still there, they decide to open a support case.

During the initial call, the engineer comes up with a solution right away:

- The FTP protocol does not block the file while a process is accessing it. It is not like an NTFS folder. This is by design and this behavior is out of the scope of BizTalk Server. In this case, as you have two host instances accessing the FTP server, it might happen that eventually both processes will access the same file at the same time. The receive location will pick up those messages and the engine will publish them as if they were different messages.

- Therefore, there are two options:

    a. You can disable one host instance from starting on one of the servers. With this action, you will ensure that no duplicated messages are published, but you will lose high availability for the FTP host.

    b. You can cluster the receiving FTP host, so only one host instance is started at a time. However, you are using NLB and clustering at the same time is not supported. To solve this situation, you have to add two BizTalk Servers to the group and cluster them. Then you could dedicate those servers to run only the receiving FTP hosts. These two new servers will be outside of the NLB.

The ACME team evaluates the options and, as this application is not mission-critical and there are budget restrictions at this time, they decide to create a new host and put the FTP receive location under it. They will start the associated host instance on server A and they will disable the host instance on server B. If there is an issue with the running host instance, they will manually start the second one and they will deal with all the associated issues reactively.

Chapter 12: The One that Sends Files Too Fast

Business users of one of the applications that sends a file to a destination system ask the BizTalk administrator if it is possible to send the files slower, like 20 messages per minute. The system that receives the files needs to consume a service (per file) that takes hours to complete and cannot handle more than a few files per minute, because it is a legacy system that cannot be scaled or changed as they do not own the source code anymore.

The BizTalk administrator automatically thinks of the `maxConnection` setting in the BizTalk Server configuration file, but then she realizes that the setting applies only to communications based on HTTP based adapters and, in this scenario, will not have any effect because the application is sending the files using the FILE adapter.

She wonders now if by adjusting the host throttling settings, they can reduce the frequency of the sending operations. She contacts then the developer team and explains the situation. The developer lead states that they can modify the rate-based throttling settings to delay the message publication or the message delivery. In both cases, the destination system will receive messages in a slower fashion.

The BizTalk administrator suggests that is better to slow down message publication. In this scenario, the files will not be stored to the MessageBox because they would remain in the file system.

The developer team agrees on that argument and starts to test the application with different host throttling configurations. After a few attempts, they get to a configuration where the BizTalk Server is picking up messages from the source folder at a rate of one every three seconds.

- **Minimum number of samples**—Default value: 100, changed to 1. By changing to this value, the host throttling algorithm will start the throttling condition in every sample (instead of 100 occurrences).

- **Sampling window duration**—Default value: 15 seconds, changed to 1 second. By changing this setting now every sample will last only one second. The throttling algorithm will consider the throttling condition every second.

- **Rate overdrive factor**—Default value: 125%, changed to 100%. By changing this threshold to 100%, the throttling condition will be raised when the number of delivered and published messages are the same.

- **Maximum throttling delay**—Default value: 300 seconds; changed to 3 seconds. The BizTalk Server engine will induce a delay of 3 seconds for every message received through this port.

- **Throttling override**—Default value: Do not override, change to a Initiate throttling condition. The throttling condition will always rise if the rate overdrive factor is reached.

However, this configuration requires you to add a new host to the environment because they need to isolate the host settings for this specific receive port.

The BizTalk Server administrator approves all the changes and decides that a production assessment is not required because this host will process messages as per the requirement now.

The application goes live, and the destination system starts receiving around 20 messages per minute.

Chapter 13: The One That Floods a Destination System

Business users start complaining about the performance of one of the web applications. They say that during peak times, the application does not return the data and they get lots of timeout errors.

The BizTalk administrator starts performance logging during the high load time, between 8AM and 10AM. Once the logging finishes, she opens the result performance monitor BLG file and starts analyzing the information. Upon examination, she notices that the following performance counters behave abnormally:

- **BizTalk: Messaging Latency**—Outbound Adapter Latency (sec). Latency increases exponentially between 8 and 10AM.

- **BizTalk: Messaging—Documents suspended/Sec**. The number of suspended messages per second increases during the whole period to 12,000 messages.

She opens the BizTalk administration console and filters suspended messages by destination URI. She notices that all the suspended messages are related to the same destination, a Web Service that is hosted internally by a different team. She contacts the administrator of that service and together they realize that the server that hosts that Web Service shows 100% CPU and it is out of memory. The administrator of that system checks the IIS logs and he sees thousands of requests with errors.

The BizTalk administrator suggests that it seems that the server is not able to deal with the load that BizTalk Server is sending. So, she decides to adjust the maxConnection setting for that URI.

She opens the BizTalk Server configuration and checks the maxConnection setting:

```
<system.net>
  <connectionManagement>
    <add address="*" maxconnection="25" />
  </connectionManagement>
</system.net>
```

She notices that every BizTalk Server destination is sending 25 messages, and that is probably the reason the destination system is flooded. She changes the maxConnection setting to open only two connections to the affected service:

```
<system.net>
  <connectionManagement>
    <add address="*" maxconnection="25" />
    <add address="http://ACMEWebService" maxconnection="2" />
  </connectionManagement>
</system.net>
```

The day after, business users say that the system is not generating timeout errors anymore and the administration of the Web Service confirms that the CPU and memory usage went back to normal during the whole day.

Chapter 14: The One with the New Application (II)

The ACME integration environment is growing. There is a new requirement to implement a new low latency application that needs to process 100 messages per second, with peaks of 200 messages.

As part of the application lifecycle, the development team introduced performance testing. The development team tests the solution in the testing environment and they get the values shown in Table 10-2 for the performance counters.

Table 10-2. *Performance Counter Data*

Performance Counter	Value
Processor: %Processor Time	32%
Spool Size	No increasing trends detected
Available Memory *	28 GB
SQL Server Disk Idle Time	68%
SQL Processor: % Processor Time	26%
BizTalk Server Disk Idle Time	75%
Documents Received /Sec	244
Documents Processes /Sec	420
Documents Sent /Sec	244

Note, the production environment has 30 GB of physical memory.

All in all, it seems that the application can perform under the agreed performance SLA with the hardware that is used in the testing and production environments. However, this test was executed while the testing servers were idle because the other applications were not tested at the same time. For this reason, the development team asks the BizTalk administrator to assess the production environment, so they can evaluate if there is enough room to run the new application on production.

The BizTalk administrator starts the performance logging for a period of 24 hours. The day after, he processes the output BLG file using the PAL tool and gets the values shown in Table 10-3 for the selected performance counters.

Table 10-3. *New Performance Counters Data*

Performance Counter	Value
BizTalk Processor: % Processor Time	45%
Spool Size	No increasing trends detected
Available Memory *	10 GB
SQL Server Disk Idle Time	58%
SQL Processor: % Processor Time	51%
BizTalk Server Disk Idle Time	45%
Documents Received /Sec	355
Documents Processes /Sec	598
Documents Sent /Sec	442

*Note, the production environment has 30 GB of physical memory.

The ACME team compares the results to estimate the maximum resource utilization in production, if they deploy the new application. The comparison is shown in Table 10-4.

Table 10-4. Performance Counters Data Comparison

Performance Counter	Testing	Production	Estimation
BizTalk Processor: % Processor Time	32%	45%	77%
Spool Size	No increasing trends detected	No increasing trend detected	Unknown
Available Memory	28 GB	10 GB	8 GB
SQL Server Disk Idle Time	68%	58%	26%
SQL Processor: % Processor Time	26%	51%	77%
BizTalk Server Disk Idle Time	75%	45%	15%
Documents Received /Sec	244	355	599
Documents Processes /Sec	420	598	1018
Documents Sent /Sec	244	442	686

Based on this comparison, the team comes to the conclusion that adding this application to the platform would not be safe, as most of the estimated calculations show that there will be a good chance that the environment would start processing messages above the MST continuously. Both BizTalk and the SQL Server show high CPU and memory consumption. The whole team gathers together to discuss the current situation, with these conclusions:

- The performance SLA for the new application has been established to 100 messages per second, with peaks of 200. The team designed the load tests to reach the maximum load and the testing platform responded smoothly to the worst load scenario, showing that it can process up to 244 messages per second continuously. Would it be acceptable to the integrated parties if BizTalk Server slows down the application under high load?

- If the integrated parties accept this, they can tune the BizTalk Server application hosts to enter the throttling state for memory consumption when the number of received messages per second is higher than 110. This situation that will not arise frequently.

- If this is not acceptable, then they will need to scale the environment by adding more hardware resources.

The integrated parties confirm that it would be acceptable to slow down processing under high load. Now the question is, how do they get the right memory threshold?

The BizTalk Server administrator suggests the following procedure:

1. Isolate the receiving location into a separated host.

2. Design a load test that will send 150 messages per second for one hour.

3. Gather the following performance counters:

   - BizTalk: MessageAgent: Process Memory Usage (MB)

   - BizTalk Messaging: Documents received/sec

4. Run the load test.

5. Analyze the Process Memory Usage (MB) counter during the full capture and perform an average calculation. This is the threshold that should be used to tune the host. So, when host instances consume this amount of memory, it is because the received documents per second is around 150.

The whole team loved this idea and proceed as suggested by the BizTalk administrator. Upon testing, they got an average value for the Process Memory Usage (MB) counter of 2.166 MB (around 2 GB of memory). That means that the host instances are consuming 6.6% of the available memory of the server (30 GB).

Using the BizTalk administration console, they set the Process Virtual threshold of the receiving host to 7 and they perform the original load test again. As the host enters the throttling state due to memory pressure, messages take longer to complete, but the processor and memory utilization of BizTalk and the SQL Servers decrease exponentially.

They approve all the changes and the application is deployed to production. The BizTalk administrator performs daily performance assessments to production and confirms that the platform is still running under the MST.

Chapter 15: The One with the High Throughput Application

A new application is ready for production. The development team has tested the solution on the testing environment and came to the conclusion that there is room for this application in production. The deployment is done over the weekend and everything works normally during the initial integration tests.

On Monday though, users complain about slowness of the platform and open an internal ticket.

The BizTalk administrator runs the BizTalk health monitor tool and finds out that the transaction log for the MessageBox database is around 40 GB (with actual data). He sends that information to the DBA and the SQL Server administrator confirms that the transaction log file for the MessageBox is growing to 40 GB. He recommends configuring the BizTalk Back Up so that the jobs run every five minutes, rather than leaving the default 15 minutes configuration. The BizTalk administrator approves the change and, upon testing, finds out that with the new job configuration, the transaction log for the MessageBox does not grow beyond 15 GB.

Summary

This chapter went through several BizTalk Server problems that frequently occur around the world. Some of them were very simple and were fixed just by adding more hardware resources to the platform. However, in my experience, it is usually better to spend time analyzing the issue to find the root cause and use the flexibility that BizTalk Server provides to customize the platform. Eventually, especially if the number of new applications is growing, you will face a situation where the only solution is to scale the platform. But because you have been squeezing the platform settings to the maximum, your BizTalk Server environment will use resources efficiently.

Index

A

Adapters, 44–45

Application Priority Levels (APL)
BPL, 148–150
HAL, 150
PBL, 151
RSL, 148
SLA, 146
TL, 150–151

Arrange-Act-Assert (AAA) pattern, 438

Atomicity, Consistency, Isolation, and
Durability (ACID), 231

B

BizTalk 360
alarm configuration
advanced pane, 403–404
basic settings, 401–402
data monitoring, 407
fields, 402–403
health monitoring alert, 406
settings, 401
threshold alert, 404–405
type, alarm, 401
automated recovery, 430
data monitoring, 400
data monitoring dashboard, 428–430
health check monitoring, 400

monitoring dashboard, 427–428
operations dashboard, 426
threshold monitoring, 400

BizTalk application
BizTalk Server counter set
counters option, 476–477
custom counter set, 475–476
mappings, 478
performance counters, 477–478
Visual Studio Solution Explorer, 475
BizTalkWCFnetTCP, 464
load test
BTSMessaging, 473–474
duration, 470
Excel reports, 485–486
graphs view, 483, 485
load pattern, 471–472
mix model, 472–473
on-premise, 469
remaining time, 480
run load test, 479–480
Spool counter data, 484–485
summary dashboard, 481–483
TestWCFNetTcp, 470
warming up phase, 480
monitoring (*see* Monitoring,
BizTalk application)
netTcpBinding properties, 467
TCP listener adapter, 463–464

© Agustín Mántaras 2019
A. Mántaras, *BizTalk Server 2016*, https://doi.org/10.1007/978-1-4842-3994-0

W

X, Y, Z

Printed in the United States
By Bookmasters